HITLER'S WAR MACHINE

THE GERMAN ARMY IN NORMANDY

EDITED AND INTRODUCED BY
BOB CARRUTHERS

Pen & Sword
MILITARY

This edition published in 2013 by
Pen & Sword Military
An imprint of
Pen & Sword Books Ltd
47 Church Street
Barnsley
South Yorkshire
S70 2AS

First published in Great Britain in 2012 in digital format by
Coda Books Ltd.

Copyright © Coda Books Ltd, 2012
Published under licence by Pen & Sword Books Ltd.

This book includes extracts from 'The Handbook on German Military Forces' and 'Cross-Channel Attack' by Gordon A. Harrison, published by the Center of Military History, US Army.

ISBN 978 1 78159 226 7

A CIP catalogue record for this book is
available from the British Library

All rights reserved. No part of this book may be reproduced or transmitted in any form or by any means, electronic or mechanical including photocopying, recording or by any information storage and retrieval system, without permission from the Publisher in writing.

Printed and bound by
CPI Group (UK) Ltd, Croydon, CR0 4YY

Pen & Sword Books Ltd incorporates the Imprints of Pen & Sword Aviation, Pen & Sword Family History, Pen & Sword Maritime, Pen & Sword Military, Pen & Sword Discovery, Pen & Sword Politics, Pen & Sword Atlas, Pen & Sword Archaeology, Wharncliffe Local History, Wharncliffe True Crime, Wharncliffe Transport, Pen & Sword Select, Pen & Sword Military Classics, Leo Cooper, The Praetorian Press, Claymore Press, Remember When, Seaforth Publishing and Frontline Publishing

For a complete list of Pen & Sword titles please contact
PEN & SWORD BOOKS LIMITED
47 Church Street, Barnsley, South Yorkshire, S70 2AS, England
E-mail: enquiries@pen-and-sword.co.uk
Website: www.pen-and-sword.co.uk

CONTENTS

INTRODUCTION 5

THE GERMAN ARMY IN FRANCE 1940-1943..........................7

BARBED-WIRE OBSTACLES 40

TYPES OF CONCRETE ANTITANK OBSTACLES 45

GERMAN DEFENSE MEASURES, 1944 48

REPORT OF THE CHIEF OF STAFF 89

GERMAN TIGER TANKS DEPLOYED IN NORMANDY 97

HOW THE GERMANS FIGHT IN WOODED AND BROKEN TERRAIN 100

A TANK-INFANTRY TEAM OBSERVED IN COMBAT 106

GERMAN MILITARY TACTICS 109

FORTIFICATIONS AND DEFENSES....................................200

SUPPLY, EVACUATION AND MOVEMENTS 223

A BATTALION COMMANDER LOOKS US OVER 274

GERMAN INFANTRY DIVISION CUT TO MEET MANPOWER SHORTAGE 277

THE GERMAN KAMIKAZES 279

EXTRACT FROM THE TELEPHONE DIARY OF THE 352ND INFANTRY DIVISION (COASTAL DEFENSE SECTION BAYEUX) 286

THE 21ST PANZER DIVISION ON 6 JUNE 1944 309

THE 711TH INFANTRY DIVISION ENCOUNTERS THE INVASION..317

THE ALLIED ATTACK: THE 6TH FALLSCHIRM REGIMENT REACTS 320

INVASION	326
LXXXIV CORPS COUNTERATTACKS WITH LOCAL RESERVES ON THE AFTERNOON OF D-DAY	327
I SS PANZER CORPS MOVES UP TO COUNTERATTACK, 6 JUNE 1944	330
GROUND TACTICS OF GERMAN PARATROOPS	338
88-MM GERMAN ANTITANK GUN USED IN FRANCE: GENERAL DATA	341
GERMAN ANTITANK TACTICS: TEXT OF A CAPTURED DOCUMENT	344
FIGHTING IN NORMANDY	348
ALLIED FIRE POWER FORCES ENEMY TO STRESS NIGHT INFILTRATION	357
TERRAIN MURALS IN A NORMAN FORT	359
GERMAN EMPLOYMENT OF HEAVY ARMORED PLATOON	360
TRANSCRIPT OF QUESTIONS PUT TO GENERALFELDMARSCHALL WILHELM KEITEL AND GENERALOBERST ALFRED JODL	364
THE INVASION BY GENERAL WALTER WARLIMONT	370
VON RUNDSTEDT EXPLAINS	376

INTRODUCTION

This book forms part of the series entitled 'Hitler's War Machine.' The aim is to provide the reader with a varied range of materials drawn from original writings covering the strategic, operational and tactical aspects of the weapons and battles of Hitler's war. The concept behind the series is to provide the well-read and knowledgeable reader with an interesting compilation of related primary sources combined with the best of what is in the public domain to build a picture of a particular aspect of that titanic struggle.

I am pleased to report that the series has been well received and it is a pleasure to be able to bring original primary sources to the attention of an interested readership. I particularly enjoy discovering new primary sources, and I am pleased to be able to present them unadorned and unvarnished to a sophisticated audience. The primary sources such as Die Wehrmacht and Signal, speak for themselves and the readership I strive to serve is the increasingly well informed community of reader/historians which needs no editorial lead and can draw its own conclusions. I am well aware that our community is constantly striving to discover new nuggets of information, and I trust that with this volume I have managed to stimulate fresh enthusiasm and that at least some of these facts and articles will be new to you and will provoke readers to research further down these lines of investigation, and perhaps cause established views to be challenged once more. I am aware at all times in compiling these materials that our relentless pursuit of more and better historical information is at the core our common passion. I trust that this selection will contribute to that search and will help all of us to better comprehend and understand the bewildering events of the last century.

In order to produce an interesting compilation giving a flavour of events at the tactical and operational level I have returned once more to post-war debriefings, of which the interview with General der Infanterie Gunther Blumentritt is reproduced here. I have also included part of the wartime US Intelligence series of pamphlets, which contain an intriguing series of contemporary articles on weapons and tactics. I find this series of pamphlets particularly fascinating as they are written in, what was then, the present tense and, as such, provide us with a sense of what was happening at the face of battle as events unfolded. Finally there is a substantial extract from the final edition of the hand book on German military forces which provides an invaluable, and surprisingly accurate, guide to the late war German forces as they were perceived by their enemies.

Thank you for buying this volume in the series we hope you will enjoy discovering some new insights you will go on to try the others in the series.

Bob Carruthers
Edinburgh 2012.

THE GERMAN ARMY IN FRANCE 1940-1943

Center of Military History, United States Army

Organization of the West

German leaders in the fall of 1943 read their newspapers and pored over intelligence reports with special interest. Crisis in the east had been reached and passed; there would be no more massed German offensives. no decisive victories. Crisis in the west was approaching. In October, news of the military conference in Moscow convinced Hitler and his staff that the opening of the second front was imminent. The conclusion was modified later as press releases from the Tehran Conference were taken to indicate a postponement of the invasion for perhaps two or three months. The best guess then was that the Allies might attack any time after February 1944, but probably in the spring. Whatever the exact time schedule, most German leaders had little doubt that invasion was close at hand.

While the Moscow Conference was going on, Generalfeldmarschall Gerd von Rundstedt, Commander in Chief in the West, was putting the final touches on a long, frank, pessimistic report on the state of his defenses. The burden of the report was that his army was not in any way prepared to resist the expected Allied attack. In three years of occupation little had actually been accomplished to make Fortress Europe a military reality.

With the conquest of France in June 1940, Hitler believed that he had won the war. He had no plans ready for the next step. He could not understand why any more victories should be necessary to convince Great Britain that it was hope less to prolong the struggle. But Britain's stubbornness, though inexplicable, was clearly a fact. Hitler noted in July that the British Government was apparently set on fighting to the finish, and he therefore began serious consideration of plans to deliver the coup de grâce. The obvious and most convincing method was invasion.

The projected invasion was given the code name SEELOEWE

(SEA LION) and Army and Navy planners set to work in a race against time to solve the manifold and unfamiliar problems of a large-scale amphibious operation. The first big problem was that there were no landing craft, and very little shipping of any description. By gathering up all the barges from inland waterways at the cost of paralyzing large sections of industry, the Germans could reckon on barely enough shipping space to put an effective force ashore in England. But towed barges at the mercy of the slightest wind-roughened seas were hardly ideal. The perils of improvisation, furthermore, would be heightened by the lack of naval protection. The only way to guard the convoys seemed to be to mass all submarines and light surface vessels on the North Sea flank and at the same time mount a diversionary expedition on the Atlantic side to draw the British Fleet away from the main crossing. The Navy was decidedly cool toward the project. Grossadmiral Erich Raeder, the Navy Commander in Chief, as early as July had uncovered so many risks that he strongly recommended against the operation except as a last resort.

Hitler agreed. Quite apart from the dangers of SEELOEWE, Hitler did not like the political implications of conquering England by invasion. He saw that the defeat of England would be followed by disintegration of the British Empire. The beneficiaries of such a collapse, he thought, would be Japan and the United States, not Germany. He wanted not the destruction but the surrender of Great Britain. To force surrender, he believed it was necessary to deprive the British finally and completely of all hope in ultimate victory. They therefore must be confronted with a solid political front on the Continent embracing Spain, Italy, and a vanquished Russia. Defeat of Russia was particularly important. Hitler thought that England drew hope chiefly from the continued independence of the Soviet Union and the United States. By knocking out Russia, the Germans would remove one source of hope and considerably dim the other; Russia's defeat would leave Japan strong in the Pacific and would probably prevent the United States from becoming an effective ally of Great Britain in Europe. "With Russia smashed," Hitler argued, "Britain's last hope would be shattered." On 31 July 1940 Hitler decided that Russia's destruction "must therefore be made a part of this struggle

Generalfeldmarschall Gerd von Rundstedt (second left)

[against England]. He set the spring of 1941 as the target date and ordered preparations made for a lightning blow to knock out Russia in not more than five months.

The decision to attack Russia resulted immediately in a reorganization and expansion of the Army. The goal set was to build up from 143 to 180 divisions. As all three of the army groups that defeated France, A, B, and C, were to be shifted to the Eastern Front by the spring of 1941, it became necessary to create a new headquarters to take over the occupation of France. This was Army

Group D, formed during September and October under command of Generalfeldmarschall Erwin von Witzleben. In order to relieve the Army High Command at once for exclusive attention to the east, a theater commander, Oberbefehlshaber West (Commander in Chief West) was designated about the same time to take charge of all offensive or defensive operations that might be mounted in the west. Field Marshal Rundstedt, still in command of Army Group A (the force earmarked for SEELOEWE), was concurrently appointed Commander in Chief West with full command over Army Group A and tactical command over Army Group D and Armed Forces Commander Netherlands (Wehrmachtbef ehlshaber Niederlande).

While these command changes were being effected, the German commanders were rapidly becoming convinced that SEELOEWE was not a sound operation of war. The Navy had set the period 20-26 September as the earliest date on which it could be ready. But readiness even on this date hinged on the ability of Reichsmarschall Hermann Goering's Luftwaffe to knock out the British Royal Air Force. In the Battle of Britain Goering tried and failed as British fighter pilots demonstrated skill and courage that took heavy toll of the attackers. There followed a succession of postponements, which gained nothing; the Royal Air Force remained unconquered and the weather, the final insuperable obstacle, only became more stormy and unpredictable as the season advanced. With an improvised landing fleet, composed largely of river barges only a third of which were self-propelled, the Germans needed a relatively long period of almost flat calm. Such periods were rare in October and could not be forecast. By the middle of October SEELOEWE had been definitely called off. Preparations were to be continued for a landing in the spring but chiefly as a deception measure to keep up the pressure on the British.

Rundstedt thus remained in France with his Army Group A during the winter of 1940-41. In April 1941 he was moved out, and command in the west passed to von Witzleben, commander of Army Group D. Witzleben was left with three armies, the Seventh and Fifteenth occupying the long coast line from the Spanish border to Antwerp, and the first disposed in the interior with headquarters near Paris.

The threat of invasion or even of damaging raids by the English against the Continent in 1941 was so slight as to be negligible. Nevertheless, Witzleben began taking certain steps to put his defense in order. In June, the former Inspector of Western Fortresses was appointed Inspector of Land Fortresses in the West and attached for tactical purposes to OB WEST. His headquarters was moved from Metz to Paris near that of Witzleben, and his first task was the inspection of the defenses of the Channel Islands.

The military reason for defending the Channel Islands was chiefly to protect coastal traffic. Hitler, however, attached to the islands a far greater political importance. He believed the British would be forced to retake them for the sake of prestige. Conversely they were precious to him as the only British territory directly under his domination. In mid-summer 1941 the 319th Division, reinforced with machine gun, artillery, anti-tank, and antiaircraft units to the strength of about 40,000 men, was ordered to the islands. This garrison comprising some of the best troops and best equipment in the west was to remain on Channel guard duty, inactive and useless for the rest of the war.

Up to the end of 1941 the only German-built fortifications on the French mainland were seven heavy coastal batteries between Boulogne and Calais emplaced for the shelling of England during preparations for SEELOEWE, a few other naval coastal batteries, and some U-boat pens. The coastal battery emplacements were built for the Navy by Organization Todt, the construction organization formed in 1938 to build the West Wall. After SEELOEWE was called off, Hitler directed Organization Todt to construct bombproof U-boat pens along the Atlantic coast, especially at Brest, Lorient, and St. Nazaire. That project, to protect what Hitler came more and more to regard as his principal offensive weapon against the Western Powers, absorbed most of the labor and materials available for fortification of the west. When Witzleben in September 1941 proposed that the Army begin work on permanent defenses, the Army High Command (OKH) had no construction battalions to give him and he had to make informal arrangements with the Navy to borrow such of their workers as were idle. Despite the difficulties, Witzleben at the end of 1941 ordered the armies, corps, and divisions under him to reconnoiter defense sites along the coast and begin construction.

This was the first step toward fortifying the west against eventual Allied invasion, but without the necessary allotment of labor and materials it could not accomplish much. The actual building of the Atlantic Wall cannot be said to have begun before the spring of 1942. By then the first Russian winter counter-offensive, coupled with American entry into the war, had forced Hitler to reckon more seriously with prolongation of hostilities and the consequent possibility of major action in the west.

Early in March 1942 Field Marshal Rundstedt was appointed Commander in Chief West to replace Witzleben. Rundstedt was one of the senior officers and leading military personalities in Germany. He had been in charge of early planning for the Polish campaign of 1939 and had commanded an army group in that campaign. In 1940 in France he again commanded an army group. After the victory over France, he was placed in charge of planning and preparations for the invasion of England. On the abandonment of that project, Rundstedt participated in the first offensive against Russia as commander of Army Group South until the end of 1941, when he was relieved because of ill health. In March 1942 he reported to Hitler that his health was restored and a week later received the command in the west.

Two weeks after Rundstedt's appointment, Hitler issued his basic order for the defense of the west. Sole responsibility for the defense of all German-occupied territory in the west including the Netherlands was given to the Commander in Chief West, and he, along with the commander in Denmark, was placed directly under the Armed Forces High Command (OKW). This extended a process begun earlier of splitting the theaters of operation between OKW and OKH, as though they were coequal commands. By the beginning of 1943 OKW had become directly responsible for all western theaters (France and the Low Countries, North Africa and Italy, the Balkans, and Scandinavia) while OKH devoted exclusive attention to the east. The division recognized, in the first place, that OKH had its hands full with the increasing difficulties of the war in Russia. It also, in part, reflected the fact that the defense of the west particularly called for co-ordination between the three services.

Co-ordination was effected, however, in name only. OKW, headed by Generalfeldmarschall Wilhelm Keitel, was no true joint staff. Naval and air force members were relatively junior officers. Reichsmarschall Hermann Goering and Admiral Raeder, furthermore, remained outside and above it in personal relationship with Hitler. Goering as Reichsmarschall outranked Keitel who, as chief of all the armed services, should have been his superior. In addition, Goering held a top Cabinet post as Minister of Aviation which further set him out of reach of OKW. Finally, the Army, wedded to the notion of Germany as a Continental power, had long opposed unification of the services on the basis of equal representation and authority. The effect of the Army view together with the independence of Goering and Raeder was to reduce OKW to the position of a second Army staff. As long as it had no direct responsibility for any one theater of operations OKW retained a certain perspective and capacity to co-ordinate the German war effort, even though the bulk of its co-ordination had to pass through Hitler himself. With the splitting of the western and eastern theaters, OKW, for all practical purposes, lost even that limited power to co-ordinate. Henceforth the only unity of command in Germany rested in the person of Hitler, who no longer had adequate machinery through which to exercise it.

In the various theaters of operations after 1940 no effective machinery was ever established to exercise unified command. In the west, during an actual enemy invasion, the army commanders in the battle areas were to have tactical control over the air force and naval units in their sectors. But the failure to give OB WEST a supreme command meant that co-ordination of the defense rested largely on such informal co-operation and liaison as the local commanders might choose to establish. The divided command would gravely handicap German preparedness. In the meantime, the chief positive result of the new top-level command organization was to free the OKW operational staff (the Wehrmachtfuehrungsstab, WFSt, under General der Artillerie Alfred Jodl) from responsibility for the war in Russia and so permit it to concentrate on the operational needs of the west, Italy, the Balkans, and Norway and Denmark.

Hitler's basic order sketched out the tactical doctrine that henceforth

Despite the ominous signs, most of the officer corps remained remarkably loyal to Hitler.

governed all planning for the defense of France. He decreed that the coast defenses should be so organized and troops so that any invasion attempted could be smashed before the landing of immediately thereafter. The main defensive preparations were to be made in the places most suitable for large enemy landings. Beaches where only small surprise landings were possible were to be defended by strong points tied in, if possible, with the coastal batteries. The rest of the coast would be patrolled. All positions were to be designed for defense to the last man of the garrison. All should be equipped with weapons and supplies so that even if overrun by the enemy they would not be forced to surrender for lack of means to continue the fight.

Five days after the issuance of this order, Hitler was profoundly shocked by the successful British raid on St. Nazaire. The spectacle of British ships, including a destroyer, sailing with impunity up the mouth of the Loire reputedly made him furious and focused his attention on the inadequacies of the French coastal defenses. The only immediate outcome, however, was the relief of Generalleutnant Karl Hilpert, OB WEST Chief of Staff. Hilpert was replaced by Generalmajor Kurt Zeitzler, who was close to Hitler, and who afterward became Chief of the General Staff of OKH.

Later more sober study of the St. Nazaire experience showed even to Hitler that the responsible commanders in France did not have the resources to deal with determined enemy forays. While Allied strength was increasing, German strength had been gradually weakened to nourish the operations against Russian. Admiral Raeder told Hitler bluntly: "We have no means of repulsing an enemy attempt." Even better defenses at St. Nazaire, in the opinion of Raeder, would not have stopped a determined Allied attack; the only thing that could have helped would have been strong naval forces and adequate air reconnaissance. Then he ventured a prophecy: "In view of the shortages everywhere and the necessity of using numerous makeshift defense measures, experience will show that there will constantly be new shortcomings in our defenses and new demands made upon them." Despite this accurate forecast of things to come, Hitler was not then, and never would be, convinced that defense could not be made invulnerable if enough concrete and resolution could be poured into it. His retort to the St. Nazaire raid was to direct that submarine bases be so well protected that successful raids on them thenceforth would be impossible.

In August 1942 he expanded his notions of a concrete coastal wall. In a conference with Field Marshal Keitel and other high-ranking Army officers he proposed that fortress construction in France should proceed with "fanatic energy [Fanatismus]" during the coming winter. The object must be to build many small strong points to house from thirty to seventy men each, armed with machine guns and "a few other weapons," chiefly antitank guns. A continuous belt of interlocking fire must be created emanating from concrete structures designed to be proof against Allied bombing and naval shellfire. Behind this emphasis on fixed defenses lay the realization of a grave shortage of troops. Already in the summer of 1942 Hitler estimated that ten to twelve more divisions were needed to establish a solid defense along the OB WEST coast J line, but reserves to make up this deficit were not available.

As the summer came to an end, prospects of victory in Russia were again clouded by the north winds. In the meantime the large-scale raid by Canadian troops at Dieppe in the latter part of August, though considered an absolute failure by the Germans, nevertheless forcibly called attention to the increasing threat of full-scale invasion by the Western Powers. On 29 September, Hitler called in Goering, Reich Minister Albert Speer (Chief of Organization Todt), Rundstedt, Generalleutnant Guenther Blumentritt (who had relieved Zeitzler as Chief of Staff OB WEST only a few days before), General der Pioniere Alfred Jacob (Chief Engineer of OKH), Generalleutnant Rudolf Schmetzer (Inspector of Land Fortresses for OB WEST), and certain other staff officers for a three-hour conference in the small Cabinet sitting room of the Reich Chancellery. The Fuehrer began by expressing his confidence that Russia would be defeated in 1943 by a German push in the spring toward Mesopotamia in the south. He then admitted grave concern over the possibility of the creation of a second front in the west. There was no question of capitulation, he said, " I must freely admit . . . that a major landing of the enemy in the west would bring us to a generally critical position." The gravest present threat was to Norway, he believed, but ultimately it was France that would be invaded because such an operation would require the least amount of shipping tonnage.

Hitler then went on to analyze the Dieppe experience. Even though the British field order for the raid, clearly specifying a withdrawal of forces after nine hours, was captured and studied by the Germans, apparently the German generals involved reported and Hitler believed that Dieppe was actually a major landing attempt that failed. On that premise he compared the introduction of large-scale amphibious operations at Dieppe to the introduction of the tank at Cambrai in World War I. In both cases, he pointed out, the British had failed through having planned only the meeting engagement, leaving the follow-up to the initiative of the field commanders who were too timid to exploit their advantage. After Cambrai both British and Germans drew the false lesson that the tank was technically a failure and so "they poured out the baby with the bath." He warned now against a false deduction on the German side that amphibious operations against the coast of France were proved impossible by Dieppe. This time, he said, the British cannot arrive at a similar conclusion, simply because they have no alternative but to try again.

The Germans must prepare the strongest possible defenses. The defenses must be prepared, furthermore, on the assumption that the Allies would enjoy air and naval supremacy. The crushing weight of Allied bombs and shells, he believed, could be withstood only by concrete. Not only that, but massive concrete works, he believed, had a psychological as well as a physical strength. Hitler pointed out that the very existence of the West Wall had deterred Daladier in 1938 from threatening military action during the Czechoslovakia crisis. The West Wall repeated along the coast would have the same deterrent effect on the Western Allies. Hitler asked for 1,000 concrete strong points for the new "Atlantic Wall" to be defended by 300,000 men. The goal was an impervious, permanent defense ring. Since the amount of time available to build it was uncertain, construction was to follow a strict priority. In Hitler's view, the most important job was to protect the U-boat bases. He listed for defense thereafter: harbors for coastal traffic, harbors suitable for enemy landings (a reflection of the Dieppe experience), the Channel Islands, and finally landing places on the open coast. Beaches deemed most likely to be used in a major invasion attempt were to be fortified first. But, as Hitler pointed out, since the Navy could not guarantee that any portion of the coast was safe, the whole would have to be walled up eventually.

It was an ambitious program. Hitler ordered that it be completed by 1 May 1943; Organization Todt thought it would be lucky to get 40 percent finished by that time. At such a rate the defense of the coast proper, having the lowest priority, became a very long-range program which would probably not be completed before the Allies struck. In any case it was fantastic to suppose that even a first-class military power could be strong everywhere along the entire coast line from the Mediterranean to Norway. It followed that defense preparations would be concentrated in accordance with estimates of Allied intentions. But German intelligence services notably failed to supply reliable information about the Western Allies. The sparseness of accurate intelligence, the plethora of rumors, and the natural jitteriness of being on the strategic defensive led to constantly revised guesses that at one time or another pointed out grave threats to virtually every section of the coast. Division commanders, corps commanders, army commanders freely contributed predictions that their own sectors had been selected for the enemy landings. They were moved sometimes by logic, more often by desire to compete for the limited supplies of troops and materiel. They seldom had any sure knowledge of what was being brewed across the Channel. Hitler's intuition was no less erratic: at various times he picked the Gironde, Brittany, the Cotentin, the Pas-de-Calais, and Norway. In late 1943 a captured British agent indicated that the Allies intended to strike in the Netherlands. He was not believed, and the Netherlands actually remained about the only sector in the west exempt from special attention as a threatened area.

Although the Germans could never be sure that any sector of the coast was safe, the necessity for concentrating their own forces led them to categorize roughly the degrees of danger. It was common consensus from the beginning that the sector of the Fifteenth Army from the Seine to the Schelde was most gravely if not uniquely threatened. This estimate, however, was based on reasoning, not on intelligence. It was thought the Allies would strike here because it was close to Germany and the Ruhr, and because the short Channel crossing would simplify the problems of air support and sea reinforcement. Strategically Allied success in this sector would cut off the whole of the German forces to the south.

The conclusion that the Kanalkueste was the most likely place for a major landing, arrived at in the early days of planning the Atlantic Wall, was never seriously shaken by any later information. Even when other sectors appeared threatened, the threats were deemed diversionary. Rationalization had a persuasiveness that the meager reports of fact never had. Furthermore, once the concrete was poured, the original estimate became peculiarly difficult to alter. During 1942, for instance, four times as much concrete was allotted the left corps of Fifteenth Army as to the LXXXIV Corps in Normandy and Brittany. By May 1943 the concentration of troops along the Fifteenth Army coast was almost three times as heavy as in Seventh Army-the army that would oppose the invasion.

In the summer of that year a new importance was given to the Pas-de-Calais area. It was here that Hitler planned to install his Vergeltungs (vengeance) weapons, the long-range rockets and pilotless aircraft from which he expected a complete reversal of the course of the war. He believed that the V-weapons would prove so dangerous to England that the Allies, whatever their previous plans might have been, would be forced to attack directly to overrun the launching sites. This estimate, of course, entailed the further conclusion that the bulk of the German defenses should be emplaced to defend the rocket sites. In June 1943 Hitler assigned construction priority to those portions of the Atlantic Wall defending rocket-launching areas.

Although by far the strongest fortified portion of the French coast, even the Kanalkueste never became anything like the impregnable fortress that German propaganda advertised. Hitler, having ordered the creation of a wall of concrete and fire which could stop any invasion at the water's edge, apparently believed that such a wall would be built and paid little further attention to it. He never saw any portion of the western fortifications. After leaving Paris in triumph in the summer of 1940 he did not set foot on French soil again until a week after the Allied invasion in June 1944. Absorbed with the struggle against Russia, he scarcely heeded the stream of memoranda in which the Commander in Chief West pointed out and reiterated the entire inadequacy of German preparations for the defense of France.

In the spring of 1943 Rundstedt went to Berchtesgaden to present his case in person. But Hitler was still not interested in bad news from the west. He was looking forward to great victories in the east. He talked of how two thousand German tanks would annihilate at least ninety Russian divisions in the new spring offensive. Rundstedt, after abrupt dismissal, returned to France and embarked on a comprehensive survey of the state of his defenses. It was this survey which resulted in the detailed report of 25 October. This he forwarded to OKW with a special request that it be brought to the personal attention of Hitler.

Impact of the Russian and Mediterranean Fronts

Rundstedt said little about the Atlantic Wall. He mentioned delays in naval construction due to a faulty priority system which had only just been straightened out. But for the most part he was less interested in the state of the permanent defenses than in the combat value of his troops. The wall, he said, was valuable for fighting as well as for propaganda, "but it must not be believed that this wall cannot be overcome." Strongly defended fortifications might be a more or less efficient means of weakening the attacking enemy by splitting his forces, but victory in the west could be achieved only by rapidly mounted, strong counterattacks.

In the light of this basic requirement, Rundstedt pointed out how thin his line of defense really was. The average coastal sector of a single division ranged from 50 miles in the Fifteenth Army sector to 120 miles in the Seventh Army sector and 217 miles along the Atlantic coast. The coastal divisions, moreover, were almost all understrength- a good many had only two regiments. Their armament, particularly in antitank weapons and artillery, was often inadequate for a maximum defense of their positions. Most serious of all, in Rundstedt's eyes, was their almost total lack of transport.

All these deficiencies were the direct result of the drain on the German war economy to maintain the Russian and Mediterranean fronts. The opening of the Russian front in 1941 had turned the west into a kind of replacement center. Toward the end of that year the Commander in Chief West was already complaining that his troops were being siphoned off at a dangerous rate. The complaint was futile; the process, in fact, had only just begun. From 1942 "the hard-pressed Eastern Front always short of forces looked with envy at the apparently sleeping army in the west, and at every crisis the higher commanders in the east . . . demanded that the reservoir be tapped. In the need of the moment these troops were usually conceded."

In 1942 the process of east-west troop exchanges was regularized. In May the Commander in Chief West issued an order concerning the reconstitution of divisions shifted from the Russian front to France emphasizing speed in re-equipping these divisions and the importance of maintaining the special toughness (Ost-Haerte) of the troops. In the same order Rundstedt warned against allowing the troops who had returned from the east to patronize those troops permanently stationed in the west. The latter, he pointed out, had done their duty and it was not their fault that they could not be used for fighting in the east. In short, it was made a matter of policy that the west should be permanently garrisoned only by troops who because of various disabilities could not be used in the hard fighting in Russia. OKH, in October, proposed a regular monthly exchange of two divisions between Army Group Center and OB WEST and one division between Army Group North and the Norway garrison. OKH listed ten infantry divisions under OB WEST command which were immediately suitable for exchange with the east. At the same time it was proposed not to transfer any mobile divisions (armored and motorized) until spring to avoid using them up in winter fighting in Russia. But that was like trying to hold on to a parasol in a hurricane. A month later, Hitler ordered the immediate transfer of the 6th Panzer Division from the west to the sector of Stalino-Volchansk. In the first eleven months after October 1942 the east-west exchange system took twenty-two infantry and six armored or motorized divisions out of the west. This was in addition to a constant weeding out of the best personnel and equipment from divisions considered unsuitable as a whole for east duty.

Thus in 1943, a year of increasing threats of attack from the west, the German armies in France had not even held their own. General Blumentritt, the OB WEST chief of staff, in September summarized the deterioration for the high command. A year ago, he pointed out, the Atlantic Wall had been garrisoned with twenty-two infantry divisions most of which had three regiments. In reserve were six infantry and seven fully mobile, first-class armored or motorized divisions. Now, he continued, in a much more dangerous situation, the garrison infantry divisions had increased to twenty-seven, but this increase was largely nullified by the reduction of most of the divisions to two regiments. In reserve were six armored or motorized divisions and seven infantry divisions, of which three were new organizations. In other words, though the holding strength remained about constant in numbers the quality had certainly declined; the striking power had decreased slightly in numbers and very substantially in mobility.

There was no appeasing the hunger of the Eastern Front. The continual protests of the Commander in Chief West and even Hitler's own resolution toward the end of 1943 to halt the weakening of the west were alike swept aside by the demands for more and more men to halt the tide of Russian victories. The German Army went into Russia in June 1941 with 3,300,000 men. By the spring of 1943, despite every effort to get replacements, the eastern army had been reduced by 600,000. Built back up to three million for the summer offensive, it suffered another net reduction of a half million by September. In 1943 alone, the Germans estimated that they had a total of 2,086,000 casualties in the east, of which 677,000 were permanent losses (that is, the killed and missing, unfit, and one-third of all wounded). The net losses continued to mount so that in the year from July 1943 through June 1944 the gap between losses and replacements amounted to 535,000.

Even these figures do not truly reflect the exhaustion of the German Army. Of 151 German Army divisions listed in the OKH order of battle for the Russian front in December 1943, ten panzer and fifty infantry divisions were "fought out" (abgekaempft) or, in other words, of negligible combat value. Eleven of the named infantry "divisions" were actually only Kampfgruppen. At the same time there were twelve full divisions in Italy, while OB WEST had forty-six divisions plus two regiments that were operational and another seven divisions in process of formation. These figures strikingly reveal the strain exerted by the Russian war: the number of divisions in the east which needed replacement and reconstitution was greater than the total number of divisions in the two western theaters.

The war in Russia was always the principal vacuum into which German resources were sucked and destroyed, but Allied attacks on North Africa in November 1942 and subsequent Allied Mediterranean operations superimposed an additional strain which contributed substantially to the weakening of the west. General der Artillerie Walter Warlimont of OKW concluded after the war that the invasion of North Africa, which came as a complete surprise to Hitler, was actually "decisive for the whole conduct of the war" for it established a "springboard for a thrust into the groin of Fortress Europe, the naturally weak and practically unprepared south flank." One immediate result of Allied landings in North Africa on 8 November 1942 was to force German occupation of the whole of France and add some four hundred miles of Mediterranean coast line to OB WEST's responsibilities.

Plans for the occupation of Vichy France were completed in July

Inside a German self-propelled gun. Ammunition supply was a crucial consideration and the German forces had to be careful to conserve their ammunition.

1942. Troops were alerted on 7 November, the day before the Allied landings in North Africa. Ten divisions under two armies (the first and Army Felber) moved across the Demarcation Line on 11 November and, without opposition from the French, occupied the Spanish border and the Mediterranean coast as far as Toulon. The area from there east and as far north as a line between Lyon and the Swiss border was taken over at the same time by the Italian Fourth Army, which moved in with six divisions and three corps headquarters. In December the units under the German first Army withdrew and first Army responsibility was thereafter limited to the Atlantic coast line as far north as the Loire River. The Mediterranean became the responsibility of Army Felber.

These arrangements lasted about six months. In June 1943 Rundstedt notified General der Infanterie Hans-Gustav Felber that Italian collapse seemed possible and he was therefore to prepare to relieve the Fourth Army. His local commanders were to try to get the Italians to continue fighting on the side of the Germans, but those who could not be persuaded were to be disarmed. Labor troops were to be formed of those willing to work, and the rest were to be regarded as prisoners of war.

During the campaign in Sicily and through the fall of Mussolini the Fourth Army held on in France. But on 10 August the Italian supreme command proposed withdrawal of the army to defend Italy against the expected Allied invasion of the mainland. Two days later Felber was relieved by General der Infanterie Georg von Sodenstern. During the next few weeks the command in the south was renamed the Nineteenth Army and preparations were completed to relieve the Italians. The relief, which absorbed four German divisions, was carried out early in September. Except for a brief fight at the Mount Cenis tunnel by units of the Italian 5th Alpini Division the relief was peaceful. But in the course of it about 40,000 Italian troops were made prisoner and sent into the interior of France as labor troops. No more than a handful volunteered to fight beside the Germans.

Southern France was only one of the vacuums created by Italian collapse. As soon as collapse seemed imminent the Germans made plans to shift troops into the Italian peninsula and into the Balkans. The total number required was not large, but the added strain was severe. The planned 1943 summer offensive in Russia (Operation ZITADELLE), becoming an exhausting defensive action, drew off so many troops that OKW in July could find only twelve divisions available for occupying Italy. All of these were already either in northern Italy or under OB WEST command. Impoverished by contributions to the Russian war, OB WEST was now to be beggared to nourish the Mediterranean. Before 1 September, Rundstedt had given up eight infantry and nine panzer divisions to Africa and Italy and one infantry and one panzer division to the Balkans. These comprised, moreover, some of the best-quality troops remaining in the west after earlier withdrawals for Russia.

Besides forcing direct contributions of troops, Allied attacks in Italy weakened the whole defense system of the west by creating invasion threats to southern France. Although Rundstedt never reckoned with a major landing on his Mediterranean coast, he did count as probable a diversionary attack tied in with a large-scale invasion in the northwest. In his October report he pointed out that the Rhone Valley was a natural invasion route to the north and that the ports of Toulon and Marseille would undoubtedly be tempting to the Allies. General

Sodenstern in August 1943 noted the clear strategic connection between thrusts from the north and south and recalled that the Rhône Valley had been a historic route to the upper Rhine for invading armies since the wars of Caesar.

The "three-front" war all but exhausted the normal German manpower reservoirs. The Germans then turned to extraordinary sources to fill up the decimated ranks of the west army. The principal last-ditch sources were foreign personnel (chiefly Russian), young recruits of the classes of 19 and 196, convalescents often with physical disabilities, organizational overhead, and troops in occupied areas comparatively safe from invasion threats, like Norway and Denmark. Divisions that remained in the west but had their rosters combed out for replacements for eastern service were replenished with men rated less fit for combat. Divisions transferred to the east were replaced with new formations, sometimes with good personnel, more often with a mixture of fit and unfit, experienced and green, German and foreign.

In June 1941 the German Army was entirely German and prided itself on its "racial purity." With the opening of the Russian campaign, German propaganda began to internationalize German war aims as a crusade against Bolshevism. At the same time the requirements for men to administer and defend vast occupied territories while well over two million men fought in the Russian battlefields made imperative the opening of almost any conceivable additional source of manpower. "Racial Germans" (Volksdeutsche), especially from Poland, were given conditional German citizenship and under this fiction made subject to the draft. As time went on the fiction was extended often to persons who could not even speak German. Recruiting was begun also in the occupied territories of Russia and units formed of the so-called Freiwilligen (volunteers). As the pressure for more and more men developed, the Freiwilligen, too, lost more and more of their volunteer character. In the late fall of 1941 Hitler authorized the employment of Russian prisoners in the German Army, formalizing a procedure already applied by field commanders. The majority of the Hilfswillige (auxiliaries) were employed as labor troops in war areas. Through increasing admixture with these three categories, Volksdeutsche, Freiwillige, and Hilfswillige, the "racial purity" of the German Army became more and more dilute. In 1944 the Army included as "volunteers" from occupied and allied territories: French, Italians, Croatians, Hungarians, Romanians, Poles, Finns, Estonians, Letts, Lithuanians, North Africans, Negroes, Asiatics, Russians, Ukrainians, Ruthenians, Kazaks, North-Caucasians, Georgians, Azerbaijani, Armenians, Turkomans, Volga-Tatars, Volga-Finns, Kalmucks, Crimean Tatars, and even Indians.

The Volksdeutschen, drawn chiefly from territories which Germany intended to integrate with the Reich, were originally classified in four categories according to the degree of their overt sympathy with the Nazi party. The majority were placed in the third category (Volksliste drei) comprising racial Germans who despite previous integration in the Polish national culture were deemed amenable to Germanization. Volksliste drei persons were given a ten-year probationary citizenship and drafted if of military age. Although integrated for the most part in the Army they were forbidden to rise above the rank of private first class.

Rundstedt, in October 1943, commented on the lower morale of the Volksdeutschen, due, he thought, not to ill will on their part but to the fact that their families were not being treated like the families of front-line German soldiers. But the reliability of the Volksdeutschen concerned him much less than that of the volunteer Russian combat battalions which his command had been forced to accept in the latter part of the year. The original idea back of the formation of the Ost (east) battalions was to employ anti-Red Russian peoples (generally prisoners of war) in the crusade against the Soviet Union. When the third great German summer offensive soured in 1943 and the German armies began a retrograde movement that had all the earmarks of final retreat, the anti-Bolshevik recruits became increasingly unreliable and it was decided to transfer them to the west in exchange for German troops. In September OKW ordered the exchange on the basis of two Ost battalions for one German battalion. At that time OKH reported that 15,800 Osttruppen were trained and that 2,000 more would be trained in November and December. During September and October, about forty-five Cossack, Georgian, North-Caucausian, Turkoman, Armenian, Volga-Tatar, Azerbaijanian, Volga-Finn, and miscellaneous

Ost battalions were brought into the OB WEST sector. The original ratio of one German for two Ost battalions was considerably modified to the advantage of the Russian theater. Plans at the end of October were to exchange thirty-two more Ost battalions for twenty-six German battalions of which OB WEST would furnish twenty and Norway and Denmark the remaining six. By May 1944 Seventh Army alone had twenty-three Ost battalions of infantry. This represented about one sixth of the total number of rifle battalions in the Army. In the LXXXIV Corps sector in Normandy and Brittany, out of forty-two rifle battalions, eight were composed of Osttruppen.

Besides recruiting prisoners of war, the Germans added to their military manpower by relaxing physical standards. At the end of 1943 the physical fitness categories were cut down from four to three. The limited service classification was abolished and men were to be graded as fit for service at the front, fit for service in Germany, or totally unfit. Those with relatively minor ear, stomach, and lung ailments were to be sent to the front. Convalescence time was ordered cut down. No accurate picture of the physical state of the German Army in the west is possible. Physical standards were unquestionably much lower than in Allied armies. But although the majority of troops in the west were considered unfit for combat in Russia, the cause of unfitness was often inadequate training, lack of transport, and lack of equipment rather than the physical condition of the men.

In the whole German Army the average age in 1944 was 31 years, four and a half years older than the average age of the German Western Front Army in 1917 and more than six years older than the U. S. Army in 1943. Of an Army of 4,270,000 in December 1943 more than a million and a half were over 34 years old. In the west the older-age classes as well as a large proportion of the relatively unfit were assigned to the static coastal divisions. Even so, repeated raids were made on the static divisions to sort out their best men for east duty. Eventually these divisions acquired a substantial number of the overage, the very young (classes of 1925 and 1926), men with third-degree frostbite, Volksdeutsche (which were used up to 8 percent of division strength), and Osttruppen. The average age of the 709th Division which held the east coast of the Cotentin was thirty-six. The fact that one whole division was almost entirely composed of men suffering from stomach ailments is dramatic, if somewhat misleading, evidence of the lengths to which German leaders went to fill up the ranks of the Army. It is misleading because, in contrast to the static coastal divisions, the offensive divisions (infantry, parachute, armored, and SS) contained excellent personnel. Though relatively new organizations, most seem to have been adequately trained and equipped by the time of the invasion.

Many of the deficiencies of the German Army in the west at the end of 1943 were substantially made up in the first six months of 1944; others were chronic and could at best only be patched over with makeshift measures. The most serious of the latter was the lack of manpower and especially of first-class combat soldiers. It should be remembered, however, that this constituted primarily a strategic weakness. While it affected the strength of the Atlantic Wall defenses both in reducing the numbers and quality of the coastal garrisons, its real importance was not for the battle of the beaches but for the campaign to follow. In naturally strong coastal defenses even a relative handful of second-class troops could give good account of themselves. The drain of the three-front war meant above all that there were no strategic reserves. Losses could not be made up. The divisions in the west could not hope for replacement when they were fought out. The defensive crust could be thickened and spiked and made very formidable indeed, but only at the expense of putting everything forward. The enemy was hollow and he would be shown so in the later phases of OVERLORD.

Rebuilding the Western Defenses

Rundstedt's report of 25 October on the weakness of the western defenses was read by Hitler; his reply was the issuance on 3 November of Fuehrer Directive No. 51, the second basic order dealing with the west. The order was, in fact, elicited not only by Rundstedt's bill of particulars but by the military reverses that the German armies suffered in the east and south in the course of the year and the growing conviction that the Allies would soon seek a decision in the west. The bitter and costly fighting of the last two and half years against

Bolshevism, Hitler wrote, had strained to the utmost German military capacities. That strain had to be borne, but now while the danger in the east remained it was outweighed by the threat from the west where enemy success would strike immediately at the heart of the German war economy. Therefore, there should be no more weakening of the west in favor of other theaters. Threatened portions of the coast line were to be strengthened by the maximum emplacement of coastal artillery, fixed antitank weapons, dug-in tanks, mines, and so on. At the same time, as security against the possibility of any enemy eruption through the coastal crust, the maximum mobile reserves should be created for rapid counterattack.

The Army would submit a plan to equip every panzer and panzer grenadier division with ninety-three Mark IV tanks or assault guns and with strong antitank defenses by the end of December 1943. Reserve panzer divisions should be fully equipped; antitank guns and machine guns were to be delivered in quantity to OB WEST units. It was forbidden to transfer armored units out of the west without Hitler's specific approval. OB WEST would conduct exercises to plan the shift of partly mobile units from portions of the coast not threatened by attack. The Luftwaffe and Navy were ordered to strengthen their defenses. Hitler concluded with an exhortation to maximum effort in preparing for the expected "decisive struggle in the west."

The order against weakening the west could not, or at least would not, be strictly carried out. On 23 November OB WEST was directed to speed up the reorganization of the 60th Panzer Grenadier Division for immediate transfer to the east. On 3 December, 10,000 men of the class of 1925 were ordered pruned from divisions in the west to be replaced with men who had been previously deferred for occupational reasons. At about the same time the number of heavy weapons allotted to the west was reduced in favor of the east. During 1944 the troop transfers would continue.

These continued transfers, however, were in the course of the first half of 1944 more than made up. The failure to adhere to the letter of Directive 51 revealed the continuing pressure of the war in the east, but more striking was the vigor and success with which the rebuilding of the west was undertaken despite that pressure. November 1943 thus

The Sturmgeschutze was an effective tank destroyer which was introduced into service in this variant, in 1942. The long barrelled 75mm anti-tank gun was soon proved to be effective against the Russian T-34. It was equally effective against the Allied Sherman tanks.

marked an important new beginning in German defense preparations in the west. The new beginning was signalized in the same month by the introduction of Generalfeldmarschall Erwin Rommel, the famed desert tactician, into the western scene. The circumstances of Rommel's selection are somewhat confused. Since the summer of 1943 Rommel had been in northern Italy at the head of Army Group B-the force that moved in when it became clear that the Mussolini partnership was on the point of collapse. Meanwhile, operations in Sicily and against the Allied landings in the south were directed by Generalfeldmarschall Albert Kesselring (OB SUED). At Hitler's wish, plans had been worked out and orders issued as early as August 1943 for the eventual assumption of command by Rommel over all German forces in Italy. The intention of making Rommel the theater commander in Italy was adhered to until the latter part of October, when, for reasons unknown, Hitler changed his mind and on the 25th appointed Kesselring instead. This choice in effect left Rommel and his staff surplus at a time when Hitler and OKW were seeking new means to strengthen the west against Allied invasion threats. Hitler himself had long been convinced of the desirability of having a high command in reserve and he seized this opportunity. Three days after Kesselring's appointment OKW had entered formal proposals for the constitution of a reserve army group headquarters under Rommel earmarked for commitment wherever the main Allied invasion should come. The new headquarters was formed from the staff of Army Group B less various special staff officers and about half of the enlisted personnel. The reduced headquarters thus formed was redesignated Army Group for Special Employment, subordinated directly to OKW and transferred temporarily to Munich pending the commencement of its new duties.

These were outlined in orders of 6 November. In preparation for his ultimate combat task Rommel was ordered to make tours of inspection of the coastal defenses of the west. He was to inspect first the defenses of Denmark and then those of Artois (roughly the Kanalkueste); thereafter he would on order examine the defense preparations in the Cotentin, the Netherlands, and Brittany. In each case he was directed to prepare operational studies for the employment of forces in defense and counterattack. He would examine the mobility, concentration, and combat readiness of all troops, but especially of the reserves. He would determine what units might be drawn from unthreatened portions of the coast, from reserve or school troops, and from home units to build a counterattacking force. He would make recommendations on the employment of armor in the operational zones.

Hitler seems to have had a number of reasons for assigning this mission to the Rommel staff. He saw it as a means of securing effective personal control of the all-important battle with the main forces of the Western Allies, and probably was responsible for the suggestion that the Rommel staff be committed directly under OKW, bypassing the theater command. Although OKW successfully argued that the proposal was not feasible in view of the smallness of Rommel's staff and the rank and importance of the theater commanders involved, the later history of the Rommel command in France suggests that the idea was only scotched, not killed. When Rundstedt was informed of the new command, OKW was careful to point out that it was not intended in any way as an abridgment of Rundstedt's authority. On the other hand, it was a recognition of the increasing burden of operational, training, and administrative responsibilities that were heaped on OB WEST in its multiple role as a defense command, an occupying force, a training command, and the base for the V-weapon war on England. The particular selection of Rommel undoubtedly had an additional morale motive. For the long-neglected west garrison troops the appointment of a commander with Rommel's reputation in combat was a stimulant and a dramatization of the new importance assigned to the west. Finally, the reserve command, considered in context with Directive 51, expressed a shift in Hitler's tactical thinking away from exclusive dependence on an impregnable wall defense toward the traditional German reliance on mobile operations. Just how far Hitler intended to depart from his earlier insistence on a pure fortress defense, in which each inch of occupied ground was to be held to the last man and the last bullet, is not clear. It is clear and of considerable importance that this directive tended in that direction and that it was so interpreted by Rundstedt. Rundstedt was thereby encouraged to re-examine ways and means of shaking his army loose from the concrete of the Atlantic Wall, and the question of how the battle for France was to be fought was posed again with a new urgency.

German defense preparations in the west and the German conduct of operations in France can be understood only against the background of disagreement over tactics among the various commanders involved. In terms of abstract doctrine the disagreement was basic and clear-cut: it opposed the notion of linear defense to defense in depth, static warfare to mobile operations, the holding of ground to battles of annihilation, the primary dependence on concrete fortifications to the primary dependence on armored striking power. In practice, however, disagreements were blurred without being reconciled by the fact that few commanders believed in simple dependence on either alternative and that, since doctrine was a the mercy of limited means, it tended to shift in response to the expected avail ability of resources. It is extremely difficult therefore to line up the commanders on either side of the argument. But, although the line was neither clear nor fixed, it was nonetheless real and significant. Since Hitler and Rundstedt at the top of the hierarchy never arrived at clear-cut decisions themselves as to the basic tactics, shifting and relatively minor differences of emphasis in the lower command resulted in confusion and unworkable compromises particularly in the disposition and training of troops. The discussion of the varying points of view that follows can do no more than suggest the bases of that confusion without attempting to describe in full the stand of any one commander.

The problem of the defense of the west was immensely complex and perhaps insoluble. Hitler at least after the possibility of defeating Russia had faded in 1943, looked forward to the forthcoming struggle in the west as his last chance to gain a decisive victory. On the other hand, his obsession with political prestige and his consequent reluctance to surrender ground voluntarily in order to gain strategic or tactical advantage committed him to a policy of rigid terrain defense not only in France but throughout the occupied territories. This basic conflict over the purpose of defense, whether it was to hold ground in perpetuum or gain military advantage for victory at arms was never decided. Plans were made, for instance, to evacuate Norway and Denmark in case of an invasion of France. OKW recommended in late 1943 that the troops in Italy be withdrawn to the north to save divisions for the main battles to be fought in Russia and France. Hitler himself, as already noted, talked in his Directive 1 of the ruthless evacuation of coastal areas not under threat of attack to feed the main battle area when the time came. But when the time did come the evacuation was not carried out, probably both because Hitler no longer believed it possible and because he could not reconcile himself to the surrender of any portion of his conquests. The policy of rigid defense, meant, in the first instance, an impossible policy of defense for its own sake.

A certain rigidity of defense in the west, however, was required by purely military considerations. It was essential to hold the Allies at arm's length from the critical industrial areas of Germany, and it was highly desirable to take advantage of the strong position afforded by the sea barrier. These military arguments in favor of a stand at the coast line, however, were subject to interpretation, and the rigidity they seemed to dictate was only relative. The decision to build an Atlantic

Wall was the initial admission that the elastic defense principles applied so successfully by the Russians in their vast territories could not be adopted in the west and that basically the German armies in the west must stand on a line. There was never any debate over the need for making this line as strong as possible through the construction of a system of permanent and field fortifications. The debate concerned only how the line was to be held: what dependence was to be placed on stopping the enemy at the line itself, and where reserves should be located and how employed.

Hitler believed in 1942 and probably again in 1944 that the line could be made so strong that the enemy landing attempt could be smashed at the water's edge within the first twenty-four hours. Rundstedt concurred that this was the ideal. He pointed out that the experiences of Dieppe and Sicily both confirmed that the enemy's weakest moment was at the time of landing. While still afloat he would be without cover and have reduced fire power. Later reports on the Salerno landings led to the same conclusion through the observation that any other defensive course was foredoomed to failure. Generalmajor Viktor Marnitz reported that at Salerno the German reserves, although located near the coast (from three to five kilometers inland), had been unable to counterattack across the open terrain under heavy Allied naval artillery fire. Allied air attacks contributed to the difficulties of forming counterattacks. Strong points along the coast had held out well but for the most part the Allies had avoided them, landing between them and infiltrating inland to seize transportation junctions. Allied troops had not been held up by any kind of natural obstacles; on the contrary they had seemed able to take advantage of all kinds of unfavorable terrain. General Marnitz's recommendations were to smash the Allied attack before landing by holding the reserves close up and withholding coastal artillery fire to the last moment. If some troops got ashore they would be forced to spread out by stubborn resistance in a number of small resistance nests. Any of the enemy forces that pierced the coastal defenses should be counterattacked by local reserves after they were beyond the range of naval guns.

Rundstedt in forwarding this report concurred in its contents, but in a later communication he made one significant addition. Smash the enemy in his boats, if possible. If he lands, counterattack immediately with local reserves. But if, despite everything, he still succeeds in getting through the first line of defense, then hold him by fire from positions echeloned in depth long enough to permit counterattack by corps and army reserves. Counterattack by purely local reserves could be considered part of the concept of static defense. Riposte by corps and army reserves introduced the concept of flexible, mobile war, particularly when limited means made it impossible to achieve both an optimum strength on the first line and an adequate pool of reserves.

General der Panzertruppen Leo Freiherr Geyr von Schweppenburg, the armored expert in the west, wanted to push the mobile tactics thus adumbrated to the point of falling back entirely from the coast with all mobile units, leaving only the static defenses to stave off the enemy as long as possible and inflict maximum losses. He wanted to seek a decision in the interior with a massed armored counterattack. The Luftwaffe, he felt, should not be committed in the battle for the beaches but saved to cover the counterattack. Sodenstern agreed, with an interesting variation which he described in reflections jotted down in the summer of 1943.[85] The relative weakness of German forces, he felt, required that they defend the coast only long enough to determine the center of gravity of the enemy attack. Strategic reserves should be assembled on both sides of the Seine northwest of Paris and on the upper Loire. The area between the Seine and Loire would be the battlefield. Since Allied air superiority would make extensive German troop movements impossible, the Allies should be compelled to maneuver into the area chosen for the battle by means of switch lines contrived to canalize the Allied attack.

The notion of gambling everything on fully mobile defense with massed counterattacks mounted inland was never seriously entertained. Rundstedt seems generally to have conceived of the main battle as taking place in the coastal area. He vacillated chiefly in the reliance which he wanted to put on mobile counterattack within that area. To make such an attack possible, German forces, of course, had to be able to maneuver freely. Salerno and Sicily had shown that armor could not fight successfully within the range of naval artillery. Rundstedt pointed out to OKW that armor therefore could not influence the battle unless German aircraft, especially torpedo planes, could interfere with the firing of Allied warships.[86] In addition, German mobility obviously depended on the quality and quantity of equipment and personnel. In his October report, Rundstedt admitted that the German divisions in the west had neither the men nor the machines to fight in open terrain against an enemy so materially strong as the Allies were sure to be. The conclusion was thus forced that the only hope of redressing Allied superiority lay in taking the maximum advantage of the water barrier. That was how the situation looked in October. After the Hitler directive in the next month, Rundstedt modified his view. If the promise to strengthen the west meant the provision of new troops and more mobile divisions, it might be possible to return to the idea of mass counterattack. He therefore proposed the formation, partly on paper, partly on the ground, of a central reserve. Specifically he suggested earmarking six infantry divisions to be withdrawn after the Allied landings from coastal zones not threatened by attack. Made mobile by vehicles contributed by each of the armies, these divisions would be organized under two corps controlled by an army headquarters. Existing panzer and panzer grenadier reserves would be commanded by a reserve panzer corps and the entire force put under the special army group headquarters that was being formed under Rommel.

There is no question that the Rundstedt plan considerably extended the ideas underlying Directive 51. OKW at once objected to the proposal to withdraw entire divisions from the unthreatened portions of the coast and suggested instead that only regimental Kampfgruppen be pulled out in order not to denude any section of its defenses. More basic objections were raised by Generaloberst Hans von Salmuth, who as commander of the Fifteenth Army defending the coast which the Germans thought most likely to be the scene of the major Allied invasion attempt occupied a key position in the command hierarchy. Salmuth criticized Rundstedt's suggestion as contravening all the hitherto accepted principles of defense in the west. It assumed, he said, that the Allies would break through the cordon defense and would succeed in establishing a bridgehead. If that happened, he believed the Allies pouring ashore unhindered would soon establish a superiority of force that would be tantamount to victory. The central reserves would take too long to assemble; it would be delayed and partially destroyed by Allied air attack. It was probable therefore that it could never be committed in mass and that late and piecemeal commitment would be ineffective. All reserves, Salmuth believed, should be held as close as possible to the coast and should be under army control. The main objection to Salmuth's argument, as Rundstedt pointed out in reply, was that it relied too much on a correct guess as to where the Allies would strike. For Salmuth this was not a very grave objection since he was convinced that the Allies would make their main attack in his sector. Rundstedt agreed that the likelihood existed, but pointed out that it was by no means a certainty.

To Salmuth's argument that the central reserves could not be assembled and committed fast enough to be of use in a decisive mass counterattack, Rundstedt made no reply. His continued advocacy of such a reserve implied a belief that if victory was to be won the difficulties had to be overcome, though precisely how was never quite clear. Rundstedt's conviction, shared by most of the commanders in the West, was that no matter how strong the Atlantic Wall was made it could be broken. The only relevant questions were what dependence to put on the wall and how to divide the available forces between local and central reserves. The Nineteenth Army commander, Sodenstern, argued that the impossibility of establishing an unbreakable cordon defense vitiated the whole concept of the Atlantic Wall since a breakthrough anywhere would make all the fortifications useless.91 Rundstedt maintained that a rigid defense in a series of strong points held to the last could so splinter and weaken the enemy that his penetrations could easily be cleaned up and the whole invasion attempt thus be defeated before the enemy's superior material force could be concentrated and gain momentum. As far as the troops defending the coastal strong points were concerned, there should be no withdrawal. Each strong point should be fought separately. But this kind of resistance would only soften up the enemy for the decisive counterattacks. To be decisive they must be mounted in force. "No dispersion," said Rundstedt, "no piecemeal commitment and no thin water soup" Divisions should be committed intact to hit the flanks of the enemy penetrations.

General der Artillerie Erich Marcks, commander of LXXXIV Corps in Normandy, was persuaded by the weakness of his forces to embrace the same tactics. He told an inspecting officer from OKW in January 1944 that even a doubling of his present troop strength would make possible only a thin screen at the coast which could still be torn at any point by the enemy. Instead of a wall defense, he therefore proposed the construction of numerous small field fortifications with some depth whose mission was not to stop the enemy but to split the attacking forces and gain time for the bringing up of German reserves. He felt that a corps reserve of armor and mobile infantry could be built up behind the coast but near enough to be committed within twenty-four hours.

OKW generally remained skeptical whether, in view of Allied superiority in the air and the limited mobility of German units, large-scale counterattacks could be mounted. But, on the whole, Jodl and his staff concurred that depth of defense was desirable. In response to repeated pleas by Rundstedt in the summer of 1943 OKW authorized the construction, if practicable, of a secondary position still within the coastal zone. In June 1943 the Commander in Chief West ordered local commanders to reconnoiter rear areas for suitable locations for heavy weapons in accordance with their own estimate of the situation and enemy intentions. He also suggested that prepared positions for antitank guns and machine guns would be of considerable importance in delaying the enemy troops that might break through the first line of defense. At the moment there was little possibility of actually starting construction. Nothing was started until the end of October, when Rundstedt ordered further reconnaissance by corps and armies and the beginning of field construction. The secondary position was to be built with maximum flexibility to include prepared switch lines and to take in already established airfields, ammunition dumps, and shelters for reserves and staffs. Antiaircraft guns would be emplaced for ground firing and all-around defense. Some 31,000 French laborers were initially used on the job.

At the end of 1943 the discussion of defense tactics had produced no unequivocal decision. Rundstedt's own orders with their dual emphasis on holding coastal positions to the last and at the same time building mobile reserves, while in one sense perfectly consistent, were nevertheless subject to interpretation as supporting either primarily static or primarily mobile defense. Since the practical problem was the allocation of limited time and resources, insufficient for the full development of both fortifications and troop build-up and training, Rundstedt's pronouncements actually straddled the issue. In the closing months of the year the doctrine of decision by counterattack in force, though qualified and not unchallenged, seemed to have achieved general acceptance in OB WEST and the apparent endorsement of OKW and Hitler. The outline of the battle as sketched by the chief of staff of OB WEST, General Blumentritt, envisaged the fighting in four main stages: first, the fire fight while the Allies were still on the water; second, the struggle on the beaches; third, the battles in the coastal zone between German local reserves and Allied units that had penetrated the main line of resistance; and, finally, the decisive beachhead battle in which OB WEST would commit large motorized units to throw the Allies back into the sea.

In accord with this outline, Rundstedt ordered a winter construction program to step up work on the fortifications with special attention to casemating coastal artillery and antitank guns; at the same time, as already noted, he began planning for the formation of the central reserve. But the latter plans would go awry chiefly because the man slated to command the reserves and conduct the battle against the invaders was to be Field Marshal Rommel. There was scarcely a general in the German Army less in sympathy with the grandiose scheme of massed counterattacks under the bomb sights of virtually unopposed Allied air fleets. Thus at the moment when the concept of mobile defense in the west seemed to enjoy highest favor, it was in reality on the point of most complete repudiation by a commander convinced that it was a dangerous fantasy.

BARBED-WIRE OBSTACLES

Intelligence Bulletin, September 1943.

1. GENERAL

With the German Army increasingly on the defensive, it is pertinent for us to know as much as possible about the enemy's employment of barbed-wire obstacles in continental Europe. A classic asset of the defense, barbed wire naturally plays an important part in the coastal and inland defense systems that the Germans are hurrying to complete in the occupied countries. The following aspects of German wire technique have recently been observed in France, The Netherlands, and Belgium.

On beaches, barbed wire is usually erected in straight lines, parallel to the shore and in front of fortified areas. Between these fortified areas, the lines of wire jut out at right angles toward the sea.

Around emplacements and fortified areas, the depth of wire obstacles varies, depending on the nature of the terrain and the importance that the Germans attach to the site. In some places the depth may range from 30 to 60 yards; in other positions, it may range from 70 to 130 yards, or may be as much as 200 yards. As a rule, the distance between the outside edge of the wire and the nearest pillbox or other firing position is at least 30 yards.

In gullies and in the crevices of cliffs, if ascent is considered at all possible, the Germans install dense wire entanglements. In front of these, the enemy sometimes places small-mesh wire, evidently for the purpose of slowing any advance in which Bangalore torpedoes might be used. Halfway up the gullies and crevices, the entanglements usually begin to thin out. Sometimes they continue as single fences running along the tops of the cliffs, near the margins.

In conjunction with road blocks, a wire fence or entanglement is often erected on each side of the road, and the gap between is closed by movable gates of various types. In many places concrete walls and other more substantial types of barriers are replacing wire entanglements as road blocks; however, wire is nearly always used on top of these wall barriers, for additional protection. Wall barriers and concrete emplacements are likely to have iron staples in them so that wire entanglements can be firmly secured.

Often the Germans use wire to fence off all sides of a minefield. Such fences consist of a single row of pickets connected by five or six strands of wire. Also, a thin belt of wire is commonly found outside antitank ditches.

The Germans are now making extensive use of a new type of barbed wire. This new type is made of a non-corrosive metal, and is thicker than ordinary wire. It is square in cross-section, rather than round. The wire, which is twisted, has 3/4-inch barbs, 4 inches apart.

2. SPECIFIC TYPES

The following are specific types of wire obstacles that the Germans are erecting in France, Belgium, and The Netherlands. Several of these types were encountered in North Africa, and any or all must be expected wherever the Germans have had an opportunity to prepare defenses. The dimensions given here an approximate.

a. Knife Rests

X-shaped metal knife rests, or "chevaux-de-frise," strung with wire, have been observed above the high water mark on beaches. Sometimes this type of obstacle consists of four trestles connected by a crossbar, and has the following dimensions:
- Height: 4 feet
- Span of trestle legs: 4 feet
- Distance between trestles: 4 to 5 feet
- Length of four-trestle unit: 16 to 20 feet

b. Apron Fences

These may be single or double aprons. They are supported by screw pickets or by angle irons embedded in concrete to a depth of about 18 inches. Often a coil of concertina wire is placed under a double apron fence, and sometimes another coil is placed along the top. The dimensions of a typical apron fence are as follows:
- Height: 4 to 5 feet
- Height (with coil on top): 7 to 8 feet
- Width: Up to 30 feet

c. Vertical Fences

Ordinary vertical fences are always installed in two or three lines, from 4 to 8 feet apart. Each fence has five or six strands of wire, and is 4 to 6 feet high. The wire is supported by wooden posts, angle irons, or screw pickets. The spaces between fences are frequently filled with wire entanglements and mines.

d. Concertina Fences

Single, double, or triple coils of concertina, supported by angle irons or screw pickets, are often used as fences. Triple coils are frequently affixed to the protecting rails of the beach promenades which are so common in the coastal towns of western Europe.

e. Trip Fences

Trip wires are often laid in front of important beach obstacles. These wires will usually be found between the high-water mark and the first barbed-wire entanglement. They are also used in the minefields in front of main defensive positions and main obstacles. Trip fences have the following dimensions:
- Height: 4 to 6 in
- Length of each diagonal or diamond-shaped section: 4 to 6 ft
- Width of whole obstacle: 12 to 20 ft

f. Alarm Wires

The Germans often place some form of alarm device in barbed-wire fences. Grenades and small explosive charges are common. Insulated live wire, which rings a bell as soon as it is cut, has also been encountered. It must be remembered that almost any kind of improvised alarm device will serve the defenders' purpose, provided that it produces enough noise to warn effectively.

g. Electrified Wire

Electrified barbed wire, attached to pickets by means of insulators, has been reported. This type of obstacle is not used on a very large scale, however.

h. Combined Fences

A typical combined fence consists of the following units, in sequence: a trip wire, a trestle fence or knife rest, and an apron fence. The apron fence is likely to be from 10 to 20 yards behind the trestle fence or

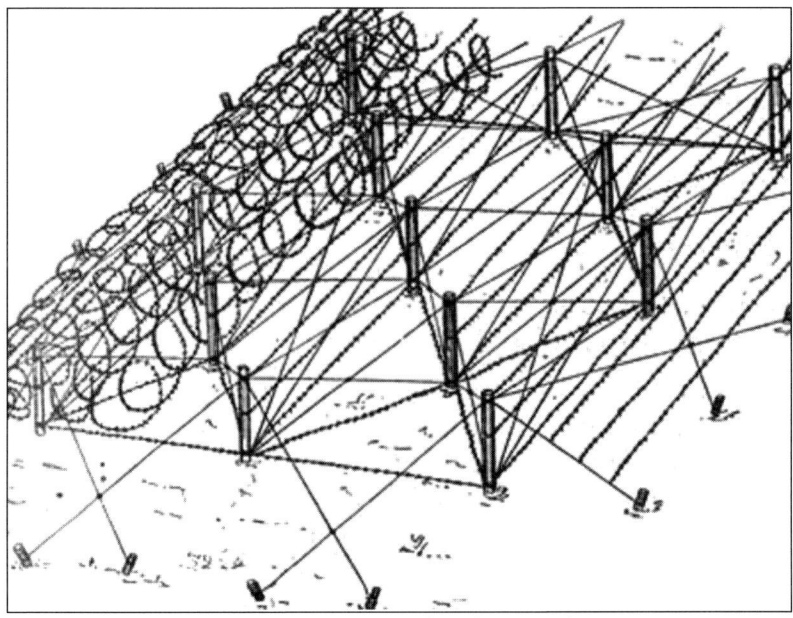

Figure 1.—German Obstacle in Depth.

knife rest, and the total depth of the whole combination may be from 30 to 60 yards. On the sea fronts of towns, the Germans usually erect an apron or knife-rest fence on the beach, and a concertina or apron fence on top of the sea (retaining) wall or beach promenade.

3. STANDARD TECHNIQUE

The *Intelligence Bulletin* distinguishes between German technique which has actually been observed, and that which is prescribed in German training documents. Some notes regarding the latter are given below.

a. Obstacle in Depth

This type of obstacle is constructed to a depth of about 33 feet. It consists of ordinary wire fences erected at intervals of about 5 feet and connected with crisscrossed plain wire (see fig. 1). The spaces between the fences are filled with barbed wire in spirals. These spirals are fastened to each other and to the pickets of the crisscrossed wire. When obstacles of this type are erected in woods, trees are often used to support the wire.

Wire obstacles in depth are usually installed in places where they will be screened as far as possible against observation by opposing forces. Woods, hollows, sunken roads, and heavily overgrown reverse slopes are sites especially favored by the enemy.

b. Wire-netting Fences

The Germans use wire netting as an emergency obstacle against infantry. They believe it to be most effective in woods and on the near side of hedges, and recommend that it be secured to the ground with wire and pickets. An obstacle of this type illustrated in a German training manual is 6 feet 6 inches high.

c. Trip-wire Obstacles

German training doctrine prescribes that these obstacles be at least 30 feet in depth. Irregular rows of wooden pickets, 2 feet high and 3 inches in diameter, are driven into the ground, and barbed or plain wire is stretched between pickets, at a height of 4 feet 8 inches. The interval between pickets in a row is 10 to 13 feet, and the interval between rows is 7 to 10 feet. Freshly cut pickets are painted to blend with the surroundings.

Trip-wire obstacles can be concealed effectively in gullies and on ground covered by low growth, especially if rusted wire is used. Mines and booby traps, equipped with pull-igniters, may be combined with these obstacles.

TYPES OF CONCRETE ANTITANK OBSTACLES

Intelligence Bulletin, September 1943.

This section deals with the principal types of concrete antitank obstacles erected by the Germans in the coastal defense zones of France, Belgium, and The Netherlands.

1. WALLS
a. General
The Germans make a practice of constructing concrete antitank walls in all coastal areas where a strong defense is planned. Walls of this type are used to block streets and roads in coastal towns, at the approaches to strategic points, and on the outskirts of towns, generally. Often the Germans prepare a continuous obstacle along the entire sea front of a town by constructing concrete walls in line with the front elevation of existing buildings. first, rough timber shuttering is erected along the site proposed for a new wall, and then the concrete is poured. Light steel reinforcement is sometimes used, but often there is no reinforcement at all. Often metal hooks project from the top of a wall, to serve as anchors for barbed wire. To improve the effectiveness of a concrete antitank wall, the Germans often dig a ditch in front of the obstacle or prepare a tank trap in the form of a pit covered with planks and gravel, or garnished netting.

In areas where there are quarries which can supply large quantities of stone, road blocks are often constructed of the native stone, instead of concrete.

b. Continuous Walls
When a continuous wall is erected along the sea front of a coastal town, a minimum thickness of 6 feet is the general rule. It is reported that the average thickness is from 8 to 11 feet. The height of such a wall is usually from 6 to 8 1/2 feet.

c. V-shaped Walls
The Germans frequently erect V-shaped walls across the roads or

tracks leading inland (through defiles between cliffs and dunes) from beaches. The point of a V-shaped wall is always toward the sea. These walls are especially common in open coastal stretches between towns. The dimensions of walls of this type are similar to the dimensions of continuous walls. It must be expected that the apex of the V will contain gun emplacements, or that the entire V will have been built to serve as a pillbox.

d. Walls with Gaps

When the Germans build a concrete wall with a gap, the gap is usually wide enough to allow only one vehicle to pass through at a time. The gap can be closed by means of girders, rails, or gates fitted into sockets imbedded in the wall.

It has been reported that in certain European coastal areas the Germans use an interesting type of staggered double road block. These obstacles consist essentially of a pair of walls or barricades, sited one behind the other, but projecting from opposite sides of a road. Each wall projects across 1/2 or 2/3 of the width of the road. These walls, which are never less than 6 feet thick, may be of masonry or concrete, or may simply consist of log barricades filled with earth or sand. The horizontal and vertical logs are about 1 foot in diameter. The vertical logs are driven deep into the ground, and additional resistance is provided by diagonal bracing. Obviously, such obstacles are intended to slow down advancing vehicles, and thereby render them much more susceptible to attack.

2. OTHER CONCRETE OBSTACLES

a. Dragons' Teeth

Concrete obstacles known as "dragons' teeth" are used by the Germans to block streets, exits from quays, and well-defined beach exits where the level of the beach is Approximately the same as that of the roads leading inland. A typical arrangement consists of four to eight staggered rows of tapered dragons' teeth, with 6 to 8 feet between the teeth in each row and 6 to 8 feet between rows. Often the bases of the teeth are connected by concrete beams, in lines parallel with the road; this is a means of reinforcing the obstacles against possible overturning. The total height of these obstacles may be from 3 to 6 feet.

b. Plain Blocks

Plain concrete blocks are used in the same way as dragons' teeth, but are also found in defiles between sand dunes, which might afford an entrance inland for vehicles even though no well-defined road exists. These blocks are arranged in from one to three rows, and are not always staggered. In dune country they are also found on forward slopes, near the crests. The blocks may be rectangular (3 feet wide on each side and 4 feet high) or cylindrical (3 to 4 feet in diameter and 4 feet high).

3. RAILS EMBEDDED IN CONCRETE

In coastal towns the Germans often use straight or curved steel rails embedded in concrete to block ramps, promenades, streets, and all other exits leading from beaches. Sometimes three or four lengths of straight rail are combined to form a skeleton pyramid, with their bases embedded in concrete and the tops bolted together. Rail-and-concrete obstacles are generally from 3 1/2 to 4 1/2 feet high.

GERMAN DEFENSE MEASURES, 1944

Center of Military History, United States Army

OKW Policy in 1944

German strategy for 1944 rested on the realization that decisive offensives could no longer be mounted in the east and that the growing strength of the Western Allies made almost certain a major invasion attempt before the end of the year. The prospective invasion of western Europe presented both the gravest danger to the Reich and the most hopeful opportunity for turning defeat into victory. If the Allies were not stopped at the landings, their attack would carry at once into the heart of Germany; if they were stopped and their beachheads annihilated, it was unlikely that a new attempt could be made for a long time to come, and as many as fifty German divisions might thereby be freed for the struggle against the Soviet Union.

Recognizing the superiority of the Allied military potential, the Germans knew that their one chance for defeating the invasion was to defeat it quickly. It was therefore vital that the maximum German force be on the spot to fight the decisive battle as soon as the Allies attacked. To stake everything on a battle whose place and timing would be entirely of the enemy's choosing was to put an all but impossible burden on the defense, demanding of it a mobility it did not have and a sure knowledge of enemy intentions it had no means of acquiring. It was one thing to decide-as Hitler did with the issuance of his Directive No. 51-to prepare the west for the critical battle to come; it was another to find the means to carry out those preparations.

Regardless of how critical the defense of the west was declared, there could be no question of withdrawing forces from the hard-pressed eastern armies to reinforce it. The best that could be hoped for was to hold on to forces already in the various occupied territories outside of Russia and devote to the west the bulk of the new resources in men and equipment that became available in the months remaining before the Allies attacked. After Hitler's November order, OKW drew up a plan providing in detail for the shift of troops to meet a major Allied invasion of any one of the western theaters of operations. If the invasion hit France-the most likely possibility-OKW planned to move three infantry divisions from Norway and Denmark, one infantry division, a *Werfer* regiment and a corps headquarters from Italy, and four mobile infantry or *Jaeger* divisions and some minor units from the Balkans. Although these troop shifts would not amount to evacuation of any occupied area, they would mean a considerable concentration of force.

Such concentration was based on the assumption that the Allies would make one main attack. In January OKW began to wonder whether the assumption was justified. All signs still pointed to an attack across the Channel, probably at its narrowest point, but there were also indications that such an attack might be preceded or accompanied by other major thrusts. OKW noticed the "astonishing" emphasis in Allied quarters on preparations for a "second front" and reasoned that these might be designed to conceal another "main blow" that would not strike across the Channel. The "other place" selected might be Portugal or the Balkans, but the choice of the latter had particular plausibility. It seemed unlikely that the large Allied forces in the Mediterranean would be committed in the slow and costly attempt to push all the way up the Italian peninsula. The Balkan area offered greater strategic prizes and was conveniently at hand.

Whatever area was threatened OKW viewed the twin facts of accumulated Allied power in the Mediterranean and comparative stalemate in Italy as a kind of strategic unbalance which might be solved by another sudden major assault. German jitteriness on this score was not calmed by a report at about this time from agents in England that the ratio of Allied seagoing landing ships to landing craft for Channel use was ten times as great as the Doenitz staff had previously estimated. This discovery seemed to confirm the guess that the Allies were planning an expedition outside the Channel.

All these fears seemed to be further confirmed by the Allied landings at Anzio on 22 January. The Anzio beachhead, in the German view, had only a slim tactical connection with the main Italian front. General Jodl, Chief of the Armed Forces Operations Staff, considering it to be an independent, self-sustaining operation, argued that it might well be the first of a series of attacks on the periphery of the Continent with the purpose of forcing dispersion of German reserves in preparation for a thrust across the Channel. This interpretation drew support from the fact (which the Germans found "surprising") that the Allies instead of at once pushing inland from the Anzio beaches paused for about a week to consolidate a beachhead, as though the object were not to gain tactical objectives but to attract German forces. Reasoning thus, Jodl told Hitler that they now had to reckon with a peripheral Allied strategy which would probably entail attacks on Portugal, on the west and south coasts of France, or in the Aegean, before the assault on the *Kanalkueste*. With regard to France, it was thought that the most likely Allied peripheral operations would be simultaneous landings on the Mediterranean and Biscay coasts to pinch off the Iberian Peninsula. This threat was taken seriously enough that during February two new infantry divisions then being formed were attached to *Nineteenth Army* for defense of the south coast and the *9th SS Panzer Division* was released from *OB WEST* and moved south into the Avignon area as army reserve. One new division went to first *Army* for defense of the Biscay coast and Spanish border.

The most important effect of the new appreciation, however, was to unsettle German plans for the defense. If the Allies were going to pursue a policy of many simultaneous or successive assaults, the Germans could not afford to weaken sectors not immediately under attack in order to concentrate on one main invasion. It would, in fact, be very difficult to discover which of many attacks constituted the major threat. Partly for this reason, and partly because the military situation both in the Mediterranean area and in Russia was shifting so rapidly during the early months of 1944 that any plans for the future were subject to almost daily changes, OKW in March canceled its comprehensive defense plans. Instead, theater commanders were advised that troop movements would be ordered in detail only at the time they were needed, presumably *after* a given Allied attack had developed into a major action. In addition, a new plan was drawn providing for a shift of certain units from the Replacement Army in Germany to any OKW front under heavy attack. *OB WEST* by this plan might get one corps headquarters, two reinforced panzer grenadier regiments, one reinforced infantry demonstration regiment, Kampfgruppen of three infantry regiments which were cadre for new divisions, a motorized artillery demonstration regiment, five *Landesschuetzen* battalions, and one *Nebelwerfer* demonstration battalion. These miscellaneous, partly green units were hardly a substitute for the eight divisions (reinforced) which would have gone to *OB WEST* under the old plan. Although OKW did not formally abandon the intention of drawing additional reinforcements from occupied areas not under attack, as a practical matter the possibility of such reinforcement had by March become negligible. With the high command admitting the possibility of not one but several landings, strategic uncertainty would evidently delay any possible concentration.

By March 1944, the German western defense had thus been weakened by a growing confusion as to Allied intentions. This confusion, however, was a relatively small element in the difficulties that multiplied for the Germans after the end of 1943. Not threats but immediate dangers in both the south and east were the principal preoccupations of the German high command. For three months after Hitler issued his order that the west was no longer to be weakened in favor of the Eastern Front, the Germans succeeded generally in holding the manpower dikes despite ominous cracks, and rising tides of Soviet victories. Just before Christmas, 1943, the Russians launched an offensive on the Kiev front which in a few days drove nearly two hundred miles west; in January, Leningrad was relieved by successful attack against the German *Army Group North*; at the end of the month, much of the German *Eighth Army* was encircled near Cherkassy; in February, the Russians attacked the German *Sixth Army* in the Ukraine in a general offensive to clear the Dnepr bend. The temptation again to corral idle divisions from the west was very great. But only one infantry division was taken from Norway, and it was replaced by a unit which, though not completely formed, was roughly equivalent in combat strength. The west suffered only minor depredations. In February, three reinforced regiments being formed in Germany and earmarked for OKW reserve for the west went east. During the same month 3,000 Russian front soldiers who were suffering from frostbite were exchanged for a like number of troops in the west. Signs of the mounting pressure of the Russian war, these borrowings still did not constitute important weakening of the west.

But at the end of January the Anzio landings had opened another small crack. The Germans reacted to the Anzio attack in force, not only because they believed it to be the first of a series of major Allied amphibious assaults, but because they saw the possibility of gaining political prestige by wiping out at least one Allied beachhead. In accordance with plans for meeting a large-scale landing in the southwest, the fully motorized *715th Division* was ordered out of France. By 4 February, however, it was seen that this reinforcement was not enough to crush the Anzio beachhead and General Jodl asked Hitler for permission to move in the *9th SS Panzer Division*, the only fully combat ready armored division in France. Hitler refused. With an eye on the large Allied reserve forces in North Africa, he feared an attack against the Mediterranean coast of France. He doubted, furthermore, whether the *9th SS Panzer Division*, even if eventually returned to France, could make up its losses in Italy, particularly in equipment. *OB WEST* thus survived that crisis. But the loss of the *715th Division*, which because of its unusual mobility had been included with the reserve armored force, was serious enough.

Much worse was to come. In March, the manpower dikes broke wide open as the Soviet Union launched a new offensive, and at the same time fears increased that Hungary was getting ready to pull out of the war. These circumstances forced temporary abandonment of the principles of Hitler s Directive No. 51. The bulk of the troops for the occupation of Hungary (carried out in the latter part of the month) were to be furnished by the Commander in Chief Southeast from the Balkans, and by the Replacement Army, but *OB WEST* had to send the *Panzer Lehr Division*, a corps headquarters, some aircraft, and a few minor units. The plan was to return all these units as soon as Hungary was firmly-in German hand! In fact, the occupation took place rapidly and smoothly and the bulk of the Hungarian Army remained under arms and continued to fight for the Germans. The *Panzer Lehr Division* thus was actually able to come back to France in May. But two divisions from the Replacement Army and two of the divisions contributed by the Commander in Chief Southeast were shuttled on to the Russian front and a third was saved only by a last-minute appeal to Hitler. The loss indirectly affected the west in that it further reduced the reserves available to meet the invasion.

With the Russian armies again on the move and threatening to collapse the whole southern wing of the German defense, the danger of invasion in the west for a time dimmed by comparison. The Russians attacked on 4 March. On the 9th Uman fell; the Germans evacuated Kherson and Gayvoron on the 14th. Still the Russian armies suffered no check. Before the end of the month they crossed the Bug, Dnestr, and Pruth Rivers. In Galicia they temporarily encircled the German first *Panzer Army*. The crisis for the Germans was too desperate to permit consideration of long-range plans. Reinforcements were needed at once and they had to be taken wherever they could be found. On 10 March the *361st Division* was ordered out of Denmark, and replaced with a division of much lower combat value. Two weeks later a similar exchange removed the *349th Division* from France and brought as a substitute a new weak division, the *331st*, from the Replacement Army. At about the same time four divisions under *OB WEST* (the *326th, 346th, 348th* and *19th Luftwaffe Field*) were ordered to give up all their assault guns, initially to strengthen Romanian forces and later to be distributed to various divisions along the whole Eastern Front. The big ax fell on 26 March when the whole *II SS Panzer Corps* with the *9th* and *10th SS Panzer Divisions* received marching orders to leave France and go to the assistance of the first *Panzer Army*.

The departure of the *II SS Panzer Corps* left *OB WEST* with only one fully mobile division (the *21st Panzer*). The OKW historian has suggested that, had the Allies invaded at that time, Rundstedt could have offered no effective resistance. This may be an exaggeration, but it is true that the end of March 1944 marked one of the low points of preparedness in the west and that during the next six weeks, with the Russian front relatively stabilized, the west did much to recoup its losses. By the middle of May four panzer divisions were ready for combat (despite deficiencies of equipment) and four more were being built up. Toward the end of the month *Panzer Lehr Division* returned from Hungary and the *1st SS Panzer Division* from the Eastern Front was attached to *OB WEST* for rebuilding. At the same time the *XLVII Panzer Corps* under General der Panzertruppen Hans Freiherr von Funck, one of the oldest and most experienced armored commanders in the German Army, was brought from the east to serve under Rundstedt.

Actually the recuperative powers of the west under the severe and continuing strain of supplying transfusions to the east were remarkable. Between November 1943 and June 1944, the total of combat divisions under Rundstedt's command increased from forty-six to fifty-eight. The increase was accounted for in part by the transfer of fought-out units from Russia but in larger part by the formation of new units. In the fall of 1942 the German Army, already sore-pressed for manpower, adopted the policy of combining training with occupation duties. The old combined recruiting and training units were split, and the recruit henceforth after induction into a recruiting unit near his home was sent to an affiliated training unit in the field. In 1943 about two-thirds of these training units were located in France, the Low Countries, Denmark, Poland, Lithuania, the Soviet Union, and northern Italy. The infantry and panzer units were organized into reserve divisions of which twenty-six (including four panzer) were formed during 1942 and 1943. Half of these were stationed in the *OB WEST* sector. Though they remained under the commander of the Replacement Army and theoretically retained their primary function of training replacements, in reality they came to be regarded as low-grade field divisions. Their time was increasingly devoted to garrison duty and on occasion to fighting Resistance forces. In order to carry out these duties, they received administrative attachments from the regular field army. As their operational responsibilities expanded and they began to occupy a permanent place on *OB WEST*'s order of battle, it became impossible for them to give up personnel for filler replacements to regular units. In short they became themselves an integral part of the field army. In recognition of this fact, most of them were eventually redesignated as infantry or armored divisions. Six of *OB WEST*'s reserve divisions, including all three reserve panzer divisions, had thus been upgraded before the invasion. Five of the remaining seven were similarly converted in the summer of 1944; the other two were disbanded.

Besides converting reserve divisions, the Commander in Chief West enlarged his army by rehabilitating German units from the east as already noted, and by activating new divisions out of miscellaneous personnel drawn in part from his own resources and in part from the Replacement Army. The effect of all this on the organization and character of the west army must be described in some detail, but in summary it may be said that the steady drain of the Eastern Front left to Rundstedt on the eve of his great battle two kinds of units: old divisions which had lost much of their best personnel and equipment, and new divisions, some of excellent combat value, some only partially equipped and partially trained. The majority of the new divisions were formed according to streamlined tables of organization designed generally to use the fewest possible men to produce the maximum fire power.

Organization for Combat

Between 1939 and 1943 the German standard infantry division contained three regiments with a total of nine rifle battalions. Each of the infantry regiments had, besides its twelve rifle and heavy weapons companies, a 13th (infantry howitzer) and 14th (antitank) company. The division had also an antitank and a reconnaissance battalion. Organic artillery consisted of one regiment of one medium (150-mm. howitzer) and three light (105-mm. howitzer or gun) battalions with a total armament of forty-eight pieces. German division artillery was thus roughly equal to that of a U.S. division. Chiefly because of the antitank and reconnaissance units, on the other hand, the division with 17,00 men was substantially larger than its U.S. counterpart.

It was also substantially larger than could be supported by the dwindling supply of manpower after four years of war. In October 1943 the division was drastically overhauled to reduce its size while maintaining its fire power. Organization charts of the new-style division (with 13,656 men) comprising three regiments of two battalions each had only just been published when further slashes were ordered. The problem (set in January 1944 by Hitler) was to trim the personnel to something like 11,000 without affecting the combat

The tense face of a grenadier as he awaits a potential Allied attack in the close confines of the Bocage. He carries with him a Panzerfaust anti-tank grenade, which made infantry very effective against tank attack.

strength. Army planners rejected this sleight of hand as impossible and contented themselves with a further cut from 13,656 to 12,769. Reductions were made chiefly in supply and overhead, and the proportion of combat to service troops was thereby raised to 75-80 percent. The result was the so-called 1944-type infantry division.

The reduction from nine infantry battalions to six was partly alleviated by the substitution of a *Fuesilier* battalion for the old reconnaissance unit. The *Fuesilier* battalion, still charged with reconnaissance duties, was organized like a rifle battalion except that one company was equipped with bicycles and the unit had slightly more horse-drawn vehicles and some motor transport. In practice the *Fuesilier* battalion came to be reckoned as a seventh rifle battalion.

Besides lopping off three battalions, the new division pruned out the rifle squad and company while at the same time increasing the proportion of automatic weapons. The basic unit, the rifle company, was cut to 140 enlisted men and 2 officers, as compared with the U.S. company of 187 enlisted men and 6 officers. Rifle strength in the German division was about 1,200 less than in the American but the total division fire power was superior. About equal in artillery, the German division enjoyed a slight preponderance in infantry howitzers, and a heavy superiority in automatic weapons.

The 1944 infantry division was set up as the basic type for new divisions as well as for the reorganization of certain old formations, as for instance, the Luftwaffe field divisions. The division which included the bulk of Rundstedt's infantry, however, the static (*bodenstaendige*) division, was exempted from reorganization unless specifically so ordered. The static divisions were formed at the request of Rundstedt in 1942 in order that he would have a nucleus of divisions not subject to transfer to the east. Though triangular with nine rifle battalions, they were substantially weaker than the normal old-type infantry division. They lacked the reconnaissance battalion and had only three battalions of artillery.

Although the static divisions were expressly designed as permanent garrison troops for the west, they were by no means safe from the periodic troop collections for the east. Actually, by the end of 1943, most of the divisions had lost their third regiments. Attempts in 1943 and early 1944 to rehabilitate the units and fill their ranks chiefly with *Ost* battalions resulted in virtual abandonment of tables of organization in favor of improvisation that reflected both the particular nature of the coastal assignments and the vicissitudes of the long struggle for manpower and equipment. In total strength and number and variety of combat units the static divisions bore little resemblance to one another. While the *716th Division*, for instance, had six battalions and only one regimental headquarters under its control on D Day, the *709th*, occupying two and a half times as long a coast line, had eleven battalions under three regiments.

Even after the 1944-type division had been standardized, experimentation continued. Certain divisions (notably the *77th* and *91st* in *Seventh Army* area) organized their six rifle battalions in two regiments. They lacked the fusilier battalion and had three instead of four artillery battalions. In the case of the *77th Division* this organic lack was partly made up by the attachment of an *Ost* battery and a Volga-Tatar rifle battalion. The *91st Division* went into combat with an attached parachute regiment. The two-regiment infantry division therefore did not operate in T/O form in the invasion area, and for the German Army as a whole it may be regarded as experimental and eccentric, designed further to conserve manpower but not accepted as a generally satisfactory solution.

The best infantry units in the 1944 German Army were the parachute divisions, administratively under the Luftwaffe but tactically always subordinated to Army command. Until the fall of 1943 German airborne forces comprised only one corps with two parachute divisions. At that time Goering proposed and Hitler approved a program intended to produce by the end of 1944 two parachute armies with a total strength of about 100,000 men. They were to be an elite arm and were put on an equal status with the SS units in recruiting, armament, equipment, and training.

Of the new parachute units created during the early months of 1944, *OB WEST* received the *3d* and *5th* Divisions and the *6th Parachute Regiment* (from the *2d Parachute Division*). Only the separate regiment and the *3d Division* were encountered during the fighting described in this volume. Both were first-rate fighting units.

The *3d Parachute Division* comprised three regiments of three battalions each and in addition had in each regiment a 13th (mortar) company, 14th (antitank) company, and 15th (engineer) company. The mortar company in the *6th Parachute Regiment* actually contained the nine heavy (120-mm.) mortars which the tables of organization called for, but in the *3d Parachute Division* weaponing was miscellaneous, including 100-mm. mortars and 105-mm. *Nebelwerfer*. The parachute division had only one battalion of light artillery (twelve 70-mm. howitzers). An order of 12 May 1944 to substitute an artillery regiment with two light battalions and one medium was not carried out before the division entered combat. The same order called for formation of a heavy mortar battalion (with thirty-six 120-mm. mortars) but this, too, was apparently not complied with. During April and May the division was able to constitute its antiaircraft battalion which had, besides light antiaircraft artillery, twelve 88-mm. guns. The total ration strength of the division as of 22 May was 17,420. The strength of the *6th Parachute Regiment* with fifteen companies was 3,457. Both were thus considerably larger than the normal corresponding infantry units. They were superior not only in numbers but in quality. Entirely formed from volunteers, they were composed principally of young men whose fighting morale was excellent. The average age of the enlisted men of the *6th Parachute Regiment* was 17 1/2. The parachute units were also much better armed than corresponding army units. The rifle companies of the *6th Parachute Regiment* had twice as many light machine guns as the infantry division rifle companies. The heavy weapons companies with twelve heavy machine guns and six medium mortars each were also superior in fire power to army units. Chief weakness of the parachute troops was one they shared with the rest of Rundstedt's army-their lack of motor transport. The *6th Parachute Regiment*, for instance, had only seventy trucks and these comprised fifty different models.

Theoretically, about on a par with the parachute divisions were the panzer grenadier divisions which, by American standards, were infantry divisions with organic tank battalions, some armored personnel carriers, and some self-propelled artillery. The only such division in the west during the invasion period was the *17th SS Panzer Grenadier Division* (*Goetz von Berlichingen*). Like all SS divisions it was substantially stronger than the corresponding army division. On the other hand, like so many west divisions, its combat strength in fact was much less than it appeared on paper. Its six rifle battalions were organized in two regiments which were supposed to be motorized; one battalion was supposed to be armored. In reality four of the battalions had improvised motor transport (partly Italian), two being equipped with bicycles. The "tank" battalion had thirty-seven assault guns, five less than authorized. The division had no tanks. Intended personnel strength was 18,354, of which on 1 June the division actually mustered 17,321. The antitank battalion, supposed to consist of three companies of self-propelled guns, had actually only one company, equipped with nine 75-mm. and three 76.2-mm. guns. The division had a full armored reconnaissance battalion of six companies, and an antiaircraft battalion. The latter contained twelve towed 88-mm. guns as well as guns of smaller calibers, but lacked almost a fifth of its personnel.

To meet the invasion in June, *OB WEST* had six army and three SS panzer divisions. Their strength and organization varied so widely that it is impossible to talk of a type. Personnel strength of the army divisions ranged from 12,768 (*9th Panzer*) to 16,466 (*2d Panzer*). The SS divisions, which had six instead of four infantry battalions, varied from 17,590 (*9th SS Panzer*) to 21,386 (*1st SS Panzer*). All the panzer divisions were thus much larger than their American counterparts, the 1st SS being more than twice as large. On the other hand they all had fewer tanks. Here again individual variations were enormous. The type organizational tables for both army and SS divisions called for a tank regiment with one battalion of Mark IV and one battalion of Mark V tanks. Each battalion was supposed to have four companies each with twenty-two tanks. The fact was quite different. Even the *2d Panzer Division*, the best prepared of the armored divisions on D Day, had less than its authorized number of the heavier Mark V's. Each of the divisions had a separate and slightly different organization which in no case conformed to the type. The *1st SS Panzer Division*, for instance, was supposed to have 45 assault guns, 21 Mark III, 101 Mark IV, and 81 Mark V tanks. It had in fact the full complement of assault guns but only 88 tanks in all, including 50 IV's and 38 V's. The table of organization for the *2d SS Panzer Division*, on the other hand, called for 75 assault guns of which 33 were on hand on 1 June; 7 Mark III tanks, none on hand; 57 Mark IV tanks, 44 on hand; and 99 Mark V's, 25 on hand.

The army panzer divisions included, in addition to the two regiments (four battalions) of infantry and one tank regiment, a self-propelled antitank battalion (armed more often with assault guns), an armored reconnaissance battalion, a towed antiaircraft battalion and an artillery regiment with one light self-propelled battalion, one light towed battalion, and one medium towed battalion. SS divisions had an additional towed light battalion.

The miscellaneous tank armament of the panzer divisions was typical of the weaponing of nearly all units in the west and reflected the long drain on the German war economy of the Russian war and the increasing production difficulties imposed by the accelerating Allied air offensive. As long as the Russian front was the main theater of war and the west was not immediately threatened, it was natural to ship the bulk of the best materiel to the east and arm the west as well

A member of the Hitler Youth Division is taken into captivity in the aftermath of the Normandy battles. Although the Hitler Youth Division fought very well in the campaign, they could not escape the inevitable end which awaited them.

as possible with what was left. The policy of equipping west divisions primarily with captured materiel was laid down in December 1941 when ten divisions were ordered so equipped. The east continued to enjoy priority on new equipment until the end of 1943, and although German-made tanks and assault guns were shipped to *OB WEST* during that time the deliveries were often more than outweighed by the transfer of armored units. first-class armored equipment remained a comparative rarity in divisions assigned to *OB WEST* until 1944. At the end of October 1943, for instance, there were in the west 703 tanks, assault guns, and self-propelled 88-mm. antitank guns (called "Hornets"). At the end of December the number had risen only to 823, the increase being largely in the lighter Mark IV tank. All the Hornets and Tiger (Mark VI) tanks had been shipped out to the Russian front, and the stock of assault guns was considerably decreased. The total of 823, moreover, compared to a planned build-up of 1,226. The new year brought a change. January showed only a slight increase, but thereafter the deliveries to the west were speeded up. Although most new Tiger tanks continued to go to the east, deliveries to *OB WEST* of the powerful Panther (Mark V) tank were notably increased. At the end of April *OB WEST* had 1,608 German-made tanks and assault guns of which 674 were Mark IV tanks and 514 Mark V's. The planned total for the end of May was 1,994.

Against the background of disintegrating German war economy, the tank buildup in the west was a notable achievement that strikingly revealed the importance assigned to the forthcoming struggle with the Western Allies. Exponents of the theories of Blitzkrieg, like Generaloberst Heinz Guderian, the Inspector General of Panzer Troops, believed that without a large armored striking force Germany could not hope to return to offensive operations essential for ultimate victory. In late 1943, therefore, Guderian proposed and Hitler approved a scheme to form a ten-division strategic armored reserve while at the same time trying to bring all armored divisions up to strength in equipment. The need, in short, was for new tanks in large numbers. But the combined pressure of the Allied air offensive and Russian ground attack was rapidly creating an economic quagmire in which the harder the enemy struggled the deeper he sank. Russian armies were destroying existing tanks while Allied bombers were making it increasingly difficult to produce new ones. The Germans tried to find an answer in diverting additional men, materials, and factory space into the manufacture of tanks. One result was to curtail the production of prime movers and parts. But without prime movers in adequate numbers the German armies in Russia were unable to withdraw their heavy guns or retrieve tanks that were damaged or out of fuel. Between October and December 1943, 979 Mark III and IV tanks and 444 assault guns were lost, in large part because they had to be abandoned in retreat. Similarly between July and December 2,235 artillery pieces and 1,692 antitank guns were captured or destroyed. General Guderian at last pointed out that there was little sense in producing more tanks and guns if they were to be thus recklessly sacrificed.

A still more important by-product of concentrating on tank manufacture at the expense of a balanced production program was the increasingly serious lack of spare parts. In June 1943 the Germans had 2,569 operational tanks with 463 in process of repair. In February 1944, only 1,519 tanks remained operational while 1,534 were under repair. During February, moreover, only 145 damaged tanks were actually returned to the front. On the first of the month, Guderian estimated that the tanks and assault guns awaiting repair equaled about nine months' new production. At the end of March, the situation had not improved; the number of operational tanks was still decreasing despite accelerated deliveries of new machines.

Although the German Army in the west on the eve of its great test was considerably weaker than planned in equipment, quality, and numbers, it was nevertheless a force strong enough to hope for victory in a battle in which Allied materiel superiority would be partly counteracted by the natural advantages of a coast line defense. Under Rundstedt's command on 1 June 1944 were 58 combat divisions of which 33 were either static or reserve, suitable only for limited defense employment. There were 24 divisions classified as fit for duty in the east by reason of their relative mobility and high-grade personnel. They included 13 infantry divisions, 2 parachute divisions, 5 army panzer divisions, and 4 SS panzer and panzer grenadier divisions. One panzer division (the *21st*), being still equipped in part with captured materiel, was not considered suitable for service in Russia, although in other respects it was ready for offensive use, and in fact had exceptional strength in heavy weapons.

All the infantry divisions were committed on or directly behind the coast under the command of one of the four armies or the *German Armed Forces Commander Netherlands*. The four armies were the first holding the Atlantic coast of France, the *Seventh* occupying Brittany and most of Normandy, the *Fifteenth* along the *Kanalkueste*, and the *Nineteenth* defending the French Mediterranean coast. The *Seventh Army*, which was to meet the actual invasion, had fourteen infantry (including static) divisions under the control of four corps.

Command and Tactics

It may be that the most serious weakness of the German defense in the west was not the shortage of men and materiel but the lack of a unified command. While Rundstedt was charged with the entire responsibility for the defense of France and the Low Countries, his powers were far from commensurate with that responsibility. He had, in the first place, no command over air and naval units. The four air corps that comprised the fighter and bomber aircraft stationed in the west were under command of the Third Air Force (Generalfeldmarschall Hugo Sperrle), which in turn was directly subordinate to OKL. Similarly Navy Group West, which under Admiral Theodor Krancke commanded the destroyers, torpedo boats, and smaller naval vessels based in the ports within Rundstedt's jurisdiction, was responsible directly to OKM. Rundstedt could issue no orders to either Sperrle or Krancke; he could only request their co-operation.

Air and naval forces were too small to have decisive effect on the battle. From Rundstedt's point of view the more important limitation of his power was the fragmentation of the command over the ground forces. Some of this fragmentation was normal and universal in the German military establishment. The *Third Air Force* had, for instance, besides command of the flying units, administrative control over parachute troops and the antiaircraft units that were under the *III Flak Corps*. *Navy Group West* controlled through regional commanders not only ships and shore installations but most of the coastal artillery, although command of the latter was mixed. The Navy had complete jurisdiction before operations on land had begun. Afterward, firing on sea targets remained a naval responsibility, but at the moment of enemy landing, in most cases, command of the batteries in the beachhead area was to pass to the Army. Virtually the whole burden of tying in the important naval batteries to the coastal defense was thus shifted to the initiative of local commanders.

A similar division of command affected the employment of the security troops which as instruments of the occupation were normally under the two military governors (*Militaerbefehlshaber*), France and Northern France (including Belgium). The military governors were directly subordinated to OKH, but for purposes of repelling invasion their security troops might be tactically under *OB WEST*. In preparation against invasion, the Commander in Chief West could only direct that the military governors co-operate with the army groups in matters affecting the latter's authority and undertake to settle any differences that might arise between them. Even this control was limited. Employment of security troops could only be ordered by the Commander in Chief West "in matters outside the scope of security."

During 1944 *OB WEST*'s authority was abridged in special ways. In November 1943, it will be recalled, Field Marshal Rommel had taken command of the *Army Group for Special Employment*, which was charged at first with inspection of the western defenses and the preparation of plans for counterattack against the main Allied landings wherever these might take place. Ultimately the Rommel headquarters was to conduct the main battle against the invading forces. About the middle of December, Rommel, having completed the first of his tasks, the inspection of the coastal defenses of Denmark, arrived in France and began a survey of the *Fifteenth Army* sector. Both he and Rundstedt recognized at once that it was neither logical nor practical for the *Special Army Group* to remain outside the theater chain of command. Its independence could only be a source of friction and inefficiency. On 30 December Rundstedt recommended that it be subordinated to *OB WEST* as *Army Group B* with command of the *Seventh* and *Fifteenth Armies* and of the *German Armed Forces of the Netherlands*. Whether the initial suggestion for this change came first from Rommel or from Rundstedt, it was clearly in the beginning agreeable to both. Since the main Allied invasion was likely to strike somewhere along the Channel coast, it made sense to put Rommel in immediate command there in order to familiarize him with his task and allow him to take such steps as he found necessary to strengthen the defense. Hitler approved but warned *OB WEST* that the Rommel headquarters was still to be considered available for commitment elsewhere. Rundstedt accepted the condition, and the reconstitution of *Army Group B* was ordered to take effect on 15 January. Rommel's subordination to OKW was at this time canceled.

His position, however, remained anomalous: whereas he had less than full command over the armies attached to him, he enjoyed an influence over the whole defense of the west which was in some measure commensurate with Rundstedt's. His orders provided that he was to be solely responsible for the conduct of operations (*Kampffuehrung*), but that in matters not directly affecting this tactical command *OB WEST* would continue to deal directly with the armies. Thus on questions of defense, training, organization and equipment, supply, artillery matters, communications, and engineer problems, the command channel might bypass the new army group. Rommel continued to be the coastal inspector for the whole of the west, and although his reports henceforth were forwarded through *OB WEST* his ability to influence coastal defense policies and practices did much to blur his subordination to Rundstedt. Moreover the binding of the Rommel staff to a geographical sector was only tentative; the headquarters was thought of still as a reserve command and as such the recommendations of its commander carried special if informal weight. Finally, and most importantly, Rommel in common with all German field marshals enjoyed at all times the right of appeal directly to Hitler. That privilege was especially important for the west because of the personalities involved. The evidence indicates that Rommel had an energy and strength of conviction that often enabled him to secure Hitler's backing, whereas Rundstedt, who was disposed whenever possible to compromise and allow arguments to go by default, seems to have relaxed command prerogatives that undoubtedly remained formally his. It is possible, of course, that he too came under Rommel's influence and failed to press acceptance of his own ideas because he was content to allow Rommel to assume the main burden of responsibility. In any case the clear fact is that after January 1944 Rommel was the dominant personality in the west with an influence disproportionate to his formal command authority.

Rommel's position, however, was not unchallenged. In November 1943 Rundstedt, thinking in terms of a large-scale counterattack against the main Allied landings, created a special staff to control armored units in that attack. The staff, designated *Panzer Group West*, was headed by General der Panzertruppen Leo Freiherr Geyr von Schweppenburg, and was directed to take over at once the formation and training of all armored units in the west and to advise the Commander in Chief West in the employment of armor. Geyr was ordered to co-operate with and respect the wishes of army group commanders. Actually, however, Geyr's ideas on the proper employment of armor were so completely at variance with Rommel's that co-operation was impossible.

In March 1944, at a meeting of the senior commanders in the west with Hitler, Rommel asked for an extension of his own authority that to all intents would have eliminated Geyr and Rundstedt as well from effective command of the defense forces. Specifically he requested that all armored and motorized units and all GHQ artillery in the west be put directly under his command and that he also be given some control over the first and *Nineteenth Armies*. The latter two armies, defending the Atlantic and Mediterranean coasts of France respectively, were at this time still subordinated immediately to *OB WEST*. In one sense, Rommel's request logically arose from his mission. Assigned responsibility for countering the major Allied invasion attempt, he required control over all the forces that might be used in the defense. It was plausible furthermore that such control should be turned over to him before the battle so that he could properly prepare and dispose the troops to fight the kind of battle he would order. Making a strong bid to unify defense policies, he asked that the Humpty-Dumpty command in the west be put together again under him. Although the method of repair naturally did not please Rundstedt, his objections were unheeded at the March meeting and Hitler approved the expansion of Rommel's command. Only after a study by the operations staff of OKW had supported Rundstedt's later written protest did Hitler reverse himself. Even then the reversal was not complete. Three panzer divisions (the *2d*, *21st*, and *116th*) were assigned to Rommel as *Army Group B* reserves, over which he was to have full tactical control while Geyr remained responsible for their training and organization. The patchwork solution solved nothing.

Young SS men captured in the immediate aftermath of the Normandy landings. The average age of the Hitler Jugend SS division was officially given as eighteen - in practice there were a fair number in the ranks who were much younger.

At the same time four other panzer-type divisions in *OB WEST*'s sector (the *1st SS Panzer*, *12th SS Panzer*, *17th SS Panzer Grenadier*, and *Panzer Lehr*) were set aside as a central mobile reserve under the direct command of OKW. The two decisions smacked of a compromise tending to preserve something of both Rommel's and Rundstedt's tactical ideas. The main effect, however, was to deprive the Commander in Chief West of the means to influence the battle directly without transferring those means to Rommel. Thus, even such inclusive authority as was possible in the German military establishment was scrupulously withheld from both high commanders in the west.

The final command change before the invasion was made in May when Rundstedt ordered the formation of a second army group headquarters to take command of the first and *Nineteenth Armies*. *Army Group G*, formed under Generaloberst Johannes Blaskowitz, took over, besides the two armies, the remaining three panzer divisions in France (the *9th*, *11th*, and *2d SS*). The reorganization provided a counterbalance for Rommel and somewhat simplified the command channels. It probably also expressed final recognition of the impracticability of the reserve high command concept.

With the establishment of Blaskowitz's headquarters, Rundstedt undertook to define his own position. He outlined for himself what amounted to an over-all ground command in his theater, subject to the restrictions already discussed. He announced his intention of granting his army group commanders the maximum freedom of action in their own sectors. He would intervene only when he fundamentally disagreed with their policies or when decisions had to be made affecting the theater as a whole. He promised to confine his directives to passing on Hitler's orders and to specifying policies that ought to be uniformly carried out by all commands.

In fact, during the critical preparatory months of 1944, general directives were few either from Rundstedt or Hitler. Hitler, far away at his headquarters in East Prussia, was so preoccupied with the Russian war that he did not even visit the west until after the invasion. Furthermore he seems not to have had any clear and consistent view of tactics himself, and his interventions in the western scene resulted more often in decisions of detail than in definitions of policy. The failure of Hitler to provide consistent guidance together with the vague demarcation of authority between Rommel and Rundstedt left the west with a vacillating leadership. Defense preparations in 1944 were increasingly scarred by compromise as the Commander in Chief West and the commander of *Army Group B* made detailed decisions in accordance with divergent aims.

The perspective from which Rommel viewed his task derived in part from his experience with desert warfare in North Africa and in part from the circumstances of his new assignment. It is important to bear in mind that Rommel came to the west only at the point when the battle was about to be fought there, and that he was assigned responsibility specifically for the conduct of that battle. He had not endured the long waiting period with its periodic alarms. He had not spent months making plans, calculating actual but shifting deficiencies against ideal needs, outlining defense systems and struggling to find the means to carry them out. The theoretical approach to tactics-the drafting of the abstractly best plan first, the search for resources second-was ruled out by the nature of his mission as well as by the limited time at his disposal. He was appointed coastal inspector and told to assess defensive capacities and make his plans accordingly. Whatever he chose to do had to be completed in three or four months. He was bound therefore to start by examining his limitations.

The experience in North Africa had convinced Rommel of the folly of trying to use massed armor as long as the enemy enjoyed air superiority. In Africa Rommel commanded some of the best trained and equipped troops that Germany produced. In France he was to command an army that was already crippled in part by inadequate training, inferior human material, and lack of mobility. Furthermore, there was still less hope in 1944 than in 1942 that the Luftwaffe could challenge the supremacy of the Allies in the air. To Rommel that meant that mobile operations were impossible in fact however desirable they might be in theory. If the German Army could not hope to maneuver on anything like terms of equality with the Allies, its only chance for a defensive success was to fight from the strongest possible natural positions. The pillboxes, entrenchments, wire, and mines of the Atlantic Wall and the waters of the Channel, in short, seemed to Rommel to offer not only the best but the only means to offset Allied superiority in mass and mobility.

Rommel therefore was led to place an exclusive dependence on fortifications that Rundstedt never advocated and that even Hitler had not contemplated in his directive of November. The battle for the west, Rommel believed, would be decided at the water's edge, and the decision would come literally within the first forty-eight hours of the Allied landings. In accord with that diagnosis, his first aim was to create a defensive belt around the entire coast with special concentration on the *Fifteenth Army* sector) extending five or six kilometers inland. Within this belt all infantry, artillery, headquarters staffs, and reserves up to division level were to be located in a series of resistance nests. Between the resistance nests mines and obstacles were to be laid so thickly as to prevent enemy penetration. Because of limited time, labor, and materials, Rommel concentrated on many simple, field-type defenses rather than on a few complex fortifications. He stressed in particular the laying of mines. He introduced, further, a defense device new to the Atlantic Wall: underwater obstacles designed to wreck landing craft. In Normandy, hedgehogs and tetrahedra located inland as tank obstacles were moved to the beaches suitable for enemy landings. They were supplemented by Belgian Gates and stakes slanting seaward. The intention was to cover every possible landing beach between high- and low-water marks with obstacles staggered to leave no free channel for even a flat-bottomed boat to reach shore. Obstacles as far as possible were to be mined. As it was considered most likely that the Allies would land at flood tide to reduce the amount of open beach to be crossed under fire, laying of the obstacles began at the high-water line and was extended in belts seaward as materials and labor became available.

To complete his hedgehog fortress, Rommel undertook to stake all fields suitable for glider landings behind the coastal zone. The stakes were to be placed close enough together so that gliders could not come down between them. They, too, were to be mined. The German estimate was that Allied airborne troops would be used in diversionary and subsidiary operations, for which Brittany and Normandy were considered the most likely target areas. Rommel therefore concentrated the erection of antiairlanding obstacles in these areas.

The general scheme of obstacle defense of the Continent was further to be extended by mine fields in the Channel. Sixteen fields, each about five miles long, were put down in the Channel between Boulogne and Cherbourg from August 1943 to January 1944. These were to be kept renewed as far as possible, but it was not believed that they would have much effect on Allied shipping. They were therefore to be supplemented by hasty mine fields laid down by all available vessels immediately before the invasion was expected. These fields would be planted without keeping open any marked lanes for German vessels. From Zeebrugge to Granville thirty-six mine fields were planned. It was also planned, when invasion seemed imminent, to sow mines from the air in British harbors. Finally along the French coast shallow-water mines were to be laid and a special seventy-kilogram concrete mine was developed for the purpose. In all these ways Rommel sought to make the expected invasion physically impossible. The Allied force entangled in the spider web of obstacles would be given the paralyzing sting by the German Army waiting at the water's edge.

Rommel's construction and mine-laying program called for a very large expenditure of labor, and labor was scarce. It has already been pointed out that Organization Todt was employed chiefly in the major port fortress areas, on V-weapon sites, and, in the spring of 1944, on railroad maintenance. In the apportionment of the remaining labor supply among the armies, *Fifteenth Army* continued to receive priority. *Seventh Army* thus had special difficulty in completing its defense works. The *LXXXIV Corps* was assigned three engineer battalions in January, two for fortress building and one for mine laying. In addition, 2,850 men of the former French Labor Service were set to work on a secondary defense line immediately behind the belt of coastal resistance points. Pleas for more construction hands were answered by attachment of two *Ost* battalions.

The only other available labor source was the combat troops. Increasingly during 1944 infantrymen were employed in work details on the Atlantic Wall with consequent serious reduction of combat training. The reserve battalion of the *709th Division*, for instance, devoted three days a week exclusively to labor duty. The time for training in the rest of the week was further reduced by transport and guard details. During the first two weeks in May the battalion was employed full time on the coastal defense in the Barfleur sector. The *709th* was an old division, but its personnel constantly shifted. The lack of continuous adequate training meant that the total combat fitness of the division steadily deteriorated through the accretion of untrained recruits.

Still worse was the effect on the new and reorganized divisions that represented a large proportion of the German striking force in the west. In *Seventh Army* all but one of the non-static infantry divisions were organized during 1944. New divisions accounted for six of the fourteen divisions under the army's command. All of these units were burdened with construction duties. In February Rommel ordered that infantry be used to lay mines and obstacles. On 25 May *Seventh Army* reported to OKH that all its units were engaged in construction projects and that consequently the necessary training was not being carried out.

The only units specially exempted from work on the fortifications were the two parachute divisions. The *3d Parachute Division* was brought into Brittany in March and stationed east of Brest. Its mission was to complete its organization and at the same time train for defense against airborne attack. The *5th Parachute Division* moved into the Rennes area between 5 and 14 May with a similar mission. Both divisions in May were put under command of the *II Parachute Corps* which, though subordinated tactically to *Seventh Army*, was administratively and for training purposes under the *Third Air Force*. Since the Luftwaffe was thus responsible for parachute unit training and, on the other hand, was not responsible to army commands anywhere in the hierarchy, Reich Marshal Goering ordered that the parachute divisions not be used for construction work except in providing local security for themselves against airborne attack. The *5th Parachute Division* had scarcely more than begun to fill out its ranks when invasion struck; but the *3d* proved one of the best prepared of the new units in *Seventh Army*.

The general stinting of training under the circumstances seems to have been inevitable and apparently did not arouse any serious protests at the time. Where Rommel's program met really effective opposition was in his efforts to concentrate reserves within the coastal zone. If it was true that the Germans had to fight on a fortified line, if they could not hope to maneuver freely, and if the crisis of the battle against the invaders would come within the first forty-eight hours, then it followed that all forces would be wasted which were not near enough to the coast to be committed at once against the first landings. This deduction was the final extension of the doctrine of static defense implicit in the original decision to build the Atlantic Wall. At least one high German commander had predicted the development and had warned against it in caustic tones. Sodenstern, commanding the *Nineteenth Army*, wrote privately in the summer of 1943 of his fear that German generalship would exhaust itself in the construction of huge masses of concrete. "As no man in his senses," he argued, "would put his head on an anvil over which the smith's hammer is swung, so no general should mass his troops at the point where the enemy is certain to bring the first powerful blow of his superior materiel." Rommel's answer, in all likelihood, would have been, first, that there was no practical alternative, second, that the first Allied blow at the point of the landings would not be the most powerful but the weakest since only a small portion of Allied fire power could then be effective, and, third, that the German general in massing his troops in fortified positions was at least giving their heads some protection against the smith's hammer.

The difference of opinion was essentially a difference in judgment of what was possible. Rommel's chief of staff has testified that Rommel would have preferred a battle of maneuver had he seen any chance of its succeeding. Rundstedt, like Sodenstern, was clearly more optimistic, perhaps because he had not had firsthand experience with the air power of the Western Allies. In any case, he did not accept Rommel's thesis and the influence of *OB WEST* was exerted spasmodically in resisting Rommel's efforts to shift the weight of the army forward to the coast, and in trying instead to free as many units as possible from bondage to the rigid defense system.

In practice any plan to introduce flexibility into the defense depended primarily on whether units could be made mobile and whether they could be organized and equipped to support themselves in combat. Through the early months of 1944 Rundstedt struggled to strengthen and provide some transport for the coastal divisions. In the *Seventh Army* area he succeeded in forming mobile Kampfgruppen (of reinforced regiments) from four of the infantry divisions (the *265th*, *266th*, *275th*, and *353d*) defending the Brittany coast. In case of a major invasion of Normandy, *Seventh Army* had plans to move these Kampfgruppen into the combat zone. In the Cotentin, the *243d Division* was converted from a static into a nominal attack infantry division. It was reorganized according to the 1944 type with six infantry battalions. Four battalions were to be equipped with bicycles. The artillery regiment, supply troops, and antitank battalion were to be motorized. Reorganization took place in late 1943, but the motorization planned to begin in May 1944 could be carried out only in very limited degree.

It should be observed in this connection that German notions of mobility in the west in 1944 hardly corresponded to American concepts of a motorized army. A mobile infantry unit in general was one equipped with bicycles, with horse-drawn artillery, and a modicum of horse and motor transport for supply purposes. It was called mobile more because of its ability to maintain itself in the field than because of its ability to move rapidly from one place to another.

For the most part the Germans lacked resources even to provide that limited mobility for the west army. Rundstedt's efforts to restore mobility to his static divisions on the whole failed. A beginning, for instance, was made to upgrade the *709th Division*, but the vehicles allotted in March had to be withdrawn in May when, as a result of the Allies' successful rail bombing attacks, *Seventh Army* began to scrape together everything on wheels to form corps transport companies.

Rundstedt's efforts to put wheels under his army were at least partly offset by Rommel's concurrent labors to dig in every available soldier and gun along the coast line. After an inspection trip in the *LXXXIV Corps* sector in February, Rommel concluded that reserves were held in too great strength too far from the coast. In particular, he felt that the *352d Division*, located near St. Lô, and the *243d Division*, near la Haye du Puits, should be regrouped so that they could be committed in the first hours after an enemy landing. *Seventh Army* therefore ordered that the divisional reserves of the *709th* and *716th Divisions* (the *795th Georgian Battalion* and *642d Ost Battalion* respectively) should be committed at the coast, that the *243d* and *352d Divisions* should move slightly northward, and that the *352d Artillery Regiment* of the latter division should be emplaced in the coastal one under the control of the *716th Division*. Similar reshuffling in Brittany put the artillery of the *275th* and *353d Divisions* into static defense positions. The shift forward of the *352d Division* meant in effect that it was no longer in reserve. On 14 March *Seventh Army* therefore proposed that the division actually take over responsibility for the left half of the *716th Division* sector. On *OB WEST*'s approval, this change was accomplished by 19 March. With the doubling of the troops on the coast, the former battalion sectors of the *716th Division* became regimental sectors. The *726th Regiment* of the *716th* was attached to the *352d*, less the *2d Battalion* which became division reserve for the *716th*. One regiment of the *352d* plus the *Fuesilier Battalion* was held in corps reserve in the vicinity of Bayeux.

Hitler, whose ideas, possibly under Rommel's influence, had undergone some change since Directive 51, wondered at this time whether all units of limited mobility which were located immediately behind the coast should not as a matter of policy be incorporated in the main line of resistance (MLR), leaving only fully mobile forces as attack reserves. General Jodl of the OKW pointed out that, except for three divisions, units were already far enough forward for their artillery to bear on the invasion beaches. To shift all troops into the coastal fortifications would be dangerous since concrete shelters were limited and field work might be destroyed by Allied bombing In Brittany and the Cotentin, moreover, it was necessary to preserve some depth of defense in order to resist probable airborne landings.

Commitment of all forces at the MLR was thus not accepted as a principle. But in practice Rommel continued to shift the weight of his army forward. In April the *21st Panzer Division* was moved from Rennes to Caen where its battalions were split on either side of the Orne River and its artillery committed on the coast. The disposition to all intents removed the *21st Panzer Division* as a unit from the pool of mobile reserves. The other two panzer divisions directly under Rommel's command were placed in position to reinforce the *Fifteenth Army*, one between Rouen and Paris, the other near Amiens. In May, another inspection tour convinced Rommel that movement of units from right to left into the invasion area would be impossible. He therefore requested that the four divisions in OKW reserve be assembled nearer the coast. Rundstedt entered an immediate protest with OKW, contending that the move was tantamount to committing the reserves before the battle. OKW agreed, and Rommel's proposal was turned down.

These four divisions (three panzer and one panzer grenadier) thus saved by OKW's intervention were the only mobile units in the west on the eve of invasion which could properly be designated strategic reserves. Three were located within easy marching distance of Normandy (easy, that is, if the Allied air forces were discounted); the fourth was far away on the Belgium-Netherlands border.

In summary, the conflict between Rommel's and Rundstedt's

theories of defense was never resolved definitely in favor of one or the other and led to compromise troop dispositions which on D Day were not suitable for the practice of either theory. The pool of mobile reserves had been cut down below what would be needed for an effective counterattack in mass; it had been removed from OB WEST's control, and, as though to insure finally that it would not be employed in force, it had been divided among three commands. While the possibility of seeking a decision by counterattack had thus been whittled away, considerable forces were still held far enough from the coast so that, if Rommel's theories were correct, they would be unable to reach the battlefield in time to influence the action. In short, operational flexibility had been curtailed without achieving a decisive thickening of the coastal defense.

The Defense on the Eve of Invasion

The scheduled completion date for the winter construction program and all troop preparations for meeting the expected invasion was 30 April. Up to that time the Germans made all arrangements to repel a major attack against the *Kanalkueste*. At the end of 1943 Hitler ordered the assembly of all available forces behind the front of the *Fifteenth Army* and the right wing of *Seventh Army*, but the latter sector was to be considered much less in peril. *OB WEST* was to release four divisions from coastal sectors of the *Seventh, first*, and *Nineteenth Armies*. Of these, the *243d Division*, released from *Seventh Army*, was to remain as a reserve division in the army area. The other three were all attached to *Fifteenth Army*. Similarly, of four reinforced regiments obtained at this time from the Replacement Army, three went to *Fifteenth Army*; one was attached to the *709th Division*. The latter attachment was made because the coastal defenses of the 709th Division were thin and enemy attack there was "possible."

That possibility, however, was not taken very seriously until the end of April. Since the German intelligence system had been supplying very little reliable information, estimates of Allied intentions continued to be based more on logical inference than on fact. Air reconnaissance was severely restricted by Allied air supremacy. Reconnaissance by sea could never be depended on. German agents in England steadily dwindled and the work of those remaining was made almost fruitless by the closing off of the English coastal areas in April 1944. News filtering through neutral countries, especially from Portugal and Switzerland, was abundant but confusing. The difficulty was not that no reliable reports got through, but that they were too few and too spasmodic to allow the formation of a convincing picture of Allied intentions, particularly since such a picture had to compete for acceptance with various preconceptions.

The best guess was Hitler's, though how he arrived at it the records do not show. While military leaders were nearly unanimous in predicting invasion in the Pas-de-Calais area, Hitler in March suddenly decided that the Allies were likely to land on the Cotentin and Brittany peninsulas. He believed they would be tempted by the ease with which defensible bridgeheads could be established there, but he apparently did not undertake any analysis of the possible military advantages.

The supposition of a special threat to Normandy and Brittany received some support a few weeks later from the Navy. On 26 April Admiral Krancke, Commander of *Navy Group West*, observed that recent air photographs showed no activity in the ports of southeast England or the mouth of the Thames, and concluded that Cap Gris Nez and the coast northeast were not threatened by Allied landings. The conclusion was reinforced by the facts that Allied air attacks against coastal batteries and radar installations were concentrated between Boulogne and Cherbourg, that Allied mine sweeping and mine laying generally blocked off the same area, and that the bombing of railroads had interrupted traffic to the Channel coast but had not affected communications with the Atlantic area. In short, Admiral Krancke felt that all signs pointed to an invasion between Boulogne and Cherbourg, probably with the main effort against the Cotentin, the mouth of the Seine, or the mouth of the Somme. This appreciation differed from previous estimates only in lopping off the Pas-de-Calais sector between Boulogne and Dunkerque as a possible landing area. The resulting difference in emphasis, however, was striking, particularly in the singling out of the Cotentin as threatened by a possible major attack. Later reports by Admiral Krancke further emphasized this threat, particularly from Allied airborne attack. Krancke's view, developed chiefly during May, was that Le Havre and Cherbourg seemed likely prime objectives for the Allied invasion forces. This conviction grew as it was seen that Cherbourg and Le Havre alone of the major French ports had been spared from heavy air attack.

Whether Hitler saw and reacted to these naval estimates or whether he had access to other information, in late April his interest in Normandy increased and he began to insist strongly on the need to reinforce the defense there. On 6 May *Seventh Army* was notified by Rommel of Hitler's concern, and the army ordered the deployment of one parachute regiment and two separate battalions in the immediate vicinity of Cherbourg. The parachute regiment selected was the *6th* and it was to be placed in the general area of Lessay-Périers. The *206th Panzer Battalion*, a separate tank battalion equipped with a miscellany of Russian, French, and German light tanks, was ordered to dig in between Cap de la Hague and Cap de Carteret. The *Seventh Army Sturm Battalion* was sent to la Haye du Puits and later shifted to le Vast, southeast of Cherbourg. Decision was made at the same time to divert to the Cotentin the *91st Division*, which was then on its way from Germany to Nantes. Orders were issued the next day switching the trains to the vicinity of la Haye du Puits. The *91st Division* was told that on arrival it would take over command of the *6th Parachute Regiment*. This movement was completed on 14 May. On 9 May Rommel ordered that the *101st Stellungswerfer Regiment,* released from *OB WEST* reserve, be committed in the Cotentin, split between the east and west coasts. On the day that this move was completed, 12 May, the *17th Machine Gun Battalion* (a well-trained unit of young men) also completed relief of the *795th Georgian Battalion* on Cap de la Hague and the latter battalion, under command of the *709th Division*, was moved on 17 May south to Bruceville northeast of Carentan. Mission of all the major units, the *91st Division*, *6th Parachute Regiment*, and *Seventh Army Sturm Battalion*, was defense against airborne landings. The 100th Panzer Replacement Battalion south of Carentan at the same time was instructed to be prepared for action against airborne troops.

The Cotentin was thus substantially reinforced and fully alerted a month before the two U.S. airborne divisions were dropped there.

While expecting airborne assault on the Cotentin, however, neither Rommel nor Rundstedt reckoned that such assault would form part of the main Allied effort. Having reinforced the actual garrison in the peninsula, therefore, they took no further steps to cope with a major landing in the area. On the contrary, a *Seventh Army* proposal on 5 May to shift the whole of the *LXXIV Corps* from Brittany to Normandy in case of large-scale landings in the *LXXXIV Corps* sector was rejected by Field Marshal Rommel. No reserves were moved nearer the *Cotentin*, and no plans were made to move them in mass in case of attack.

As for the Navy, having called its opponent's trumps it relaxed under the curious delusion that the Allies might not play at all. Krancke's thesis seems to have been that unless the invasion were preceded by large and devastating attacks on the coastal batteries it could not succeed. He noted on 31 May that such attacks had indeed increased, but they were, he thought, still too limited to insure the success of landings. Actually, from his point of view, he was right. Despite his prognostications about the threat to the Cotentin he continued to believe that large-scale landings would strike the Pas-de-Calais. Here the coastal batteries were formidable. The Allied air attacks had hit them more often than they had hit any other sector of the coast, and yet the attacks up to the eve of D Day had eliminated only eight guns. In the Seine-Somme sector five had been destroyed, and three in Normandy. The Navy thus remained confident that its artillery could still knock the Allied invasion fleet out of the water-provided of course it sailed where it was expected. That confidence was further nourished by the fact that, despite heavy air attacks on radar stations, the radar warning system remained virtually intact as of 31 May. In fine, reviewing the situation on 4 June Admiral Krancke was driven to the conclusion that not only was attack not imminent but there as a good chance that observed Allied preparations were part of a huge hoax. The mixture of bluff and preparation for a later invasion would keep up, the naval chief thought, until German forces were so weakened in the west that landings could be attempted without great risk.

The contrast between Krancke's optimism about enemy intentions and his sober accounting of the helplessness of his own forces in the face of enemy overwhelming superiority was the most striking aspect of his last report before the invasion. His fleet of combat ships was so small that it could scarcely be talked about in terms of a naval force and even what he did have was for the most part bottled up in the ports by what he called "regular and almost incessant" Allied air sorties. His main offensive units in June were a flotilla of destroyers (which on 1 April had two ships operational), two torpedo boats, and five flotillas of small motor torpedo boats (*S-Boote*) with thirty-one boats operational. In addition he had a few mine sweepers and patrol craft. Fifteen of the smaller submarines based in French Atlantic ports, though not under Krancke's control, were scheduled to take part in resisting the invasion. Midget submarines and remote-controlled torpedoes were being developed but they never got into the fight. Even this tiny fleet could not operate. Krancke reported thirty Allied air attacks on his naval forces during May and added that even in dark nights his units got no relief. He predicted an enforced reduction of effort and heavy losses in the future. In the meantime he found himself unable to carry out his plan for blocking off the invasion coast with mine fields. Delivery of all types of mines had been delayed chiefly by transportation difficulties. Up to the end of April there were on hand only enough concrete shallow-water mines to put in two mine fields in the Dieppe area.

In May, more mines became available. But in the meantime the mine-laying fleet had been depleted by Allied attacks, and increased Allied air surveillance of the sea lanes made all German naval activity difficult.

"The anticipated mining operations [Kranke reported on 4 June] to renew the flanking mine fields in the Channel have not been carried out. On the way to the rendezvous at Le Havre T-24 fell behind because of damage from [a] mine, "Greif" was sunk by bombs, "Kondor" and "Falke" were damaged by mines, the former seriously. The 6th MS-Flotilla [mine layers] likewise on its way to Le Havre to carry out KMA [coastal mine] operations reached port with only one of its six boats, one having been sunk by torpedoes and the other four having fallen out through mine damage, air attack or sea damage. The laying of KMA mines out of Le Havre therefore could not be carried."

In fact during the month only three more coastal mine fields could be laid and all these were put down off the Kanalkueste. The essential mining of waters around the Cotentin could scarcely be begun. Naval defense preparations were actually losing ground. The program of replacing the 1943 mine fields in mid-Channel finally had to be abandoned in March 1944 because of lack of mines and because of Allied radar observation. Krancke estimated that the deepwater fields would all be obsolete by mid-June. Some hasty mine fields were laid in the Bay of the Seine during April but their estimated effective life was only five weeks. The dearth of materials and adequate mine layers continued to disrupt German plans. Krancke's conclusion on the eve of invasion was that mining activity of E-boats could only provide a "nonessential" contribution to the German defenses.

If Admiral Krancke's forces were helpless in naval action, they were scarcely more effective on land, where their assigned task of casemating coastal batteries dragged along past the completion date with no end in sight. Hitler had ordered in January that all batteries and antitank guns were to be casemated by 30 April. On that date Admiral Krancke reported that of 547 coastal guns 299 had been casemated, 145 were under construction; remaining concrete works had not been begun. Like all other defense preparations, this effort had been concentrated along the Kanalkueste. In the Pas-de-Calais and Seine-Somme sectors, 93 of the 132 guns had been casemated. Normandy had 47 guns, 27 of which were under concrete at the end of April. As for the fixed antitank positions, 16 of the 82 guns had been covered in the *Fifteenth Army* area. The nine guns in the *Seventh Army* sector were all open.

The Army's construction program, of course, suffered along with the Navy's and was far from completion on D Day. Shortage of materials, particularly cement and mines, due both to production and to transportation difficulties affected all fortification work. The shortage of cement, critical even at the outset of the winter construction program, was greatly intensified by the Allies' all-out rail bombing offensive. Late in May *LXXXIV Corps*, for example, received 47 carloads of cement in three days against a minimum daily need of

The wreckage of the 1st Rifle Brigade's transport column, and a 6 pounder anti-tank gun, on the road between Villers-Bocage and Point 213

240 carloads. Two days after this report was made, the flow of cement to the *Seventh Army* area stopped altogether as trains had to be diverted to carrying more urgently needed ordinary freight. During May the cement works in Cherbourg were forced to shut down for lack of coal. Plans were then made to bring up cement by canal to Rouen and ship by sea to the *Seventh Army* area, but this was a last-minute solution and could never be tried out.

On 15 May *Seventh Army* reported that its defense preparations were to be considered complete, its beach obstacles and antiairlanding obstacles set, and its troop dispositions made. This was, to say the least, an exaggeration, analogous to a claim that a bombing program was complete as soon as all targets had been hit. In fact, a week later *LXXXIV Corps* estimated that the construction program was only half complete. The corps was particularly concerned that not even the fortification of the immediate MLR along the water's edge nor the naval and army coastal batteries were finished. The so-called *Zweite Stellung*, which Rundstedt in late 1943 ordered to be built a few kilometers in from the coast line in order to get some depth of defense, had progressed still more slowly, even though, being largely a system of prepared field positions constructed by the French, it took relatively few priority materials or labor. In March *LXXXIV Corps* reported the position 65 percent finished, but the more critical fact was that only thirty-one of the planned eighty-eight resistance nests and strong points were actually fully ready for defense. In the sector of the *709th Division*, defending the vital east coast of the Cotentin, only one of forty-two planned positions was fully prepared. Rommel decided in April that the *Zweite Stellung* was wasting time and effort that were vitally needed for reinforcing the main line of resistance. He therefore ordered all work discontinued except where the *Zweite Stellung* lay close to the coast and could be considered part of the primary defense. Thus the last chance to secure some depth of defense was lost.

But the sacrifice of depth did not result in solidity for the main line. Despite *Seventh Army*'s report that obstacles on the shore line and in fields suitable for airborne landings were complete by the middle of May and needed only deepening, it was precisely that deepening which alone could have made them effective. Rommel's inspection of the antiairlanding obstacles on 18 May convinced him that, far from being complete, they had only just been begun. Few were mined and his goal was to have them all mined. For that purpose he required 13,000 shells for Normandy alone. As for the shore obstacles, they had been completed only along the high-water mark and a few yards seaward. Admiral Krancke warned against continued acceptance of earlier estimates that the Allies would land at high tide. If landings were made near low tide they would not be materially hindered by the obstacles already in place. This was true but increasing their number was inevitably a slow process. A measure of the difficulties faced by the German Army was the experience of the *352d Division*, which had to cut stakes for obstacles by hand in the Foret de Cerisy some ten or twelve miles inland, haul the wood by cart to the beach, and drive the stakes, again by hand, into the tidal flats.

Mining of the coastal zone had made considerable progress but was still far short of the goal. In the first six months of 1944 Rommel succeeded in tripling the number of mines in the coast defense zone. But the five or six million mines laid by D Day contrasted with Rommel's own minimum estimate of fifty million needed for continuous defense belts. For the *352d Division* sector alone ten million were needed to cover a thirty-mile front actually received about ten thousand antipersonnel mines during 1944 and no Teller mines at all.

Similar incompleteness marked the fortifications on D Day. On the east coast of the Cotentin, strong points and resistance nests were spaced about 875 yards apart; between the Orne and Vire Rivers they were 1,312 yards apart. Most of them were field fortifications, sometimes with concreted troop shelters and sometimes embodying concrete gun casemates. Of the installations in the *352d Division* sector only 15 percent were bombproof; the remainder were virtually unprotected against air attack. The fortifications had no depth whatsoever. According to the commander of the *716th Division* the forty to fifty fortified resistance centers in his sector were beaded along the coast like a string of pearls. Generalmajor Horst Freiherr Treusch von Buttlar-Brandenfels, OKW operations staff officer, had warned after his inspection trip of Normandy defenses in January that if the enemy broke through one strong point there would be a gap of three or four kilometers into which he could advance unhindered. The abandonment of the *Zweite Stellung* meant that to a large degree this condition still prevailed in June.

Rommel's inability to complete the Atlantic Wall undoubtedly contributed to the general ineffectiveness of German resistance to the Allied landings on 6 June. A stronger wall would have meant a harder crust, and in cracking it the Allies would unquestionably have suffered heavier losses. But it also seems likely that such a difference would not have proved decisive. The critical weakness, as Rommel had seen, was the German inability to maneuver. And the most important cause of that was the unchallenged supremacy of the Allies in the air. The Luftwaffe had not only been beaten before D Day; it had been all but annihilated.

The story of what happened to Gringo's air force, which four years before had been the world-famed spearhead of blitzkrieg, cannot here be told in detail. Among the causes of its decline there was at least an element of bad judgment. Through 1942 Hitler persisted in believing that the end of the war was just around the corner of the next campaign; at the same time he refused to recognize the tremendous productive capacity of the Western Allies, particularly the United

States. Although in 1940 the Germans had pioneered in the use of specially developed attack aircraft for support of ground operations, after the end of the French campaign they neglected to develop the tactics further. They turned instead first to creating a bomber fleet to knock out England and later to producing fighter forces to protect the homeland. Their efforts on both scores were inadequate. In the meantime the development of an Air Force to co-operate with the Army went by the board. In 1944 the Luftwaffe depended for the most part on two fighter types: the Focke-Wulf 190 and the Messerschmitt 109. The attack plane, the twin-engined Junkers 88, was available in such small quantities that the tactical air commands were equipped mainly with the standard interceptor aircraft. Not only did this mean less offensive power in land warfare but, more important, it entailed competition between the demands for air support and the demands for the defense of Germany against the ever intensified Combined Bomber Offensive. Thus the Germans faced the same dilemma in the allocation of air forces that they did in the division of their ground troops between the west and east. In both cases the compromise effected between the rival claims resulted only in establishing inferiority to the enemy on all fronts. And this, in turn, produced a spiral of attrition and increasing inferiority, spinning inevitably to disaster.

In the beginning of 1944, when it was already too late, Reich Minister Albert Speer tried to halt the spiral by concentrating on fighter production. Under the impetus of the Speer program monthly production of fighters rose steadily in 1944 despite all the Allied air forces could do to destroy aircraft and ball bearing factories. In the three months before D Day between seven and eight thousand fighters were produced. Since losses continued to mount, the net gain was only about a thousand planes. But even this gain was not reflected in a stronger air force. Increase in the number of available aircraft only emphasized the critical shortage of qualified pilots. This in turn resulted primarily from a lack of gasoline which compelled a progressive shortening of the pilot-training period from about 260 hours in 1942 to 110 and even in some cases to 50 in 1944. The green pilots accelerated the deterioration of the Luftwaffe as a whole, since their inexperience increased their own losses and the losses of their planes. Moreover the planes themselves, mass produced in haste, were inferior. During 1943 an average of 500 aircraft a month had been lost or damaged because of mechanical or pilot failures. In February 1944 the losses from these causes soared to 1,300, accounting, in short, for about half the month's new production. This was unusual, but looses through accidents continued to be as important as losses through enemy action. In May, for instance, 712 aircraft were destroyed or damaged by the Allies, while 656 were lost in flying accidents.

On D Day there were about 400 fighter planes in the west under *Third Air Force*. But only about half of these were available to oppose Allied air forces supporting the invasion. The 400 planes were grouped under *II Fighter Corps* and divided between two subordinate commands, the *4th Fighter Division* with headquarters at Metz and the *5th Fighter Division* located near Paris. The mission of the *4th Division* was to intercept Allied heavy bombers entering or leaving Germany. Thus tactically its planes belonged to the Reich defensive system. In case of invasion they were to be diverted to intercept Allied planes over the invasion area, but with bases so far from the scene of operations they were unlikely to be very effective, and would not be on hand on D Day.

Despite the accepted thesis that the first hours of the landings would be the critical period for the defense of France, the Luftwaffe made no comprehensive plans to be on hand in strength during those hours, mostly because with its limited supply of planes and pilots it could not afford to hoard reserves in idleness while waiting for the Allies to strike. In December 1943 the *II Air Corps* was transferred to France from Italy to take over control of all the fighter aircraft to be used in support of the German Army. On D Day, however, the *II Air Corps* was still only a headquarters without any planes. In case of invasion, it was to get ten wings (*Geschwader*) from Germany. Actually only about six wings arrived, and these trickled in with the result that they could never be employed in a concentrated effort. None were on hand on 6 June. The wings earmarked for *II Air Corps* were then just being refitted in Germany. The majority of the pilots were new graduates of the accelerated training programs. Not only did they have no battle experience; they were barely able to handle their planes. Most of them were not familiar with France and did not know how to read maps. The commander of the *II Air Corps*, Generalleutnant Alfred Buelowius, aware of their inexperience, proposed that he send planes out to guide the reinforcements into the flying fields prepared for them. Responsibility for the movement, however, rested with the German Home Air Command (*Luftflotte Reich*) and Buelowius was not consulted. The result was that on D Day the units were scattered and lost on their flights from Germany and many were forced to make emergency landings. Few arrived at their assigned bases.

Thus for one reason or another the planes that should have been in France on 6 June to shield Rundstedt's army against intolerable Allied air supremacy were not there. The 50 to 150 planes that did fly to the attack in the critical hours of the defense could achieve nothing, and the German Army faced the massed blows of Allied combined arms alone.

REPORT OF THE CHIEF OF STAFF

By General der Infanterie Gunther Blumentritt

1. OB West Situation Prior to Invasion

During the period 6 June-24 July 1944, I was the Chief of Staff, OB West. OB West, under OKW, was responsible for the areas of Holland, Belgium, and France only with regard to coastal defense. Directly subordinate to OB West were Army Group B (Fifteenth Army, Seventh Army, and troops in Holland) and Army Group G (First Army, Pyrenees security forces, and Nineteenth Army). Third Air Force and Navy Group West were subordinate only for the tactical defense of the coast. The Militärbefehlshabers (military commanders) of France and Belgium-northern France were under OB West only for defense against invasion. However, the Militärbefehlshaber of Holland was not subordinate.

The chain of command was very complicated and muddled; there was no absolute responsibility as was given to Field Marshal Montgomery or General Eisenhower. The C-in-C West was responsible only for the defense of the West Front against invasion. Only the elements of the Heer (Army Group B and Army Group G, with their subordinate units) were directly under OB West. Third Air Force, Navy Group West, and the two Militärbefehlshabers were independent, being under OKL, OKM, and OKW, respectively. All of these commands not under the Heer had a direct channel to their superior command and without having to contact OB West. The C-in-C West could give direct orders to these non-Heer commands only on matters pertaining to the coastal defense.

The Waffen SS, subordinate to the various commands for tactical purposes only, were in direct contact with RF-SS Himmler, over the head of the Heer. The Militärbefehlshabers had their own security troops, responsible to them only. The C-in-C West could only *request* the service of these troops. For the Heeres troops, there was no court martial jurisdiction above Army level. The Navy, Luftwaffe, SS, and

Militärbefehlshabers had their own military courts, with independent jurisdiction. OB West had no courts and no jurisdiction.

Moreover, OB West had only limited authority, and this only in strategic and tactical matters pertaining to the defense of the area against invasion. The C-in-C West was actually only the senior strategic head, not a commander-in-chief—*primus inter pares* in strategic matters. As a result, responsibility for the area and for all strategic and tactical measures was made considerably difficult. The commanders-in-chief of the Navy, Luftwaffe, and SS (Dönitz, Göring, Himmler) were close to Hitler and their wishes received more attention than those of the C-in-C West, who had no such representation in OKW.

A dictator does not favor putting too much power in the hands of one man. *"Divide et impera!"* Let this example be a warning of how not to organize the high-level commands. Formerly the German principle was "The man in whom I put my trust will have power over all in order to accomplish his mission, but he will also be absolutely independent and will have full responsibility. If he is not equal to the task, then another shall take his place." It was otherwise in Germany in 1939-45.

Headquarters
- OB West - St Germain (northwest of Paris)
- Army Group B - Castle at La Roche-Guyon (on the Seine river, northwest of Paris)
- Army Group G - North (?) ofToulouse
- Navy Group West - Paris
- Third Air Force - Paris
- Militärbefehlshaber for France - Paris
- Militärbefehlshaber for Belgium-Northern France - Brussels

The first three commands had forward command posts which were temporarily occupied as the situation demanded.

In OKW strategic reserve were Panzer Lehr Division and the 12th SS Panzer (Hitlerjugend) Division, west of Paris Approximately in the area northeast of Le Mans, and the 1st SS Panzer (Leibstandarte) Division, in the vicinity of Brussels. OB West had no strategic reserves. (The possibilities in the event of invasion had been

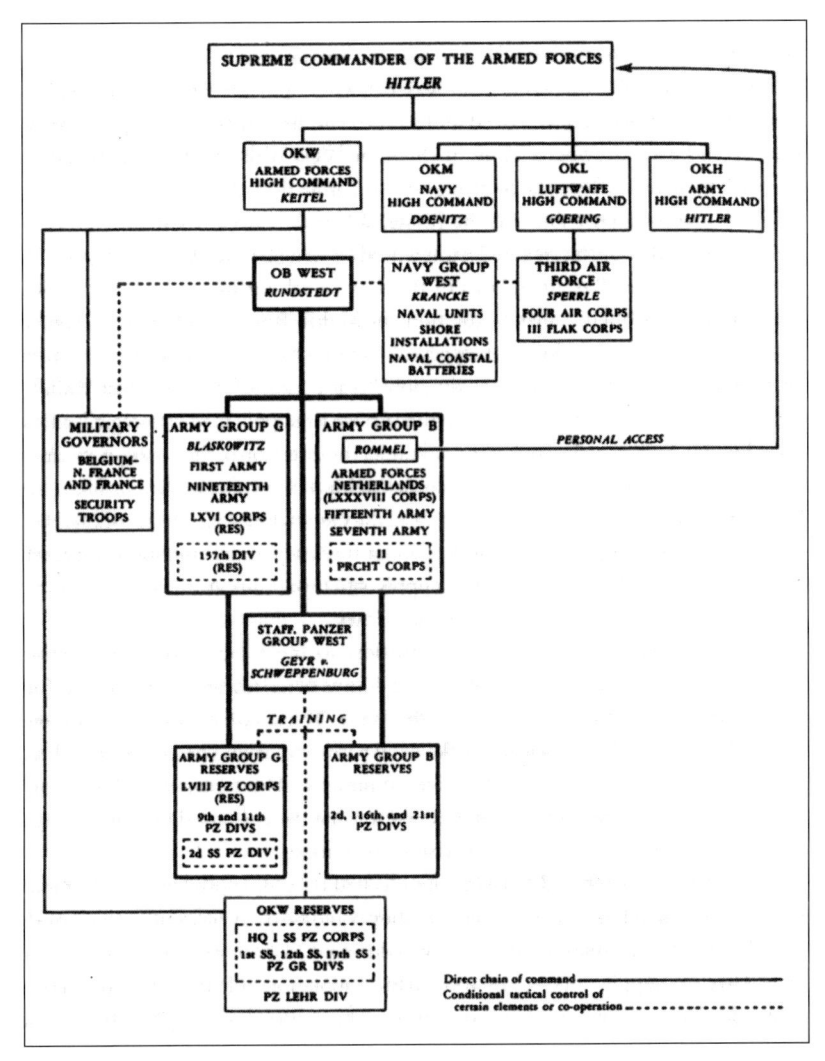

```
                    SUPREME COMMANDER OF THE ARMED FORCES
                                   HITLER

      OKW              OKM              OKL              OKH
   ARMED FORCES        NAVY          LUFTWAFFE           ARMY
   HIGH COMMAND    HIGH COMMAND    HIGH COMMAND      HIGH COMMAND
      KEITEL          DOENITZ         GOERING           HITLER

                           NAVY GROUP       THIRD AIR
         OB WEST              WEST            FORCE
        RUNDSTEDT            KRANCKE         SPERRLE
                          NAVAL UNITS     FOUR AIR CORPS
                             SHORE        III FLAK CORPS
                         INSTALLATIONS
                         NAVAL COASTAL
                           BATTERIES

  MILITARY      ARMY GROUP G     ARMY GROUP B
  GOVERNORS     BLASKOWITZ         ROMMEL                  PERSONAL ACCESS
  BELGIUM-      FIRST ARMY      ARMED FORCES
  N. FRANCE     NINETEENTH      NETHERLANDS
  AND FRANCE      ARMY          (LXXXVIII CORPS)
  SECURITY      LXVI CORPS      FIFTEENTH ARMY
  TROOPS          (RES)         SEVENTH ARMY
                157th DIV            II
                  (RES)         PRCHT CORPS

                          STAFF, PANZER
                          GROUP WEST
                            GEYR v.
                          SCHWEPPENBURG

                            TRAINING

              ARMY GROUP G      ARMY GROUP B
                RESERVES         RESERVES
              LVIII PZ CORPS
                  (RES)
              9th and 11th      2d, 116th, and 21st
                 PZ DIVS             PZ DIVS
              2d SS PZ DIV

                          OKW RESERVES
                          HQ I SS PZ CORPS
                        1st SS, 12th SS, 17th SS
                             PZ GR DIVS           Direct chain of command ————
                                                  Conditional tactical control of
                          PZ LEHR DIV             certain elements or co-operation ----
```

considered. The fronts not under attack were to free certain previously designated divisions for OB West use. OB West, after obtaining permission from OKW, would then be able to commit these divisions in the invasion area. These preparations were made in detail on all fronts.) Army Group B and Army Group G had their own divisions or units in reserve.

The rear positions in Holland were the Grebbe Line and the Yssel Position. In all of Belgium and France there was no prepared rear position. Once the Allies had broken through the coastal defenses, there would be nothing to stop them until they reached the West Wall on the German frontier.

On the map (only on paper) there was a line Abbeville-Amiens-Compiegne-Soissons-Reims-Chalons-sur-Marne-St Didier- Chaumont -Langres-Gray-Dole-Swiss border, following the Somme, Aisne, Marne, and suitable high ground. However, this position was never constructed; there was no labor or material available and no time. Even if the position had been constructed, there were no troops available to occupy it. For political and psychological reasons, OKW permitted only a "secret" reconnaissance of the position, but no actual construction. We were to hold the coast and not to think of "rear" positions. (The same principle applied on the Eastern Front.) Only after the invasion was this position to be hastily constructed by Gen Fl Kitzinger. At that time, of course, construction was still less possible.

The West Wall, built before 1939, was close to the Western frontier of Germany and ran south of Aachen-Belgium-Luxembourg border-along the Saar to Saarbriicken-south of Pirnasens-Bienwald-Rhine river-along the east bank of the Oberrhein to the east of Basel. The West Wall was built primarily for political reasons. It was not nearly as strong as propaganda abroad purported. Since the fortifications were erected before 1939, they were unable to withstand aerial bombs of1944; their concrete works were too weak. The West Wall was only a chain of bunkers and lacked the depth that every defense must have. Once through the weak, thin line, the enemy would find no fortified defense in depth. After 1940, the West Wall was neglected and no longer improved upon. Permanent weapons were removed and sent to the fronts. Wire entanglements were taken up and used elsewhere. Thus, in 1944, the West Wall was not a strong position; above all, it lacked sufficient occupying troops for its defense.

The last rear defense line was the Rhine. When the Allies crossed this river there would be no further obstacles and the war would be virtually over. Only the Upper Rhine (West Wall) between Rastatt and east of Basel had weak fortifications. The Middle and Lower Rhine were not fortified. In addition, the Middle Rhine is so narrow that between Bingen and Andernach it does not represent a strong barrier. Moreover, there were no permanent security troops. Actually the only "rear position" was the West Wall.

The unusual command channels in the service of supply made strategic leadership more difficult. Supply of the entire area was under the direction of the Oberquartiermeister West in Paris (Gen Finch, previously Gen Eckstein). This officer was subordinate to OB West, the Militärbefehlshaber for France, and the Generalquartiermeister of OKH (Gen Wagner, later Gen Toppe). Thus, he was under three separate commands and received orders from three different men! The supply situation, during the invasion from the high-level standpoint of OB West, was as follows:

a. There was not enough motorized transport to meet the needs of the action in Normandy. OB West had no motorized columns of its own and therefore was forced to borrow these from the armies in the West. These columns were composed of purchased French and Belgian trucks of all types and ages. The drivers were French civilians, insofar as they would drive voluntarily. The transport columns of the Seventh Army were in no way sufficient. Only the Panzer-type divisions had organic transport columns; the infantry divisions had none.

Since the French and Belgian railroads had been disrupted by Allied air attacks and the French Resistance movement, they could be used very little. On many days, only seven to ten trains could be moved during a 24-hour period. These trains also had to carry supplies of coal and food to the population of Paris and southern France in addition to troops and tracked vehicles. This railroad net, crippled by air attacks on the Seine and Loire bridges and on important railroad yards, could therefore transport only a small percentage of the supplies. Thus, the few motor transport columns were even more burdened. The crippled rail net forced us to unload troops and supplies far behind the front and resulted in an extraordinarily long supply line. As the Allied air force destroyed many moving convoys, the available transportation dwindled more and more.

b. The supply of fuel was so critical that our few planes were unable to fly because of the shortage of gasoline. The fuel requirements for Panzer-type divisions, for the Luftwaffe, and for the Navy (U-boats) were so great that, even with the available motor transport, gasoline supply was insufficient. (Fuel requirements for the Eastern Front, the Balkans, and Italy were also very great.)

c. There was no shortage of small-arms ammunition, but artillery ammunition, particularly for light and medium field howitzers (Model 1918), was very critical. The great number of foreign weapons with varied types of ammunition increased the difficulties of ammunition supply.

d. Medical and veterinary services in general were adequate.

e. Spare parts for the much too many types of tanks and motorized vehicles were often unavailable. Tank and vehicle repair often took weeks because the required spare parts were not in stock.

The OB West right boundary was the German-Dutch border to the mouth of the Ems river on the North Sea. Adjacent on the right was the North Sea Naval Command at Wilhelmshaven. The left boundary of OB West was the Franco-Italian border at Menton (Mediterranean). The adjacent command on the left was OB Southwest in Italy (Genfldm Kesselring).

The mission of OB West was as follows: "OB West is to prevent any hostile landing in its area. The MLR is the high tide line on the coast. Should the enemy land at any place, they are to be immediately thrown back into the sea."

Essentially this was the text of the order given by the Führer (OKW). The order would have been of value only if OB West were permitted freedom of action to carry it out in detail. OB West should have been able to order the disposition of divisions and should have reserved full freedom to bring up, without approval, all divisions suitable to the existing situation. However, this was not the case, and every detail was ordered or approved by the Führer (in East Prussia!). Thus, command leadership of the type in which we had been schooled was made impossible.

We had been educated to work according to general operational instructions issued by responsible high command, which gave the commander a free hand. From 1942 until the Spring of 1944, OB West had requested similar general instruction several times, the last time in late June 1944 when the Führer was in the West for 24 hours. (The

Führer's headquarters were northeast of Soissons, on the Soissons-Laon road.) These instructions were not issued. In accordance with our training, these instructions could have been Approximately as follows:

"The mission of OB West is to prevent a hostile landing on the coast of its area. Should the enemy, contrary to expectations, succeed in landing, they are to be thrown back immediately with all free and available forces. In the event of an enemy breakthrough deep into the OB West area, they are to be defeated by a fluid field operation under the direction of OB West, even if southern France has to be given up. If this operation does not achieve results, then OKH will issue further instructions according to the situation. In the closest circle of the OB West staff, a planned retreat to the West Wall in order to conserve forces should be contemplated. This plan is to be kept secret and is not to go beyond OB West. In any event, the final decision rests with OKW."

Thus, our best strategist, Genfldm von Rundstedt, would have been free to conduct operations in the manner taught by Moltke, Schlieffen, and Hindenburg-boldly and independently.

I shall evaluate the divisions in the West only from the high-level viewpoint of OB West. We had a total of about 60 divisions of all types and all degrees of efficiency.

a. The bulk of the SS Panzer divisions and Heeres divisions were the best. A few SS and Heeres Panzer divisions had not yet completed their reorganization and were inadequately equipped with tanks. The 21st Panzer Division (Feuchtinger) was an expedient, having been assembled and organized with obsolete French armored vehicles. The personnel were better. The Panzer Lehr Division (Bayerlein) and 2nd Panzer Division (von Lüttwitz) were probably the best equipped. Both divisions were combat-experienced and energetically and well led. The command leadership of most of the SS divisions was less satisfactory. By 1944, all divisions had been employed both in the East and in the West. They had been reorganized several times and were not the divisions of 1939-40. Because of the fuel shortage, tank drivers were not sufficiently experienced and therefore were not good enough to drive in rough terrain and were responsible for the large number of tanks dead-lined.

b. The Fallschirm divisions were next in the evaluation. These divisions did their best under the proved, experienced leadership of Gen Meindl (II FS Corps). (These divisions, however, had no parachutes!) The Panzer and Fallschirm divisions were preferential units with the best personnel, the best equipment, and the longest rest periods.
c. In third place came those infantry divisions which were not employed in the coastal fortifications. However, these divisions were for the most part newly reorganized, only hastily trained, and weakened by combat in the East. These were horse-drawn divisions. Their personnel and equipment were much less suitable for a large-scale war of materiel than the Panzer and Fallschirm divisions.
d. In last place were the coastal divisions. Most of these divisions had only two organic infantry regiments, weak artillery, and very limited mobility. For a long time they had been occupying a rigid defense of a broad front and were unaccustomed to mobile warfare in open terrain. Most of the officers and men had been wounded and were in limited assignment status. Their weapons were no match against a modern, well equipped enemy. One division was composed only of men with stomach ailments.
e. The Luftwaffe Feld divisions varied in quality; some were good, some were inferior. The men and equipment were good, but the personnel did not have adequate training in ground combat.

In 1944, there were Approximately 25 waves of divisions-meaning 25 types of divisions which varied in organization, artillery, and composition. Before committing any division it was necessary to know to which wave the division belonged. On this subject there was a large, red book marked "Secret." It does not follow that the first wave was the best and wave 25 the worst. In 1943-44, OB West had to release the best infantry divisions to the Italian Front. The morale of these heterogeneous troops, considering the serious situation in general in 1944, ranged from very good to satisfactory. There were no moral difficulties; the troops did their best as far as their varied composition, equipment, and leadership permitted. Further details can best be given by the respective division and regimental commanders.

GERMAN TIGER TANKS DEPLOYED IN NORMANDY

The Panzer VI Tiger tank has become synonymous with the German army and is particularly associated with the Normandy campaign and the exploits of Michael Wittman. The popular conception is of a mass of German heavy armour arrayed against a plucky allied force. In reality, rather like its real life counterpart, the Tiger was actually a very rare beast. Only three German schwere Panzer Abteilung (Heavy Tank Battalions) were equipped with Tiger I or II tanks and are actually known to have fought in Normandy against Allied invasion forces. One was a Wermacht formation and two were Waffen SS, in addition, a small number of Tiger I tanks may have also reached Normandy with the Panzer Lehr (Training) Division although the precise information remains sketchy.

s.Pz.Abt. 503

We know for certain that s.Pz.Abt. 503 was transferred to Normandy equipped with 33 Tiger I's and 12 Tiger II's, reaching action in early July 1944. The 33 Tiger I's were all shipped to the unit in June 1944.

A knocked out Tiger I of s.SS-PzAbt. 101 lies abandoned in the ruins of Villers Bocage.

Photographs of the unit's Tigers are very rare and identification is not helped by the fact that the technical features of the machines are very similar to late Tigers shipped to the other units. However, possible distinguishing features include the fact that spare tracks were apparently never mounted on the front plate, spare tracks were stowed outside the hull MG mount and driver's visor, and were attached to the Pilze sockets on turret roof. Camouflage patterning too was very similar to other units in the field, but on at least some vehicles, the Balkankreuz is a distinguishing feature from the fact that they were exceptionally large by comparison with other units. Surviving photographs are all black and white, so an element of conjecture is required, but it is apparent that all tactical numbers in this unit were applied using a thin and very neatly stencilled white outline and a very dark, most probably black, interior.

s.SS-Pz.Abt. 101

It is also known that s.SS-Pz.Abt. 101 took delivery of 45 Tiger I's in time for the Normandy battles, ten were delivered from the factory to the unit in October 1943, a further nine reached it in January 1944, and a final batch of twenty five reached the unit in April 1944. The unit arrived in Normandy in early June and Michael Wittmann and the 1st and 2nd Kompanie took part in the celebrated battle of Villers-Bocage on 13th June 1944. It was this engagement which, more than any other, has forged the reputation of the Tiger. We know that the unit's Tiger I's included both the rubber-wheel and steel-wheel variants. Identification is made easier from the fact that in this unit spare track was customarily mounted on the front plate on the majority of the unit's Tigers. Further identification is made easier by the fact that each Kompanie carried the distinctive Leibstandarte unit marking of crossed keys in a shield, on the front and rear. A further indicator of the unit's identity is the fact that the 1st Kompanie also carried a panzer lozenge with an "S" and a small "1" on the front and rear plates. Tactical numbers were fairly large and dark with white outline with the exception of the command tanks.

A second SS Heavy Tank unit, s.SS-Pz.Abt. 102, also took part in the battles for Normandy having been transferred to the Normandy front with forty five Tiger I's, and reaching action in early July. The unit was equipped with the Tiger at a comparatively late stage in the war and difficulties with supply dictated that initially only six Tiger I's were available for issue in April 1944 with the remaining thirty nine Tigers only being issued to the unit in May 1944. Understandably photographs of this unit's Tigers are very rare and difficulties in identification are compounded by the fact that technical features appear to be identical to the later Tigers which shipped to s.Pz.Abt. 503 and s.SS-Pz.Abt. 101 which also took part in the Normandy fighting. However, one possible clue to help in the identification of this unit from s.SS-Pz.Abt. 101 is that it appears not to have been the practice to mount spare track on the front plate. The summer camouflage pattern was applied large patches of color which on some vehicles leads to the appearance of lines of the original dunkelgelb. Tactical numbers were thin, neatly stencilled with white outline and dark interior. Tactical numbers on the turret sides were often sloped, being aligned with the slope of the turret roof. Some Tigers of s.SS-Pz.Abt. 101 carried a single underlined "S" rune painted on the zimmerit on the front and/or rear plates.

Panzer Lehr Division

It is known that the Panzer Lehr Division (Training Division) was issued ten Tiger I's in September-October 1943 and five Tiger II's in February-March 1944. Of the ten Tiger I's, three Tiger I's were listed as still with the division in summer 1944. The division reported six of eight Tigers operational on 1st June 1944 and three Tigers were certainly operational on 1st July 1944. Whether any Tiger I's actually travelled and fought with the division to Normandy, and the eventual fate of the Tiger I remains tantalisingly unclear.

HOW THE GERMANS FIGHT IN WOODED AND BROKEN TERRAIN

Intelligence Bulletin, January 1945

The Germans recognize that operations in wooded and broken terrain require special combat methods both in the attack and in the defense. In such terrain the Germans try to control all roads and trails, so as to ensure the movement of support weapons and supplies. The heaviest fighting therefore generally takes place in the vicinity of these roads and trails.

GENERAL PRINCIPLES

In the attack the Germans maintain careful protective fire as they advance along the roads and trails; when they are obliged to move across open stretches, this protective fire becomes continuous. Roads are opened up as rapidly as possible, and are covered with antitank guns. Special attention is paid to the formations adopted during movement and in battle, to correct employment of fire power, to appropriate communication methods, to the problem of maintaining direction, and to supplying forward elements with an adequate amount of ammunition.

In the defense it is considered essential to block roads and trails. Snipers are posted in trees. Centers of resistance are established at curves, bends, and defiles, and whenever a road climbs to higher ground. Firing positions are prepared just off roads and trails, to command open fields of fire.

METHOD OF ADVANCE

In the approach march, squads and platoons advance on a narrow front, deployed in depth along roadside hedges and scrub growth, and in hollows running in the desired direction. The leading squads, on contact, serve as scouts and patrols. They advance in extended order, with a light machine gun leading. While the squads immediately behind the forward squads deploy less deeply at intervals of 30 to

"In the defense it is considered essential to block roads and trails. Snipers are posted in trees. Centers of resistance are established at curves and defiles, and whenever a road climbs to higher ground."

40 paces, the subsequent squads follow in squad columns so as to have all-around observation and protection. Special observers are detailed to watch out for tree snipers.

The Germans believe that when battle is joined, the same formations employed during the approach march should be maintained as far as possible. Fire cover is provided by the support weapons, especially the mortars, which advance with the forward troops. However, the Germans recognize that further deployment of squads and platoons may be necessary. It is a German principle that after resistance has been crushed and hostile strong points eliminated, the original formations should be resumed immediately.

The reserve platoon advances, employing the same close formation,

"In the approach march, squads and platoons advance on a narrow front, deployed in depth along roadside hedges and scrub growth."

in the rear of the platoon which gains the most ground. The commander of the reserve platoon arranges for all-around protection, particularly to repel surprise attacks which may be made by hostile forces from centers of resistance not yet engaged. These protective measures also include protection of the rear.

USE OF FIRE POWER

To eliminate centers of resistance, the Germans employ all available light and heavy weapons, especially mortars.

Since observation in close country is difficult, the Germans not only keep their support weapons well forward, but often use their heavy machine guns as light machine guns.

Terrain conditions are likely to have a definite effect on German employment of mortars. Sometimes observers can work only from treetops. Every effort is made to place observers close to the mortar positions so that corrections can be passed accurately and rapidly to the mortar detachment. The employment of message runners is not considered practicable in the heat of battle; instead, disk signaling is preferred. The Germans try not to site their mortars too close to the roadside scrub growth.

The commanders of the support weapons are required to report their availability to the leading rifle company commander and his platoon commanders, and to remain in their vicinity.

The antitank guns follow without orders in the rear of the infantry, as soon as the roads have been cleared. Their principal mission is to take over the job of preventing hostile tanks from using the roads. In addition, so far as their principal mission permits, the antitank guns take part in attacks on Allied centers of resistance, using antitank high-explosive shells.

"Sometimes observers can work only from treetops."

"In the heat of battle, disk signaling is preferred."

"The antitank guns take over the job of preventing hostile tanks from using the roads."

Protected by the fire of the support weapons, the infantry works its way forward as close as possible to the Allied centers of resistance. As soon as the support weapons cease firing, the infantry breaks through, hurling hand grenades. The Germans are scrupulously careful in regulating the time when the support weapons are to cease firing—first the medium mortars and then the heavy machine guns—and the time when the breakthrough is to be attempted. The points at which the breakthrough is to be made are sealed off on the flanks by squads especially detailed for this job. Hostile positions along hedges or other roadside growth are mopped-up after the breakthrough.

MISCELLANEOUS PRECAUTIONS

Platoons and squads detail men for the express purpose of maintaining contact with neighboring units. These men indicate the headquarters of their own units by means of pennants and by signaling with lamps to flanking squads and platoons. It is a rule that pennants marked "Front Line" always be put up. Identification panels are laid out, when necessary, to indicate the advance of the front line.

Because the opportunities for unobserved movement are very good in terrain of this type, the Germans make considerable use of runners. Radio-telegraphy and smoke cartridges also are used, in addition to the light signals.

Higher headquarters are continually kept informed about the

situation, to permit smooth coordination of the attack.

Since the problem of maintaining direction is difficult in closely wooded and unevenly wooded terrain, squad leaders are given specific rendezvous on roads and paths. Compass directions are issued before the departure.

Because of terrain difficulties, the Germans find it useful to equip squads with ladders, axes, good knives, and sharp spades. Since ammunition supply is likely to be slow and cannot be relied upon, a generous quantity of ammunition, including hand grenades, is issued to the men before the departure.

"Compass directions are issued before the departure."

"Because of terrain difficulties, the Germans find it useful to equip squads with ladders, axes, good knives, and sharp spades."

A TANK-INFANTRY TEAM OBSERVED IN COMBAT

Intelligence Bulletin, December 1944.

For a period of 36 hours in the last days of July, an officer of an Allied army group staff had an excellent opportunity of observing German tanks and infantry attacking an Allied force in France. The following notes, which are based on his report, describe the tactics that the Germans employed.

The general situation was fluid at the time of the attack. The Germans advanced westward in three parallel columns, each consisting of tanks accompanied by infantry. The center column followed a main road, firing rapidly and moving at a brisk rate. It went from hill to hill, with the accompanying infantry dog-trotting through the fields on each side of the road and over the hedgerows. The infantry was deployed over no more than the width of a single field on each side. The center column had a total of only about eight track-laying vehicles. At least three of these were tanks, one or two probably were self-propelled guns, and the remainder probably were half-track personnel carriers.

Although the total German strength which had been sent to capture and hold an important crossroads at St. Denisière consisted of two companies of infantry and probably not more than ten tanks, the Allied officer observed only the track-laying vehicles previously mentioned and possibly a platoon of infantry.

The Infantrymen Moved Fast

The leading tank fired its 75 rapidly, getting both graze and air bursts, while its machine guns, supplemented by those of the vehicles behind it, sprayed the top of every hedgerow. The noise was terrific, and the bursts in the shrubbery and the tops of trees and hedgerows were certainly impressive. Even before the shock of the guns discharged at close range, and the garden-hose spray of machine-gun bullets, had taken full effect, German infantrymen were over the hedgerow and into the field and were advancing toward the next field with determination and courage. They knew where they were going, and went there fast.

At night the Germans reacted forcefully, with fire and limited movement, whenever they detected any sign of an Allied approach. The German tanks moved slowly, and made very little noise. Immediately after firing, each tank moved to a new position 25 to 50 yards away. It should be emphasized that the noise discipline of the German tank crews and the accompanying infantry was superior. There was no talking or shouting; except for machine-gun and cannon fire and the starting of motor, no sound carried farther than 100 yards.

On the other hand, the approach of U.S. tanks and the passing of most U.S. motor convoys was rapidly identifiable by the loud shouting, talking, and issuing of orders by the U.S. troops who approached or passed the general vicinity of a German position. The propensity of U.S. tank drivers to "gun" their motors was a dead giveaway, whereas the Germans always eased their tanks forward, traveled in low gear, and were remarkably quiet in all operations except the firing. They used long bursts of their rapid-firing machine guns to discourage guests. If pressed at all, they sent up flares to obtain German artillery and mortar fire on their flanks. The way they handled their tanks was bold and sure. They acted as if they knew exactly what their destination was, and by which route they wished to proceed.

A U.S. Tank "Got the Works"
At 0230, the darkest part of the night, a German tank moved out and headed toward the northernmost German column, making as little noise as possible. Later it turned out that a lone U.S. tank on reconnaissance had pushed up against the nose of the ridge that the German tanks had organized, and the Germans were quietly laying plans to place a terrific amount of fire on it. Before long, it got the works.

Because there were so few German infantrymen, and because they were interested only in reaching and holding the team's objective, their mopping-up activities were negligible. Thus, of the Allied troops overrun in this fashion, a large percentage was neither killed, wounded, captured, or missing during the first two or three days. The ease and rapidity with which this small attacking force made its penetration, reached its objective, sat on the objective, and cut traffic on an important road is of more than ordinary interest. Also, it is reasonable to assume that the Germans will employ small groups for similar missions in the future.

GERMAN MILITARY TACTICS
Handbook on German Military Forces

I. GENERAL TACTICAL DOCTRINES

1. Basic Doctrines

An outstanding characteristic of the German nation is its fondness for everything connected with militarism. This is based not only on traditional sentiment but also on long-range and intense education that glorifies the military spirit. This gives the German military leaders the essential foundation for aggressive military operations.

The Germans believe that only the offensive can achieve success on the field, particularly when combined with the element of surprise. German military literature, for the past century, has emphasized the need for aggressiveness in all military operations.

The Germans have been thoroughly aware of the psychological component in warfare and have developed systematic terrorization to a high degree.

At the same time they have placed considerable reliance on novel and sensational weapons such as the mass use of armor, the robot bomb, and the super-heavy tank. Their principal weaknesses in this regard have been their failure to integrate these new techniques with established arms and tactics—German field artillery, for example, did not maintain pace with German armor—and their devotion to automatic weapons at the expense of accuracy.

A highly trained officer corps and a thoroughly disciplined army are the necessary elements to implement this aggressive philosophy. German tactical doctrines stress the responsibility and the initiative of subordinates. The belief of former years that the German Army was inflexible and lacking in initiative has been completely destroyed in this war, in which aggressive and daring leadership has been responsible for many bold decisions. Yet, while the Germans have many excellent tacticians, they tend to repeat the same type of maneuvers, a fact which has been fully exploited by Allied commanders.

The German specialization in particular types of warfare such as mountain, desert, winter, or the attack on fortified positions, showed thorough preparation and ingenuity. At the same time the Germans had been quite willing to learn from their opponents and on numerous occasions have copied Allied tactics and weapons.

2. Recent Tactical Trends

From the time when the German Army was forced on the defensive by the Allied armies, German tactical doctrines have undergone modifications such as renunciation (except in unstated instances) of air support, and the substitution of linear defense for elastic offensive defense.

The primary goal of Germany today is to gain time and to achieve victory in a political sense, since the Germans are no longer capable of a military victory. Of necessity their military operations now supplement this effort and have become a large-scale delaying action.

3. Exercise of Command

The U.S. and German doctrines applied in exercise of the command are virtually identical. The Germans stress the necessity of the staff in assisting the commander to evaluate the situation and in preparing and disseminating orders to the lower units. They emphasize that the commander should be well forward with his units not only for the purpose of facilitating communication, but also because his presence has a salutary effect on the troops.

II. RECONNAISSANCE

1. General

a. PURPOSE.

The purpose of reconnaissance and the types of units employed to obtain information are similar in the U.S. and the German Armies. German tactical principles of reconnaissance, however, diverge somewhat from those of the U.S. The Germans stress aggressiveness, attempt to obtain superiority in the area to be reconnoitered, and strive for continuous observation of the enemy. They believe in employing reconnaissance units in force as a rule. They expect and are prepared to fight to obtain the desired information. Often they assign supplementary tasks to their reconnaissance units, such as sabotage behind enemy lines, harassment, or counter-reconnaissance.

b. TECHNIQUE.

Only enough reconnaissance troops are sent on a mission to assure superiority in the area to be reconnoitered. Reserves are kept on hand to be committed when the reconnaissance must be intensified, when the original force meets strong enemy opposition, or when the direction and area to be reconnoitered are changed. The Germans encourage aggressive action against enemy security forces. When their reconnaissance units meet superior enemy forces, they fight a delaying action while other units attempt to flank the enemy.

c. CLASSIFICATION.

Reconnaissance is classified by the Germans as operational, tactical, and battle reconnaissance—corresponding to the U.S. distant, close, and battle reconnaissance.

2. Operational Reconnaissance (Operative Aufklarung)

Operational reconnaissance, penetrating over a large area in great depth, provides the basis for strategic planning and action. This type of reconnaissance is intended to determine the location and activities of enemy forces, particularly localities of rail concentrations, forward or rearward displacements of personnel, loading or unloading areas of army elements, the construction of field or permanent fortifications, and hostile air force concentrations. Identification of large enemy motorized elements, especially on an open flank, is important. Operational reconnaissance is carried out by the Air Force and by motorized units. Aerial photography units operate at altitudes of 16,500 to 26,500 feet. Since missions assigned to operational air reconnaissance units are generally limited to the observation of important roads and railroads, reconnaissance sectors and areas normally are not assigned. The motorized units employed for operational reconnaissance have only directions and objectives assigned.

3. Tactical Reconnaissance (Taktische Aufklarung)

a. PURPOSE.

Tactical reconnaissance, carried out in the area behind the operational reconnaissance, provides the basis for the commitment of troops. Its mission embraces identification of the enemy's organization, disposition, strength, and antiaircraft defense; determination of the enemy's reinforcement capabilities; and terrain reconnaissance of advanced sectors. Air Force reconnaissance units and motorized and mounted reconnaissance battalions are employed for tactical reconnaissance. Their direction and radius of employment are based upon the results of the operational reconnaissance.

b. AIR RECONNAISSANCE.

Tactical air reconnaissance is normally made from altitudes of 6,500 to 16,000 feet. As a rule, air reconnaissance units are assigned specific reconnaissance areas, the boundaries of which normally do not coincide with sectors assigned to ground units. Reconnaissance planes generally are employed singly.

c. GROUND RECONNAISSANCE.

Sectors of responsibility are assigned to ground tactical reconnaissance battalions. In order to make them independent or to facilitate their change of direction, battalions may be assigned only reconnaissance objectives. In such instances, boundary lines separate adjacent units. The Germans avoid using main roads as boundary lines, defining the sectors in such a way that main roads fall within the reconnaissance sectors. The width of a sector is determined by the situation, the type and strength of the reconnaissance battalion, the road net, and the terrain. In general, the width of a sector assigned to a motorized reconnaissance battalion does not exceed 30 miles.

d. ORDERS FOR TACTICAL RECONNAISSANCE.

Orders issued to a reconnaissance battalion or its patrols normally contain, in addition to the mission, the following:

(1) Line of departure.
(2) Information concerning adjacent reconnaissance units.
(3) Sector boundaries or direction of operation.
(4) Objectives.

(5) Phase lines.

(6) Instructions for transmission of reports.

(7) Location of immediate objectives whose attainment is to be reported.

(8) Instructions regarding air-ground liaison.

(9) Time of departure, route, and objective of the main force.

e. TACTICAL RECONNAISSANCE PROCEDURES.

When a motorized reconnaissance column expects contact with the enemy, it advances by bounds. The length of bounds depends on the cover the terrain offers as well as on the road net. As the distance from the enemy decreases, the bounds are shortened. The Germans utilize roads as long as possible and usually use different routes for the advance and the return.

The reconnaissance battalion commander normally sends out patrols which advance by bounds. Their distance in front of the battalion depends on the situation, the terrain, and the range of the signal equipment, but as a rule they are not more than an hour's traveling distance (about 25 miles) ahead of the battalion. The battalion serves as the reserve for the patrols and as an advance message center (*Meldekopf*), collecting the messages and relaying them to the rear. Armored reconnaissance cars, armored half-tracks, or motorcycles compose the motorized reconnaissance patrols, whose exact composition depends on their mission and on the situation. Motorcycles are used to fill in gaps and intervals, thereby thickening the reconnaissance net.

When the proximity of the enemy does not permit profitable employment of the motorized reconnaissance battalion, it is withdrawn and the motorized elements of the divisional reconnaissance battalion take over.

Divisional reconnaissance battalions seldom operate more than one day's march (18 miles) in front of the division, covering an area Approximately 6 miles wide.

4. Battle Reconnaissance (Gefechtsaufklarung)

a. GENERAL.

Battle reconnaissance as a rule is begun when the opposing forces begin to deploy. All troops participating in battle carry out battle reconnaissance through patrols, artillery observation posts, observation battalions, and air reconnaissance units. The information obtained on the organization and strength of the enemy provides the basis for the conduct of the battle.

b. ARMORED CAR PATROLS.

The Panzer division dispatches armored reconnaissance units equipped with armored vehicles and numerous automatic weapons. The armored reconnaissance unit is fast and has a wide radius of action.

Armored car patrols normally are composed of three armored reconnaissance cars, one of which is equipped with radio. An artillery observer often accompanies the patrol so that in an emergency fire can be brought down quickly. This type of patrol usually is organized for missions lasting one to two days. Tasks are defined clearly, and nothing is allowed to interfere with the patrol's main objective. If enemy forces are met, action is avoided unless the force is so weak that it can be destroyed without diverting the patrol from its main task. If enemy action is anticipated, the patrol is reinforced with self-propelled guns and occasionally with tanks. Engineers and motorcyclists are often attached to the patrol to deal with road blocks and demolitions.

While scouting a woods, a favorite German ruse is to drive the leading car toward its edge, halt briefly to observe, and then drive off rapidly, hoping to draw fire that will disclose the enemy positions.

At road blocks, the leading car opens fire. If fire is not returned, men dismount and go forward to attach tow ropes to the road block. If necessary, the patrol dismounts and proceeds with machine guns to reconnoiter on foot.

A patrol is never split up, but in open country distances between cars may be as much as 200 to 300 yards.

c. OBSERVATION BATTALION AND AIR RECONNAISSANCE.

The German observation battalion locates enemy artillery and heavy weapons positions by sound and flash ranging and evaluated aerial photographs. The Air Force assists in battle reconnaissance by observing the distribution of the enemy's forces, his artillery, bivouac and movements, reserves, tank assemblies, and any other special occurrences behind the front. In general, air battle reconnaissance is executed under 6,000 feet.

d. BATTLE RECONNAISSANCE PATROLS (Spähtruppen).

The Germans send out reconnaissance patrols, consisting of a noncommissioned officer and three or four men, to get such information as the location of enemy positions and minefields. They generally avoid contact and retreat when fired on.

e. COMBAT PATROLS (Gefechtsspähtruppen or Stosstruppen).

These consist of at least one noncommissioned officer and eight men, but are usually much stronger. As a rule the combat patrol is commanded by a sergeant who has under him 15 to 20 men, organized in two equal sections, each commanded by a section leader. These are raiding patrols, and their mission often includes bringing back prisoners of war. Since Allied air supremacy has neutralized German air reconnaissance to a great extent, the Germans have placed increased importance on prisoners of war, especially officers, as a source of information on enemy strength, dispositions, and intentions.

Combat or other types of patrols are often sent out to test the strength of enemy outposts. If an outpost proves to be weakly held, the patrol attacks, occupies the position, and remains there until relieved by troops from the rear. If the patrol is strongly garrisoned, the patrol attempts to return with a prisoner of war.

f. SPECIAL PATROLS (Spähtruppen mit besonderen Aufgaben).

These vary in strength in accordance with their special mission. Special patrols are sent out to carry out such tasks as demolitions, engaging of enemy patrols that have penetrated German positions, and ambushing enemy supply columns.

g. MISCELLANEOUS PATROLS.

Engineer patrols are employed to reconnoiter approaches to fortified areas, defiles, or rivers. Artillery patrols, usually consisting of an officer and a few mounted men, reconnoiter routes of approach, observation posts, and firing positions.

h. TERRAIN RECONNAISSANCE (Geländeerkundung).

The Germans place great emphasis on terrain reconnaissance, realizing the influence terrain has upon the conduct of operations. Most of their usual reconnaissance missions include terrain reconnaissance tasks. Terrain may be so important at times as to require reconnaissance by special units. Ground and air reconnaissance units give special attention to the road net—its density, condition, road blocks, mines, and demolitions—as well as to the terrain itself, particularly tank country.

i. EQUIPMENT AND SUPPORT.

The Germans equip their ground battle-reconnaissance patrols with machine pistols and one or two light machine guns that are used to cover the patrol's approach or withdrawal. Engineers often are attached to guide a patrol through German minefields and to clear a way through enemy wire or mines. Artillery support is given in the form of harassing fire put down just before the patrol reaches its objective. Sometimes the artillery fires into adjacent sectors to mislead the enemy as to the actual area to be reconnoitered. In other instances, artillery and mortars that have registered during the previous day shell during the night the area to be reconnoitered. As soon as the barrage is lifted, the patrol advances under cover of machine-gun fire from flanking positions.

III. MARCHES

1. General

The formations and the organizations of the march column in day or night advances are the same in the German Army as in the U.S. Army and are governed by the same principles. For a smooth functioning of the march the Germans stress: systematic training and practice; attention to physical welfare; care of vehicles and equipment; previous reconnaissance of routes; warning orders; and the issue of detailed march orders.

2. Organization and Control of the March Column

In order to secure the march column against enemy attacks, the Germans divide the column in the same manner as U.S. doctrine prescribes, namely into Advance Guard (*Vorhut*), Main Body (*Gros*), and Rear Guard (*Nachhut*). German equivalents for the U.S. terms are:

Advance Guard
- Spitze: Point
- Spitzenkompanie: Advance party
- Vortrupp: Support
- Haupttrupp: Reserve

Rear Guard
- Nachspitze: Rear point
- Nachspitzenkompanie: Rear party
- Nachtrupp: Support
- Haupttrupp: Reserve

The issue of orders for march and traffic control is the responsibility of the higher command. Movement by road of formations from battalion strength upwards is carried out in the Zone of the Interior at the orders of the Army High Command (OKH) or a headquarters acting on the orders of the Army High Command. In the Theater of War such movements are controlled by Army Headquarters, which issues orders in accordance with instructions from Army High Command or the Army Group. Movements in the areas of military commanders of line-of-communication areas are controlled by orders of the commanders of such areas.

Orders for movement are issued to the formations of fighting troops by the operations group of headquarters; those to supply services and units in the line-of-communication area emanate from the supply and administrative group.

The Germans set up a well organized traffic control service which is under the orders of the operations group. All traffic control services usually wear orange-red brassards, while the members of the military police are distinguished by metal gorgets.

The Germans allot to each front-line division its own road or sector of advance, usually marked by advance parties. General Headquarters or any other troops directed simultaneously on the same roads, are subordinated to the division for the duration of the move. All-weather roads usually are allotted to motorized or armored divisions, while subsidiary roads are assigned to infantry divisions.

3. Conduct of the March

When a German infantry division advances along several routes, an infantry element normally forms the head of each main body. The commander of the main body usually marches at or near the head of the main body. The motorized elements of the division, unless employed on reconnaissance or security missions, are organized into one or more motor echelons which follow the march column by bounds, or move in a column along a separate road. Before the march begins, the division signal battalion lays a trunk telephone line as far forward as the situation permits and extends this line while the march proceeds. The leading signal unit usually marches with the support of the advance guard and establishes telephone stations at important points. In a march along several roads the trunk line normally is laid along the route of the division commander and his staff. In addition to the construction of the trunk line, the Germans stress radio communications to the rear and flanks, as well as the use of messengers mounted on horses, bicycles, or motorcycles.

4. Security of March Columns

As a rule the Germans allot motorized units for the protection of the flanks and rear of march columns. However, a smaller unit, such as a battalion, may advance without flank security detachments.

The Germans are very much concerned about antiaircraft protective measures and often march in open columns (*Fliegermarschtiefe*); an advance in deployed formation (*Fliegermarschbreite*) is seldom practical. Antiaircraft defense is concentrated at important terrain features, such as bridges, crossroads, and defiles. Because of Allied air supremacy the Germans now instruct their troops to conduct movements and the transport of supplies only at night, and without lights. They also order their troops to leave burned out vehicles standing on the road to attract fresh attacks by enemy aircraft.

IV. OFFENSIVE

1. General

The fundamental principle of German offensive doctrine is to encircle and destroy the enemy. The objective of the combined arms in attack is to bring the armored forces and the infantry into decisive action against the enemy with sufficient fire power and shock. Superiority in force and fire power, the employment of armored forces, as well as the surprise element, play a great part in the offensive.

Coordination between the combined arms under a strong unified command is, the Germans emphasize, an absolute requisite to the success of these shock tactics. This has become more and more true as the Allies have developed effective antitank weapons and have adopted deeper defenses, limiting the self-sufficiency of German tanks. To counter these measures, the Germans have increased the mobility and armor protection of their motor-borne infantry, and have mounted a large proportion of both their direct and indirect heavy support weapons on self-propelled carriages.

In attempting thoroughly to paralyze the defender up to the moment of the tank-infantry assault, the Germans realize that even the most formidable forces are never sufficient for overwhelming superiority on the entire front. They therefore select a point of main effort (*Schwerpunkt*) for a breakthrough, allotting narrow sectors of attack (*Gefechtsstreifen*) to the troops committed at the decisive locality. There they also mass the bulk of their heavy weapons and reserves. The other sectors of the front are engaged by weaker, diversionary forces. In selecting the point of main effort, the Germans consider weaknesses in the enemy's defensive position; suitability of the terrain, especially for tanks and for cooperation of all arms; approach routes; and possibilities for supporting fire, especially artillery. Although the Germans select a point of main effort in all attacks, they usually also make plans for shifting their main effort if they meet unexpected success elsewhere. To allow such shifts, sufficient reserves and a strong, unified command are organized.

An attack on a narrow front, according to German doctrine, must have sufficient forces at its disposal to widen the penetration while maintaining its impetus, and to protect the flanks of the penetration. Once the attack is launched, it must drive straight to its objective, regardless of opposition.

2. Types of Attack

a. FLANK ATTACK (Flankenangriff).

The Germans consider that the most effective attack is against the enemy's flank. The flank attack develops either from the approach march—sometimes through a turning movement—or from flank marches. It attempts to surprise the enemy and permit him no time for countermeasures. Since mobility and the deception of the enemy at other positions are required, the flank attack is most successfully mounted from a distance; the troop movements necessary for the maneuver can be executed in close proximity to the enemy only with unusually favorable terrain or at night. Attacks are launched on both flanks only when the Germans consider their forces clearly superior.

b. ENVELOPMENT (Umfassungsangriff).

The envelopment is a combination flank-and-frontal attack especially favored by the Germans. The envelopment may be directed on either or both the enemy's flanks, and is accompanied by a simultaneous frontal attack to fix the enemy's forces. The deeper the envelopment goes into the enemy's flanks, the greater becomes the danger of being enveloped oneself. The Germans therefore emphasize the necessity of strong reserves and organization of the enveloping forces in depth. Success of the envelopment depends on the extent to which the enemy is able to dispose his forces in the threatened direction.

c. ENCIRCLEMENT (Einkreisung).

An encirclement, the Germans think, is a particularly decisive form of attack, but usually more difficult to execute than a flank attack or an envelopment. In an encirclement, the enemy is not attacked at all in front, or is attacked in front only by light forces, while the main attacking force passes entirely around him, with the objective of maneuvering him out of position. This requires extreme mobility and deception.

d. FRONTAL ATTACK (Frontalangriff).

The Germans consider the frontal attack the most difficult of execution. It strikes the enemy at his strongest point, and therefore requires superiority of men and materiel. A frontal attack should be

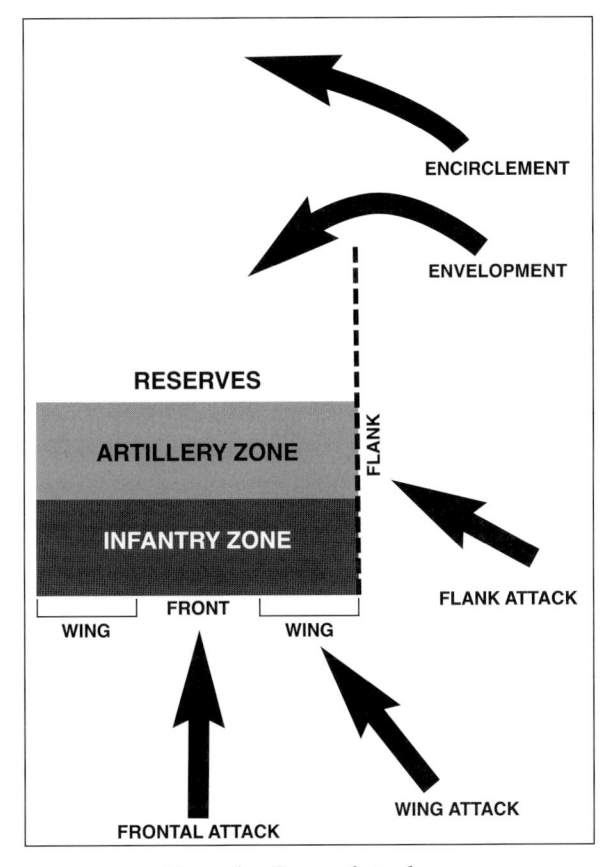

Figure 1.—Forms of attack.

made only at a point where the infantry can break through into favorable terrain in the depth of the enemy position. The frontage of the attack should be wider than the actual area (Schwerpunkt) chosen for penetration, in order to tie down the enemy on the flanks of the breakthrough. Adequate reserves must be held ready to counter the employment of the enemy's reserves.

e. WING ATTACK (Flügelangriff).

An attack directed at one or both of the enemy's wings has, the Germans teach, a better chance of success than a central frontal attack, since only a part of the enemy's weapons are faced, and only one flank of the attacking force or forces is exposed to enemy fire. Bending back one wing may give an opportunity for a flank attack, or for a single or double envelopment.

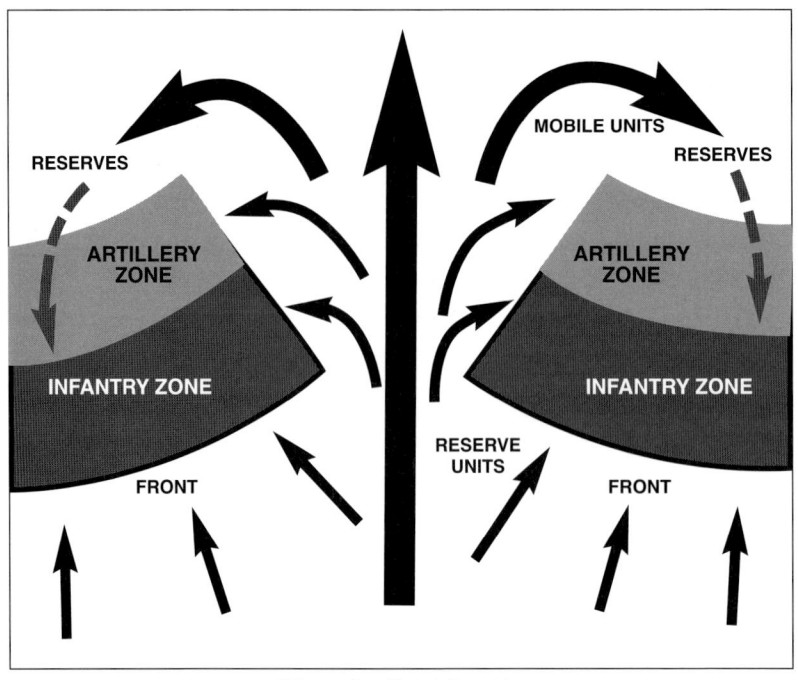

Figure 2.—Breakthrough.

f. PENETRATION (Einbruch) AND BREAKTHROUGH. (Durchbruch).

These are not separate forms of attack, but rather the exploitation of a successful attack on the enemy's front, wing, or flank. The penetration destroys the continuity of the hostile front. The broader the penetration, the deeper can the penetration wedge be driven. Strong reserves throw back enemy counterattacks against the flanks of the penetration. German units are trained to exploit a penetration to the maximum so that it may develop into a complete breakthrough before hostile countermeasures can be launched on an effective scale. The deeper the attacker penetrates, the more effectively can he envelop and frustrate the attempts of the enemy to close his front again by withdrawal to the rear. The attacking forces attempt to reduce individual enemy positions by encircling and isolating them. The Germans do not consider a breakthrough successful until they overcome the enemy's artillery positions, which usually is the special task of tanks. Reserve units roll up the enemy's front from the newly created flanks.

The Germans often refer to this maneuver as *"Keil and Kessel"*.

3. Organization of the Attack

a. ATTACK ORDER.

The attack order (Angriffsbefehl) generally contains the objective of the attack, the disposition of the infantry, unit sectors and boundaries, disposition and support missions of the artillery, location of reserves, and the time of attack. The order is not drawn up in accordance with any stereotyped form, but as a rule follows this pattern:

(1) Estimate of the situation (disposition of hostile and friendly troops).
(2) Mission.
(3) Assembly areas for the forward companies; objective; sector boundaries; orders for the continuation of combat reconnaissance.
(4) Instructions for the preparation of the heavy-weapons fire support, especially for massed fire.
(5) Orders to the artillery for fire preparation and coordination.
(6) Assembly areas for the reserves.
(7) Time of attack.
(8) Instructions for rear services (medical service and supplies).
(9) Location of command posts.
(10) Miscellaneous.

b. SECTORS OF ATTACK.

The width of a sector assigned to an infantry unit in the attack depends on the unit's mission and battle strength, on terrain conditions, on the available fire support of all arms, and on the probable strength of enemy resistance. Normally the sector assigned to a platoon is between 165 and 220 yards. A company attack sector is about 330 to 550 yards. A battalion sector is 440 to 1,100 yards, while a division sector may be 4,400 to 5,500 yards. These sectors also provide the boundaries for the other arms, especially for the artillery in support of the infantry, although the artillery may utilize favorable observation positions in neighboring sectors. This also applies to the heavy infantry weapons.

For large units the sectors are determined from the map; for smaller units, from the terrain. These sectors extend as deep into enemy territory as the plan of battle may require. As the situation develops, changes are frequently made. Important points always lie within units' sectors, unless they are to be attacked by several units. The Germans

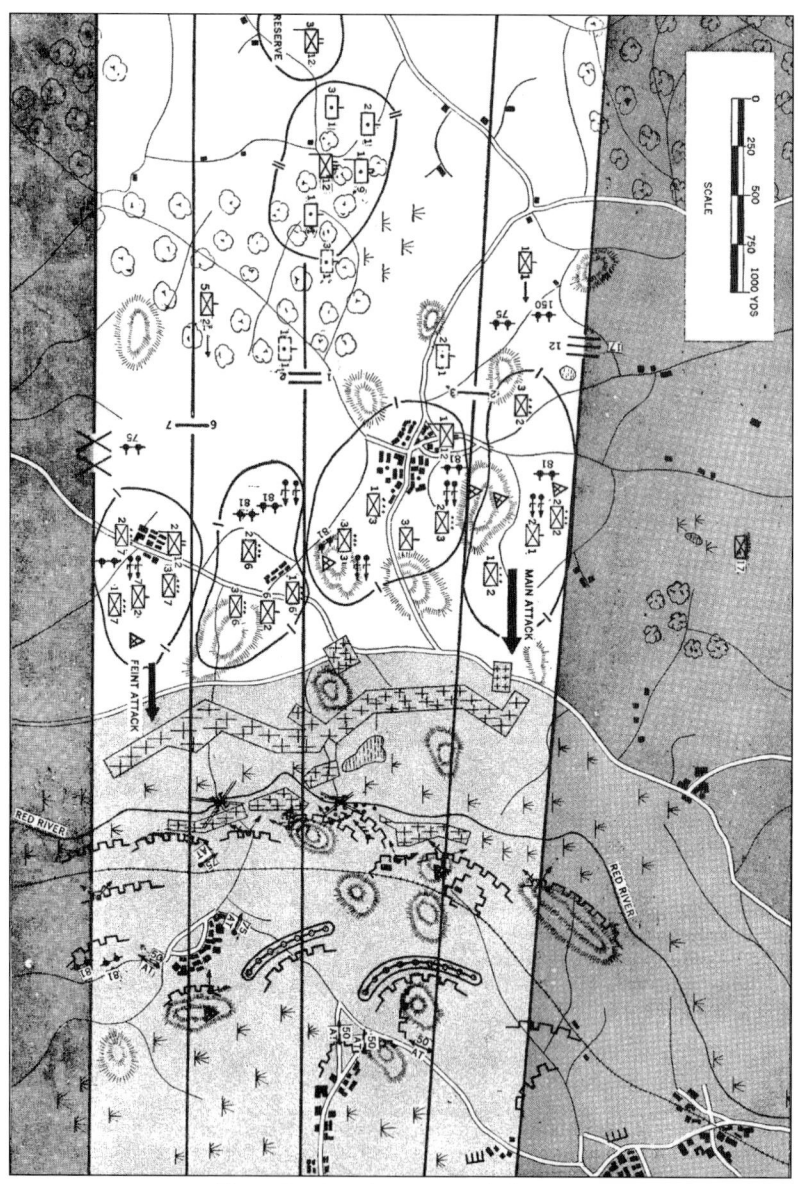

Figure 3.—Attack sectors and objective.

do not consider it necessary to occupy the whole width of the sector with troops. Open flanks ordinarily are not bounded.

c. FIRE PLAN.

Fire superiority is achieved through coordination of the infantry and artillery weapons. The basis for the fire plan (Feuerplan) is the regulation of the commitment of all weapons.

The fire plan includes the following:

(1) Assignment of combat missions.
(2) Distribution of observation sectors and fields of fire for the infantry and the artillery.
(3) An estimate of capabilities of the artillery for effective execution of the combat mission.
(4) Orders for the commencement of fire and fire schedules.
(5) Orders for the preparation for massed fire.
(6) Instructions for ammunition supply.

The Germans stress the coordination of flat and high trajectory weapons so that all dead spaces are covered by fire. Lack of signal equipment, however, often hinders the application of this principle.

4. Conduct of the Attack

a. GENERAL.

Most of the German successes in the present war have been achieved with armored formations. Years of secret training and equipping were devoted to the development of the Panzer division. The original German Blitzkrieg tactics were based on the belief in the irresistible power of tank formations operating independently with the support of dive-bombers. Considerable modifications have taken place in this theory over the past few years. At the present time, the offensive tactics of the Germans are less spectacularly bold than they were in 1939, but the fundamental theory behind them has changed remarkably little, though in their armored tactics they stress more tank-infantry coordination since unlimited air support is no longer at their command.

The main weight of all major German attacks since 1939 was borne by the *Panzer* division. Where infantry divisions have been employed, they were limited to local attacks on a comparatively minor scale or to mopping up in rear of the *Panzer* divisions. The Germans never envisaged a full-scale attack by infantry formations on fixed defenses. German tactics have been to outflank or encircle the main area of the enemy defenses with tank formations and to have the infantry roll up the defenses from the rear, or to break frontally through the enemy defenses with massed tanks and develop the famous *"Keil und Kessel"* maneuver.

The Germans learned at heavy cost the futility of charging a hostile antitank defense with tank concentrations and of engaging in tank-versus-tank combat without having superiority in range and armament. They have learned that large formations of tanks cannot achieve a breakthrough, opposed by an effective screen of antitank guns, without the assistance of other arms. Therefore attention has to be given to the combined tactics of tanks and *Panzer Grenadiers*, the mechanized or motorized infantry who accompany the tanks.

Great emphasis in German offensive theory is laid on the role of the artillery, but in practice the artillery-support role has devolved to an ever-increasing degree on the tanks and assault guns. Nevertheless, the principle that the supporting fire should be concentrated on a narrow frontage where the tanks and infantry are most likely to achieve a breakthrough has been retained.

The fact that a part of the enemy resistance is likely to remain undisclosed until the attack has already begun has caused the Germans permanently to decentralize a portion of the field artillery. This tendency has led to the emergence and continual development of the assault guns, whose main function is the close support of infantry and tanks in the attack. Their armor and mobility allow them to operate much farther forward than the field artillery.

The tendency to detach field artillery battalions from their field artillery regiment remains strong. In fact, this tendency is so prevalent that a concentration of massed artillery preceding an attack seldom is achieved, necessitating, as it does, a great degree of centralized control. The Germans, however, replace the massed artillery fire to a large extent with the fire of multi-barreled mortars and rocket projectors, though these latter have not the accuracy of the former.

The Germans make a clear distinction between an attack made from movement and an attack from a prepared position, which is the more common of the two.

b. ATTACK BY MECHANIZED AND MOTORIZED FORCES.
(1) The attack.

In armored-force operations, the Germans stress the need for the concentrated employment, at the decisive place and time, of the entire

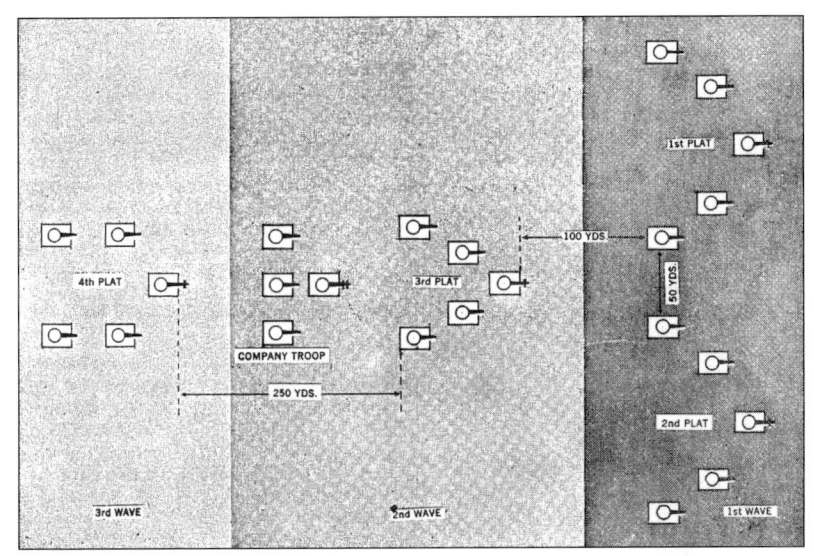

Figure 4.—German tank formation, battalion in "Blunt Wedge".

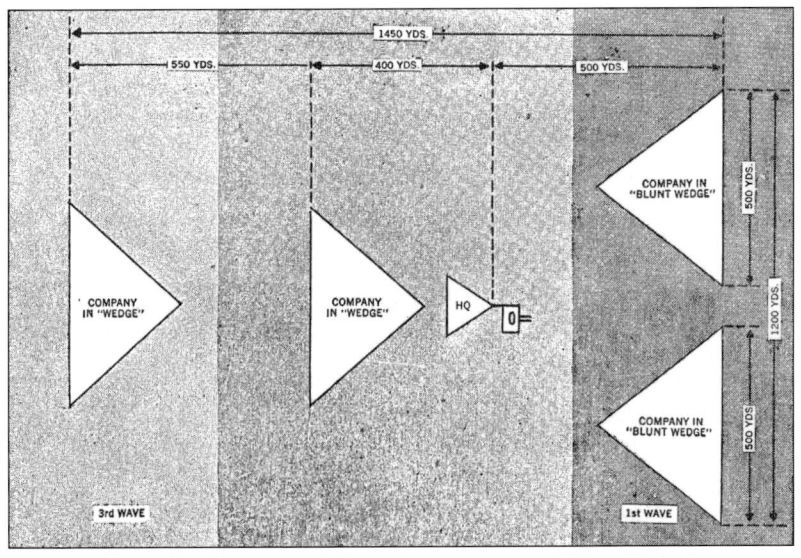

Figure 5.—German tank formation, company in "Blunt Wedge".

combined command of tanks and other arms, less necessary reserves. The tanks constitute the striking force of such a command and normally advance as the first echelon of the attack. Their primary mission is to break through and attack the enemy artillery, rather than to seek out and destroy enemy tanks, which can be more effectively engaged by antitank units. The mission of the other arms is to assist the tanks in their advance, and particularly to eliminate antitank weapons. The smallest combat unit in such a force of combined arms is the company.

The basic formation for the tank platoon, company, and battalion are file, double file, wedge, and blunt wedge. The type of formation used for a specific task depends to a large extent on terrain conditions and the strength of enemy opposition. A German tank platoon normally consists of one command tank and two tank squads of two tanks each.

The tank regiment normally attacks in waves, in either of the following manners:

The tank regiment is echeloned in depth, one tank battalion following the other. The regimental commander's location is between the two battalions. This formation has the advantages of a sufficiently wide front (about 1,100 yards), and close contact by the commander of his units in the conduct of the attack. The normal depth of such a formation is about 3,000 yards. This is the usual form of the tank attack. When two tank battalions are attacking, one behind the other, it takes them about half an hour to pass their own infantry.

When the two-battalions-abreast formation is employed, it is almost essential that another tank regiment form the following wave. This formation usually has the disadvantage of being too wide. The regimental commander cannot observe his units, and he has no units of his own behind him which he can commit in a decisive moment. The attack normally proceeds in three waves.

The first wave thrusts to the enemy's antitank defense and artillery positions.

The second wave provides covering fire for the first wave, and then attacks the enemy's infantry positions, preceded, accompanied, or followed by part of the *Panzer Grenadiers*, who dismount as close as possible to the point where they must engage the enemy. The objectives of the second wave are the remaining antitank positions, positions of heavy infantry-support weapons, and machine-gun emplacements which hold up the advance of the infantry.

The third wave, accompanied by the remainder of the *Panzer Grenadiers*, mops up.

These three waves now often are telescoped into two, the first wave speeding through the enemy's position as far as his gun positions, the second crushing the enemy's forward positions in detail and mopping up the opposition not dealt with by the first wave or which has revived since the first wave passed through.

A typical attack formation of this type might be divided up among the *Panzer* division's units as follows: the first wave, on a frontage of about 2,000 to 3,000 yards, might consist of one tank battalion, two companies forward, supported on the flanks by elements of the assault gun battalion. Close to the rear of the first wave usually follow one or two *Panzer Grenadier* companies in armored half-tracks. About 150 yards to the rear of the first wave moves the second wave, formed of the second tank battalion in the same formation, closely followed by the remainder of the armored *Panzer Grenadiers*, who are in turn followed at some distance by the motorized *Panzer Grenadiers*. The flanks are protected by antitank guns which normally operate by platoons, moving by bounds. The artillery forward observer travels in his armored vehicles with the first wave, while the artillery commander of the supporting artillery units usually travels with the tank commander. Assault guns normally also accompany the second wave.

The tanks help each other forward by fire and movement, medium or heavy tanks taking up hull-down firing positions and giving covering fire while the faster tanks advance to the next commanding feature. Then the latter give covering fire to the former moving forward to their next bound.

Once the first wave has reached the rear of the enemy's forward defenses, it pushes straight on to attack the enemy's artillery. As soon as these positions have been neutralized, the tanks reform beyond the artillery positions and either prepare to exploit the attack or form an all-round defensive position on suitable ground.

The tank unit commander, as the leader of the strongest unit, is in most cases in command of the combat team, and all the other participating arms (*Panzer Grenadiers*, artillery, engineers, and antitank units) are placed under him. The Germans realize that a strong and unified command is an essential feature of any military operation.

For certain missions, however, tank units are attached to another arm, in which case the tank commander is consulted before the final plans for the operations are made.

(2) Infantry-tank cooperation.

When the enemy has well prepared positions with natural or constructed tank obstacles, the German infantry attacks before the tanks and clears the way. The objective of the infantry is to penetrate into the enemy position and destroy enemy antitank weapons to the limit of its strength and the fire power of its own support weapons, augmented by additional support and covering fire from the tanks and self-propelled weapons sited in their rear.

Only after the destruction of the enemy antitank defense can the tanks be employed on the battle line to the fullest advantage.

When the tank obstacles in front of the enemy position already are destroyed, and no additional tank obstacles are expected in the depth of the enemy's main defensive position, the infantry breaks through simultaneously with the tank unit. The infantry attack is conducted in the same manner as it would be without the cooperation of tanks. Heavy infantry weapons are kept in readiness to fire at possible newly discovered antitank positions. Of particular importance is protection of the open flanks by echeloning the flank units and employing heavy weapons at the flanks.

In most cases, the infantry follows the tanks closely, taking advantage of the fire power and paralyzing effect of the tanks upon the enemy's defense. The Germans normally transport the infantry to the line of departure on tanks or troop-carrying vehicles in order to protect the infantry and to increase its speed. The infantry leaves the vehicles at the last possible moment, and goes into action mainly with light automatic weapons.

The tanks advance by bounds from cover to cover, reconnoitering the terrain ahead and providing protective fire for the dismounted *Panzer Grenadiers*. The tanks do not slow their advance to enable the infantry to keep continuous pace with them, but advance alone and wait under cover until the infantry catches up with the advance. Terrain that does not offer sufficient cover is crossed with the greatest possible speed.

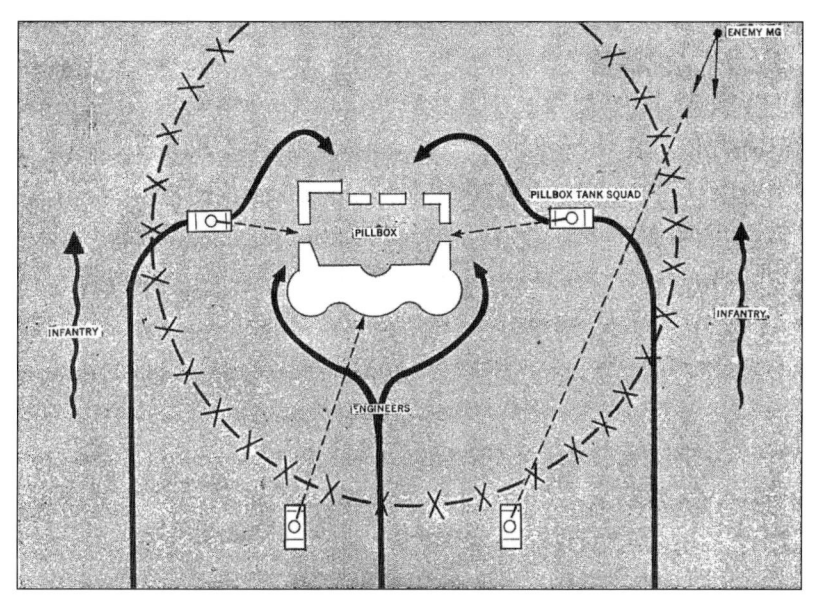

Figure 6.—Attack against an enemy pillbox.

The infantry attacks in small formations also by bounds under the fire cover of its own heavy weapons and of the tanks, staying away from individual tanks because they draw the strongest enemy fire.

When a tank company attacks with infantry, there are normally two platoons on the line, one platoon back, and the fourth platoon in reserve. The interval between tanks is usually 100 to 120 yards. The tank's machine guns usually engage infantry targets at about 1,000 yards range and under, while the tank guns engage targets at 2,000 to 2,500 yards.

The coordination between tanks and *Panzer Grenadiers* moving into combat on armored half-tracks is similar to the technique employed in a purely armored formation, since the armored half-tracks are not only troop-carrying vehicles but also combat vehicles. When the terrain is favorable for tank warfare, the *Panzer Grenadiers* in their armored half-tracks follow immediately with the second wave, after the first tank wave has overrun the opponent's position. A deep and narrow formation is employed. After the penetration, the main mission of the *Panzer Grenadiers* is to overcome the enemy positions which survived the first wave.

In attacking enemy pillboxes the Germans use combat groups

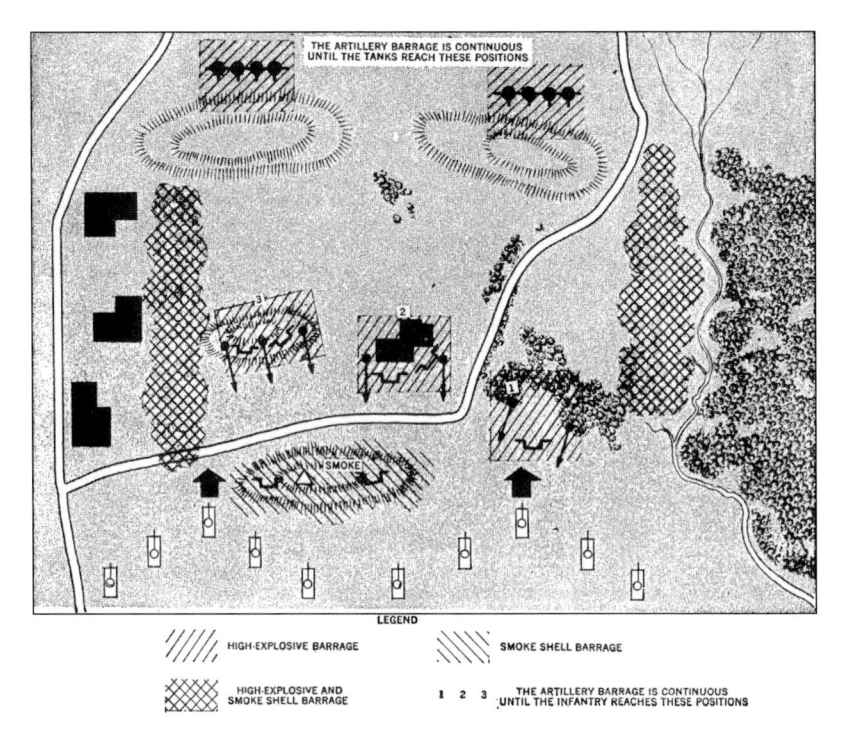

Figure 7.—Artillery support during a tank attack.

consisting of tanks, infantry, and engineers, assisted by artillery. The normal composition of a combat group attacking one bunker is one platoon of tanks and one platoon of infantry reinforced by one squad of engineers. Before the combat group is committed against the enemy pillbox, artillery fires high explosives and smoke shells at the neighboring pillboxes to isolate them, shells the terrain between pillboxes, and conducts counterbattery fire. Under the protection of this fire, the combat group advances close to the pillbox while other infantry units attack the enemy in the terrain between the pillboxes.

One tank squad covers the advances of the other tank squads and the infantry platoon by direct fire against the pillbox, particularly against the observation and weapons' openings. The first tank squad halts under cover whenever possible and covers the advance of the second tank squad.

When the combat group reaches a barbed wire obstacle surrounding the pillbox, the two tank squads have different missions. One tank squad remains in front of the pillbox, and its tanks are driven into a position from which they can overlook the terrain, and watch out for antitank guns and machine gun emplacements, while the other tank squad (the pillbox tank squad) rolls across the obstacle to enable the infantry and engineers to get close to the pillbox. The pillbox tank squad then fires on the pillbox at close range. The infantry squad meanwhile takes the surrounding terrain and covers the engineers who blast the entrance of the pillbox with TNT.

(3) Artillery-tank coordination.

Artillery support is of decisive importance for the preparation and the successful conduct of a tank attack. A unified command for the entire artillery controls the artillery fire as long as the infantry and tank units are fighting on the same line. When the tanks break through the enemy forward defense lines, the self-propelled artillery or any other artillery battalion designated for the support of the tank unit is placed under the command of the tank unit commander.

The Germans believe that the artillery fire must not check the momentum of the attack. Consequently the heaviest fire must fall well ahead of the tanks or outside their sector.

The mission of the artillery preparation before the attack is to destroy, or at least to neutralize, the opponent's antitank defense in the area between the line of contact and the regimental reserve line. Continuous counterbattery fire prevents the enemy from shelling the tank assembly area and from breaking up the preparation of the tank attack.

The artillery has the following missions before the tank attack:
- Counterbattery fire on enemy artillery located in positions which command the ground over which the tank attack is to be made.
- Concentrations on enemy tanks in assembly areas.
- Harassing fire on all areas in which the antitank units are located or suspected. Fire is heaviest on areas in which tanks cannot operate but from which they can be engaged effectively.
- Adjusting fire with high explosives on probable enemy observation posts commanding the sector to be attacked. These observation posts are blinded with smoke as soon as the attack begins.

Experience has taught the Germans that the flanks of a tank attack are

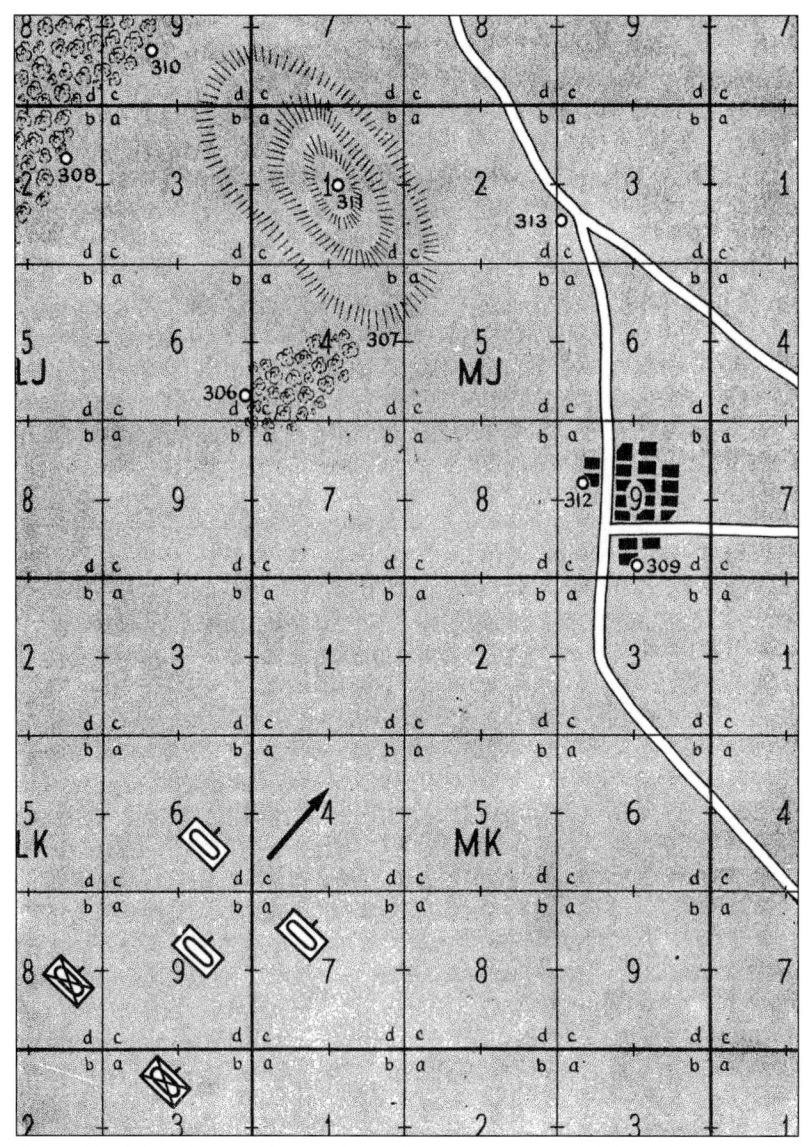

Figure 8.—Map with superimposed coordinate system and artillery reference points used by tank commanders.

vulnerable. Therefore they assign to the artillery and the rocket projector units the task of protecting flanks by barrages using high explosives and smoke shells.

The artillery has the following missions during the tank attack:
- Counterbattery fire.
- Blinding enemy observation posts.

- As the attack progresses, engaging successive lines of antitank defense, especially areas to the rear and flanks of the sector attacked.
- Screening the flanks of the attack with smoke and neutralizing the enemy's infantry and rear areas.
- Delaying the movement and deployment of enemy reserves, particularly tanks.

The Germans stress that this wide variety of tasks must not lead to the wholesale dispersal of effort. The main task of the artillery is at all times the destruction of the enemy's antitank weapons, tanks, and artillery.

Liaison between artillery and tanks during the attack is established by the commanding officers and the artillery liaison group, which normally moves with the first wave. Artillery forward observers, if possible in armored observation posts, ride with the most forward elements. A German field expedient is for the tank unit to take along a forward observer in one of its tanks. It often happens that the tankman himself has to take over the observation for the artillery. He himself can request artillery fire and shift concentrations when the situation requires such changes. Figure 10 represents a map with superimposed coordinate system and artillery reference points used by tank commanders to help them in this task.

c. THE INFANTRY DIVISION IN THE ATTACK.

(1) General principles for employment.

German teaching envisages infantry divisions being employed to make a penetration in the enemy defensive positions through which armored and mechanized formations can pass. During the course of this war, however, no major attack has been carried out by infantry divisions without the support of *Panzer* divisions. In fact, more major attacks have been carried out by *Panzer* divisions, with only a minimum of ordinary infantry elements. Infantry divisions have been employed almost entirely in a role of consolidation, following up the armored and mechanized formations, systematically eliminating centers of resistance bypassed by the latter, or exploiting the latter's success by mopping up demoralized enemy defenses to the flanks of the armored breakthrough—in short, consolidating and holding the ground won by the mechanized formations.

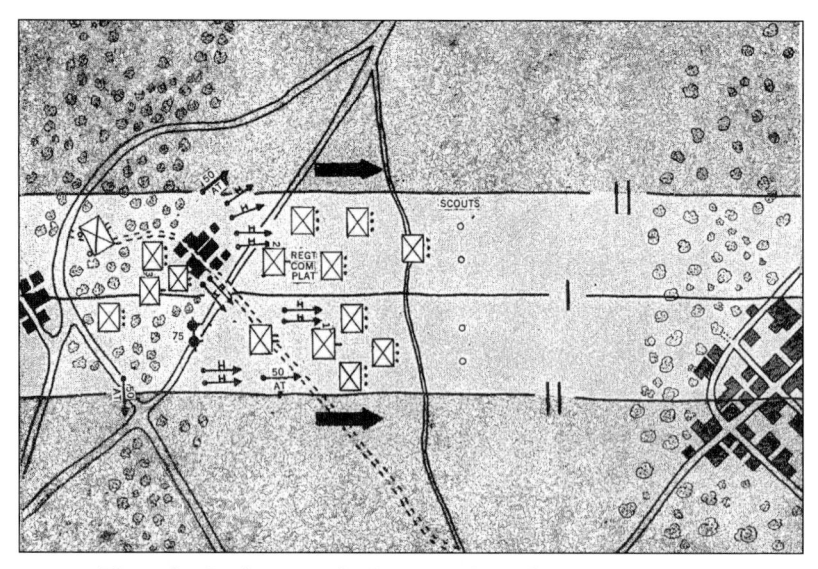

Figure 9.—Deployment of a German infantry battalion (1st stage).

In view of the unspectacular role allotted to the infantry division it is difficult to give information about other than minor infantry tactics, such as attacks on a small scale.

(2) Preparation for the attack.

The method of forming up for an infantry assault on a prepared position is similar to that employed by the *Panzer* division. While the infantry is in assembly positions, the artillery makes all preparations for the support of the attack. It draws out hostile artillery fire and executes counterbattery fire against known enemy batteries. Large troop concentrations and especially-important targets are taken under fire at great ranges. In order not to betray their full strength and intentions, the Germans withhold a portion of their batteries from these missions. They also try to deceive the enemy as to their intentions by covering other sectors simultaneously with fire. When possible, preparation for an attack is avoided during the day in order to prevent Allied observation. Occasionally, to obtain a success by surprise, the Germans launch attacks without artillery preparation. Surprise attacks also are launched under cover of darkness or fog.

The Germans normally occupy their line of departure by means of infiltration in order to avoid losses. Their orders direct what actions have to be taken when companies run into enemy defenses; when enemy fire is opened from the flank; when an enemy counterattack is launched; when objectives are reached; when companies appear to be getting dispersed; when part of a company pushes too far ahead of neighboring units or is held up.

The heavy machine guns of the rearward company and some of the mortars and heavy mortars are assigned to deal with enemy flanking fire.

The commander of the heavy company is normally at the battalion headquarters, from which he can control the fire of the infantry heavy support weapons.

(3) Deployment.

(a) *First stage*.

The Germans carry out deployment in two stages. They call the first stage *Entfaltung* or "shaking out", which is equivalent to the development of a march column according to U.S. procedure. In the first stage (*Figure 9*), an infantry regiment normally deploys down to battalions, although the procedure may go down to companies if a high state of preparedness is necessary. Features of the first stage of deployment are as follows:

Companies retain their combat vehicles until their weapons and equipment arrive at the off-carrier position, which is located as far forward as the situation permits.

The Germans often place only one company forward, the main strength of the battalion being kept under control of the battalion commander as long as possible so that he may employ it in the most advantageous direction for attack.

If the condition of the terrain and enemy fire cause a change of intervals between units, the normal intervals are resumed as soon as possible.

Support weapons are used to cover the "shaking out" phase of deployment and the subsequent advance, the weapons being kept within the march column between the companies or behind the battalion.

After the first stage of deployment has been carried out, the leading elements of the battalion may be ordered to seize important tactical features.

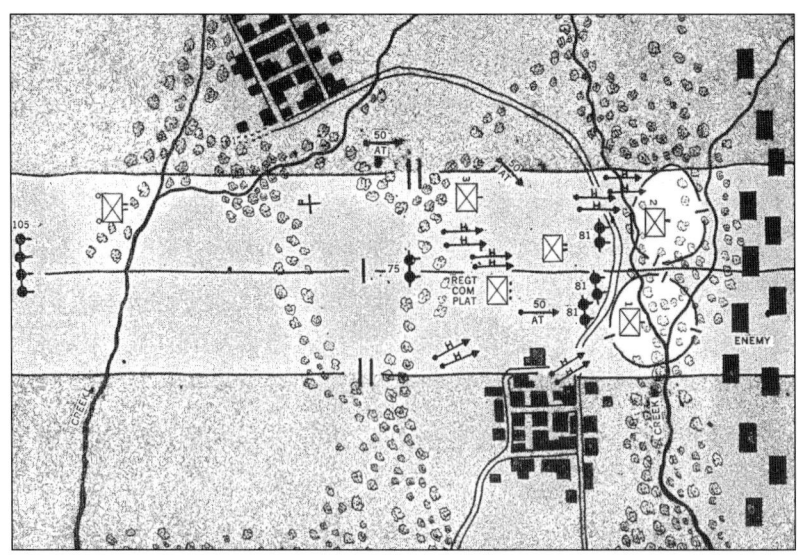

Figure 10.—Deployment of a German infantry battalion (2nd stage).

When deploying by night or in woods, a careful reconnaissance is made, routes are marked, and strong protection is placed forward. Intervals between units are shorter.

After the first stage of deployment has been completed, the battalion commander marches with the leading elements and normally will send reconnaissance patrols ahead or reconnoiter the enemy position himself. The commanders of support weapons accompany him, reconnoitering for firing positions.

(b) *Second stage.*

The second stage (*Figure 10*), called *Entwicklung* (development), is deployment in detail, which is the final action of the company extending itself down to platoons and squads. Features of the second stage of deployment are as follows:

The companies deploy in depth as soon as they come within range of artillery fire. An advance in columns of files is considered desirable because it affords a small target and the company is easier to control, but before adopting this formation the danger of enfilade fire is weighed.

If enemy fire and difficult terrain necessitate further deployment, the companies disperse in depth by sections. Reserves and support weapons also adopt open formations, but they remain far enough behind to avoid coming under the fire directed at the leading elements.

When the rifle companies are deployed, they exploit all possible cover as they advance, employing column-of-file formations with irregular distances. The leading elements are not extended until they are to engage in a fire fight. The elements that follow continue advancing in file.

In determining when to deploy, the Germans take into consideration additional physical strain placed on men when they march cross-country.

(4) Technique of attack.
The infantry attack on prepared positions is made in the same sequence as that of the *Panzer* division, namely penetration, breakthrough, exploitation by the reserves. In the infantry attack, however, the first phase is a series of local attacks by so-called assault detachments (*Stosstrupps*) with the aim of overcoming key points in the enemy defenses, so that wedges into the enemy's forward positions can be established from which the attack can be driven forward into the depth of the enemy position, or rolling up the positions on either flank of the wedge.

Assault detachments normally are composed of infantry with engineers attached. A typical assault detachment consists of the following: one officer; obstacle clearing party, consisting of two to six men for each lane to be cleared, equipped with small arms, wire-cutters, and bangalore torpedoes and other explosives; embrasure-blasting party consisting of three or four men equipped with grenades and demolition or pole charges. This party may also include, though it may work independently, a flame-thrower party, consisting normally of two men; covering parties, normally two or three parties of varying size from three men with one light machine gun to full platoons; smoke party consisting of two or three men equipped with smoke candles or grenades; supply party, carrying reserves of equipment and ammunition, their strength depending on the size of the assault detachment.

Attacks most often are made at dawn, and are preceded normally by heavy artillery preparation, one purpose of which is to make shell holes which afford cover for the advancing assault detachments as they move forward. When the latter reach the wire obstacles surrounding the enemy position, Very signals are fired, calling for available artillery fire to be brought on the position to seal it off, from flanking positions. If, by reason of proximity of the assault detachment to the artillery's danger zone, the former cannot be protected by covering fire, the smoke party may lay a smoke screen. The obstacle-clearing party then cuts one or more lanes through the wire, using wire cutters or bangalore torpedoes. The embrasure-blasting party passes through and attacks the embrasures. Flame throwers, if employed, are not intended by themselves to cause the surrender of the position, but to cover the advance of the embrasure-blasting party with its explosive charges which are considered the decisive weapon.

Antitank guns may be used to give close support to the embrasure-blasting party, being man-handled from cover to cover. They will attack the embrasure with armor-piercing ammunition and also give protection against possible tank-supported counterattacks.

It is probable that several such operations will be in progress on any one sector at any one time before an attack, in the first place to probe for weak spots, and in the second place to keep the enemy in uncertainty as to the final point of main effort of the attack. German feint attacks have often been delivered in such strength or with such violence as to be indistinguishable from the main attack.

Once a wedge has been firmly established in the enemy positions, the second phase of the attack begins. Troops so far held in their assembly area, or slowly making headway under cover of the artillery fire supporting the first phase of the attack, advance to cut the enemy position in two and to roll up the positions flanking the wedge.

Because the Germans anticipate enemy defenses organized in depth, and because these are unlikely to be fully disclosed until after the beginning of the attack, they do not make detailed plans for close-support covering fire, which would be hard to work out in advance, but tend to decentralize their support weapons and artillery for the second phase of the assault, in which reinforced battalions, companies, or platoons fight their own way forward, independently of their flanking units, until they have gained their final objective.

Attack on lightly defended positions is more similar to the conduct of the attack by the *Panzer* division. The first phase is likely to be a deployed attack on a two-regiment front, the third regiment in reserve.

The Germans believe that in the advance extended formation of units is advantageous because it forces the enemy to scatter his fire.

To counteract the overwhelming Allied superiority in artillery and planes which frequently knock out the attack before it is under way, the Germans have been known to use the following method. Small groups of less than platoon size infiltrate mainly at night over a period of three to four days into the hostile battle position or at least well behind the advanced positions. During the day the infiltrated groups conceal themselves, but if caught pass themselves off as ordinary patrols to avoid raising suspicion. When the actual attack is launched these units try to give the impression that the defender is surrounded and often cause great confusion.

When the Germans go over from the attack to the defense, even if only temporarily, they concentrate the supporting weapons around the commander of the unit that is to be supported, so that he can control the fire plan.

(5) Infantry-assault gun coordination.
The assault guns are organized in assault gun battalions and are under the control of the division commander. The Germans regard their self-propelled assault guns as decisive weapons to be employed particularly at the point of main effort. In cooperation with infantry they facilitate the penetration and breakthrough. These weapons, the Germans believe, complement artillery fire by their ability to follow the infantry right up to an objective. Their use for small actions before an attack is forbidden so as not to betray their presence. Surprise is sought by bringing them into position by night and camouflaging their assembly area. Used primarily to neutralize enemy support weapons at short ranges over open sights, assault guns are preferably employed in concentrations; to employ them singly or in comparatively small number is frowned upon by the Germans.

German assault guns advance with or just behind the infantry; they never go ahead of the infantry. When an objective is reached, the assault guns do not remain with the infantry while the position is being consolidated but retire about 1,000 yards to await further assignment.

In close combat the assault guns are rather helpless and therefore it is the task of the infantry to keep the enemy away from the assault guns. Newly-organized assault-gun escort batteries have the same task.

(6) Artillery.

The Germans employ their field artillery in general support (*Allgemeine Unterstützung*) or in direct support (*Unmittelbare Unterstützung*), in the same manner as the U.S. Army. The Germans consider the battalion as the firing unit. Splitting up an artillery battalion into batteries and placing batteries under an infantry battalion is the exception justified only when the infantry battalion has an independent mission (for example, flank protection) or when the terrain does not permit unified fire control by artillery battalion commanders. Single commitment of guns is against German tactical doctrine. Various recent reports, however, describe deviations from the prescribed practice. Normally the Germans do not employ single field artillery pieces for direct fire, as, for instance, the Russians do. But much use is made of roving guns (*Arbeitsgeschütz*), and of guns firing from alternate positions to make identification more difficult. Standing German orders call for the preparation of alternate firing positions, which, however, are used now only in cases of very heavy counterbattery fire, as the gasoline shortage keeps all movements to a minimum. The Germans often designate the number two piece as the roving gun, and, unlike the other pieces, it normally is not dug in. It frequently changes its position, which is about 250 to 300 yards from the rest of the battery.

The German artillery often engages a target from a lateral position. This deception, particularly identified with longer range weapons, is extended by employing another gun, often of lighter caliber, in a carefully coordinated attack on the same target. Flash simulators also increase the difficulty of visual location of active guns.

The first step to obtain infantry-artillery coordination is taken in the attack order and is assured by direct contact between the commanders, artillery liaison units (*Artillerieverbindungskommando*), and direct contact between artillery observers and infantry units.

The Germans also employ forward observers (*Vorgeschobene Beobachter*), who have the same task as their U.S. counterpart.

The signal equipment necessary for communication between units, liaison units, and observers is only partly organic. The Germans keep most of the signal equipment centralized in the division signal battalion, which allots equipment as needed to the various units.

In the attack the greater part of the artillery supports the main effort. The remainder of the artillery is assigned the mission of flank protection against possible enemy counterattacks.

5. Meeting Engagement (Begegnungsgefecht)

In the meeting engagement the Germans believe that the advantage lies with the side which succeeds first in making effective preparation for the attack and thereby deprives the enemy of his freedom of action. When both adversaries attack immediately from march columns, the decisive factors are the initiative of the junior officers and the efficiency of the troops. The senior commander quickly coordinates the functions of the various officers, while the advance guard secures for him freedom of action and the opportunity for a speedy deployment of his troops.

6. Pursuit

U.S. and German tactical doctrines on pursuit are very much alike. Pursuit begins when the enemy is no longer able to maintain his position and abandons the combat area with the bulk of his forces. The object of the pursuit is the complete annihilation of the retreating or routed enemy. Effective pursuit requires great initiative from commanders of all echelons of command, who must not hesitate to start pursuit immediately, even when their troops are exhausted. The enemy must be given no time to pause to reorganize his forces and reconstitute his defense.

The pursuit is conducted on a broad front by means of fire and movement. When making for distant objectives every effort is made to get around the enemy's flanks and effect a surprise attack in his rear. However, care must be taken that enemy attack on one's own flank does not cause deflection from the original direction.

Fast-moving troops are used in the pursuit. These troops often are organized into pursuit or advance sections. The infantry scatters the enemy and by-passes resisting enemy strongpoints, leaving their destruction to units following in the rear. Part of the artillery places concentrations at the avenues of retreat, while the remainder displaces forward in echelon, providing continuous support for the units in front. The Germans emphasize that a pursuit without the necessary artillery support may lead to disaster. Assault guns travel well forward with the rapidly advancing infantry, their comparatively heavy armament enabling them to crush quickly and decisively any enemy forces attempting to make a stand. Combat aviation bombs routes of retreat and strafes the hostile forces in direct support of the ground attack. Combat engineers repair damaged roads, facilitating the continuous flow of supply and troops.

Pursuit, after a successful breakthrough, is regarded by the Germans as an ideal mission for the *Panzer* division. *Panzer Grenadiers* in armored half-tracks or in unarmored vehicles and tanks supplement each other in pursuing the enemy. During the advance on roads, the tanks form the point. However, through wooded areas or larger villages the *Panzer Grenadiers* take over the point. Tanks and *Panzer Grenadiers* stay close together so that either, according to the situation, can be committed as soon as enemy resistance is encountered. Tanks are normally not used in units of less than company strength.

V. DEFENSIVE

1. General

In German doctrine the object of the defense (*Verteidigung*, or *Abwehr*) is to halt the hostile attack, or to gain time pending development of a more favorable situation for resumption of the offensive. Thus German and U.S. doctrine are essentially the same: only the offensive leads to decisive successes.

In the last two years German defensive operations have become increasingly passive in nature. The Germans formerly placed the greatest stress on immediate and violent counterattacks as effective means of destroying the attacking enemy. This required great mobility and large reserves. At present more emphasis is placed on the construction of defensive positions, and counterattacks are frequently local in character. It is most likely that this passive type of defense is only an expedient due to German shortages of mobile equipment and manpower.

2. Organization for Defense

a. GENERAL.

The Germans attempt to break a hostile attack in front of the main line of resistance (Hauptkampflinie), at the forward limit of the battle position (Hauptkampffeld), or to force the enemy to abandon his attack.

As in U.S. practice, the commander usually determines from the map the main battlefield and assigns a general line as guide for the location of the main line of resistance, to ensure continuity of the defensive position. Lower echelon commanders fix the main line of resistance on the ground, since only on the terrain, after thorough reconnaissance, can the details of the defense be decided. A recent official German directive states, however, that reconnaissance must not delay the construction of defensive positions.

Organization of the defensive position follows a conventional pattern and includes an advanced position (*Vorgeschobene Stellung*), and an outpost position (*Gefechtsvorposten*), both of which usually are under immediate command of the area commander. A reserve position may also be provided.

The width and depth of a German defense area depend upon the terrain and the proportional strength of friendly and hostile forces. In general, however, the width of a defensive sector assigned to a unit is Approximately twice the width of the sector when the same unit attacks. Normal sectors are: platoon, 220 to 550 yards; company, 440 to 1,100 yards; battalion, 880 to 2,200 yards; regiment, 2,200 to 3,300 yards; division, 6,600 to 11,000 yards.

b. ADVANCED POSITION.

The Germans organize the advanced position 5,000 to 7,000 yards in front of the main line of resistance, within the range of their medium artillery. A position is selected which will prevent seizure by the enemy of important terrain features, provide good observation points for friendly artillery, and, if possible, deceive the enemy as to the location of the main line of resistance. Troops manning these positions attempt to make the enemy deploy his forces prematurely and, if possible, in the wrong direction.

The forces in the advanced position are usually reconnaissance detachments, which include machine-gun, armored-car, and antitank-gun units, the fire power and mobility of which make them suitable for this type of employment. In general they occupy important features, such as railroads, river crossings, cross-roads, and commanding ground. Forces in advanced positions are not expected to hold at all cost; in the face of superior enemy fire they retire along predetermined routes under over of their medium artillery.

c. OUTPOST POSITIONS.

Outpost positions normally are established 2,000 to 5,000 yards in front of the main line of resistance. When the fronts are stabilized, the outpost position is the only position forward of the main line of resistance. The location, which depends upon the terrain, is always within range of friendly light artillery.

German outpost positions are occupied in strength varying from platoons to companies, depending upon the mission, terrain, width of the sector, and the number of troops available. Often they are only weakly occupied as long as the advanced positions are in front of them. Ordinarily outposts are established by infantry units drawn from the main battle position, supported by the fire of close-support weapons, such as mortars and infantry guns.

Antitank guns often are attached to these outpost units to repel hostile armored reconnaissance units. The main weapon, however, is the light machine gun which opens fire at ranges of about 1,300 yards, while riflemen commence fire at about 850 yards.

Firing positions are selected by the Germans to facilitate unobserved withdrawal of the outposts to the main battle position when hostile pressure becomes too strong. Several alternate positions are prepared for each weapon, and shifts are made by day and night to make it difficult for the opponent to detect and dislodge the outpost troops. Positions normally are selected at the edges of woods, villages, hedgerows, or hills. A good field of fire is considered mandatory, and the organization of firing positions is simple. Numerous dummy positions are constructed, including knee-deep trenches filled with leaves to simulate depth and occupancy. During the day, positions are manned by guards; at night, advanced listening posts, particularly alert at dusk and dawn, warn the troops of the enemy's approach. Small, prepared attacks with limited objectives under the protection of the outposts are utilized to interfere with the hostile preparations and secure information.

Withdrawal of the outposts is conducted so as not to hinder the fire of the main battle position. After the outposts are abandoned, they are likely to be covered by carefully registered fire of heavy weapons in order to prevent their occupation by the enemy.

d. MAIN LINE OF RESISTANCE.
The Germans organize their battle position in depth, with individual strongpoints connected to form an uninterrupted belt. The strongpoints, constructed for all-around defense, and surrounded by barbed-wire obstacles and mine belts, contain one or more heavy weapons supplemented by machine guns, mortars, and riflemen. The smallest strong-point is occupied by a reinforced squad. Squad strongpoints normally are incorporated into platoon strongpoints, and the latter into company strongpoints, etc.

The Germans make the maximum use of reverse slopes in their defensive positions. Forward-slope positions are usually avoided as they are detected too early by the enemy and are likely to be destroyed by massed fire. Since organization of a position in woods requires much time and labor, and strong occupation is requisite to compensate for poor observation, the Germans also avoid woods when time is short and labor scarce. Battle positions are laid out so that woods are neither in, nor directly in front or in rear of, defense installations. The Germans believe, however, that when it is possible to establish a well prepared position in a woods, a position so located offers the same advantages as a reverse slope.

When the Germans decide to construct defensive positions on terrain divided by a stream, they organize bridgeheads on the bank on the hostile side where the terrain facilitates crossings. Where the river forms a re-entrant bend into enemy-held terrain, a second position is constructed at the base of the bend. On narrow rivers and creeks, the entire German main line of resistance is on the hostile side of the river,

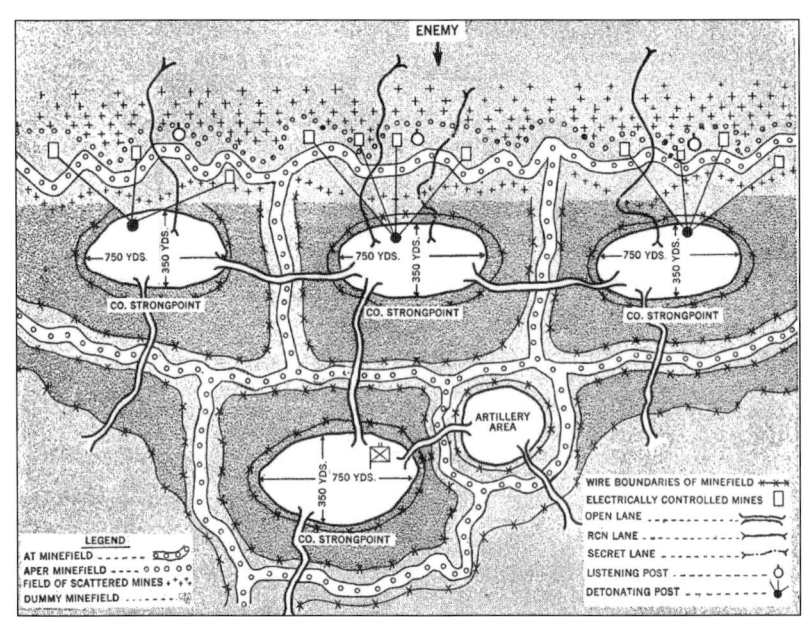

Figure 11.—Typical layout of a reinforced battalion strongpoint.

and the stream becomes the tank obstacle of the position. (See antimechanized defense.) When the friendly side of the river consists of swampland, it is used as an obstacle, and the hostile bank is not included in the defense system.

The Germans endeavor to provide all parts of their position with strong support from artillery and heavy infantry weapons. A detailed fire plan is prepared in advance by the infantry and coordinated with the artillery plan. Provision is made for fire in front of the forward limit of the battle position, which is partly protected by minefields and other obstacles. Alternate positions are dug so that support weapons may be shifted and fired rapidly. The mass of the artillery lays concentrated fire both close to and well in front of the main line of resistance, and is sited to cover the spaces between the effective fire zones of front-line units.

The Germans in general adhere to the principle of "effect before cover" in determining priorities for constructing the various installations in a defense position. first they build combat trenches; erect infantry obstacles such as barbed-wire fences; and construct machine-gun positions, dugouts, foxholes, and antitank positions. They clear fields of fire by careful cutting of underbrush but try to avoid cutting down trees in order to preserve concealment of the position. The underbrush is left in front of the position as far as 1 to 3 yards. They organize observation posts for artillery and heavy infantry weapons, increase the depth of the battle position, dig communication trenches and emplacements for the heavy infantry weapons, and build command posts. Finally, they construct emplacements for the artillery, dig antitank ditches within the battle position, and build dummy positions.

The Germans insist on thorough camouflage. Whenever practicable, trenches and wire obstacles are placed along natural terrain lines such as rows of brush or edges of fields. Trenches are dug zig-zag at obtuse angles, 330 to 660 yards long, depending on the terrain. Machine-guns are emplaced in trenches 1 to 3 yards in length. To avoid silhouettes, the Germans heap more earth behind the trenches than in front. Dugouts for riflemen and for machine-gun positions normally provide sufficient protection against enemy artillery and mortar fire. Whenever possible, three layers of logs and earth are used as cover.

e. RESERVE POSITION.

Occasionally a reserve position is organized and troops in the main battle position retire to it, but only under heavy pressure. This reserve position is constructed far enough to the rear to compel hostile artillery to displace forward in order to bring it under fire. Motorized reserve

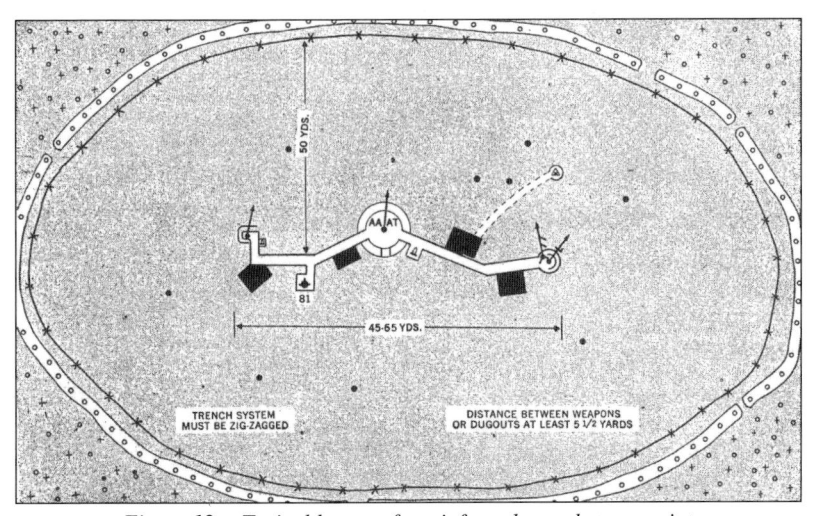

Figure 12.—Typical layout of a reinforced squad strongpoint.

units normally are kept there for counterattacks which are planned in advance.

f. ANTIMECHANIZED DEFENSE.

In constructing a defensive position the Germans stress construction of obstacles and antitank defenses. If possible they select tank-proof terrain, and natural tank obstacles, such as steep slopes, are improved. Very steep forward slopes are made at least 8 yards deep, while uphill slopes are made 2 to 3 yards high. Originally the Germans constructed antitank ditches well forward of the main line of resistance, but experience taught them that such ditches offered favorable jumping-off positions for hostile infantry and also revealed the location of the main line of resistance. At the present time, therefore, antitank ditches normally are dug in the area between the main line of resistance and the artillery positions. They are built in an uninterrupted line to avoid leaving passages that can be exploited by the enemy.

All crossings essential to assure the maneuverability of friendly troops are built so that they can be blown up on the shortest notice.

The Germans are aware that obstacles of any kind are effective only when covered by fire from various weapons. Consequently, there usually are trenches behind the antitank ditches from which machine-gun and antitank-gun fire can cover the entire length of the tank obstacle.

The Germans learned that dense minefields in front of their positions were an inadequate tank obstacle, because the enemy usually neutralized them by massed artillery fire or by concentrated air bombardment before launching a large-scale attack. Now German minefields normally are laid within the main battle position, and only single mines are dispersed in pattern at wide intervals in front of the main line of resistance. Particular stress is placed on the mining of roads. Routes of withdrawal which have to be left open are prepared for mining, and, if time does not permit placing of actual mines, dummy mines are installed.

The Germans employ many kinds of tank obstacles. They recently have used static flame throwers dug into the ground. Usually sited in pairs and in conjunction with other tank obstacles, they are fired by well concealed personnel as soon as hostile tanks come within range.

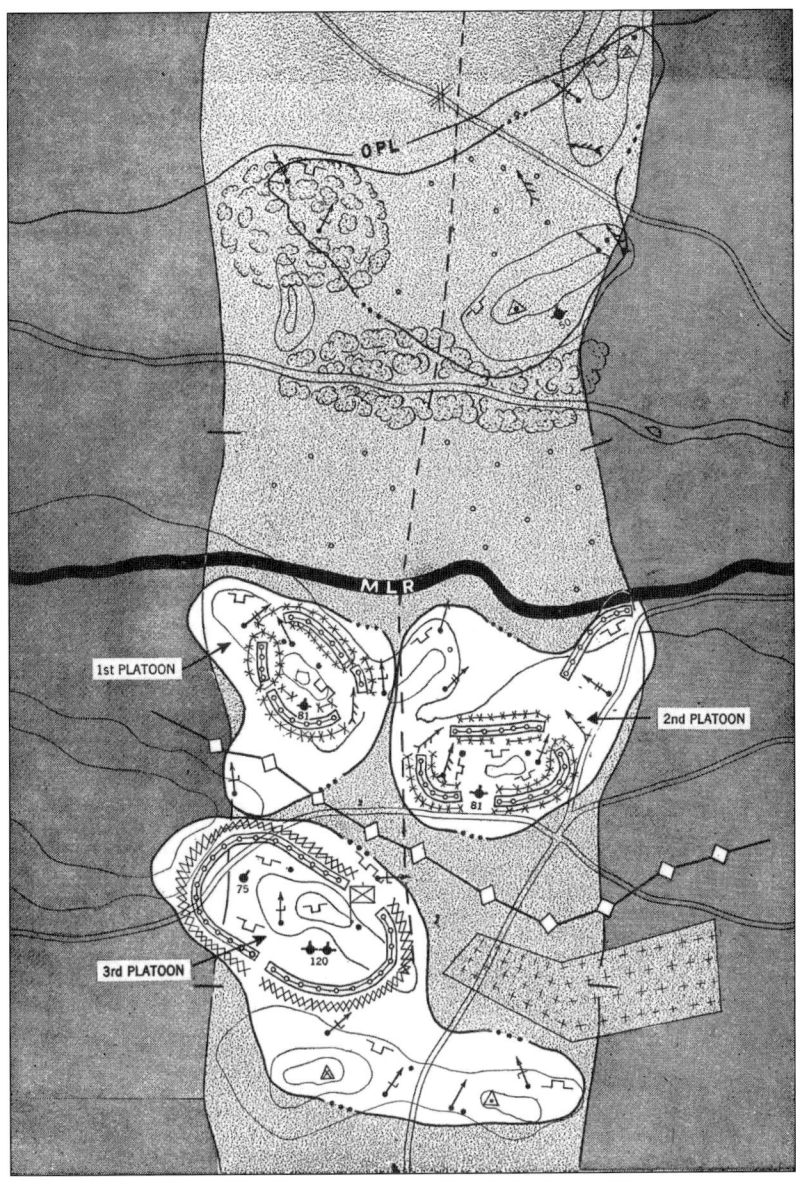

Figure 13.—German company in a defensive position.

German antitank guns are disposed in depth, with some well forward. They often are dug in and carefully concealed to prevent the enemy from discovering the location and strength of the antitank defenses prior to attack. In emplacing antitank guns, the Germans prefer positions in enfilade or on reverse slopes. They normally employ two to three antitank guns in each position, protecting them from infantry attacks with light machine guns. Ranges at which the Germans open fire upon hostile tanks vary according to the caliber of the gun and its position. Although single antitank guns sometimes engage enemy tanks at ranges up to 1,000 yards, main antitank defenses usually hold their fire until the range is reduced to about 150 to 300 yards. The employment of close-combat antitank teams supplements the antitank defense. When the hostile tank attack is repulsed, the antitank guns move to alternate positions.

The Germans emphasize that the use of smoke can be of great assistance in defeating enemy tank attacks. Smoke shells are fired into the attacking formation about one-third the distance back from the leading echelon. Thus the Germans avoid blinding their own antitank gunners, and leading hostile tanks not only are left without adequate support but are silhouetted against the smoke. The Germans also rely on the smoke being sucked into the tanks and forcing the crews to dismount.

3. Conduct of the Defense

German defense of a position, whether hastily prepared or complete in all details, is conducted on the same principles. Unless they are compelled by manpower and materiel shortages to rely on the strength of their positions, the Germans prefer heavy concentrations of fire and powerful, coordinated counterattacks by mobile reserves of all arms. They apply the principle of selecting a point of main effort (*Schwerpunkt*) to the defense as well as to the attack. This principle necessarily is applied in reverse order in the defensive, the main effort being made opposite the point where the enemy is making his main attack.

German artillery attempts to disrupt a hostile attack before it reaches the defensive positions. The Germans state that it is invaluable to install observation posts simultaneously in the main line of resistance, in the advanced position, and in the immediate vicinity of the gun position. Thus they try to keep a hostile force constantly under observation and fire even when it achieves a penetration. The artillery regiment commander controls the fire as long as possible, although requests for artillery barrages may be made by unit commanders as low as platoon leaders. Capabilities of German heavy mortars, which like all other support weapons usually are sited on reverse slopes, are exploited, with a present trend toward mortar-fire concentration.

When a part of the battle position is lost, the area is taken under artillery fire to annihilate enemy forces which have penetrated it. The Germans normally organize reserve units, even when only relatively few troops are available. Immediate local counterthrusts by infantry elements and support weapons near the penetration endeavor to hurl back the enemy before he has an opportunity to establish himself. These small counterthrusts, which normally closely follow the artillery fire, preferably are directed at the flanks of the penetrations.

When the enemy succeeds in making a large penetration or breakthrough, the German higher echelon commander decides whether a general counterattack should be launched to restore the position or whether the main battle position should be reestablished farther to the rear. The counterattack is directed against the hostile flank, where possible, and is prepared thoroughly. Assembly area, time, objective, zone, artillery support, and employment of tanks, self-propelled artillery, assault guns, and air units are controlled by one commander.

German antiaircraft defense, which is unable to give adequate protection everywhere because of Allied air supremacy, is concentrated at important points. The main mission of the light and medium antiaircraft artillery is the protection of roads. Accuracy of Allied air reconnaissance compels the German antiaircraft artillery to change positions from day to day, the changeover being made during the night. The Germans also enforce a preliminary two-hour fire silence in the new position to try to trap enemy fighter-bombers. Searchlights often are placed parallel to a protected road to prevent enemy aircraft from illuminating the road by flares. This is particularly important since the Germans normally bring forward their relief troops, rations, and ammunition during the night.

4. Defense of Towns

The Germans regard towns and villages as excellent strongpoints, particularly if the buildings are of masonry. Towns also are regarded as excellent antitank positions because of the considerable infantry-artillery effort necessary to neutralize them.

In defending a town or village, the Germans locate their main line of resistance well within the built-up portion; the edges of the town, which provide easy targets for artillery fire, are believed to be too vulnerable. The main line of resistance is laid out irregularly in order to develop flanking fire, and every effort is made to conceal its location until the last possible moment. Minor strongpoints are maintained forward of the line in order to break up attacks and provide additional flanking fire. Cul-de-sacs are organized and attempts made to trap attacking forces in them for destruction by counterattacking mobile reserves. These reserves are kept in readiness within the town itself, but other reserve forces are held outside the town to prevent hostile flanking maneuvers.

Both occupied and unoccupied buildings are booby-trapped in organizing the defended positions. Entrances to buildings are blocked, and all windows opened so as not to disclose those from which fire is maintained. Rooms are darkened, and passages are cut in the walls between buildings. To avoid detection, the Germans fire from the middle of the rooms, and frequently change their positions, while communication is maintained through cellars and over roofs. Machine guns are sited low, usually in basements, to provide better grazing fire. Chimneys and cornices are used as cover for men on roofs; tiles may be removed to provide loopholes. Searchlights are mounted to illuminate fields of fire; in their absence vehicle headlights may be used as substitutes. When houses collapse, the defense is carried on from cellars, and rubble heaps of destroyed areas are organized into strongpoints.

Tanks are considered to be ineffective within a defended town, although the Germans have used them in static, dug-in positions at crossroads and squares. As a result of their experiences on the Eastern Front, the Germans believe single tanks are too vulnerable to Molotov cocktails, magnetic mines, and explosive charges. When the Germans themselves use these antitank weapons, they employ them from foxholes dug outside the perimeter of the town. Efforts are made to destroy enemy tanks immobilized by antitank action, either within or outside the town, in order to prevent their recovery or use as artillery

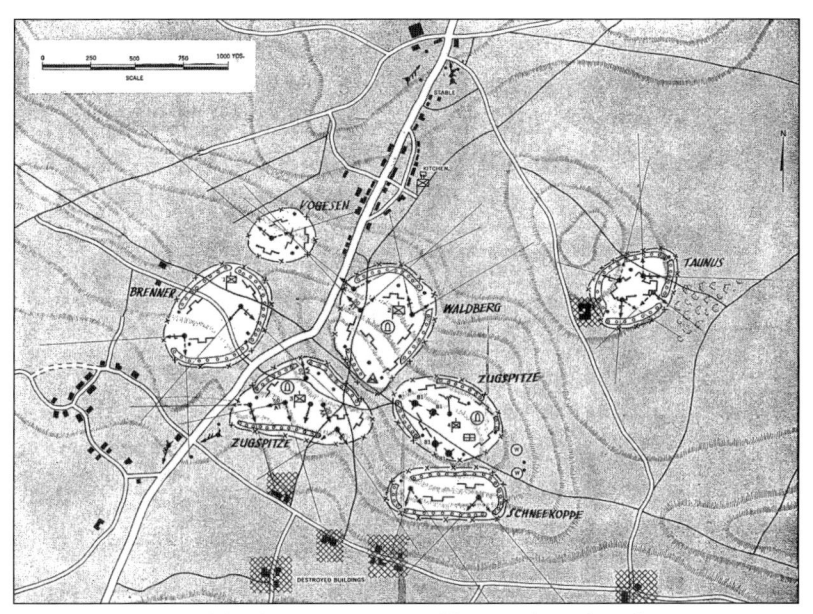

Figure 14.—Strongpoint manned by an infantry battalion.

observation posts and machine-gun nests. Antipersonnel mines are interspersed in antitank minefields because the attacking infantry are considered the chief menace.

Assault guns may provide direct defensive support fire if attacking forces break through and disorganize the German position. To secure the added protection afforded by masonry walls, the Germans may locate assault guns or tanks within buildings and use them against hostile armored vehicles and infantry. Counterattacks, supported by assault guns or tanks, will not be withheld until the situation has become desperate; indeed, surprise counterattacks may be launched at any time.

For the defense of village strongpoints special battle commandants (*Kampfkommandanten*) are appointed. The battle commandant is usually the senior officer and the tactical commander of all military forces, emergency units, and civil organizations in his area. He has the disciplinary power of a regimental commander.

In the case of fairly small villages, consolidation of the place itself is usually deemed sufficient. For larger localities an outer defense system is constructed in addition to the inner defenses.

The inner defense system consists of a number of concentric

positions which are broken down into perimeter positions, intermediate positions, and the inner ring position. The inner defense system is divided into sectors, each forming a strongpoint system in itself, with the strongpoints protected by all-around antitank and infantry obstacles and connected with each other by trenches.

The perimeter ring position is the most important part of the inner defenses and consists of one or more continuous trench systems, each with a deep main battle zone. The forward edge often is beyond the outskirts of the village, unless this creates unfavorable conditions for the antitank defense, in which case it is within the village itself. Artillery and heavy support weapons are employed as whole units in support of the perimeter ring position, although single guns may be detached for the defense of strongpoints and roads. The nearer the fighting approaches the inner ring, the more likely it will be that the Germans will split up the support weapons units for close cooperation with infantry assault groups.

The outer defense system likewise consists of a number of concentric positions, Approximately 4 to 6 miles apart, so as to force the enemy artillery to displace to engage each one. For defense of larger towns the Germans organize the outside ring about 12 1/2 to 18 1/2 miles beyond the outskirts whenever feasible. Beyond this outside defense ring, about 2,200 yards forward, are the advanced positions, with covering units still further forward on main roads and railways.

Patrols of all types, including motorized and cyclist patrols, give early warning of the enemy's approach and keep him under continuous observation. Non-military outposts, such as police sentries, party officials, and local farmers also are used for these duties.

Sector boundaries for companies and battalions are defined from the outside defense ring to the center of the town or village. Usually they do not coincide with vital main roads, which always are defended by entire companies or battalions. Every strongpoint, defense block (combined adjacent buildings), and sector has local reserves; mobile reserves, consisting of combat groups comprised of infantry, tanks, assault and self-propelled guns, are employed for counterattacks of a larger scale.

In addition to regular military units the Germans employ emergency

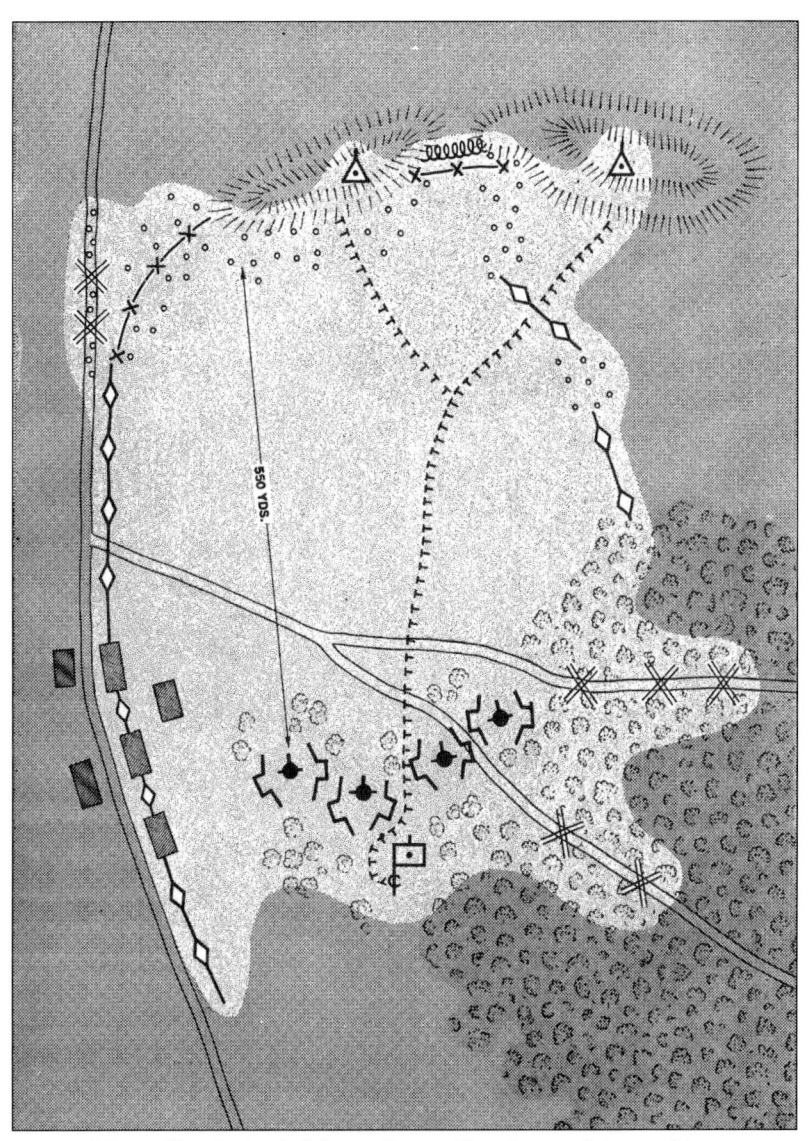

Figure 15.—Antitank defense of an artillery battery firing position.

units, organized from personnel of Army, Navy, and Air Force in town defense. Besides these regularly organized emergency units, improvised emergency units are formed from stragglers, remnants of formations, and units in process of reorganization. Utilization of emergency units is only temporary. Their main tasks, of local nature, are protection of headquarters, supply points, airfields, etc., and garrison service in fortifications.

5. Doctrine of Westwall System

The Germans consider economy of force the fundamental principle in planning zones of permanent fortifications. They originally built the Westwall as a protective barrier along the French frontier to permit commitment of maximum forces offensively in the East. Thus, in 1939, they were able to hold in the West with Approximately 20 divisions, while employing 40 to 50 divisions against Poland.

When Westwall construction ceased in 1940, German strategy in the West was offensive, envisioning an invasion of France by a wide envelopment, with the bulk of the German forces in the North, where the Westwall defenses were relatively weak. The pivot of maneuver was south of the Moselle River, where the Westwall defenses were strongest.

The Germans never have discarded the principle that offensive action is the best protection. When their armies were forced back to the Westwall in 1944, they used this defensive system as a base for offensive operations in selected areas, as in the Saar and the Eifel. Advantage also was taken of this protected zone for the free lateral movement of troops; shelters were utilized for the cover and concealment of reserve forces, weapons, and supplies.

German Westwall tactics are based on a stubborn defense of individual fortifications, local counterattacks against areas of penetration, and counterattack by general mobile reserves against areas of deep penetration. German troops are not permitted to develop a static-defense complex which might foster the idea that a position once surrounded is lost. Bunker garrisons are taught to continue resistance even though surrounded, because their perseverance impedes the attackers' advance and facilitates counterattacks. Troops are trained in the principle that the decision usually is achieved by the infantry in the open between bunkers. Organic heavy infantry weapons and artillery are the backbone of German defense in the Westwall, just as in mobile warfare. Reserves habitually are left under cover until the time for counterattack arrives.

Surprise is always attempted. For example, bunkers and heavy weapons frequently are sited on reverse slopes, not only for concealment and protection in defilade, but also to open fire suddenly

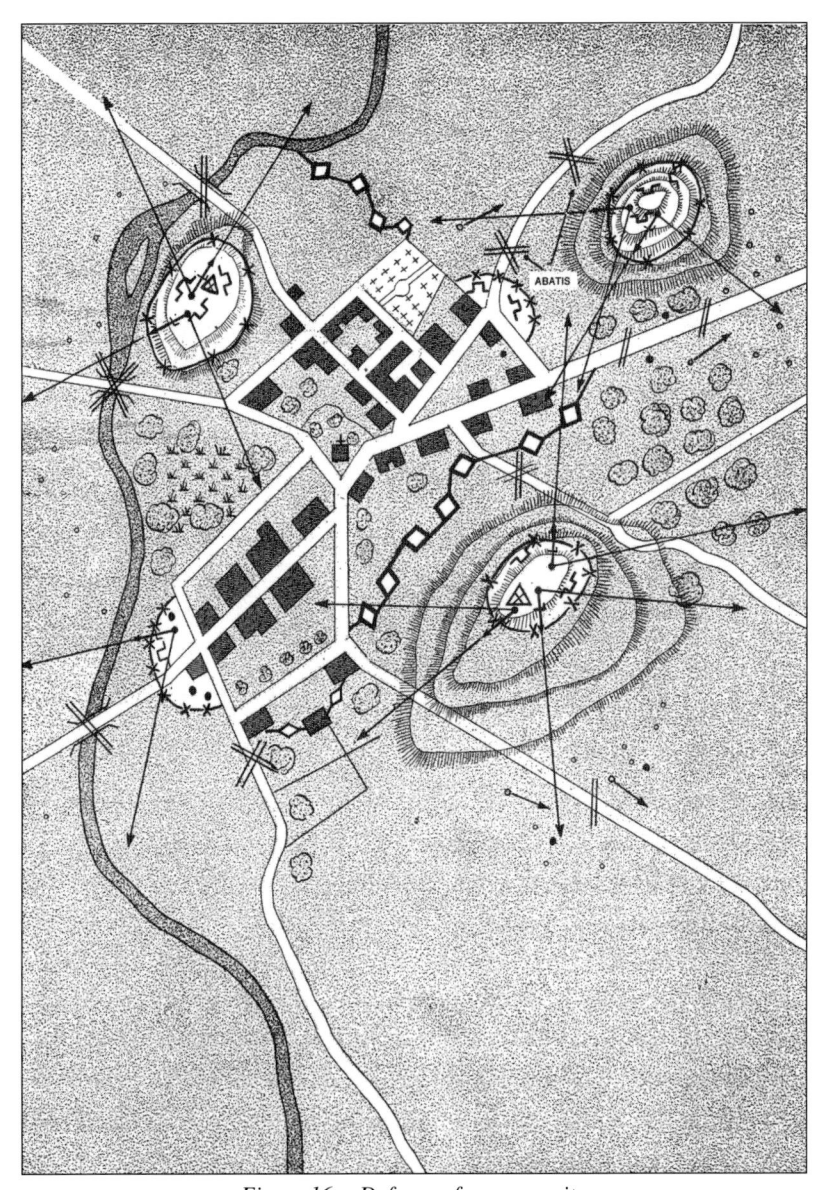

Figure 16.—Defense of a community.

upon the unwary attacker crossing the crest or moving around the nose of a hill. The attacker penetrating the Westwall defense system must be prepared to cope with unexpected resistance flaring up in his rear areas, surprise by accurate flanking and enfilade fire at short and medium ranges, sudden counterattacks by forces not known to be in the areas, and counterattacks in increasing strength as the penetration progresses.

German doctrine prescribes that the intact portion of the defenses must continue the battle, regardless of the situation at the penetrated area, until the appropriate command orders a readjustment of the line. Penetrations normally are dealt with as follows: by mobile reserves which seal them off frontally; by counterattack or counteroffensive from protected flanks to threaten the rear areas of the penetrating force; or by both, as in the Aachen area. At any rate, the Germans will attempt to destroy the penetration before the attacker has reorganized and consolidated his gains. Here again the principle of economy of force is generally followed. German troops may be taken from strongly protected and little threatened areas in order to concentrate on adequate counterattacking or counteroffensive force. Hence the attacker should have sufficient strength to ward off strong countermeasures and at the same time exploit the advantages gained by a penetration.

VI. RETROGRADE MOVEMENTS

1. Withdrawal from Action (Abbrechen des Gefechts)

a. GENERAL.

The Germans break off an engagement for one or more of the following reasons: when it has served its purpose; when conditions require the employment of the troops, or part of them, on another front; when a continuation of the battle gives no promise of success; or when defeat is imminent.

When an attack exhausts itself without attaining its objective, the Germans assume the defensive as the first step in withdrawing from action. If the defense must be continued in a rearward position, the breaking of contact, the retirement, and the resumption of the defense are carefully planned beforehand. Positions in the rear are prepared for the reception of the troops, particularly if they have been engaged in heavy fighting. The retirement is made in conjunction with that of adjacent units, and stress is placed on maintaining the cohesiveness of the retiring forces.

By maintaining the usual fire of all arms, the Germans try to deceive their enemy as long as possible as to the continued occupation in force of their original position.

In view of the severe losses inflicted by Allied planes and armored forces on German troops during daylight disengagements, the Germans try to await darkness before withdrawing from action. At night they break off combat on a wide front and move back along routes as nearly perpendicular as possible to terrain features suitable for fighting delaying actions. When the situation forces them to withdraw during daylight, they do so by unit sectors, coordinating the movements of adjacent units.

b. ORDERS.

The German company commander follows this outline in drafting his orders for breaking off an engagement:

- General instructions. Rearward movement of supplies, ammunition-carrying vehicles, and equipment.
- Reconnaissance and marking of routes of withdrawal.
- Detailed instructions. Combat orders for the covering forces (reconnaissance units, heavy support weapons, medical personnel, infantry combat wagons, and infantry engineers).
- Type, time, and march order for the withdrawal of the rifle platoons and heavy weapons.
- Assembly areas.
- Location of the company commander.

2. Retreat (Ruckzug)

a. GENERAL.

Retreat is a forced retirement which is ordered by the Germans only when all possibilities for success are exhausted. The objective is to place enough distance between friendly and hostile forces to enable the former to conduct an orderly withdrawal and to occupy new positions to the rear.

b. COVERING FORCES.

The German usually organize covering forces from troops in closest contact with the enemy—either whole tactical units or elements from several. These forces attempt to make the enemy believe that the position is still fully occupied. Engineers prepare additional obstacles, minefields, and booby traps forward of and within the positions to be held. A portion of the artillery and heavy infantry weapons support the covering forces. They maintain as long as possible their former fire activity to deceive the enemy, even when fulfilment of their mission means the loss of individual guns. The sector assigned to a covering force is usually too wide to be under effective control of a single commander, but the actions of the various commanders are closely coordinated. Orders specify whether the covering forces are to remain in contact with the hostile forces until they begin to advance, or to follow the main body after a specified interval.

c. REAR GUARD (Nachhut).

(1) As the distance from the enemy increases, the retiring troops form march columns. Where possible, a division's retirement takes place along two parallel routes. The freshest troops available are used as rear guards. Since the rear guard cannot expect support from the retreating main body, it must be relatively strong. It is composed of infantry units. Generally the divisional field artillery retires with the main body, none being assigned to the rear guard. Self-propelled and heavy infantry-support guns, and even howitzers, are frequently attached to the rear guard. Tanks also may be assigned. A typical rear guard for each route in a division retirement is one infantry battalion to which are attached elements of the reconnaissance unit, to protect the flanks, and of the engineer unit, to prepare demolitions.

(2) The rear guard infantry battalion normally employs only one of its rifle companies on active rear guard tasks. The three rifle companies perform this function in turn as long as their strength remains Approximately even. If the terrain demands it, two companies are employed at a time. Two or more antitank guns and half of the self-propelled or heavy infantry guns allotted to the full rear guard support the rearmost rifle company or companies. When pressure becomes too strong, the single rifle company is withdrawn through the two remaining rifle companies which are supported by the remainder of the attached weapons. Variations of this leapfrogging progress are repeated until darkness, when a general disengagement takes place and the original formation is resumed.

(3) Rear guards withdraw by bounds to selected but not prepared

positions. The extent to which positions eventually can be prepared depends on the proximity of the pursuing forces, the length of time each particular position is likely to be held, and the decision of the individual company and platoon commanders. During each stage of the retreat, the commander of the rear company can order a withdrawal to the main rear guard position, but withdrawal from each main rear guard position is ordered by the commander of the main body. Frequently the speed of withdrawal is based on a time-distance schedule. During the withdrawal from a certain town, rear guards were instructed to retire not more than 3,000 yards a day.

(4) Experience has shown that in certain types of country a reinforced rear guard company generally can hold up very superior forces on a front as wide as three miles. In one instance of a withdrawal from a defensive position along a river line, a German *Panzer* division, which had one *Panzer Grenadier* battalion and attached elements as its rear guard, was covered by one rifle company reinforced by a company of tanks, four infantry guns (including two self-propelled), and a battery of medium howitzers. The tanks were mainly used to cover the withdrawal of the rifle elements. On another occasion a similar rear party had a number of heavy mortars attached. These covered the infantry withdrawal with the help of four tanks, which also carried the mortars back to the next bound.

(5) Particularly suited for rear guard tasks, because of its armor and high fire power, is the armored reconnaissance battalion of the *Panzer* division. When employing the armored reconnaissance battalion in terrain that affords cover, the Germans site well camouflaged, armored half-tracks in wooded areas, flat reverse slopes, or high grain fields, and open fire with all weapons at very close range. The armored half-tracks then penetrate into the confused enemy and, after repulsing him, retreat to previously organized alternate positions.

3. Delaying Action

a. BASIC PRINCIPLES.

The Germans make a distinction between "delaying engagements"

(Hinhaltendes Gefecht) and "delaying action" *(Hinhaltender Widerstand)*. A delaying engagement is primarily the general plan of the higher commander for holding back the enemy. Delaying actions are the measures taken by lower units to carry out the higher commander's plan.

The purpose of delaying actions is to enable the main German force to disengage itself from battle, retire in order, and establish a new defensive position. Delaying actions therefore seek to deceive the enemy as to German strength, dispositions, and intentions; to prevent the enemy from committing the main German forces; and to prevent close pursuit of the main forces by the enemy. These measures are accomplished by rear guards, special battle groups, and strongpoints, all of which are characterized by high automatic fire power, mobility, and economy in numerical strength.

Delaying actions are organized not in a main defensive belt, but on lines of resistance (*Widerstandslinien*). The distance between such lines is great enough to prevent the enemy from engaging two of them from the same artillery position. He is compelled to displace and move up his artillery to engage each line. These lines of resistance are normally established along forward slopes to facilitate disengagement and withdrawal under cover. The delaying actions are fought forward of the lines of resistance with mobile forces. Furthermore, battle outposts are organized forward of each line.

The main delaying weapons are machine guns, mortars, and self-propelled weapons. Tanks are used in small groups.

Maintenance of contact is a most conspicuous principle in the Germans' conduct of a withdrawal and delaying action. The size, composition, direction, and intention of the attacking enemy force are observed at all times.

b. CONDUCT OF THE DELAYING ACTION.

During a delaying action, wide sectors are covered by artillery units widely deployed—guns are sited by sections if necessary—and by widely distributed infantry-support weapons. The defense is then further organized by establishing strongpoints manned by small groups.

The positions from which delaying actions are fought are

characterized by very slight depth. As a general rule, a unit is responsible for double the front normally allocated in defensive fighting. A company sector is 650 to 1,300 yards; a battalion sector 1,750 to 4,400 yards; a regimental sector 4,400 to 6,600 yards; and a division sector 13,000 to 22,000 yards.

In leaving a line of resistance, German covering forces attempt to disengage by night. If that is not possible, their actions are governed by the following principle: the enemy is not allowed to come closer to them than they are from their next line of resistance. The troops must be able to reach the new position before the enemy reaches the old one, or their losses will be excessive.

The troops therefore do not retire in the face of enemy patrols—every effort is made to destroy such patrols—but only when the enemy mounts an attack. If it can be ascertained that the enemy is preparing for a massed attack, the Germans make a timely withdrawal to avoid exposing the troops to enemy artillery concentrations. Advance elements employ smoke to enable them to make a getaway in a critical situation. Riflemen cover the disengagement of heavy weapons, which move back by bounds. Every opportunity is taken to make limited counterattacks in order to inflict casualties on an enemy who advances recklessly.

Fire is opened at extreme ranges on an enemy advancing for a major attack. Enemy reconnaissance forces are allowed to approach, however, and then an effort is made to destroy them.

Counterattacks on a large scale are avoided, except when the enemy threatens to penetrate the line of resistance. When that occurs, the Germans counterattack with the main forces of the rear guard and seek to restore the situation in order that the program of staged withdrawal may be continued. Local counterattacks are made for the protection or retention of some feature essential to the safe conduct of the main withdrawal, or to gain time for the preparation of the line of resistance or phase line.

The area between the lines of resistance is called the intermediate area (*Zwischenfeld*). Explicit orders are given as to whether the intermediate area is to be covered in one bound or is to be fought over. The latter necessity arises especially when the next line of resistance has not been fully prepared and time must be gained. Detachments must reach the line of resistance early enough to insure that all the main positions are occupied in time.

The supply of ammunition is carefully organized. A great deal of ammunition is required for delaying actions because a few weapons on a broad front must do as much as or even more than the normal number of guns in a defensive position. When ammunition is scarce, the Germans specify, down to sections if necessary, the quantity of ammunition that may be used at each position. Every commander maintains a supply of ammunition for emergencies.

The Germans stress the importance of deceiving the enemy by every means. Artillery and heavy weapons are moved continually to give an impression of greater strength. Dummy positions and camouflage are also widely used.

So that isolated groups may be adequately directed, signal communication receives special attention.

In delaying actions in mountainous terrain, the Germans make greater use of their reconnaisance and engineer units than of any other component. Reconnaisance units are almost continuously in contact with advance and flanking enemy elements, and participate in most rear-guard and battle-group engagements.

c. STRONGPOINTS TN DELAYING ACTION.

The Germans cover the rear guard's resistance or phase lines by a system of strongpoints or defended localities. Just as it is a function of the rear guards to prevent a pursuing force from making contact with the main body while it is on the move, so it is the function of strongpoints to prevent the penetration of resistance or phase lines until the main body has withdrawn to its next position.

In manning strongpoints, the Germans show the same economy of force they show in forming rear guards. Typical fire power of a strongpoint in close country is one or two self-propelled guns, two heavy mortars, and up to six machine guns. In open country, one self-propelled gun is normally employed, supplemented by three tanks and a small party of infantry with mortars and machine guns in armored half-tracks.

Strongpoints generally are organized on the hedgehog principle.

Provision is made for all-around fire, but the strongpoints are not necessarily mutually self-supporting. They are normally located on commanding features, and sometimes on the forward edges of villages or hamlets if these dominate road or terrain bottlenecks. In flat country, however, villages usually are not occupied except by snipers, but positions are occupied in the rear of the villages to engage enemy vanguards debouching from them. Weapons are not dug in, and positions are frequently changed. Counterbattery fire thereby is rendered very difficult as there are no prepared positions to be spotted from the air. The Germans thus force their enemy to launch a full-scale attack supported by artillery to dislodge the garrison of the strongpoint, which normally withdraws just before the attack can materialize. Approaches to strongpoints which cannot be covered by fire are frequently mined. Extensive minefields are frequently laid at the heads of re-entrants in hilly terrain.

d. BATTLE GROUPS IN DELAYING ACTION.

Battle groups normally are organized for the execution of some specific task in the withdrawal, such as a local counterattack or the defense of some particular feature whose retention is necessary for the security of the main withdrawal.

Battle groups, which the Germans employ for offensive and defensive as well as delaying missions, vary in size from a company or two, with attached close support weapons, to a regiment or several battalions reinforced with tanks, artillery, antiaircraft, engineer, and reconnaissance elements. In all cases the Germans seek to make them as self-sufficient as possible in combat. In actual practice, however, the composition of German battle groups appears often to have been dictated less by the theory of what units should be put together to form a self-sufficient combat force, than by the demands of an emergency situation which commanders have been forced to meet with the insufficient and normally disassociated units at their disposal.

German battle groups may be organized for short, long, or changing missions. They are usually known by the name of their commander.

e. DEMOLITIONS AND OBSTACLES.

To prevent the pursuing enemy columns from approaching close enough to engage even their rear guard elements, the Germans continually employ demolitions and obstacles of all kinds. The thoroughness with which engineer operations have been carried out has increased steadily throughout the war. Culverts and bridges are completely destroyed. Roads and all natural detours are mined, cratered, or blocked by felled trees; in streets and villages, streets are blocked by the wreckage of buildings. Vertical rail obstacles are placed to obstruct main routes; mines often are laid for 30 yards around the edge of the obstacle. Wooden box mines are used to a large extent as demolition charges, and aerial bombs and artillery shells are sometimes similarly employed.

Frequently rear parties are committed to a delaying engagement in order to cover the preparation of demolitions immediately behind them. During static periods in the general withdrawal, when the Germans occupy their line of resistance or phase line, engineer units prepare demolitions in the rear. After the withdrawal, these demolitions are covered by sniper fire, machine guns, and self-propelled weapons as long as possible.

VII. MINEFIELDS

1. General

The Germans make extensive use of mines which they consider a most effective defensive weapon. Minefields are utilized chiefly to cover defensive actions and retreats, although limited use is made of them in offensive actions for flank protection. In a static situation the Germans regard minefields as an element of the front-line position, laid out according to an over-all mine plan developed in close conjunction with that for the fields of fire of all weapons. Within recent months, standard German doctrine for minefield location has been modified. Instead of laying dense minefields in front of the main line of resistance, dispersed mines are laid there, while the minefields proper are sited within the main battle position.

2. Surveying of Minefields

The Germans consider it necessary to survey the location of minefields and individual mines within the minefields. German engineers are instructed to choose reference points (*Festpunkte* or *FP*) for minefields which easily can be identified. At a grade crossing, at the intersection of two improved roads, at the edge of a village, or some such favorable location, this can be done without any difficulty. In some instances, however, the Germans are forced to use "guide wire" and auxiliary fixed points (*Vermessungspunkte* or *VP*). A type of auxiliary fixed point that has proved practicable is the center of an equilateral triangle with sides 15 to 25 feet long. The corner points and the fixed point itself may be stakes, rails, or concrete or steel girders about 3 feet in length connected with barbed wire. Such a fixed point can be reestablished easily because even heavy shelling will rarely destroy more than one or two stakes.

A minefield is limited by the four corner points A_1, A_2, A_3, and A_4. The corner points are marked clockwise, A_1 and A_2 forming the base line on the German side. The survey of the field refers to one or both points of the base line. Auxiliary fixed points, called "mine stakes" (*Minenpfähle*), are used if necessary. Fixed points may be reference points found on the map or auxiliary fixed points established by the troops. Distances are measured in meters; azimuth readings are taken on the German issue compass—divided into 6,400 mils like the U.S. compass but read counter-clockwise, and marked with the letters *KZ* (*Kompasszahl*). The new-type compass called "march compass" has clockwise graduation and is indicated with the letters *MKZ*. The Germans use the magnetic azimuth and always proceed in their survey from the friendly toward the enemy side.

The Germans believe that it is advantageous to lay a continuous chain of reference points 600 to 900 feet apart, through a division sector. This chain can be used to determine the location of ditches, trenches, obstacles, and pillboxes, as well as minefields. Individual points are designated with Roman numerals, starting on the right flank of the division sector.

3. Laying of Minefields

a. PATTERNS.

To assure the greatest possible effect, minefields normally are laid out in definite patterns. The Germans make an exception to this practice, however, in sectors where they do not intend to undertake offensive actions. There they disperse the mines irregularly in the areas between defensive positions.

The main belts of a major antitank minefield laid in uniform pattern normally consist of anti-tank mines with a sprinkling of antipersonnel mines in the forward edge of the field. Both types may be fitted with anti-lifting devices, and some of the antipersonnel mines have trip wires attached. In some instances, these mines are placed in the intervals between the diagonal wires of a double-apron fence, with trip wires fastened to the diagonals.

A number of antitank mines are laid in the forward edge of antipersonnel minefields to prevent armored vehicles from detonating the main belt of antipersonnel mines. The forward edges of minefields of all types often are sown with explosive charges placed in wooden boxes fitted with pressure fuzes. These act as both antitank and antipersonnel mines, and discourage the use of detectors to locate the mines.

Forward of most regular fields, and particularly in front of lanes, mines may be found widely spaced or scattered at random in unmarked groups. Mines also are laid in spaces running out at right angles from the forward edge of the minefield to damage vehicles moving along the field in search of lanes.

All pressure-type antitank and antipersonnel mines are laid in lines. For measuring distances and spaces, the troops use a mine-measuring wire (*Minenmessdraht*) which they themselves make from old telephone wire. (See *Figure 15*.) The mine-measuring wire is 24 meters (about 25 yards) long, and every meter (3 feet 3 inches) is marked with a piece of wood. The rings on the ends are about 5 inches in diameter. The measuring wire, in addition to measuring the distance between fixed points, serves to lay out right angles by staking out a triangle with sides of 6, 8, and 10 meters respectively. Spaces between mines are determined by reference to the marks on wire; the four rings on one end are used to offset the rows.

The density of a minefield depends upon the interval between mines and the number of rows. The table opposite represents the density.

Mine lanes are left open for patrols, and passage lanes for assault

Type of Mine	How Laid	Interval between Mines	Number of Rows	Density per 1 Meter of Front
T-Mine 35	Buried	4 m (4.4 yds)	8 12 16	2 3 4
T-Mine 42 T-Mine 43	Laid on surface	4 m (4.4 yds)	8 12 16	2 3 4
	Buried	2 m (2.2 yds)	4 6 8	2 3 4
R-Mine 43	Buried or laid on surface	about 4 m (4.4 yds)	2 4	1/2 1
S-Mine 35	Buried	4 m (4.4 yds)	4 8 12	1 2 3
		2 m (2.2 yds)	2 4 6	1 2 3
Schti-Mine 42	Buried	1 m (1.1 yds)	1 2 3	1 2 3
		1/2 m (0.55 yd)	1 2	2 4

troops. For permanent patrols new lanes are made from time to time, and the old ones closed. A mine-free safety strip is provided on the Germans' side.

The Germans normally lay mine belts in individual sections 80 by 105 feet. The sections usually are staggered, and, for extensive mine belts, they are combined in units of three or four to form forward or reverse arrowheads, or echelons. Minefields arranged in echelon are surveyed by using corner posts on the hostile side of intermediate minefields as survey points.

The Germans emphasize that minefields must be covered by fire, although during a hasty withdrawal they often do not follow this principle. It is common for a regular minefield to have a listening post with two men at the rearward edge; about 70 or 80 yards farther to the rear there usually is a covering party of four or five men armed with one or two light machine guns.

When the Germans are in hasty withdrawal, they usually lay a large number of small nuisance minefields. These fields contain many different types of mines, which often are unmarked and show every evidence of hurried laying. The consequent lack of pattern uniformity makes their detection and clearance a laborious and dangerous task. Though no consistency is noted in layout and types of mines used in such fields, the Germans show certain preferences in their choice of sites for them.

b. LOCATION.

In general, mines are laid either close to, or on, roads; on airfields and railways; and along telegraph routes. Surfaced portions of roads usually are avoided by the hasty mine layer, but khaki-painted T-Mines sometimes are placed on the surface at dips in the road, in the hope that drivers will be unable to check their vehicles in time to avoid them. The Germans also place mines along the shoulders of the road opposite narrow places where drivers have to detour to pass, and at the entrances to defiles where they have to pull off the road to wait for vehicles moving in the opposite direction. Other places usually sown with antitank mines are turnouts, sharp bends, the unsurfaced islands sometimes found at crossroads, berms, and well worn wheel ruts.

c. CONCEALMENT.

The Germans, with great ingenuity, attempt to make their mines difficult to detect. They bury them as much as 24 inches below the surface where they explode only after passage of a number of vehicles has compacted the earth cover sufficiently to operate the fuze. They put explosives in wooden boxes to prevent the effective operation of ordinary mine detectors, and mark tire prints in the earth on top of the mine by drawing a detached axle and wheels over it.

The Germans also show considerable ingenuity in siting random antipersonnel mines on the line of the hostile advance. Road demolitions are plentifully sown with S-Mines, and kilometer posts at points where vehicular drivers have to dismount to read directions are similarly treated. S-Mines also are placed in ditches, often close to to the trip-wire peg of another mine.

Nuisance fields on lines of communication generally are closely spaced, occasionally so closely as to cause sympathetic detonation. This is particularly possible when mines are laid with their pressure plates almost flush with the surface of the ground and only lightly covered with earth.

German dummy minefields take various forms. In some cases a trip wire is laid to give the appearance of a minefield perimeter wire, with the usual lanes, and the ground is disturbed at regular intervals. Scrap metal, often dispersed with real mines, is placed in shallow holes to cause a reaction in the mine detector. Dummy mines often are wired in and connected with booby traps.

4. Marking of Minefields

The Germans stress the marking of minefields and attempt to mark them in such a manner that they cannot be recognized by the enemy but can easily be found by their own troops. Their methods of marking minefields are not uniform. The front edge of a field often is unmarked and unwired; the rear edge seldom so. Some fields have been found unmarked, but because of many accidents caused by their own minefields, the Germans issued orders within recent months making proper marking obligatory.

The following are typical examples of markings by the Germans, the type used depending on the situation and terrain: corner-post marking stakes; double-apron fence on the enemy side and a single trip wire on the friendly side, or the reverse; single knee-high wires; cattle fencing; empty mine crates; and signs.

The length of marking stakes varies with the terrain. They are flattened on one side for a length of about 8 inches. The flat surface is painted red, with the letter M (*Minen*) in black. Such stakes are used

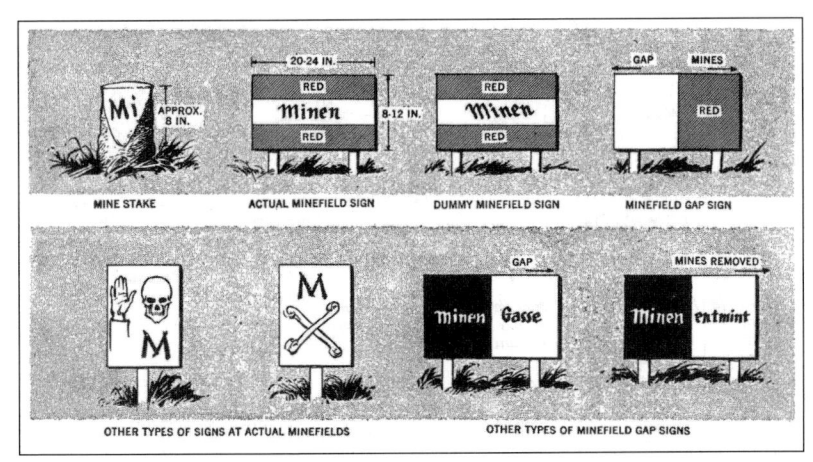

Minefield signs.

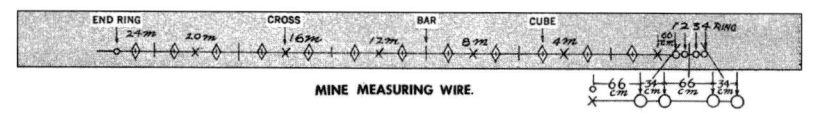

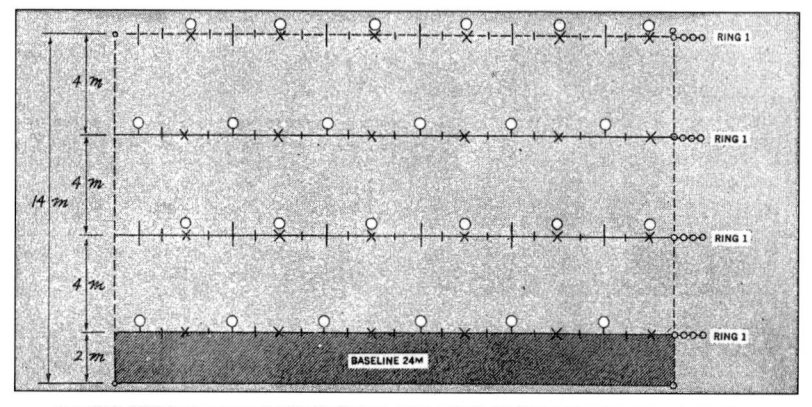

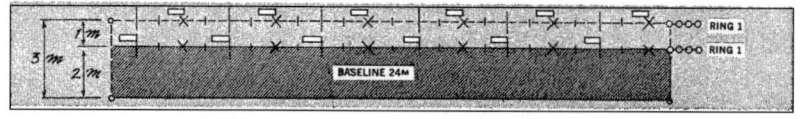

Figure 17.—Mine Measuring Wire and Minefield Patterns.

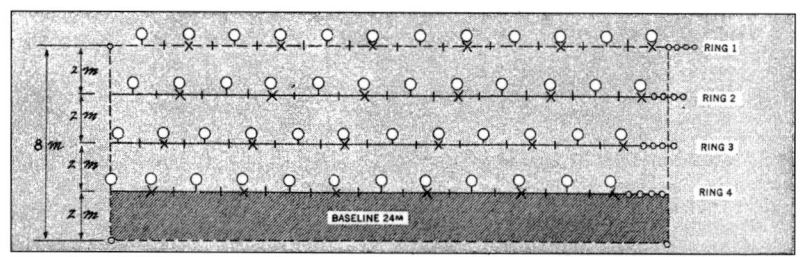

only on the friendly edges of minefields.

Signs are painted in red and white on boards or pieces of sheet metal, and fastened to two stakes. The edges of minefields are marked with signs showing horizontal stripes. Edges of lanes through the fields are shown by vertically divided signs with the white portion on the side of the lane, and the red portion on the side of the minefield (danger). The reverse side of the signs (the side toward the enemy) is

painted olive drab. If red paint is not available, the Germans substitute black-and-white signs. They are painted with the following words:
- *Minen*—for mines
- *Gasse* or *Gassen*—for mine lanes
- *Entimint*—for an area cleared of mines.

Minefields are marked with vertical lettering, dummy minefields with slanting letters. This distinction, however, is supposed to be made known only to the German engineer troops because other troops may divulge the location of dummy minefields by crossing them.

5. Mine Plans, Sketches, and Reports

A German mine plan shows one or more fields in all necessary technical details. A German mine map, on the other hand, shows all mine obstacles within one front sector and their tactical significance, but without technical details.

The Germans use a number of different forms for their reports and sketches, although all are based on the same principle. Figure 17 shows a very commonly used form. The upper third of the mine map form provides space for written specifications and a small situation sketch. The drawing is made on the blank space provided. It is the engineers' responsibility to draw up mine maps, and to keep them up to date. Additional remarks sometimes are placed on the back of the sheet.

a. DETAILS OF MINE MAP.

The German mine map usually shows the following details:

(1) Name of the obstacle and designation of the unit which laid it.

(2) Name of the area in which the obstacle is located.

(3) Grid reference and particulars of the map sheet referred to.

(4) Obstacle shown in the little sketch in red.

(5) Date minefield was laid.

(6) Name and rank of officer or noncommissioned officer in charge of laying field.

(7) Day of survey and instrument used (old or new compass—German issue).

(8) Name and rank of officer or noncommissioned officer in charge of survey.

b. MINE DATA IN MAP.

The following data are given on the mines:

(1) Number, type and igniter. (Example: 72 T-Mine with *T-Mi.Z. 42*, booby-trapped.)

(2) Whether or not the mines are dug in.

(3) Number of rows, and number of mines per row.

(4) Fence (Example: warning fence on friendly side.)

(5) Special features (Example: destroyed enemy tank in center, on enemy side.)

c. MINEFIELD-TYPE IDENTIFICATION IN MAP.

Colored lines drawn diagonally across the upper right-hand field of the mine map identify the type of the minefield as follows:

(1) A red diagonal line designates fields which cannot be cleared because some or all mines are booby-trapped.

(2) A yellow diagonal line designates fields which can be cleared by using data from mine document.

(3) A green diagonal line designates dummy minefields.

(4) Mines taken up or exploded are marked in red.

The number of the minefield plan and unit designation appears on the upper right-hand corner of the sheet. Battalion, regiment, and division engineers make their notes in the space provided for them.

For S-Mines laid 50 meters (55 yards) from the German lines, a note is made in red letters: *VORSICHT, NUR 50 METER ABSTAND!* (Caution, only 50 meters distance!)

In case electrical ignition is provided, a note is made showing how the igniters will be disposed of, if the unit which has laid the minefield is relieved.

d. INFORMATION IN MINEFIELD DRAWING.

The drawing of the minefield is made in the blank space on the lower part of the sheet. The scale is from 1:500 to 1:2,000 whenever possible. The following information is included:

(1) Shape and size of minefield.

(2) Pattern.

(3) Location of booby-trapped mines.

(4) Location of survey points with azimuth and distances.

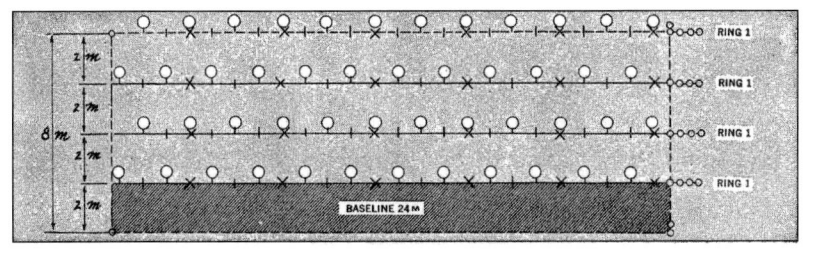

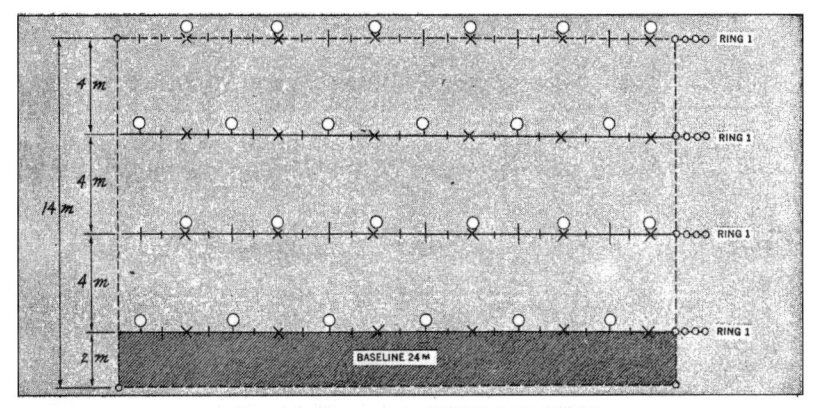

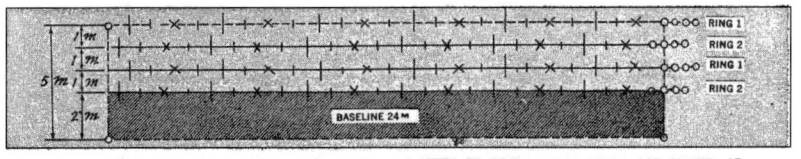

Figure 18.—Minefield Patterns.

(5) Type and location of warning fence.

(6) Location of the front lines and fortifications.

(7) Neighboring minefields, mine lanes, terrain features, special features.

The Germans believe that it is not necessary to mark on the minefield drawing the location of every single mine, if a partial drawing is sufficient. The German mine plans contain the detail symbols shown in Figure 18, while simple tactical signs are sufficient for minefield maps.

The Germans complete their mine plans at company or battalion command posts, based on sketches and data compiled while the field

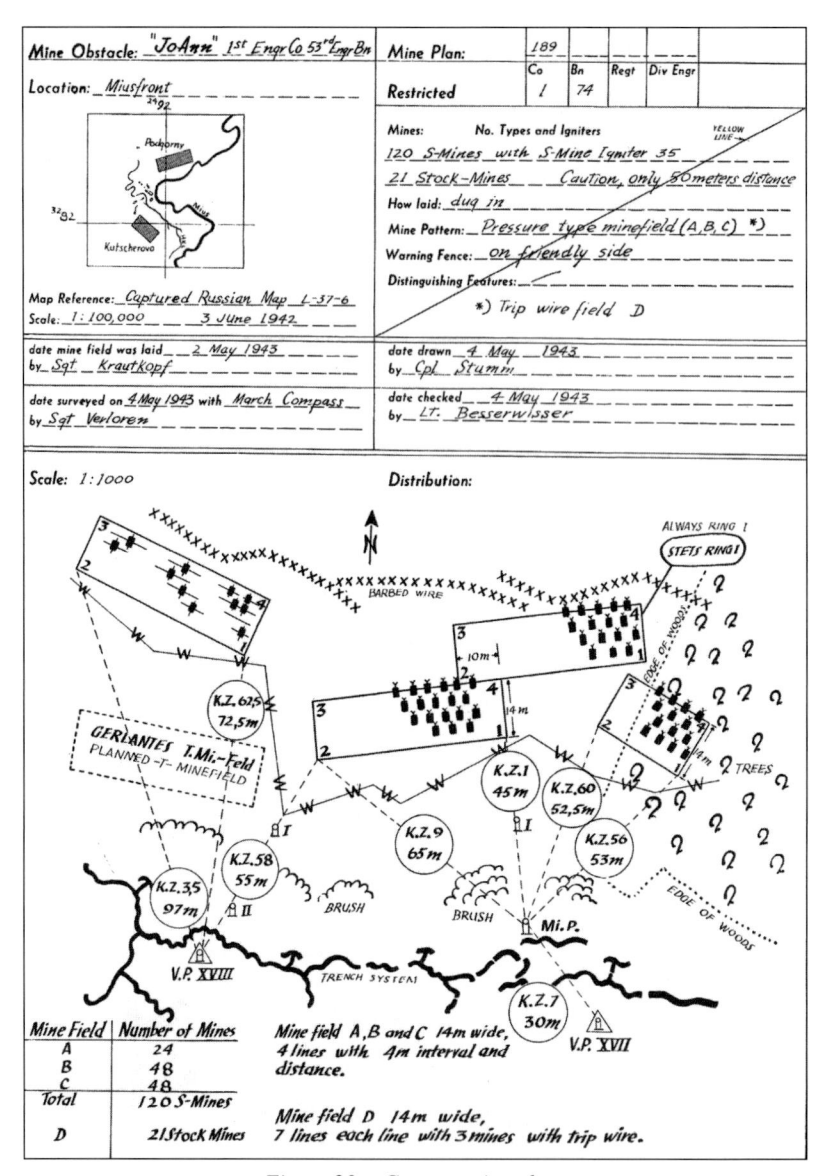

Figure 20.—German mine plan.

is being laid out. They make five copies of all mine plans and distribute them as follows: One for engineer company which is in charge of the minefield; two for division; one for army; one for central file in *Dessau-Rosslau*.

Changes in the minefield are recorded on the back of the mine plan. After three changes a new mine plan is drawn.

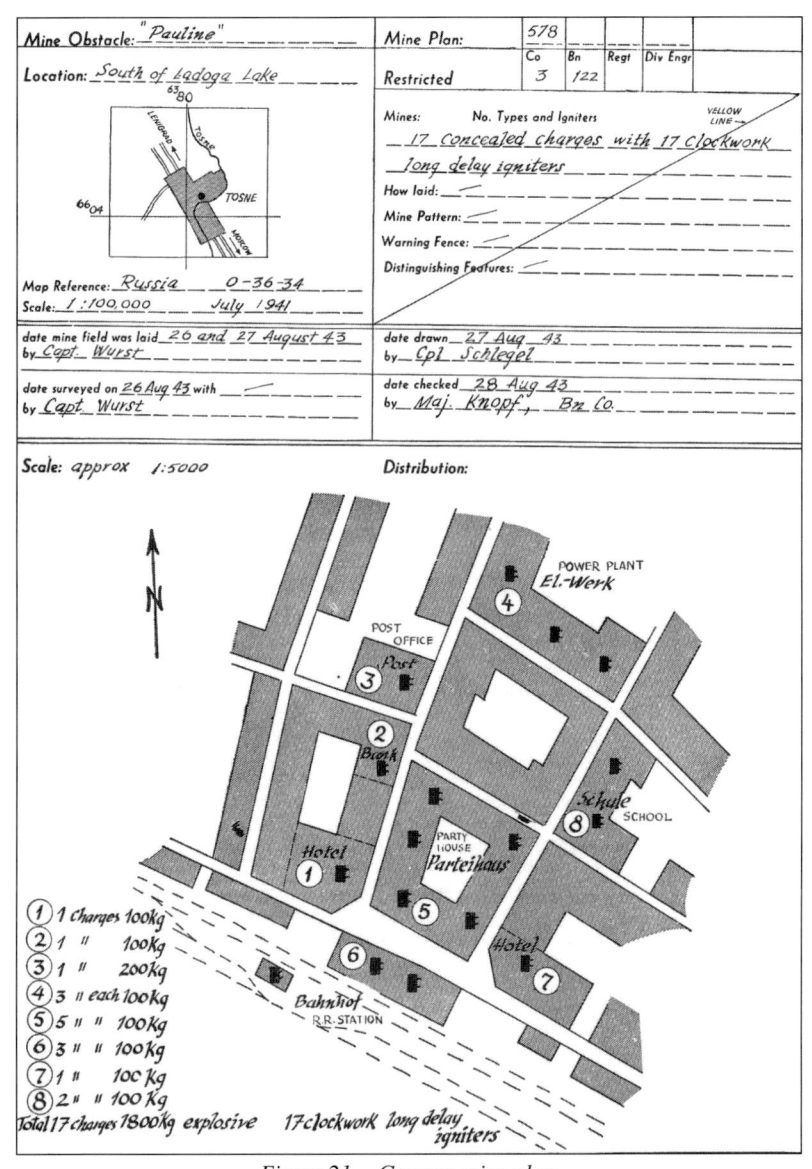

Figure 21.—German mine plan.

A mine sketch is a simplified mine plan used to transmit information on a minefield as rapidly as possible. It is not drawn to scale, and is drawn whenever the tactical situation, bad weather, or other circumstances prevent the preparation of mine plans.

Front-line troops receive from the engineers instructions or sketches showing the approximate location and extent of the minefield. These

CONVENTIONAL SIGNS FOR MINE MAPS

Terrain impassable for tanks

Antitank ditch or obstacle

Antitank mine field

Antipersonnel mine field

$\left.\begin{array}{l}3\\4\end{array}\right\}$ Mines per meter width of front

CONVENTIONAL SIGNS FOR MINE PLANS AND SKETCHES

Antitank mines

Index number to be used only if different types of mines are laid in the same field.

Improvised antitank mines

S-Mines

Stock Mines

Schu-Mines 42

Improvised antipersonnel mines

Small hidden charges

Large hidden charges

Observation mines

Booby-trapped mines

Taken-up or destroyed

Scattered mines

Deliberate mine field

Mines lying on the surface

Mines below the surface

Mine field cleared or destroyed

Gaps through mine fields

Dummy mine fields

Built-in hidden charges

Survey points (VP) and Fix points (**FP**)

Warning fences

Direction of enemy attack

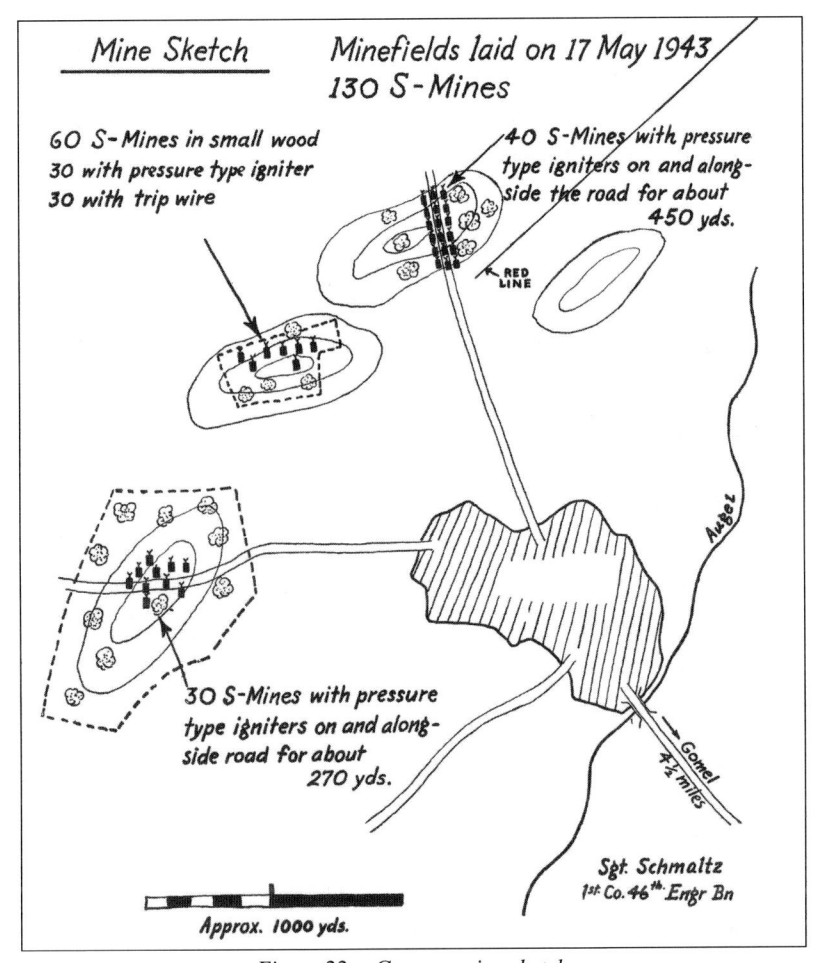

Figure 22.—German mine sketch.

sketches, as a rule, do not contain details on types of mines or igniters, pattern, and survey points.

Engineer units in charge of minefields keep records of changes in minefields under their care and keep these records with their units, while mine plans are turned over to the relieving units.

e. MINE REPORTS.

Armies generally designate certain areas for fields of scattered mines. In this case mine reports take the place of mine plans. Normally, mine reports contain:

(1) Number of the order authorizing scattering of mines.

(2) Designation of units scattering the mines.

(3) Name and number of field containing scattered mines.

(4) Map location of scattered minefield.

(5) Number of mines scattered, subdivided by types and igniters.

(6) Number and type of booby-trapped mines. kind of booby trap.

VIII. SPECIAL OPERATIONS

1. Town and Street Fighting

In attacking a town or village, the Germans employ flanking and encircling tactics. They attempt to cut off water, electricity, gas, and other utilities. While carrying out the flanking maneuver, they pin down the defenders with heavy artillery fire and aerial bombardment. When it is necessary to make a direct assault, the Germans concentrate all available heavy weapons, including artillery and air units, on one target. They favor as targets for their massed fire the forward edges of the community, especially detached groups of buildings and isolated houses. During the fire concentration the infantry assembles and attacks the objective immediately upon termination of artillery fire. Tanks and assault guns accompany the infantry, and with their fire immobilize any new enemy forces which may appear. They also support the infantry in sweeping away barricades, blasting passages through walls, and crushing wire obstacles. Guns and mortars are used against concealed positions, and antitank guns cover side streets against possible flanking operations. Machine guns engage snipers on roofs.

The immediate objective of the Germans is to divide the area occupied by the enemy. These areas then are isolated into as many smaller areas as possible, in order to deny the enemy freedom of movement.

Another form of attack employed by the Germans is to drive through a community and establish good positions beyond the town to block the retreat of the defender. Then they try to annihilate the enemy within the community.

The assaulting troops are divided into a number of columns and make a series of coordinated parallel attacks. Attacks from opposite directions and conflicting angles are avoided, since they lead to confusion and to firing on friendly troops. The columns are subdivided into assault and mop-up groups. Assault detachments of engineers, equipped with demolition equipment, flame throwers, and grenades, accompany the infantry. Where possible, the Germans blast holes through the walls of rows of buildings along the route of advance in order to provide the infantry with covered approaches. These passages afford protection for bringing up supplies and evacuating casualties. Houses are cleared of defenders by small-arms fire. Streets are avoided as much as possible by the Germans who infiltrate simultaneously through back yards and over roofs. They attempt to further the advance by seizing high buildings which offer dominating positions and wide fields of fire.

When compelled to advance through streets, the Germans move in two files, one on each side of the thoroughfare. The left side is preferred as it is more advantageous for firing right-handed from doorways. Consideration is given to the problem of fighting against defenders organized not only in depth but in height. Consequently the men receive specific assignments to watch the rooms, the various floors of buildings, and cellar windows. Side streets are immediately blocked, and at night searchlights are kept ready to illuminate roofs.

As soon as a building is occupied, the Germans organize it into a strongpoint. Windows and other openings are converted into loopholes and embrasures. Cellars and attics are occupied first in organizing for defense.

Even buildings which have been completely destroyed are kept under constant observation to prevent their reoccupation by the enemy. From occupied buildings the Germans deliver continuous machine-gun and rifle fire with the object of denying the enemy the opportunity to occupy alternate positions.

Underground corridors and sewers, which provide excellent cover for defenders, are attacked with determination. When immediate clearance or smoking-out is not possible, the entrances are barricaded, blasted, or guarded.

Aware that their tanks and assault guns are vulnerable to attacks by tank-hunting units, the Germans assign infantry to protect them. Barricades and obstacles are cleared by infantry and engineers. All able-bodied civilians, regardless of danger, are summoned to clear the streets of debris.

When a section of a town is occupied, the Germans close up all side streets leading from the occupied area, block all exits of houses, and then begin a house-to-house search with details assigned to special tasks, such as mopping up roofs, attics, basements, courtyards, and staircases.

2. Attack on Fortified Positions

The Germans realize the difficulty of attacking a strongly fortified enemy position and prepare such an attack well in advance of the actual operation. Before attacking a large and intricately fortified position covering a large area—a classical example was the assault on the Belgian Fortress Eben Emael—the Germans attempt to secure, in addition to information obtained through normal reconnaissance, its exact plan by the employment of agents and fifth columnists. When time permits, they construct a duplicate of the fortification on similar terrain well in the interior of Germany, as they did with Eben Emael. In building such installations for intensive rehearsal training of specially-organized combat teams, the Germans spare neither labor nor expense. These special combat teams usually consist of combat engineers, reinforced by infantry, antitank, and chemical warfare units.

The attack on the fortress usually is preceded by an intensive dive-bomber bombardment and long-range heavy-artillery fire. The purpose of these bombardments is to destroy obstacles and minefields, and to create bomb craters which not only provide cover for assaulting troops but also may be converted into firing positions. Often paratroopers land in close proximity to the fortification just prior to the assault, immediately establishing radio communication with the combat-team headquarters.

The climactic phase of the operation is the assault. Its primary objective is to get the engineers forward to certain selected works. During the approach, and until the engineers reach the fortifications, the artillery delivers fire of maximum intensity. Antitank guns lay direct fire against the embrasures, and chemical-warfare units employ smoke to blind forts and adjacent supporting works. The infantry covers the embrasures with rifle and machine-gun fire and remains in readiness to move forward and consolidate any success the engineers may gain. Engineers crawl forward, utilizing shell holes for cover. They are equipped with hand grenades, blocks of TNT, and submachine guns. Some groups use bangalore torpedoes, some pole-charges, while still others are armed with heavy flame throwers. With TNT and pole charges, they attempt to demolish systematically the weaker works, such as embrasures, ports, turrets, joints, and doors.

3. Combat in Woods

When attacking in woods, the Germans usually divide the area into company sectors. The Germans stress constant reconnaissance to discover the most weakly manned enemy position. This reconnaissance is carried out, even though company strength becomes temporarily reduced. Reconnaissance patrols usually move clockwise from their original position. The company commander reviews the reconnaissance reports in detail with his platoon and section leaders.

The company usually deploys in wedge formation when advancing. In order to achieve surprise, the Germans often leave the roads and advance cross-country.

As soon as the point of the wedge of the company is in sight of the enemy, the Germans creep forward to close-combat range, always keeping contact with adjacent and supporting units. The company then storms the enemy's position, using the greatest possible number of hand grenades, pole charges, and close-combat weapons. The advance elements attempt to break into the hostile position as deeply as possible, the body of the wedge widening the peneration on both sides. The company commander then decides whether to roll up the enemy position on the more important flank or to hold the ground until reinforcements arrive before continuing the attack.

Each platoon details at least one observer, armed with an automatic weapon, to neutralize enemy treetop snipers. The Germans believe that bursts of fire, rather than single shots, are necessary to deal effectively with such snipers.

The Germans consider fighting in wooded areas as the primary task of riflemen and machine gunners, since the employment of heavy-support weapons often is impossible. The Germans occasionally dismount heavy machine guns and use them as light machine guns. Antitank guns of small caliber and light infantry howitzers sometimes are brought forward manually, and when indirect fire is not possible they engage targets directly. Light mortars are employed individually. From Finnish troops, the Germans learned a successful method of using mortars in woods. The mortar observers, accompanied by a telephone operator, move with the advanced element. The line back to the mortar crew is exactly 200 yards long. One man is detailed to see that the line does not get hung on the way and as far as possible runs in a straight line. When the advanced element contacts the enemy, the observer judges the distance from himself to the target and adds the 200 yards to the mortar range. Bracketing of fire for adjustment is considered too dangerous because of the close proximity of friend and foe.

When the Germans leave a woods or have to cross a large clearing within the wooded area, the troops work themselves close to the edge of the woods. Then all the men leave the woods simultaneously, rushing at least 100 yards before seeking cover.

4. Combat in Mountains

a. GENERAL.

The German principles of combat in mountain areas correspond in general to those employed on level terrain. The peculiarities of mountain terrain, such as limited routes, extreme weather conditions, and difficult communications, necessitate additional considerations in the tactics employed. The greatest differences occur in the higher mountains, where the Germans utilize specially trained mountain troops, which include the renowned Tyrolean and Bavarian mountaineers.

The Germans emphasize that all operations will be of longer duration in mountainous country than in lowlands, and therefore make proper allowance for the factors of time and space. For every 330 yards ascent or 550 yards descent they add 1 hour to the time estimate for covering a given distance on the map. Movements, command, and supply in mountain areas represent sources of difficulty, according to the Germans.

b. TACTICAL CHARACTERISTICS OF MOUNTAIN WARFARE.

The Germans divide their units into numerous marching groups, which normally consist of a reinforced infantry company, an artillery battery, and an engineer platoon. In this manner the Germans counteract the danger of ambush, since each group is able to fight independently. The Germans locate their engineer units well forward with the advance guard so that they may assist in road repairs. The Germans realize that small enemy forces can retard the advance of a whole column and therefore they have single guns sited well forward. They also organize stationary and mobile patrols for flank protection.

The skill and leadership of junior commanders are severely tested in mountain warfare, as forces generally are split into small groups, the efficient command of which requires a high standard of training and discipline. Columns often are separated by large areas and impassable country, and since lateral communication is often very difficult, command of deployed units becomes much more complicated than over level terrain.

Normally supplies are organized in two echelons, the mountain and valley echelon.

The Germans make extensive use of high-trajectory weapons in mountain fighting, although antitank guns and heavy machine guns are used for covering road blocks. The effectiveness of the mountain artillery depends on carefully selected observation posts which are in communication with the single gun positions.

Radio is the primary means of communication, since the laying of telephone wire is not considered feasible.

c. MOUNTAIN TACTICS.

Attacks across mountains are made to protect the flanks of the main attack, to work around the enemy rear, or to provide flanking tire for the main attack. The Germans attempt to seize commanding heights and mountain passes.

The Germans select their assembly areas as close to the enemy as possible to make possible a short assault. Supporting weapons are attached to companies, and where feasible, to platoons.

In defense, the Germans organize their advance positions on the forward slope, while the main battle position with heavy-support weapons is located on the reverse slope. The greater part of a unit often is held in reserve. This necessitates the organization of relatively narrow sectors, which, however, results in an organization of ground favorable for counterattacks.

5. Winter Warfare

Many of the techniques of German winter warfare were developed from those of the mountain troops, which were adapted easily to conditions of extreme cold.

Ski patrols are the chief means of reconnaissance in snow-covered terrain. As a rule, the strength of the patrol is a squad, reinforced by infantry soldiers trained as engineers, artillery observers, and a communication detachment. In addition to normal reconnaissance missions, patrols obtain information as to the depth of the snow, load capacity of ice surfaces, and danger of avalanches. These ski patrols normally blaze trails by marking trees or rocks and by erecting poles or flags. Stakes are used to indicate the extremities of roads.

Under winter conditions, German units keep support weapons and artillery well forward while on the march. Their antitank weapons are distributed throughout the entire column. Ski troops are organized to guard the flanks. Sleighs are added for the transport of weapons and supplies.

The Germans assign to trail units the task of cutting tracks for the formations that follow. The strength of the trail unit of a company is one or two squads; that of a battalion up to two platoons. In difficult terrain their strength may be doubled. Trail units are divided into a number of trail detachments consisting of six to ten men, echeloned behind the first of the trail units. The march formation of ski troops is generally single file; usually parallel trails are used to reduce the length of the column.

In winter warfare, attacks with limited objectives are the rule. The Germans attempt wherever possible to combine frontal and flank attacks under conditions of extreme cold and snow. They employ support weapons as far forward as practicable. Attacks often are made by ski troops; because of the difficulty of transporting artillery, ski

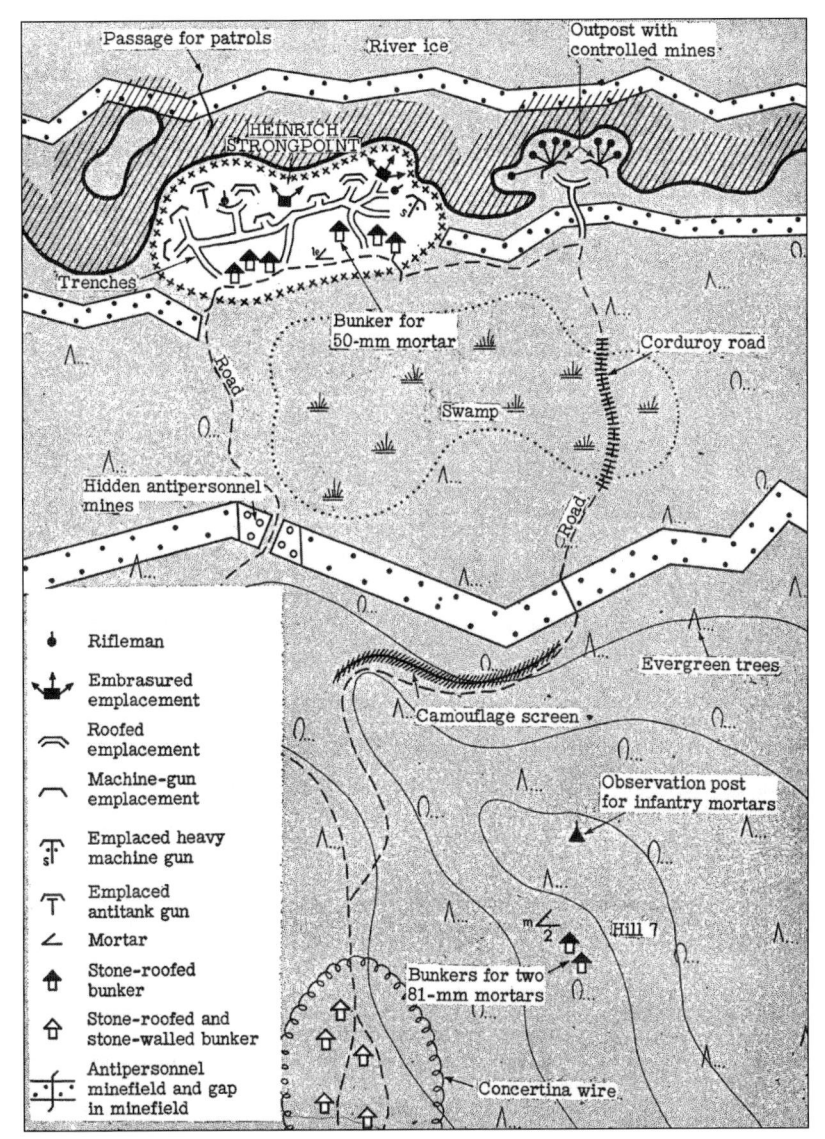

Figure 23.—Typical German winter position along a river in Karelia.

troops frequently have to dispense with artillery support. For this reason the Germans consider it all the more necessary to concentrate heavy and light infantry weapons at points of main effort and to coordinate high and flat trajectory weapons. When pack howitzers are available, they can be dismantled and brought forward on sledges. Assault guns can effectively support ski troops in snow under 16 inches deep. They either accompany the attack as far as road conditions allow or move into positions at effective range, not exceeding 3,500 yards, on specially cleared paths away from roads. They occupy their positions just before the attack. As a rule attached assault guns are employed in platoon and company strength; single commitment is avoided. Tank units are attached only in exceptional circumstances.

Organization of a defensive position in deep snow or on frozen ground takes considerable time, for it is necessary to move weapons into position, lay out foot paths and roads, and build strong outposts and strongpoints with all-around defense. Camouflage is particularly stressed under such conditions. Since normal units used as reserves in deep snow have only limited mobility, the Germans employ ski troops for reserves wherever possible. These ski units are used for immediate counterattacks which are directed, where possible, against the flank of the attacking enemy. The Germans also use the ski troops as raiding parties to harass the enemy's front and rear.

6. Partisan Warfare

a. GENERAL.

In order to understand German anti-partisan measures, it is necessary to discuss briefly the characteristics of Allied partisan organizations and their fighting techniques. The following discussion is based entirely on official German sources. The principles involved may be accepted by the Germans and find their way into actual practice in the near future.

b. TASKS OF PARTISAN WARFARE.

The Germans consider that the strategic mission of the Allied partisans was to inflict maximum injury on the German Armies of Occupation. Means employed to accomplish this task were as follows:
- Raids on individual drivers, resting places, troop and supply trains, headquarters, airfields, and ammunition and supply dumps.
- Demolition of bridges, roads, and railway tracks.
- Destruction of wire communications and railway systems.
- Destruction of industrial installations and crops.
- Terrorization of collaborators.
- Undermining the morale of locally recruited auxiliary troops.

c. ORGANIZATION OF PARTISANS.

(1) *General.*

Allied partisan forces were organized partly prior to German occupation and partly during the occupation when dispersed army personnel and civilians rallied around a common leader. The Germans list the following elements as sources for the recruitment of Allied partisan units:

- Remnants of Allied units which escaped destruction during military operations.
- Individual stragglers.
- Smaller units or individual members of Allied forces who infiltrated through the German lines.
- Allied parachutists.
- Escaped prisoners of war.
- Deserters from locally recruited auxiliary services.
- Civilian volunteers.
- Terrorized civilians.
- Women, who may be employed either as combatants or auxiliaries in the supply, medical, or signal services.

(2) *Russian partisan units.*

The Germans outline the composition of Russian partisan units as follows:

- Diversion groups of three to ten men.
- Combat units of 75 to 100 men, divided into two or three companies, each of two or three platoons.
- Battalions.
- Regiments, consisting of several battalions.
- Brigades of several hundred men.
- Units of several thousand men, of varying composition and fighting value.
- Divisional headquarters in command of operational groups.
- Corps headquarters controlling a certain number of brigades or regiments.
- Scouting and reconnaissance detachments.
- Higher intelligence headquarters.

In addition the Russians had signal organizations and special formations for demolition works and bridging, mounted detachments, and in some cases even artillery and antitank guns. A special ground organization was set up to serve the air forces which supplied the partisans.

(3) *French partisan units.*

The composition of the French partisan forces, according to the Germans, is:
- The squad consisted of four or five men.
- The platoon consisted of Approximately 30 men.
- The company had Approximately 100 men.
- A battalion consisted of three or four companies.

(4) *Weapons.*

The weapons of the partisans included rifles, light machine guns, light mortars, pistols, machine pistols, hand grenades, explosives and incendiary material. Battle units also had heavy machine guns, heavy mortars, and guns.

(5) *Uniforms.*

Partisans had no standard uniform. They wore civilian dress and the most diverse uniforms of their own and enemy forces. Stocks of uniforms were maintained by raiding German supply depots.

(6) *Camps.*

The partisans located their camping areas in inaccessible terrain such as dense forests, marshes, wooded mountains, and caves. The camps usually were fortified with field works, dugouts, tree platforms, and minefields. Normally a number of camps were set up in adjacent areas with alternate camp sites prepared. The camps were complete with dumps, slaughtering facilities, bakeries, dressing stations, and weapon repair shops. These camps were well guarded, the personnel of the guard being composed of partisans or of volunteers from nearby communities.

d. PARTISAN TACTICS.

(1) *General.*

Higher headquarters would issue directives of a general nature, and the leader of the smaller detachments would determine the method of execution. In accordance with their strategic function, partisans almost always avoided pitched battles. If trapped and forced to fight, they would follow different courses according to their strength. Large bands would fight it out, whereas smaller units endeavored to disperse by small groups, infiltrating through the lines of the attackers or disguising themselves as harmless and peaceful civilians. Defensively, partisans fought with determination, even ferocity, from behind well fortified and camouflaged positions, allowing the attackers to approach to close range, and then delivering concentrated surprise fire. In Warsaw, Polish partisans fought in building areas for weeks with much skill, inflicting considerable losses on the Germans.

(2) *Fighting methods.*

The partisans carried out guerrilla operations by conducting surprise raids against headquarters, camps, and weapon depots of the occupation army or by ambushing military transportation facilities, columns, or convoys.

When raiding columns, the partisans constructed obstacles along the route and then destroyed the first and last vehicle of the column. Railway trains were destroyed by exploding the roadbed or removing trackage. Troops trying to escape from trucks or trains were taken under fire. Before an attack partisans usually destroyed all telephone communications.

Partisan bands often changed their field of operations in order to carry out a given task, to secure supplies, or to evade discovery and prevent encirclement. Strict discipline on the march was maintained. Marches were generally at night, by routes known only to the local population. Partisan bands have marched 40 to 45 miles daily.

A common ruse was to give the appearance of greater strength by disseminating false information concerning partisan strength and armament. Partisans frequently used military uniforms of the occupation army for purposes of reconnaissance and requisitioning.

For successful operation the partisans needed secret agents who could be found in almost every village. The intelligence service of the partisans, of necessity, employed large numbers of women and children. In addition to collecting information, they were used as messengers between various partisan groups. (Local civilian populations usually were summoned to give assistance to the partisans.)

e. GERMAN ANTI-PARTISAN MEASURES.

(1) *General.*

The Germans divide the measures to be adopted against partisans into offensive action and passive defense measures. Both constitute specialized types of activity, brought about by the particular methods employed by the opponent. Since the partisans are inferior in armament, regular troops are inclined to underrate them and to act without due care and precaution. According to German doctrine, dealing with partisans demands increased vigilance, boldness, and aggressiveness in order to meet their extraordinary cunning and cruelty. In addition, the Germans considered that special training was necessary for their own troops in order to overcome difficult types of terrain such as woods, marshes, mountains, and built-up areas as well as for fighting at night or under winter conditions. Experience taught the Germans that the success of their anti-partisan measures depended on proper coordination between the German Armed Forces, *SS*, police, and the civil administration, ignoring, when necessary, territorial boundaries.

(2) *Offensive action.*

The Germans centralized the command and control of their anti-partisan measures and made arrangements in regard to the fields of responsibility between the supreme command of the armed forces, the *SS Reichsführer* and the Chief of Police. While in 1942-1943 the responsibility for the organization and direction of these measures rested with the supreme command in operational areas and with the *SS Reichsführer* in the so-called *Reichskommissariat*, the latter, upon acquiring increased powers, assumed complete responsibility.

Subordinate to the *SS Reichsführer* were the Chief in Command of Anti-partisan Formations (*Chef der Bandenkämpfverbande*) and the senior *SS* and police commanders, under whose command Army and Air Force units occasionally are attached.

All German troops and, in emergency, civilian establishments were prepared to engage partisans. The Germans employed the following army units in combat against partisans: divisions, independent task forces, cavalry units, motorized units, armored trains, service troops, emergency units, and locally recruited units. In addition to these organizations, the Germans employed Navy and Air Force units, as well as *SS* and police formations, including the security service (*Sicherheitsdienst*) and Secret Field Police (*Geheime Feldpolizei*).

The Germans emphasized the equipping of their anti-partisan units with easily transportable and quick-firing weapons, such as small arms, machine pistols, automatic rifles, rifles with telescopic sights, light and heavy machine guns, light and medium antitank guns, light infantry guns, light antiaircraft guns, and light flame throwers. Heavier artillery, antitank and antiaircaft guns, tanks, and armored cars, although they effectively strengthened the forces, could not be employed in all situations and terrain.

Clothing and equipage were designed to enable the unit to operate in all types of terrain and under all weather conditions.

The Germans realized the necessity of intensive intelligence work for successful anti-partisan measures. Higher commanders kept situation maps based on information concerning the partisans transmitted by all headquarters and units of the armed forces, and by civilian establishments. Systematic observations were made by security branches, such as the security service, the secret field police, and the military intelligence (*Abwehr*); information was disseminated and exchanged by adjacent establishments.

To provide all the necessary data for the tactical employment of anti-partisan forces, the Germans conducted intensive reconnaissance preceding their operations. This was carried out by collaborators, by mobile patrols. or by reconnaissance aircraft. Collaborators were the only means of reconnaissance employed when the projected operation had to be kept absolutely secret. The interrogation of prisoners was considered one of the best sources of information. The Germans therefore abandoned their original practice of shooting captured partisans on the spot.

When the Germans had adequate forces available they attempted to encircle and annihilate partisan units. The planning for this operation included the determination of the ground to be encircled, usually limited to the area actually known to be held by partisans. The assembly area was well removed from the areas to be encircled and was occupied in such a manner that the offensive intention was not disclosed. All forces taking part in the operation moved from the assembly area so that they reached the encircling lines at the same time. Lines were chosen which could be defended easily, such as lines of hills or forest paths across the direction of the advance.

The Germans normally kept sufficient local and mobile reserves armed with heavy support weapons. The consolidation of the encircling line was considered decisive for the outcome of the operation, because partisan fighting patrols tested the German lines with the object of breaking out through weak spots. The consolidation of the encircling line followed the usual principles for defense, such as disposing forward battle outposts, drawing up fire plans for light and heavy support weapons, fortifying strongpoints for all-around defense, and keeping mobile reserves in readiness. The precise method by which the encircled partisans were annihilated depended on the forces the Germans had available, on the terrain, and on the reaction of the trapped unit. One method employed was the gradual compressing of the encircled pocket, possible only in restricted areas, because in large areas the encircling forces could not advance at the same rate, thus creating gaps through which partisans could escape. Another method employed was to exert pressure from one side of the pocket while the troops on the opposite side confined themselves to defense. This method was used when the partisans held ground easy to defend, such as a river course, a ridge of hills, or edges of woods. The Germans also utilized powerful wedges and split up the defense pocket into several smaller pockets which were mopped up separately. Another method was to attack from the encircling line by strong assault groups formed from reserves, in cases where battle reconnaissance indicated that the partisans intended to defend their center position.

When time and forces for an encirclement were not available, the Germans attempted to defeat partisan bands by surprise attacks, intending to pursue and wipe out single detached groups. This method proved to be of value where a partisan formation had not been able to consolidate its position. The German actions therefore were dependent on the methods adopted by the partisans. When they committed their forces for battle, the German attack was carried out systematically with concentrated forces and fire. When the partisans attempted to avoid contact, the Germans pursued them frontally, while other units carried out enveloping movements. When the partisan formation dissolved, however, the Germans had to undertake reconnaissance to locate their new assembly area before a new action could begin. The primary target in such actions was the leader of the partisans, and the Germans usually placed a premium on the head of the leader to encourage his capture or death.

The Germans employed large numbers of heavy support weapons, tanks, assault guns, self-propelled antitank guns and heavy howitzers, when fighting the partisans in communities, and concentrated all available heavy weapons against a single objective. The tactics employed followed the German combat methods for street fighting and combat in towns.

The Germans also employed combat patrols against the partisans, copying the latter's methods with the object of harassing the bands and hindering their assembly and supply. Areas which were used regularly by the partisans for food requisitioning, or which they crossed on raids or sabotage expeditions, offered good opportunities for the deployment of German combat patrols. These patrols consisted of hand-picked, tough, well trained "Partisan Hunters" of platoon to company strength. They often wore civilian clothes or partisan uniforms.

(3) *Protection measures.*

Offensive anti-partisan operations were supplemented by vigilant protective measures designed to safeguard troops; road, rail, and waterway communications and traffic; industrial, administrative, and signal installations; and growing crops and forest preserves.

The Germans designated the security of troops as a command responsibility. As a rule the Germans did not billet units of less then company strength in lonely districts. All billets and camps were organized for all-around defense, and all guard rooms were made into strongpoints. Maps showing the local partisan situation were consulted before the march.

To protect railway installations the Germans organized special protection forces whose task included patrolling in addition to the protection of communication centers. Strongpoints were constructed inside all installations and often along the tracks.

The Germans also organized special forces for the protection of roads and waterways. These forces, *"Sicherungstruppen"*, were supplemented by military police detachments on the roads and water police on the waterways.

The ruthless methods employed by the Germans to maintain law and order are too well known to be discussed in this book. From the killing of individual suspects to the wholesale slaughter of whole communities and the burning of villages there is one long line of German atrocities and brutality.

f. GERMAN PREPARATION FOR PARTISAN WARFARE.

Beyond doubt the Germans prepared and are still preparing fanatical members of the National Socialist Party, *SS*, and armed forces for partisan activities as the territory occupied by the Allies increases. One of Heinrich Himmler's main duties as commander-in-chief of the Home Army is supervising the establishment of partisan organizations and stay-behind agents in areas about to be occupied by the Allies. The Germans have built up large stores of ammunition and supplies, particularly in the mountainous areas of the country, and have established at various localities training centers for future German *SS* Partisans. Women are included in this training program. As to the methods which the Germans are most likely to employ, no definite information can be revealed at this time. However, it is recommended that a study of the Allied partisan combat methods be made to obtain an approximate conception of possible German partisan activities.

7. Anti-Airborne Operations

The Germans consider the use of mines and wire obstacles particularly effective against enemy airborne operations. They block landing fields and areas where landings might be made with S-mines, stakes, ditches, piled earth, stone, and wood, nondescript vehicles without wheels, and other barricades. They also construct minefields and dummy minefields.

For the protection of important installations against airborne attack, the Germans organize an all-around defense, giving particular attention to covering avenues of approach with machine guns. Observation posts are set up on high points, such as church towers and terrain features to give early warning of hostile landings. Such posts are located also in rear areas, and are especially important in thinly populated localities, since wire communications are particular targets of enemy airborne troops. Special signals by church bells, drums, or bugles are arranged for alarming the German mobile reserve units. These units, specially organized for the task of counteracting enemy airborne invasions and partisan activities usually consist of motorized troops with machine guns and antitank guns mounted on their vehicles. Although the Germans consider it an error to delay in committing these units, they stress that care should be used to avoid enemy deceptive maneuvers such as the dropping of dummy parachutists.

The Germans usually withhold rifle fire until descending parachutists are at close range, using machine-gun fire at greater distance. They believe that fire is most effective immediately upon the landing of the hostile force, before a consolidation of position has been made. Enemy transport planes are considered particularly good targets since they must reduce speed just prior to the jump of the troops.

The Germans appreciate the importance of immediate action against airborne troops and when no alternative is possible they will commit inferior forces to combat the hostile aerial invasion, hoping to delay the attack until reserves can be brought up.

FORTIFICATIONS AND DEFENSES

Handbook on German Military Forces

I. DOCTRINE OF FORTIFICATIONS

1. Economy of Force

The Germans regard economy of force as a fundamental principle in designing fortifications. In conformity with this view, they employ defense works to permit a relatively smaller force to defend a line than otherwise would be required. German troops are taught that fortifications exist not for their personal safety but to enable them to fight more effectively, although fortified works, especially those of reinforced concrete, naturally make for a lower casualty rate. The German doctrine of offensive warfare therefore is not affected by the construction of strong systems of defense. Such systems in fact may be considered to be offensive rather than defensive in purpose, since they make it possible to concentrate a relatively large proportion of the field forces for action at any given point. In September 1939, the Westwall (Siegfried Line) [The Germans do not employ the term "Siegfried Line".] enabled the Germans to hold their Western Front with Approximately 20 divisions, while employing 40 to 50 divisions against Poland. These latter troops, in turn, could be concentrated on the northern and southern parts of the Polish border for a double envelopment of the Polish forces, since the vulnerable central sector due east of Berlin was protected by the so-called Oder Quadrilateral, a zone of permanent defense works constructed between 1935 and 1939. Again, in May 1940, the Westwall played an important role— this time in the envelopment of the Maginot Line—for, while the French border was held with relatively weak forces, the bulk of the *Wehrmacht* wheeled through Belgium and Luxembourg.

2. Organization of Defenses

a. PRINCIPLE OF DEPTH.

The Germans believe that a fortified line should consist of small works organized in great depth. This principle, embodied in the Westwall, is directly opposed to that of the French Maginot Line, which was a continuous wall of mammoth forts with little, if any, depth. The German idea is that a fortified line should not be employed to present an unyielding front to an attacker, but rather to act as a shock absorber and gradually slow down the advance. Then, when the attack has lost its momentum, counterattacks can be launched to destroy the penetration before the attacker has reorganized and consolidated his gains. The importance the Germans attach to counterattack is shown by the fact that they keep their best assault troops for this purpose and man the concrete positions with inferior soldiers. In order to impede the enemy's advance as much as possible and to facilitate the counterattack, troops manning the fortifications are taught to continue fighting even though their positions are overrun.

b. ZONES OF DEFENSE.

The Germans achieve depth in a fortified line by constructing successive zones of defense. In a typical segment of the Westwall, there are three independent zones from front to rear.

(1) The Forward Zone (*Vorfeldzone*) contains field fortifications including trenches, barbed-wire entanglements, machine-gun emplacements, and observation posts.

(2) The Main Defense Zone (*Grosskampfzone*) comprises fortified structures such as pillboxes, casemates and shelters, and antitank obstacles covered by antitank guns. In addition, this zone has intermediate areas, front and rear, in which isolated works are placed at critical points along natural avenues of enemy approach.

(3) The Rear Defense Zone (*Rückwärtige Zone*) is much the same as (2), but is not as strong.

c. STRENGTH.

It is the German practice to provide the weakest terrain with the strongest and most numerous defense works arranged in the greatest depth. But the defended zone is everywhere made as strong as the available resources permit, and no terrain is left entirely without the protecting fire of some permanent defense works.

d. SITING OF DEFENSE WORKS.

Pillboxes and casemates in a fortified line are so spaced as to provide interlocking fields of fire between adjacent works, yet they are not so close together that hostile artillery fire which misses one structure will hit another.

In view of the German theory as to the purpose of fortifications, the principle of "effect before cover" is applicable; that is, a wide field of fire is considered more important in siting a position than cover or concealment. When possible, pillboxes and casemates may be sited to permit both frontal and flanking fire. This is particularly important since German doctrine directs that fortified positions be held even after the defensive line is overrun by the enemy. The fire plan of field artillery may be coordinated with the belts of fire from the fortifications so that concentrations can be laid on the areas where fire coverage from the fortifications is relatively weak.

e. FIELD WORKS.

In accordance with German doctrine, concrete and steel pillboxes, and casemates are supplemented by extensive field fortifications to lend flexibility and mobility to the defense, to engage the enemy before he gets close enough to assault the main works, and to facilitate counterattack. Such field works are interspersed liberally throughout the Westwall and include minefields, obstacles, fire trenches for infantry weapons, and open emplacements for field artillery. Although open gun emplacements are intended to give supporting fire to pillboxes and casemates, they also can cover dead areas between the main works.

f. SHELTER.

The German practice is to provide all troops with adequate shelter against weather and hostile fire. Concrete pillboxes and casemates often have accommodations for the gun crews, and open field works have underground shelters or dugouts adjacent to the firing positions. In a fortified line, underground shelters are provided in the rear of the battle zone for the reserves who are assigned to the counterattack. This is in accordance with the German doctrine that reserves should be committed as a unit, fresh, and without having had to sustain casualties or endure the strain of hostile aerial and artillery bombardment while waiting to attack. Personnel shelters enable the reserves to be kept close to the front so they can begin the counterattack with minimum delay.

g. COMMUNICATIONS.

German fortified works commonly are linked together with communication trenches to facilitate relief of personnel, ammunition supply, and the care and evacuation of the wounded. In some cases a group of defense works is connected by a system of tunnels. Signal communication is provided by telephone cables buried in the earth, and often telephones communicate between the outside and the inside of a structure. Speaking tubes are installed in many of the works in case of failure of the telephone system.

II. CHARACTERISTICS OF FORTIFICATIONS

1. Principles of Design

The basic considerations in the design of German fortifications are fire effect, cover, and concealment. Fire effect has first priority; natural concealment is used as much as possible by blending positions with the surrounding terrain. Personnel and supply shelters, in the construction of which fire effect need not be taken into consideration, are completely below ground level, or as low as the water-table level permits. In order to present as small a target as possible to high-angle fire and bombing, emplacements, pillboxes, and casemates are built no larger than necessary to permit crews to operate their guns.

2. Construction

a. GENERAL.

All permanent, fortress-type works and many field works are of concrete reinforced with steel. Some field works, however, are of masonry, brick, or timber. Steel also is used in concrete structures for beams, turrets, cupolas, gun shields, machine-gun loopholes, and doors. These installations are prefabricated and are assigned code or model numbers. The concrete works themselves are designated by type number and are constructed from plans prepared in the Army Ordnance Office.

Figure 1—German three-way reinforcing rods and wooden forms ready for pouring in concrete.

b. THICKNESS OF CONCRETE.

The usual thickness of concrete walls and roofs is 6 feet 6 inches (2 meters); smaller thicknesses are found as a rule only in the small field works. In casemates the minimum thickness of the walls and roof is 6 feet 6 inches, and generally increases commensurately with the caliber of the gun.

c. REINFORCEMENT OF CONCRETE.

Most German concrete fortifications are reinforced with steel bars running in three dimensions to form cubes of 10- or 12-inch sides. The diameter of the bars, which are hooked at both ends, varies from 3/8 inch to 5/8 inch, the most common size being 1/2 inch.

The roof over the interior compartments in most structures is supported by steel I-beams, encased in the concrete roof. The size of the beams depends on length of the span. Steel plates laid between the I-beams, and resting on the lower flanges, form the ceiling of the structure. These plates prevent the inside of the roof from spalling if the structure sustains a direct hit from artillery shells or aerial bombs. In some cases, the roof is supported by reinforced-concrete beams instead of the steel I-beams, apparently to save critical material.

3. Open Emplacements

a. "TOBRUK" TYPE.

From experience in the North African campaign the Germans derived a type of open, circular pit lined with concrete, which they called a "Tobruk". Hitler subsequently ordered Tobruk pits to be used as defense works in the field, and instructions for building them were distributed down to divisions. A Tobruk pit, which consists of a concrete weapon chamber with a neck-like opening at the top, is built entirely underground. The concrete usually is reinforced. Tobruks vary in size, depending on the weapon mounted in them, but the diameter of the neck is kept as small as possible to reduce the risk of direct hits. Instructions to German troops insist that a Tobruk should not have a concrete roof, since this would reveal the position to the enemy. A board of irregular shape, used as a lid, camouflages the circular opening and keeps out rain.

b. TOBRUK 58c.

The most common type of Tobruk is designated *58c* by the Germans (see Figure 2). It also is called a *Ringstand* from a rail that runs around the inside of the neck. The rail provides a track for rotating a machine-gun mount, thus giving the gun a 360-degree traverse. This type of Tobruk has an ammunition chamber, which also serves as an underground entrance.

c. MORTAR EMPLACEMENT.

A Tobruk used as a mortar emplacement, such as Type *61a* (see Figure 3 overleaf), is larger than a *Ringstand* and has a concrete base in the

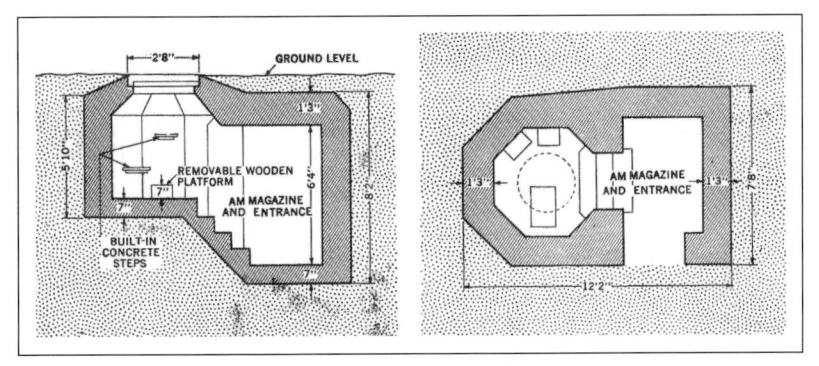

Figure 2.—Ringstand.

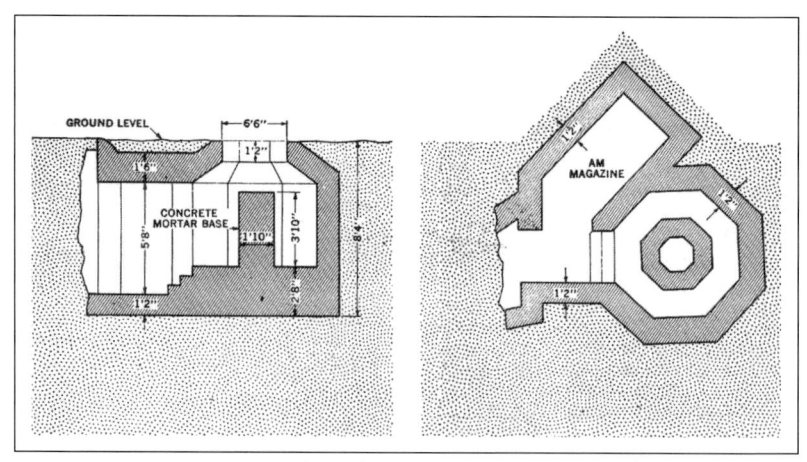

Figure 3.—Tobruk for 50-mm mortar.

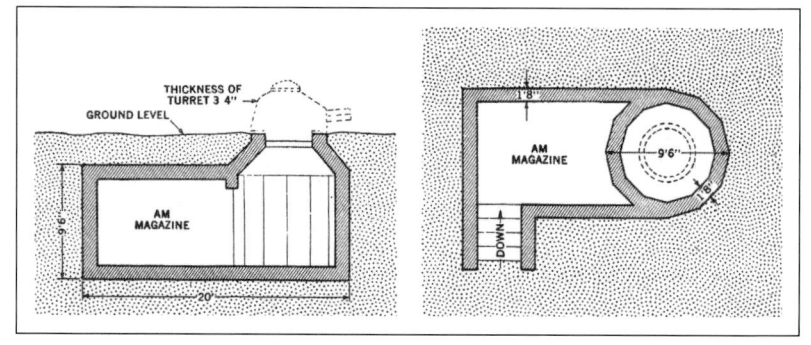

Figure 4.—Panzerstellung.

center of the pit for mounting the mortar. This type also is combined with an ammunition magazine.

d. PANZERSTELLUNG.

The German also have used a Tobruk as a base for a tank turret, usually taken from a French *Renault 35* (see Figure 4). Such an installation, called a *Panzerstellung*, has a turret armed with an antitank gun and a machine gun coaxially mounted. The turret is bolted to a circular metal plate, which is rotated by hand on wheels around a track in the top of the pit affording a 360-degree arc of fire.

4. Pillboxes and Casemates

a. CONSTRUCTION.

(1) *General.*

Although the Germans have a number of types of pillboxes and casemates, most infantry and artillery weapons are installed in open rather than closed emplacements. In accordance with German doctrine, pillboxes and casemates are supported by open field works. Pillboxes may have wall and roof thicknesses of as little as 2 feet; indeed, some of the earliest examples built on the Westwall had thicknesses of only 1 foot. This was increased, however, until all pillboxes had at least the standard thickness of 6 feet 6 inches. Casemates, which house guns of large caliber, have at least the standard thickness of 6 feet 6 inches. Pillboxes and casemates usually have a stepped embrasure to prevent bullets from richocheting into the gun opening. In addition, a steel gun shield may close the opening.

(2) *Type 630 pillbox.*

Figure 5 overleaf illustrates a newer type of pillbox for the light antitank gun, Type 630, which has 6 feet 6 inches of concrete in the roof, front wall, and side walls; and 6 feet 4 inches in the rear wall. A machine gun firing through a loophole in the rear provides close defense, and a loophole in the interior wall at the foot of the stairs has an opening for a machine gun to keep attackers from entering the pillbox. A Tobruk pit is built into the front wall as an observation or machine-gun post.

(3) *Local designs.*

Some pillboxes are found which do not conform to standard types and are apparently of local design. The Germans often construct a pillbox by mounting a steel turret on an open emplacement, and many pillboxes along the French coast were built by mounting a tank turret over a pit in the sea wall.

(4) *Type 685 casemate.*

Figure 6 overleaf illustrates a typical German casemate, Type 685, for the 210-mm or 128-mm antiaircraft guns. Most casemates are of this simple design, consisting of a gun room with recesses for ammunition, but some may provide quarters for the gun crew. The walls and roof of Type 685 are 11 feet 5 inches (3.5 meters) thick. The embrasure permits a traverse of 60 degrees and an elevation of 45 degrees. A number of similar casemates (Types 683, 684, 686, 688, 689, 690, 692, and 694) have embrasures for a traverse of 90 degrees or 120 degrees. Additional protection and camouflage are afforded by banking the

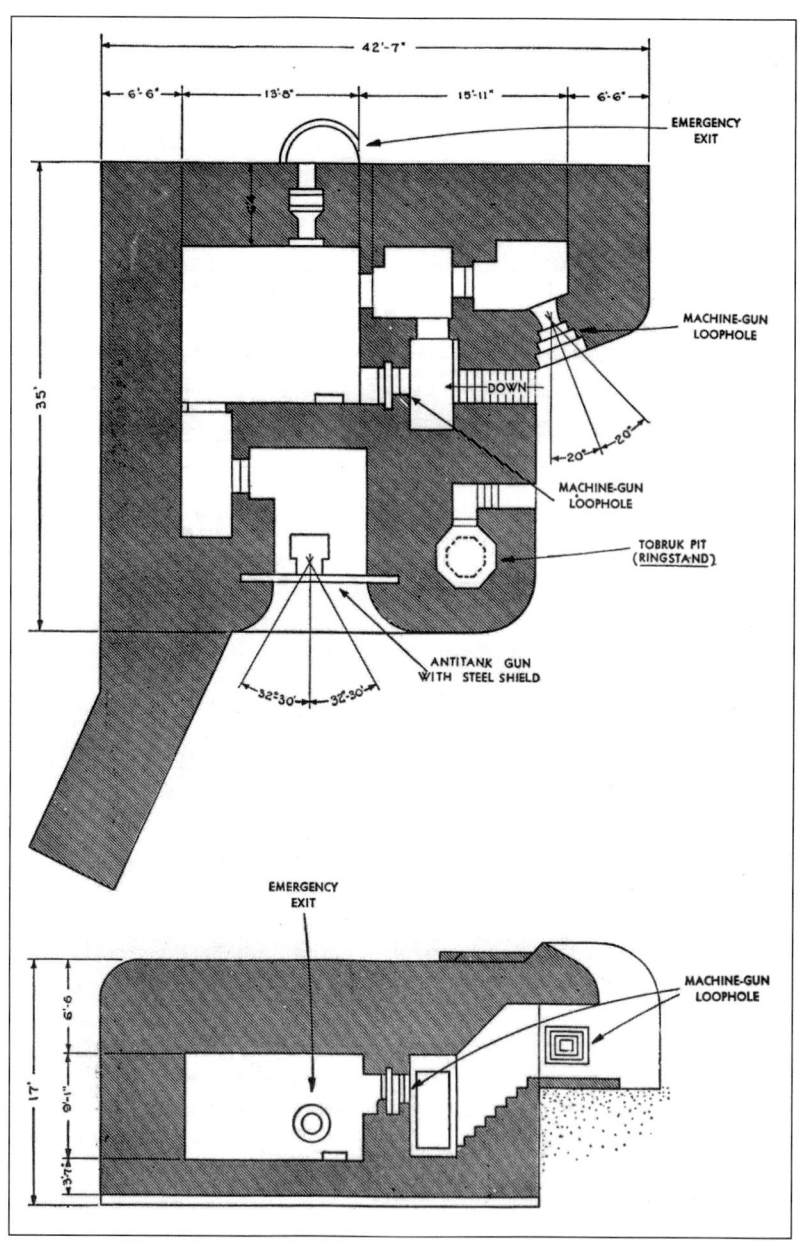

Figure 5.—Typical pillbox, Type 630 for light antitank gun.

sides and by covering the top with a 2-foot 6-inch layer of earth.

(5) *Type 677 casemate*.

The Germans often site a casemate to deliver flanking fire. For this purpose, a wing wall is provided on the side toward the enemy to

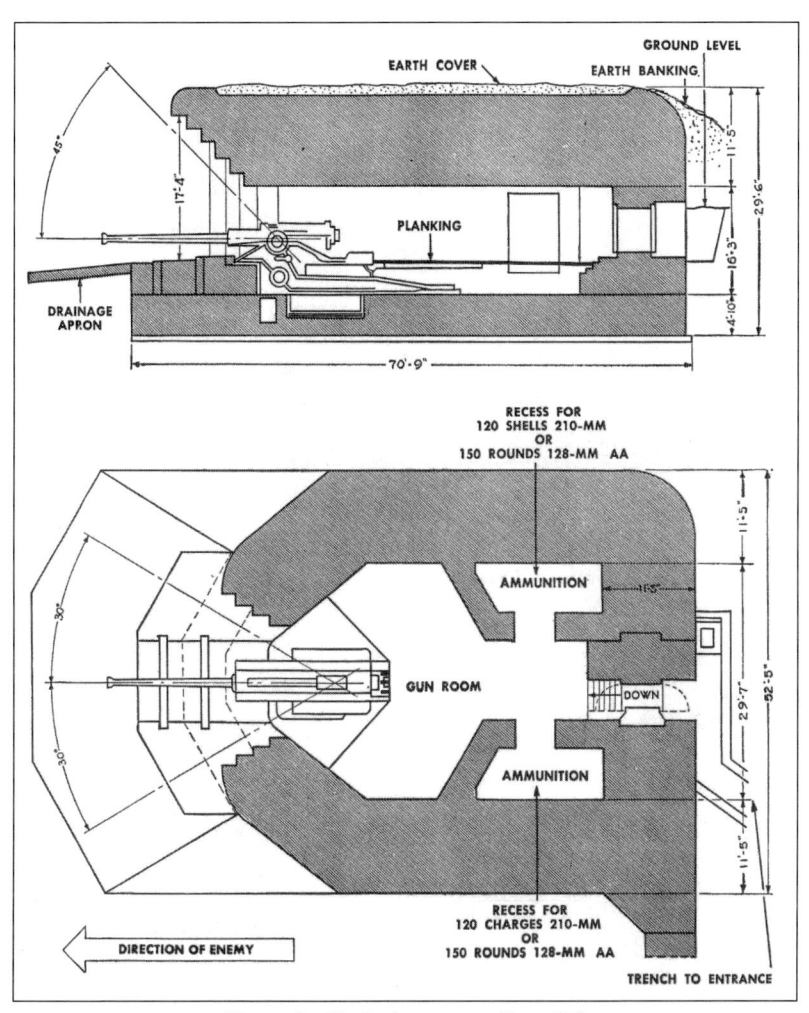

Figure 6.—Typical casemate, Type 685.

shield the embrasure from hostile fire, as in Type 677 for 8-cm gun (Figure 7 overleaf). The length of this wing wall depends on local ground conditions. The casemate can be built to fire to the right flank by constructing the wing on the opposite wall.

b. CAMOUFLAGE.

To camouflage pillboxes and casemates, earth is banked over the sides and top, the entrance in the rear is covered by a flat-top, and a camouflage net may be hung in front of the embrasure while the gun is not in action. In the case of small pillboxes, branches may be placed over the embrasure. The Germans also conceal pillboxes and

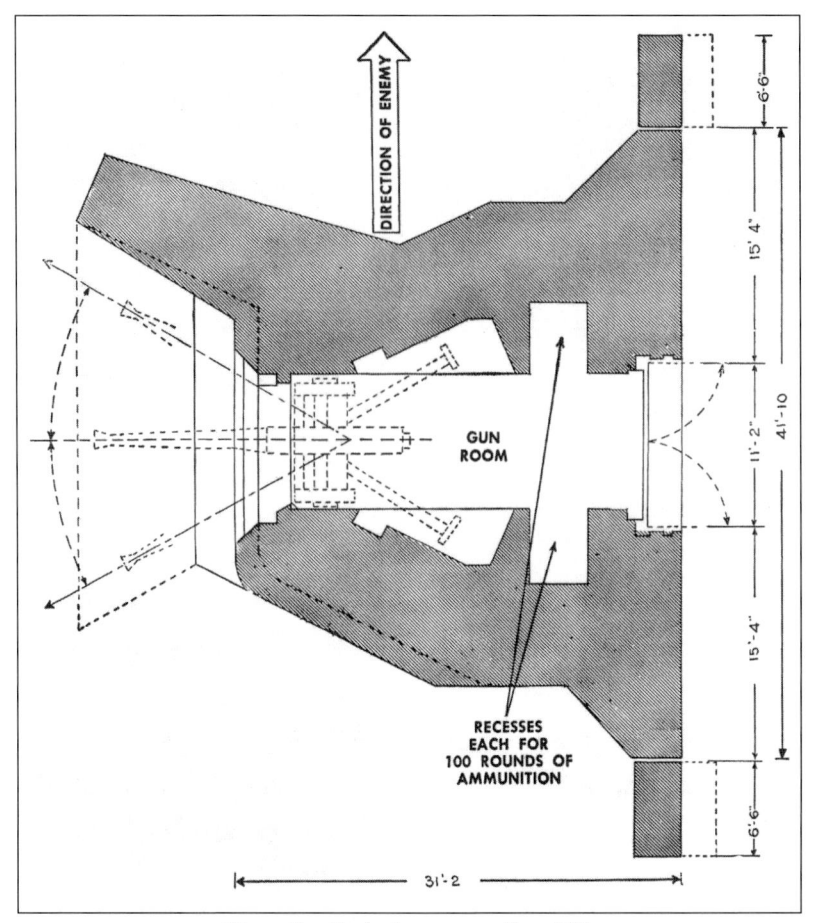

Figure 7.—Typical casemate, Type 677.

casemates by enclosing them in wooden structures resembling ordinary houses. The guns then are fired through false doors or windows, or a section of the wall over the embrasure is made to drop out of the way. Pillboxes also are built into the cellars of existing buildings. German instructions to troops insist that no cover or concealment should obstruct the field of fire of the gun.

c. MOBILE STEEL PILLBOX.

The Germans also have a mobile steel pillbox (Figures 8, 9, 10, 11) which is armed with a machine gun and manned by two men. The pillbox is constructed in two sections, a top half and a bottom half welded together. The top half contains the aperture, armament, air vents, and entrance door. Thickness of the armor varies from 5 inches

Figure 8.—Emplacing a mobile steel pillbox.

Figure 9.—German mobile steel pillbox.

Figure 10.—Interior of mobile steel pillbox showing machine-gun mount.

Figure 11.—View through doorway of mobile steel pillbox.

at the aperture to 2 inches at the sides and top. The bottom half is only 3/4 inch thick, but is entirely below ground level when the pillbox is in place.

The total weight of the pillbox without armament or ammunition is 6,955 pounds. The aperture, which is seen on the left side in the photograph, is divided into two parts: the lower part for the gun barrel; the upper for sighting. The machine gun has an arc of fire of

Approximately 45 degrees. The aperture cover is operated manually from the interior of the pillbox. Entry is through a door, 20 inches by 23 inches, in the back of the upper half. The door can be seen hanging open on the right in the photograph. There are two openings in the top for periscopes, one over each seat.

A blower operated by a pedal provides ventilation. The ventilation holes on both sides of the pillbox also enable an axle to be passed through the pillbox. Wheels are fitted to the ends of this axle and the pillbox can then be towed upside down. When installed for use, the sides and top are banked to blend with the surroundings.

5. Shelters

a. PERSONNEL SHELTERS.

(1) *Purposes.*

The Germans stress the desirability of adequate shelter for all troops. Personnel shelters are built in the rear of a fortified line to house the reserves and also in individual defense positions for the troops who man the installation. Some personnel shelters have accommodation for two sections, or 20 men, but it is the usual German practice to house no more than ten men in one shelter. A personnel shelter also may serve as a headquarters, a command post, a medical station, or a signal center. Types provided for these purposes are similar in design and differ mainly in size and number of interior compartments.

(2) *Type 621 shelter.*

One of the most common personnel shelters (Type 621, for one infantry section) is illustrated in Figure 12. It is constructed of reinforced concrete, with the standard wall and roof thickness of 6 feet 6 inches (2 meters). It is entirely underground, with an earth covering of 1 foot over the roof. Seventeen steel I-beams, 13 feet 2 inches long, support the ceiling over the interior compartment. Steel plates resting on the bottom flanges of the I-beams provide an all-steel ceiling. Shorter I-beams support the ceiling over the doors and entrance stairs. A camouflage flat-top is stretched over the trench in the rear, which gives access to the entrance stairs, to conceal it from air observation. To secure one side of the flat-top, a row of hooks is cast into the roof along the rear side of the shelter. A Tobruk pit is built into one of the

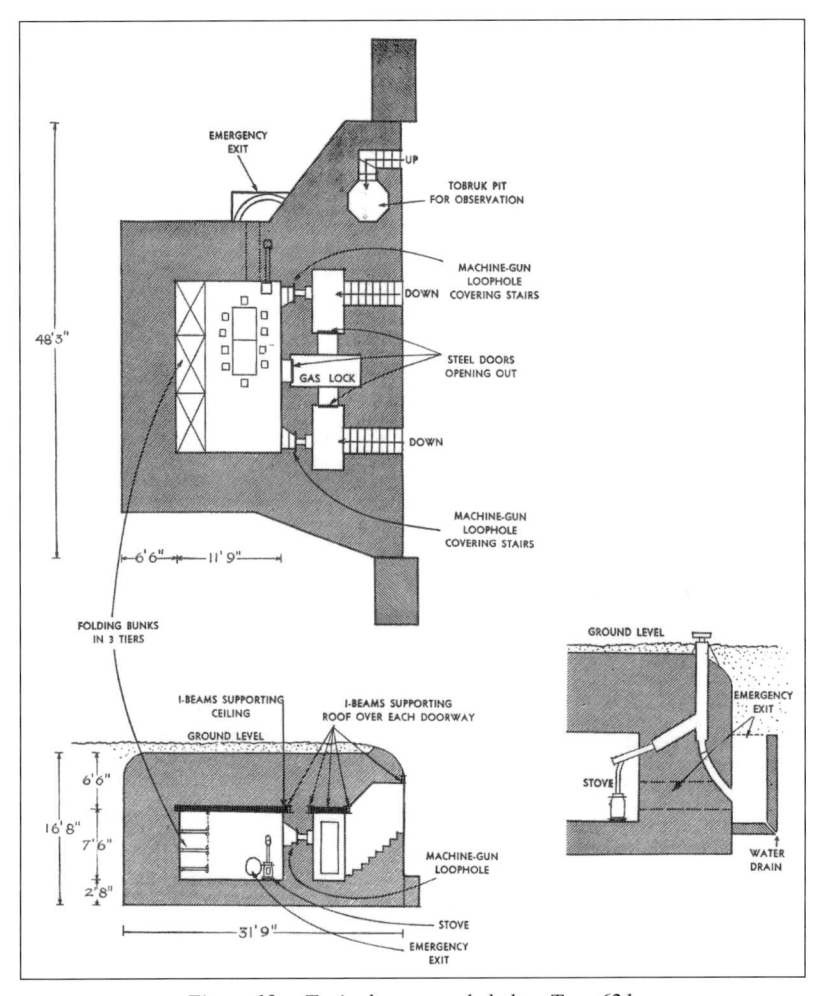

Figure 12.—Typical personnel shelter, Type 621.

wings in the rear for observation. Although the shelter accommodates only ten men, two entrances are provided to enable the section to deploy rapidly when they are to man their positions nearby or launch a counterattack. Each of the entrance stairs is covered by a machine gun firing through a loophole in the interior wall at the foot of the stairs. Both entrances converge into a gas lock, sealed by three steel doors each about 1 inch thick. All doors open out. To make the chimney grenade-proof, the vertical shaft is continued below the stovepipe and curved outward into the space used for the emergency exit. A grenade dropped into the chimney thus will not enter the shelter

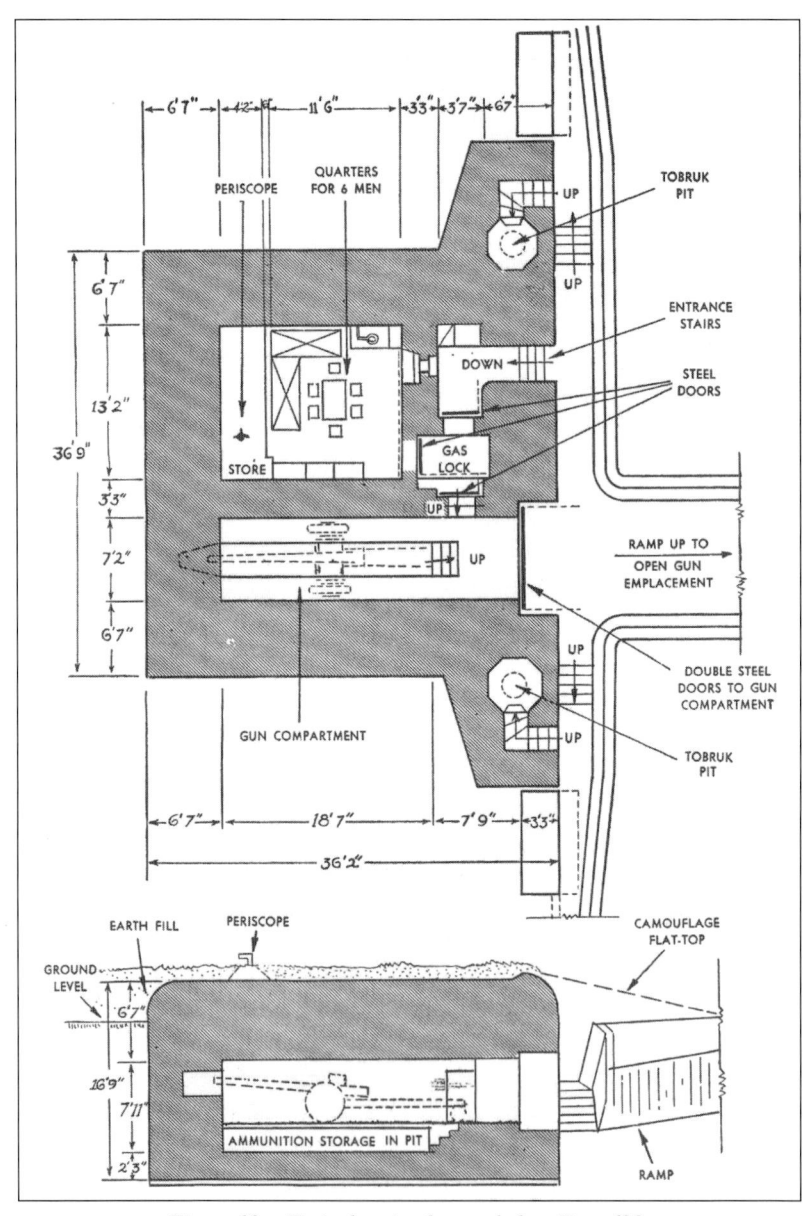

Figure 13.—Typical antitank-gun shelter, Type 629.

but will fall outside the sidewall and explode harmlessly. There are four ventilation shafts opening into the rear wall between the entrance stairs. Two of these are dummies to mislead attackers who try to introduce smoke into the ventilating system to drive out the occupants. The blower is driven by an electric motor, but the Germans usually make provision for manual operation as well, in case of power failure. To communicate with the interior of the shelter, there is a telephone at the head of one of the entrance stairs, and both a telephone and a speaking tube in the Tobruk. A telephone cable, buried deep in the earth, leads to neighboring installations.

(3) *Modifications in design.*

Modifications may be made in the plans in order to adapt the shelter to the terrain; for example, the Tobruk may be built into the other rear wing, or the emergency exit may be installed in the opposite side wall. Such changes are at the discretion of the local construction authorities. Some types of personnel shelters have a steel turret built into the roof for observation, and sometimes a machine gun is mounted in the Tobruk. However, the Germans insist that troops are not to fight from shelters, but are to use them merely as protection while not engaged in combat.

b. ANTITANK-GUN SHELTERS.

The Germans provide a special shelter for antitank guns and their crews. Figure 13 shows a typical antitank gun shelter, designated by the Germans as Type 629. Accommodation for the men is similar to that of other personnel shelters, but there is a separate compartment for the gun and ammunition. Double doors in this compartment enable the gun to be rolled out of the shelter and up a ramp (slope 1:6) to an open emplacement in the rear of the shelter from which it fires over the top of the shelter. The shelter has two Tobruk pits (*Ringstände*) in which machine guns appear to he installed to support the antitank gun. These Tobruks are connected by telephone and speaking tube to the crew's quarters. The shelter also is equipped with a periscope.

c. COMBINED SHELTER AND EMPLACEMENT.

Figure 14 overleaf shows a personnel shelter, with an open emplacement on the roof, known as Type L 409 ("L" stands for *Luftwaffe*). This type will accommodate nine men, and its details are similar to those of other personnel shelters. Type L 409 is for a light antiaircraft gun, but in others of the L 400 series the roof emplacement is used to mount a searchlight (L 411), or a radio direction finder (L 405). In some types, the shelter below the gun emplacement is used as a battalion command post (L 434) or an ammunition magazine (L 407).

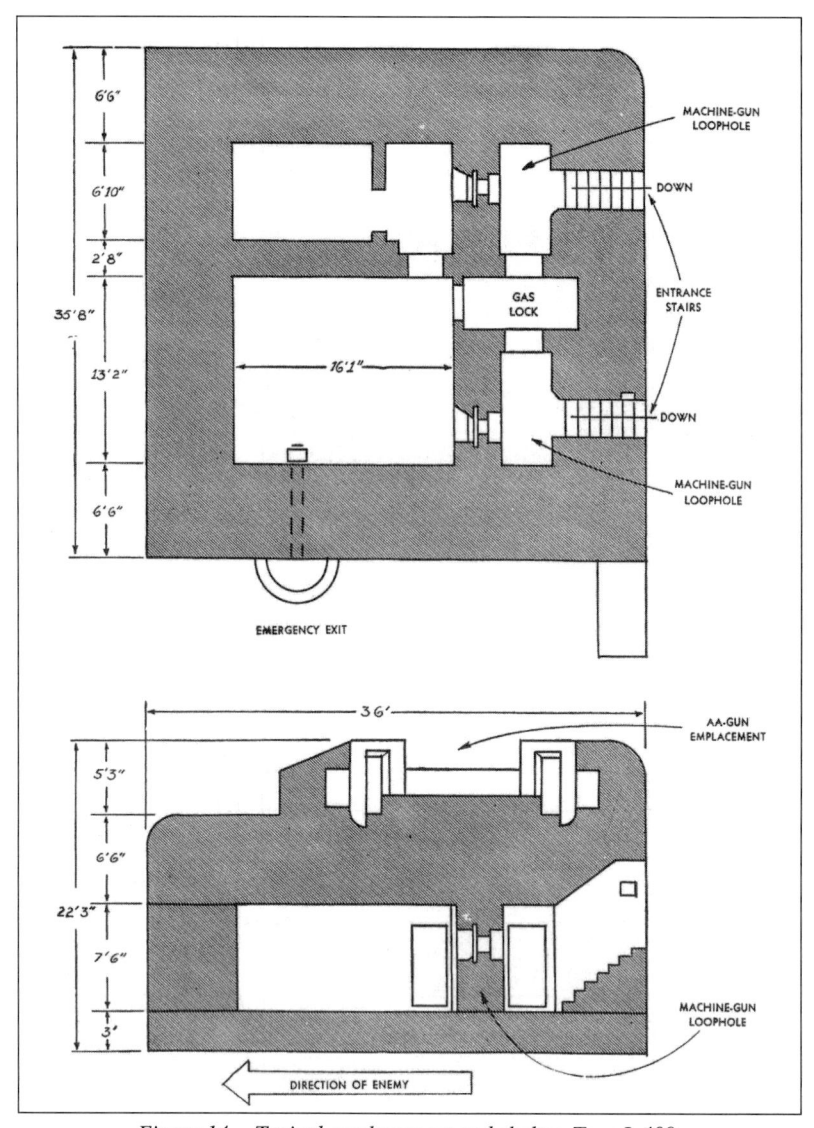

Figure 14.—Typical emplacement and shelter, Type L 409.

d. SUPPLY SHELTERS.

The Germans have designed a number of shelters for the storage of supplies, ammunition, and drinking water. Such types usually are entirely underground and may have a wall and roof thicknesses less than the standard 6 feet 6 inches. Shelters designed for supplies may have only one entrance; they ordinarily have no emergency exit, machine-gun loopholes, or Tobruk.

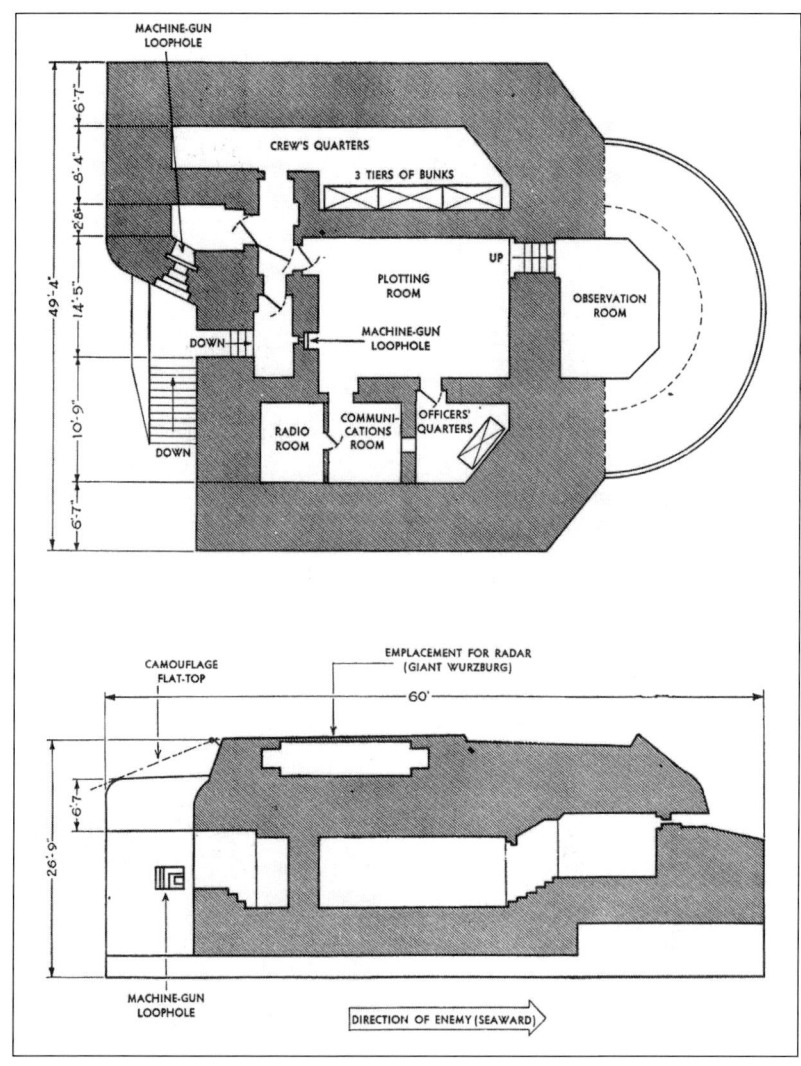

Figure 15.—Typical observation post, Type 636.

6. Observation Posts

The Germans have constructed special works of reinforced concrete as coast artillery observation and command posts. A typical observation post, Type 636 (for Army Coast Artillery), is shown in Figure 15. Separate rooms are provided for observation, plotting, radar, officers' quarters, and enlisted men's quarters. A Giant *Würzburg* radio direction finder is mounted in the emplacement on the roof. For close defense, there are two machine-gun loopholes covering the rear

Figure 16.—Dragon's teeth showing concrete foundations.

entrance: one in the exterior wall, and one in the interior wall at the foot of the stairs. There are quarters for two officers and nine enlisted men, but since this does not accommodate all the personnel on duty at the observation post, a personnel shelter for one section is built nearby.

Field artillery observation posts in a permanent defense line are similar to personnel shelters, with the addition of a steel cupola for the observer.

7. Obstacles

The German tactical use of obstacles differs from the U.S. Army in that they install them within the main battle positions. Obstacles are covered by fire from concrete pillboxes and open emplacements. The Germans employ both fixed and movable permanent obstacles, constructed for the most part of steel, concrete, or both. The most common types are described below.

a. ANTITANK OBSTACLES:

(1) *Dragon's teeth.*

A prominent feature of the Westwall is the anti-tank obstacle called by the Germans "dragon's teeth". These are truncated pyramids of reinforced concrete, arranged in irregular rows of four or five. The height of the teeth varies successively from 2 1/2 feet in the first row on the enemy side to 5 feet in the rear row, so that a tank is made to belly on the obstacle. The teeth are cast in a concrete foundation running from front to rear, and sometimes also along each row, to prevent the teeth from being toppled over.

Dragon's teeth are usually sited in long continuous lines, broken only where roads pass through the line of obstacles and where the terrain is considered unsuitable for tank activity.

(2) *Elements C*.

The Germans adopted the Belgian de Cointet antitank obstacle, more often called "Elements C", which is illustrated in Figure 17. Here a number of units have been fastened together to form a continuous antitank wall, but since the units have rollers in the front and rear, the Germans also use them singly as movable blocks.

(3) *Curved-rail obstacle*.

Similar to the "Elements C" is the curve-rail antitank obstacle, which the Germans used extensively along the Westwall. The curved rail, which slopes upward to a steep angle at the rear, faces the enemy, so that tanks attempting to climb over the obstacle tip over backward. It usually is made in sections 6 feet high, 3 feet wide, and 10 feet long.

b. ROAD BLOCKS.

(1) *Steel bars*.

A road passing through a barrier may be closed by horizontal steel bars arranged successively higher in reinforced concrete slots or by steel rails set upright into the road.

(2) *Tetrahedra*.

The Germans also block roads with tetrahedra, which consist of steel frames or solid concrete blocks with four faces. The height of a tetrahedron varies from 2 1/2 to 4 1/2 feet, and its purpose is to belly a tank.

Figure 17.—German Elements "C" joined to form antitank obstacles.

Figure 18. Slots in the concrete pillars hold steel bars across the road to serve as a block.

Figure 19. Concrete tetrahedra used as antitank obstacles.

Figure 20. Road passing through Westwall dragon's teeth. Note (right) uprights for horizontal steel bars which can be placed across the road as a block.

Figure 21. Line of dragon's teeth of Westwall. Note steel antitank barrier set an at angle in the road.

c. BARBED-WIRE OBSTACLES.

A German double-apron fence is illustrated in Figure 22 overleaf. The fence is 4 to 5 feet high. (2) Knife rests, or *chevaux de frise*, strung with barbed wire, can be seen to the right of the fence where the road passes through the obstacles. The Germans call knife rests "Spanish

Figure 22. German double-apron barbed wire. Note knife rests in the background (right).

riders" and use them as road blocks. German knife rests are about 4 feet high and have angle-iron or timber frames. (3) Concertina wire (*S-Rolle*) often is used by the Germans either in single, double, or triple coils. Sometimes it is wired to concrete posts, fixed on top of walls, and interwoven with double-apron fences or between concrete dragon's teeth. (4) The Germans also use an obstacle consisting of trip wires (*Stolperdraht*) arranged about 30 feet in depth. The wire is stretched from 4 to 8 inches above the ground on irregular rows of wooden pickets. The interval between pickets in rows is 10 to 13 feet and between rows 7 to 10 feet.

SUPPLY, EVACUATION AND MOVEMENTS

Handbook on German Military Forces

I. HIGHER ORGANIZATION OF SUPPLY

1. Government Direction of Production

Economic production in Germany is highly centralized and under complete governmental control. The Ministry for Armament and War Production (*Reichsminsterium für Rüstung und Kriegsproduktion*) under Albert Speer controls production of war material and ammunition; the Ministry for Economic Affairs (*Reichswirtschaftsministerium*) controls all other industrial production; the Ministry for Food and Agriculture (*Reichsministerium für Ernährung and Landwirtschaft*) controls food production. Among them these three ministries control production of the supplies for the German Armed Forces and, within the limitations imposed upon Germany by the insufficiency of her natural resources and the effects of the Allied advances and bombings, they are able to gear the production to the needs of the war machine.

2. Estimate of Needs and Placing of Orders.

These are essentially General Staff functions, since they involve present and future operations and capabilities. On the basis of High Command directives, the detailed estimates of the number or quantity of each article of supply are worked out by the technical branches concerned; they must be adjusted to the industrial, labor, and raw material potentialities of the nation.

The three branches of the Armed Forces and the *Waffen-SS* establish their procurement policies on an interservice basis and coordinate the use of railways, canals, and roads for military traffic. In addition, for a number of particularly critical items, the Armed Forces High Command has created special depots which are at its exclusive disposal (*Verfügungsdepots*).

Within the Armed Forces the lines of distinction between the Armed

Forces High Command and the Army High Command are not always clearly drawn as far as procurement is concerned. The Army being by far the largest branch of service, the Army High Command (*OKH*) may in certain cases act for the Armed Forces High Command (*OKW*). In addition, the Army procures a proportion of the materiel used by the *Waffen-SS*. The bulk of this materiel is transferred to the *Waffen-SS* through Army channels of supply and not through the system of depots maintained by the *SS* High Command.

3. The Army

The Army High Command (*OKH*) has the direct responsibility for a well functioning army supply system. Its wartime supply functions are divided into two distinct phases. The first phase, centering in the Zone of the Interior, is supervised by the Chief of Army Equipment and Commander of the Replacement Army (*Chef der Heeresrüstung* and *Befehlshaber des Ersatzheeres*) who organizes the procurement of supplies; their storage in suitably placed depots, and their distribution to home and field units. It is his duty to interpret high command directives on an overall nationwide basis. He determines what proportion of supplies is essential for use by garrison and training units, what amount can be sent to the front, and which areas are in the best position to issue supplies. The second phase, the Field Army (*Feldheer*) supply system, is controlled by the Chief of Field Army Supply and Administration (*Generalquartiermeister* or *Gen. Qu*) who administers the sending of requisitions to depots established by the Chief of Army Equipment and the receipt, storage, and distribution of supplies in the field.

II. SYSTEM OF SUPPLY WITHIN GERMANY

1. Production, Acceptance, and Distribution of Equipment and Ammunition

[The term "equipment" refers to the group of materials handled by equipment depots and equipment parks, in contrast to the individual equipment (*Ausrüstung des Mannes*) and clothing handled by clothing depots.]

a. DESIGN AND DEVELOPMENT.

This is primarily the responsibility of the Army Ordnance Office (*Heereswaffenamt*). In particular, its Weapons and Equipment Manufacture Group (*Amtsgruppe für Industrielle Rüstung*) includes ten sections dealing with the main categories of equipment and known as armament sections one to ten (*Waffenrüstungsabteilungen 1-10*). The Ordnance Office also has a Research Branch (*Forschungsabteilung*) and a Development and Testing Branch (*Amtsgruppe für Entwicklung und Prüfung*). In addition, the Ordnance officer coordinates the activities of numerous army-owned and semi-private research institutes and experimental stations throughout the country. Suggestions for design and development are also received from all the technical branches of the Army.

b. PRODUCTION.

On the production side the Ministry for Armament and War Production has, through its regional Armament Inspectorates, a decisive influence on the selection of firms, coordination of armament orders with other orders, labor questions, and scheduling and supervision of production.

c. ACCEPTANCE.

The testing of weapons, equipment, and ammunition, and their acceptance at the armament factory is the responsibility of the Army Acceptance Organization (*Heeresabnahmewesen*), which is a branch of the Army High Command/Army Ordnance Office (*OKH/Heereswaffenamt*). There is one Acceptance Inspector (*Abnahmeinspizient*) in each corps area who acts through acceptance commissions located at the factories.

d. DISTRIBUTION OF EQUIPMENT AND AMMUNITION TO ARMY UNITS.

After acceptance at the factories, the flow of equipment and ammunition to field and home units may take a number of routes:

- By way of equipment and ammunition depots.
- By way of equipment parks.
- Direct from the factory.
- Through SS depots.
- Through special Armed Forces High Command (*OKW*) depots.

2. Main Army Equipment and Ammunition Depot Organization

a. ORGANIZATION.

The agencies responsible for most of the storage, issue, and repair of equipment and for the storage, issue, and salvaging of ammunition belong to a separate branch of the Army, the Ordnance Branch (*Feldzeugwesen*). The branch is headed by the Chief Army Ordnance Officer (*Feldzeugmeister*), who works through his staff, the Ordnance Inspectorate (*Feldzeuginspektion*) in the General Army Office (*Allgemeines Heeresamt*). From the Ordnance Inspectorate the chain of command leads through three regional commands, called Ordnance Groups (*Feldzeuggruppen*), with headquarters in Berlin, Kassel, and Munich, to the Ordnance Headquarters (*Feldzeugkommandos*) which are at the level of the corps areas but not affiliated with the latter. There is one Ordnance Headquarters in each corps area, where it controls a varying number of equipment and ammunition depots. The Ordnance Headquarters is the lowest controlling agency for the storage and issue of equipment and ammunition, and it is important to note that below this level equipment and ammunition are handled by two separate types of depots. The Ordnance Headquarters is designated by the number of the corps area. It and the depots it controls are not, however, part of the corps area organization, although the auditing of their books is done by the Corps Area Administration.

In addition to the Ordnance Headquarters designated by the corps area numbers, there exist an Ordnance Headquarters XXX, which is in charge of a great number of subterranean ammunition depots in central Germany, and a special Tank Ordnance Headquarters (*Panzer-Feldzeugkommando*), created in 1943 in order to centralize the supply of all types of armored fighting vehicles and their spare parts throughout Germany.

b. EQUIPMENT DEPOTS.

Army Equipment Depots (*Heereszeugämter* or *HZa*) and Army Branch Equipment Depots (*Heeresnebenzeugämter* or *HNZa*), controlled by the Ordnance Headquarters, handle weapons, tanks, tank spare parts, motor transport, assault boats, radio apparatus, anti-gas equipment,

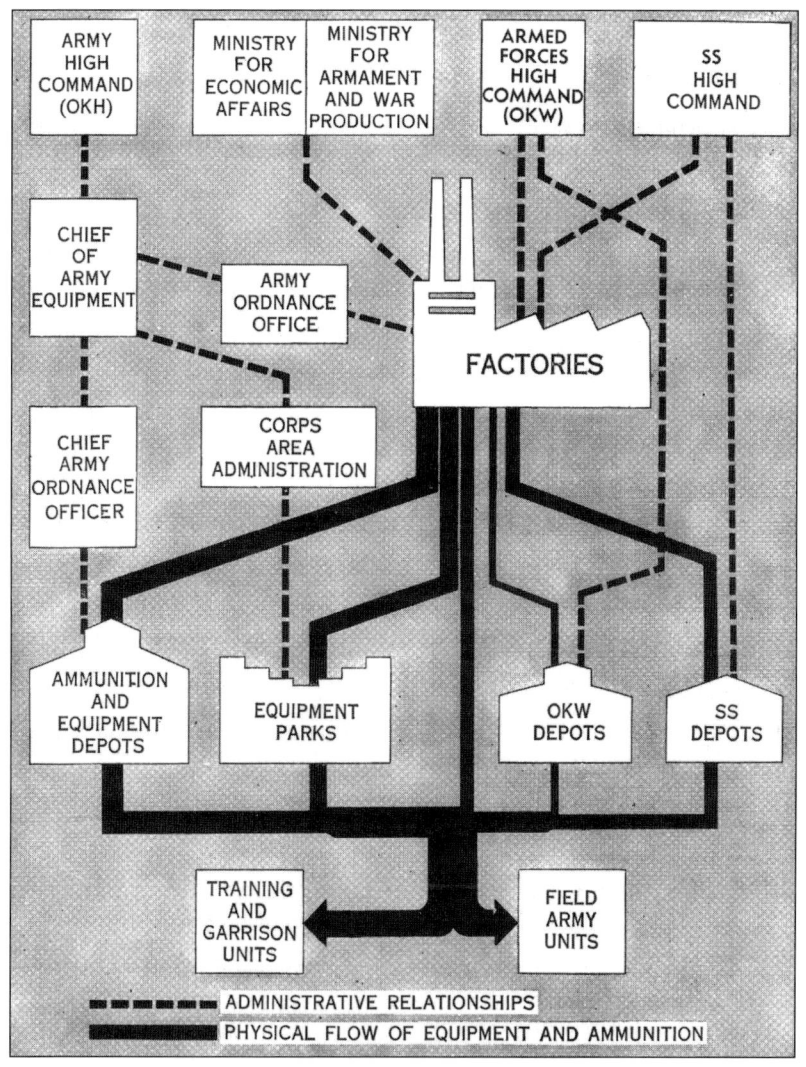

Figure 1. Supply of equipment and ammunition

bridge materials, special clothing, concrete mixers, and manuals, as well as many other articles. They do not furnish ammunition, fuel, rations, clothing (other than special types), medical and veterinary equipment, horses, or most types of individual equipment.

Although the depots normally handle a great variety of items, they sometimes concentrate upon particular types. For example, air reconnaissance has revealed large concentrations of motor transport at the Chemnitz *HZa* and large artillery stores at the Berlin-Spandau

Figure 2. Munchen Main Equipment Depot (HZa). Photographed early in 1943 after a bombing. Chief features are four very large standard equipment buildings (averaging 590' x 155') typical of Main Equipment Depots; 21 smaller standard equipmrnt buildings (about 270' x 70'); a gun park containing about 300 guns; and about 55 miscellaneous buildings in the depot area.

HZa. It is known, however, that these centers also hold large stores of equipment which cannot be seen from the air. When depots specialize in only one type of equipment, they have their specialties incorporated into their names. This group includes the Army Tank Equipment Depot (*Heerespanzerzeugamt* or *HPZa*) at Magdeburg-Königsborn; the

List of known Army Equipment Depots (branch depots not included):		
Corps Area	Installation	Location
I	HZa	Königsberg
II	HZa	Güstrow
II	HZa	Stettin
III	HZa	Berlin-Spandau
III	HZaNachr	Berlin-Schöneberg
IV	HZa	Chemnitz
IV	HZa	Xaumburg
V	HZa	Ulm
VI	HZa	Unna
VII	HZa	Freilassing
VII	HZa	Ingolstadt
VII	HZa	München
VIII	HZa	Breslau
VIII	HZa	Brieg
VIII	HZa	Kotzenau
IX	HZa	Kassel
X	HZa	Hamburg-Glinde
XI	HZa	Hannover
XI	HZa	Magdeburg
XI	HPZa	Magdeburg-Königsborn
XII	HZa	Mainz-Kastel
XIII	HZa	Amberg
XVII	HZa	Wels
XVII	HZa	Wien
XVIII	HZa	Hall (in Tirol)
XVIII	HZa	Salzburg
XX	HZa	Graudenz
XXI	HZa	Posen

Army Branch Tank Equipment Depots (*Heerespanzernebenzeugämter* or *HPNZa*) at Frankfurt an der Oder, Naumburg, Bielefeld, Breslau, Oppeln, Kassel, Altengrabow, and Olmütz; the Army Signal Equipment Depot (*Heereszeugamtnachrichten* or *HZaNachr*) at Berlin-Schöneberg; and the Army Branch Signal Equipment Depot (*Heeresnebenzeugamtnachrichten* or *HNZaNachr*) at Wien-Strebersdorf (Vienna).

In addition to their storage functions, the *HZa* and *HNZa* adjust and test newly arrived materials and repair damaged equipment. Several of the *HNZa* are engaged almost entirely in repair functions, and most equipment depots maintain ordnance, signal, and engineer equipment servicing sections for inspecting newly manufactured equipment and repairing damaged equipment. Specialization in items repaired may occur: thus the tank equipment depots repair tanks and armored vehicles which have been so badly damaged that they cannot be repaired in the field.

The equipment depots are staffed by officers and noncommissioned officers of the Ordnance Branch who control the workers, usually civilians or soldiers serving a prison sentence.

An Army Equipment Depot is divided into two parts: the storage depot (*Lager*) and the workshop (*Werkstatt*). The storage depot is subdivided in departments (*Bezirke*), each of which specializes in one type of equipment. Depending on the type of equipment handled, the workshop will have separate sections like an arms workshop (*Waffen-Werkstatt*), an optical instruments workshop (*Optische-Werkstatt*), etc.

The Army Equipment Branch Depot is organized along the same lines as the Army Equipment Depot.

Associated with equipment depots are the Armed Forces depots attached to motor transport manufacturers. The main function of these is to facilitate transfer of vehicles from factories to equipment depots.

As the number of *HZa* is relatively limited and as they are perhaps the largest supply depots within Germany, they have been heavily bombed by Allied air forces. Despite much damage, the *HZa* have shown great recuperative powers. The importance of many *HZa*, however, has diminished, while that of the *HNZa* has increased through the dispersion of stores among the smaller supply centers.

c. AMMUNITION DEPOTS.

Army Ammunition Depots (*Heeresmunitionsanstalten* or *HMa*) and Army Ammunition Branch Depots (*Heeresmunitionsnebenanstalten* or *HMNa*) are the main German centers for the storage and issue of ammunition. Frequently they concentrate upon particular types of ammunition; for example, the *HMa* at Münsterlager, Celle, Dessau, Augsburg, and Neu Ulm are probably principal centers for the storage of chemical warfare ammunition.

In addition to storing and issuing ammunition, the *HMa* and *HMNa* participate in its production by assembling and filling shells and by manufacturing fuzes and other accessories.

Like the equipment depots, the ammunition depots are staffed by personnel of the Ordnance Branch. Employees include civilians, soldiers, prisoners of war, and large numbers of foreign laborers. An *HMa* usually has the following departments:

- Administration
- Manufacture (filling and packing of shells)
- Shipping
- Personnel administration
- Motor pool

Because of the large number of well distributed ammunition depots, many of them underground, Allied air attacks have not interfered materially with their functioning. But the increased number of foreign laborers employed by these depots undoubtedly has lowered their productivity.

d. AREA OF DISTRIBUTION.

Generally a depot is allocated a definite geographical distribution area. The depot may be the exclusive German distributor of a particular item, or it may be merely the exclusive distributor within an allotted area. Thus the Ulm *HZa* distributes types of engineer equipment to all areas, while it issues Czech small arms to less than half of the corps areas. In addition, a depot may be assigned to a particular army for the supply of materiel replacements and the repair of its damaged materiel.

3. Corps Area Equipment Park Organization

a. GENERAL.

The corps area parks complement the equipment depots in the handling of motor transport, engineer equipment, and anti-gas equipment, and form the principal centers for the distribution of horses, veterinary equipment, and medical equipment. Requisitions for repairs reach the parks from both home and field units. Primarily, a park is responsible for servicing its allotted area; usually it also is charged with the supply and maintenance of designated units of the Field Army.

b. MOTOR TRANSPORT PARKS.

The Home Motor Transport Parks (*Heimatkraftfahrparke* or *HKP*) received damaged or impounded vehicles such as motorcycles, trucks, and staff cars, but do not handle tanks and armored vehicles, or any newly manufactured vehicles. There are several such parks in each corps area, controlled by the Home Motor Maintenance District Headquarters (*Heimatkraftfahrbezirk*) of the corps area.

Most of the vehicles repaired belong to the *Wehrmacht* and the *SS*; but vehicles from semi-military and civilian agencies are also repaired. The *HKP* vary widely as to the number of vehicles repaired daily and the average number held. At Berlin, where there are three *HKP*, each may hold as many as 1,000 vehicles and repair 30 daily. Most *HKP*, however, hold 60 to 100 vehicles and have a daily repair average of probably less than ten vehicles. Since many of the vehicles received are damaged beyond repair and must be scrapped or cannibalized, the daily repair averages are not as inefficient as may appear upon initial glance.

A typical *HKP* includes a reception point where vehicle defects are inspected, a large number of workshops, and final inspection points where vehicles are either dispatched to units or sent back for further repair. Frequently there are branch administrative offices (*Zweigstellen*) and workshops located as far as 40 miles from the Main Office (*Hauptstelle*). The number of *HKP* in a corps area varies greatly: at one time Corps Area VI was known to have nine *HKP*, while Corps Area V had only four.

Supplies of spare parts and tires are procured from Central Spare Parts Depots (*Zentralersatzteillager* or *ZEL*) and Tire Depots (*Reifenlager*) which are controlled by the *HKP*, or direct from factories.

c. MEDICAL PARKS.

The Berlin Main Medical Park (*Hauptsanitätspark*) and the Corps Area Medical Parks (*Wehrkreissanitätsparke*)—one per corps area— receive all types of surgical apparatus, drugs, bandages, and dispensing equipment from factories and hold them for distribution to hospitals within their corps areas and to Medical Collecting Parks (*Sammelsanitätsparke*). The latter are subsidiaries of the Corps Area

Medical Parks and serve as collecting points for medical supplies to the field forces. In certain cases the Main Medical Park and Corps Area Medical Parks may deliver their supplies direct to the field forces.

The Main Medical Park in Berlin occupies a special position as it holds critical drugs and hospital supplies for distribution to Corps Area Medical Parks and Medical Collecting Parks. In addition it tests newly developed pharmaceutical preparations and medical equipment and furnishes the Corps Area Medical Parks with "standard" samples of medical equipment. The Main Medical Park is subordinate to the Chief Army Medical Inspector, and the Corps Area Medical Parks are subordinate to the Corps Area Surgeons; there is thus no chain of command leading from the Main Medical Park to the Corps Area Medical Parks.

There is also a group of Medical Booty Collecting Points (*Sanitätsbeutesammelstellen*) that are centers for the collection of captured medical equipment. This is sorted and tested prior to shipment to the medical parks for distribution.

Although the medical parks participate in the repair of damaged medical equipment, it is very likely that much of the recovery work is done by the manufacturers.

d. VETERINARY PARKS.

Veterinary supplies are procured through veterinary parks. The Army Main Veterinary Park (*Heereshauptveterinärpark*) is directly subordinate to the Veterinary Inspector. It is the central procurement agency for veterinary equipment. Upon orders from the Veterinary Inspector the Army Main Veterinary Park will supply the Home Veterinary Parks (*Heimatveterinärparke*) with veterinary equipment either directly or by ordering it for these parks from commercial manufacturers. Horse-shoeing equipment is always ordered from civilian factories.

The Home Veterinary Parks, numbering one in each corps area, and the Army Main Veterinary Park receive veterinary equipment such as shoeing equipment and veterinary medicines from the manufacturers and issue it to units and horse hospitals, besides repairing and salvaging damaged veterinary equipment received from units.

e. HORSE PARKS.

Young horses purchased by the Army are sent to Army Remount Depots (*Heeresremonteämter*) for their maintenance and training until they are suited for field use. They are then delivered direct to corps area riding schools, to home units, or to Home Horse Parks (*Heimatpferdeparke*) which forward horses to Field Army units.

As the occupied territories formerly furnished most of the horse replacements for the German Army, their loss will greatly aggravate the already noticeable animal shortage at a time when the German Army is becoming increasingly dependent on horse transportation.

f. OTHER PARKS.

A sizeable number of Home Engineer Parks (*Heimatpionierparke*) have been reported functioning within the corps areas, supplying home and field units with engineer equipment. In addition, there are at least five special Home Fortress Engineer Parks (*Heimatfestungspionierparke*), which supply fortress engineer units; a number of Home Railway Engineer Parks (*Heimateisenbahnpionierparke*); and a few Gas Defense Equipment Parks (*Gasschutzgeräteparke*).

4. Clothing and Individual Equipment Supply Organization

a. PROCUREMENT AND ADMINISTRATION.

Procurement of raw materials is the special function of the Armed Forces Clothing and Equipment Procurement Office (*Wehrmachtbeschaffungsamt Bekleidung and Ausrüstung*) at Berlin. The raw materials are then issued to the clothing depots of the three branches of the Armed Forces and the *SS* which manufacture, store, and issue clothing and various items of individual equipment. In addition, damaged, captured, or impounded clothing may be sent to the clothing depots for repair and reissue.

In the Army the highest administrative echelon is a section in the staff of the General Army Office (*Allgemeines Heeresamt/Stab/Bekleidung*) which issues all directives on clothing and equipment. It controls the work of the Army Clothing Depots (*Heeresbekleidungsämter* or *HBA*). Within each corps area the supply of clothing is directed by Section E (*Sachgebiet E*) of the Corps Area Administration

(*Wehrkreisverwaltung*). Thus for all practical purposes the normal Army Clothing Depot is subject to a dual control.

b. CLOTHING DEPOTS.

One or more Army Clothing Depots are generally found in each corps area. These *HBA* receive raw materials from which they manufacture clothing, insignia, shoes, tents, canteens, blankets, and other items of individual equipment. They exercise control over Testing and Repair Sections (*Verwaltungsund Instandsetzungabteilungen*), which repair damaged clothing, and Army Clothing Dumps and Branch Dumps (*Heeresbekleidungslager und Nebenlager*), which assist in the forwarding of clothing to the field forces.

Specialized types of clothing depots include Collecting Points for Winter Clothing (*Sammel-Stellen für Winterbekleidung*), Army Clothing Repair Workshops (*Heeresbekleidungsinstandsetzungswerkstätten*) which presumably do not handle newly manufactured clothing, and Clothing Processing Centers (*Durchschleusungsstellen*) which are believed to be centers to which reinforcements requiring refitting are routed before their departure for the front. In addition, rations depots may store and issue clothing for certain areas.

c. AREA OF DISTRIBUTION.

The *HBA* issues clothing and individual equipment to units within its assigned territorial area. Many *HBA* are also responsible for the supply of particular armies in the field; to facilitate the transfer of clothing to field units, issues may be made to Army Clothing Dumps and Branch Dumps which in turn issue clothing and individual equipment to field units.

5. Rations Supply Organization

a. GENERAL.

The German Army depends for its transportation to a large extent on horse-drawn vehicles; forage is therefore considered to be of equal importance to human rations, and the supply of both is handled by the same agencies. In the following description of the supply organization the term rations includes forage as well.

b. PROCUREMENT AND ADMINISTRATION.

The over-all planning of rations and the laying down of policies for

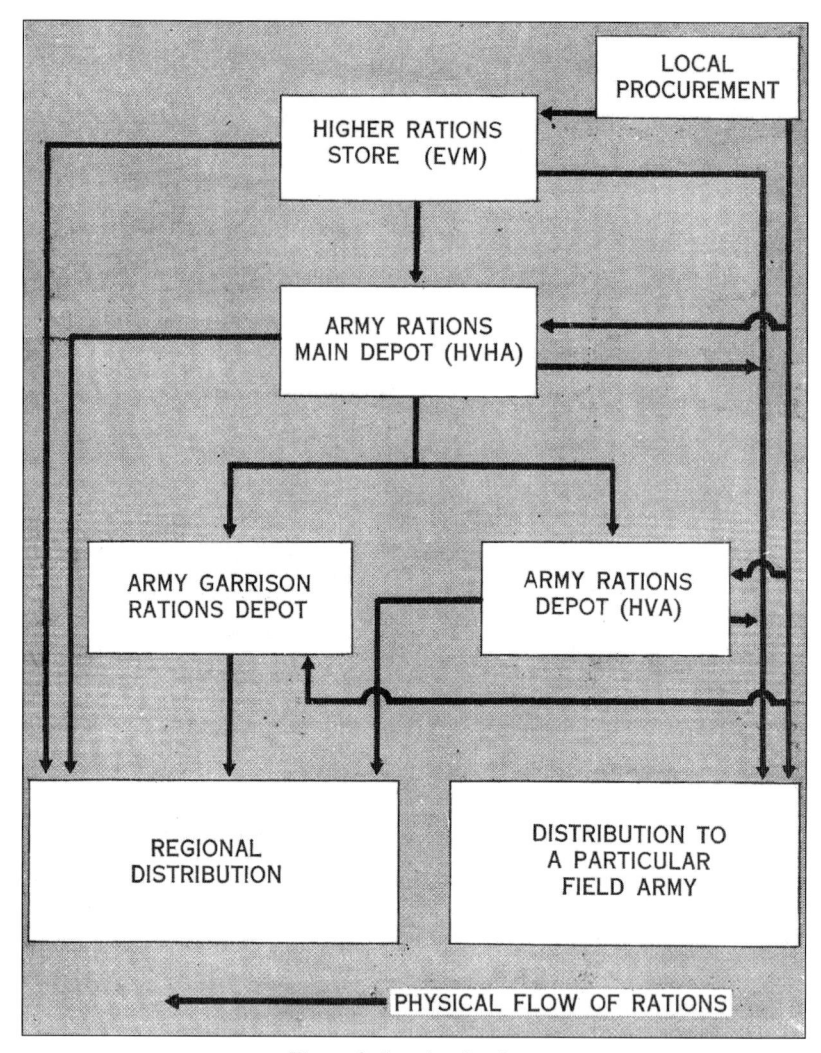

Figure 3. Supply of rations

the procurement and organization of supplies is done for all branches of the Armed Forces at the Rations and Procurement Group (*Amtsgruppe Verpflegung und Beschaffung*) of the Army High Command/Administration Office (*OKH/Heeresverwaltungsamt*). At the same time the Rations and Procurement Group directs the supply of rations to the Field Army and to the Replacement Army. Regional control of supply is exercised by Section C (*Sachgebiet C*) of the Corps Area Administration.

Although all rations depots procure a proportion of their supplies direct from local producers, they draw most of them from the Higher Rations Stores (*Ersatzverpflegungsmagazine* or *EVM*) to which they are subordinate. In procuring rations for distribution, the *EVM* purchases food from all parts of the corps area in which it is located and arranges for the exchange of goods with other corps areas. In many instances procurement of a particular rations component, such as flour or fodder, may be delegated to one of the depots subsidiary to the *EVM*.

c. RATIONS DEPOTS.

While in peacetime the troops purchased their rations mostly through commercial channels and only bread and forage were procured from the Army bakeries and rations depots, in wartime the supply of rations from Army depots has become the rule. To fulfil this task, the Higher Rations Stores or *EVM* were formed at the outbreak of war from many of the already existent Army Rations Main Depots (*Heeresverpflegungshauptämter* or *HVHA*).

The most important type of rations depot is the *EVM*. The *EVM* control Army Rations Main Depots (*HVHA*) which in turn control Army Rations Depots (*Heeresverpflegungsämter* or *HVA*) and Army Garrison Rations Depots (*Heeresstandortverwaltung Verpflegungsabteilungen*). Although the number of such installations in a corps area varies, one corps area is known to have two *EVM*, three *HVHA*, nine *HVA* and at least 12 Army Garrison Ration Depots. There are probably 40 *EVM* in Germany, 36 of which are listed below.

The echelon of the depot generally determines its size and stock. Each *EVM* is expected to maintain stock sufficient for one month's rations for 300,000 men; this would amount to over 10,000 tons of food. An *HVHA* retains food reserves of perhaps 3,000 tons, while an *HVA* usually stocks several hundred tons. An *EVM* almost invariably has a bakery and good rail facilities; lower echelon depots may lack bakeries and may have only road connections.

The rule as to size of depots is not inflexible. A large share of the stores normally retained by the *EVM* may be divided among *HVHA* and *HVA* for additional protection from air raids and to facilitate the loading of rations trains. In other instances, Army Garrison Rations Depots handle more stores than *HVHA* or *HVA* of the same corps area

List of known Higher Rations Stores (EVM):	
Corps Area	Location
I	Insterburg
I	Königsberg
I	Lötzen
II	Stettin
III	Berlin
III	Potsdam
IV	Dresden
IV	Halle
IV	Leipzig
IV	Torgau
V	Aalen
V	Ulm
VI	Minden
VI	Münster
VII	München
VIII	Breslau
VIII	Liegnitz
VIII	Oppeln
IX	Erfurt
IX	Frankfurt am Main
IX	Kassel
X	Bremen
X	Hamburg
X	Rendsburg
XI	Hannover
XI	Magdeburg
XII	Mainz
XIII	Bamberg
XIII	Nürnberg
XVII	Linz
XVII	Wien
XVIII	Graz
XX	Danzig
XXI	Posen
B.u.M	Olmütz
B.u.M	Prag

due to abnormal troop concentrations in their particular garrison areas.

While specialization is not typical of the rations depots, since both human and animal rations are found in all types, a limited number of *HVHA* and *HVA* tend to have concentrated stores of a particular rations component. As an example, one *HVHA*, now captured, maintained a reserve of thousands of tons of oats in addition to its stores of troop rations. In certain farming districts Fodder Collecting Points (*Rauhfuttersammelstellen*) specialize in the collection and storage of forage.

d. AREA OF DISTRIBUTION.

The depots maintained by the Army supply food and forage to Army, *SS*, and Air Force units present in their localities. Naval units generally are supplied by Naval Rations Depots (*Marineverpflegungsämter*). The process of local supply is relatively simple, as units contact the nearest rations depot and thereafter automatically are attached to a depot for their supply of rations. If a depot finds itself unable to provide full rations to all units in its area, it receives assistance from other depots in the corps area.

In addition to supplying local needs, the *EVM* are the principal centers for the supply of rations to the Field Army. Ordinarily, a group of *EVM* becomes responsible for the rations supply of a particular army; then the *EVM* must make certain that the army has about 10 days' supply of rations on hand at all times, based upon an estimate of the probable rations strength prepared by the army 28 days in advance.

Lower echelon depots may become involved in the supply of the field armies in a number of ways:
(1) When an *HVA* or *HVHA* is delegated to assist the *EVM* in storage of field army rations.
(2) When an *HVHA* is assigned the function of procuring and storing a particular component of the ration for the entire corps area.
(3) When any of the depots located in the theater of operations are turned over to a field army to be used as an Army Rations Depot (*Armeeverpflegungslager*).

6. Fuels and Lubricants Supply Organization

a. GENERAL.
Because of the critical condition of German fuel supply, the collection and distribution of fuel have largely been retained by the Ministry of Economic Affairs through its Central Petroleum Office. Both the Central Petroleum Office and the Armed Forces High Command exercise authority over the *WIFO* (Economic Research Company), which is the organization responsible for the administration of depots supplying fuel to the armed forces.

b. PROCUREMENT.
The Ministry of Economic Affairs, in collaboration with the Armed Forces High Command, establishes the proportional allotment of fuel to the Armed Forces and to civilian users. The refineries, producers, and importers then are directed to ship supplies either to the *WIFO* Depots or to air force, naval or commercial storage depots.

c. TYPES OF DEPOTS.
The main *WIFO* depots controlled by the Central Petroleum Office consist of Main Strategic Depots (*Zentralhauptlager*), which are usually underground, and of Main Transit Depots (*Zentralumschlaglager*), which store supplies for transshipment. In addition to supplying the largest share of fuel received by army fuel depots, these depots handle a portion of the fuel used by the Air Force

and Navy. The Main Strategic Depots have storage capacities ranging into hundreds of thousands of tons of oil. For this reason the Allied air forces have bombed them with great consistency. The importance of the Main Transit Depots has decreased since the cutting off of Rumanian petroleum imports.

The smaller *WIFO* depots, controlled by the Armed Forces High Command, consist of Army High Command Fuel Supply Depots (*OKH Nachschubtanklager*) and subsidiary Army Fuel Supply Depots (*Heeresnachschubtanklager*). These depots are directed solely to the supply of Army units. Very likely, commercial storage depots situated in the Theater of Operations have been converted into *WIFO* depots of this sort.

Not controlled by *WIFO* are the depots situated near the producing plants (*Marschtanklager* or Fuel Replacement Depots) which send fuel supplies to the depots mentioned above as well as direct to the Field Army.

7. Waffen-SS Supply Organization

a. RELATION TO ARMY SUPPLY.

While the *Waffen-SS* is generally self-sufficient in its Zone of the Interior supply, it depends upon the Chief of Army Equipment for most of its tanks, self-propelled guns, and other heavy equipment and for the repair of many of its vehicles. Indeed, *Waffen-SS* units have a higher priority on heavy equipment than do army units. To what extent the *SS* reciprocates by supplying army units has not been determined.

b. SS DEPOTS.

Of the *SS* depot centers; Oranienburg is the most important as it contains the Main *SS* Equipment Depot (*SS-Zeugamt*), the *SS* Central Distribution Center (*SS-Zentralzulassungstelle*), the *SS* Signal Equipment Depot (*SS-Nachrichtenzeugamt*), and an *SS* Motor Transport Depot (*SS-Kraftfahrzeugdepot*). Other important *SS* depot centers are Berlin, Dachau, and Prague. Since the *SS* depots supply the other branches of the *SS* as well as the *Waffen-SS* with rations, clothing, and certain types of equipment, they cannot be considered as purely military depots.

8. Transportation

All military transportation by rail or on inland waterways comes under the direction of the Chief of Transportation (*Chef des Transportwesens*) at the High Command of the Armed Forces (*OKW*). He works through a chain of transportation headquarters which are usually subordinate to the Army but act for the whole of the Armed Forces. The activities of the transportation headquarters cover the occupied territories as well as Germany.

The Transportation Headquarters (*Transport-Kommandanturen*) are regional liaison offices of the Armed Forces with the German State Railways (*Deutsche Reichsbahn*) and the authorities controlling the transportation on inland waterways. The Transportation Headquarters are located at the seat of a Railway Directorate (*Reichsbahndirektion*) and control the area of one or more Railway Directorates.

The Transportation Headquarters are the basic units through which all military agencies must deal if they require rail or water transportation for units, freight, or casualties. The Transportation Headquarters make the transportation facilities available and issue orders as to how and when they are to be used.

The staff of the Transportation Headquarters is organized into:

Section Ia:
- Troop movements for the Armed Forces
- Auxiliaries of the Armed Forces
- Transportation of prisoners of war

Section Ib:
- Freight for the Armed Forces
- Armament goods
- Armed Forces travel

Section IVb:
- Hospital and convalescent trains

Subordinate to the transportation headquarters are railway station headquarters (*Bahnhofskommandanturen*) and officers stationed at inland harbors (*Hafenoffiziere*). These headquarters and officers are stationed there for the maintenance of order and as liaison officers with the local railway and harbor officials.

III. SYSTEM OF SUPPLY OF THE FIELD ARMY

1. General

The supply system of the Field Army is simple and flexible. Its main objective during combat is to replace all supplies used during one day of combat by the beginning of the next day. Rules and regulations are not mandatory; much discretion therefore remains with the supply officers who are encouraged to move supplies as far forward as possible without reloading, to salvage all usable materiel, and to limit expenditure of supplies as far as possible.

2. Staff Control

a. SUPPLY DIRECTIVES.

The commanders of Field Army units conduct supply within their commands in accordance with directives laid down by the Army High Command. For this purpose their general staffs are provided with staff officers, analogous to our G-4's, who are called *Ib* and who are responsible for all matters of transport and supply. When the *Ib*, acting in the name of his commander, issues supply directives, their execution usually falls to the following:

(1) Arms and Equipment Section (*W* and *WuG*).
(2) Intendance Section (*IVa* or *Intendantur*), dealing with rations, clothing, and pay.
(3) Medical Section (*IVb*).
(4) Veterinary Section (*IVc*).
(5) Motor Transport Section (*V*).
(6) Supply Troop Commander (*Kommandeur der Nachschubtruppen*), commanding the organic or attached supply troops.

b. STAFF OFFICERS AND DUTIES.

The staff officers concerned with supply in the Field Army and their duties are as follows:

(1) At Field Army headquarters, the Chief of Field Army Supply and Administration (*General Quartiermeister*) is directly responsible to the Chief of Staff of the Field Army and constantly is kept informed of the supply situation of the various armies. One of his

main functions is forwarding the requirements of the armies to the Chief of Army Equipment. He regulates the evacuation of prisoners and wounded, and the use of communications in the theater of operations. Large stocks of materials, including captured materials and mobile supply trains, are under his control. Important repair centers are also maintained under his control.

(2) At army group headquarters, the Army Group *Ib* intervenes only when a critical situation requires action, since army groups are not in the normal chain of supply. Normally his most important function is the supervision of security units which safeguard supplies in the communications zones. Units attached to an army group are supplied through the army in whose area they are located.

(3) At army headquarters, the Army *Ib* (*Oberquartiermeister*) administers the collection and forwarding of requisitions, the receipt of supplies from Zone of the Interior depots, the distribution of supplies to lower echelons, and the maintenance of important dumps and repair centers.

(4) At corps headquarters, the Corps *Ib* (*Quartiermeister*), who always has been a link in the chain of requisitioning, recently has been assigned a role in the chain of supply, although the larger proportion of supplies still pass direct from army dumps to divisions. In addition to handling the supply of organic corps troops, the Corps *Ib* supervises the distribution of supplies from corps dumps to lower echelons.

(5) At division headquarters, the Division *Ib* makes his requisition to the Corps *Ib* on the basis of requisitions and reports from the troop units. He controls the division services of supply and provides a systematic supply of reserves of all kinds for the troops. Like the Army *Ib*, he is in the normal chain of supply.

3. Requisitioning and Procurement

a. REQUISITIONING.

(1) The normal channel of requisitioning is from troop units through regiment, division, and corps to army.

(2) An army generally sends requisitions for ammunition, fuel, motor transport, horses, weapons, spare parts, and most other types of

equipment to the Field Army, while requisitions for rations, clothing, medical equipment, and veterinary equipment go direct to home depots assigned to the army. While these are the usual channels, many variations are known to occur. For instance, an army may send a requisition for certain special weapons and chemical warfare equipment directly to the Chief of Army Equipment, or an army may send a rations requisition to the Field Army in addition to forwarding the requisition to a home depot.

(3) Requisitions arriving at the Field Army usually are forwarded to the Chief of Army Equipment, who passes them down to a designated home depot. In some cases, however, the Field Army may send requisitions directly to a home depot without routing them through the Chief of Army Equipment.

(4) A requisition may be filled at any level by the echelon which has the necessary supplies available in its storage centers.

b. PROCUREMENT.

Requisitioning is supplemented by two methods of field procurement: living off the land and the use of captured materiel.

(1) Living off the land may be accomplished either by local purchase or by outright confiscation of local supplies. Such procedure seldom is sufficient to supply all the requirements of units. In some areas, nevertheless, it has considerably lessened the German supply problem, as in Italy where much food, clothing, ammunition, and equipment is locally procured.

(2) The employment of captured materiel has always been a favored practice in the German Army. In the offensive beginning in December 1944, directed against the Americans holding the St. Vith-Bastogne area, the Germans apparently expected to keep their tanks operating by the seizure of American fuel dumps. The German soldiers frequently were clothed with American uniforms and operated with liberal amounts of captured Czech, British, French, and Russian, as well as American weapons and equipment.

4. Principal Installations

a. REARWARD OF RAILHEADS.

(1) *Collecting stations (Sammelbahnhöfe)*.

Shipments of less than a rail carload are sent to these stations and combined into carloads and train shipments before being routed to the railhead.

(2) *Forwarding stations (Weiterleitungstationen).*
Rail shipments that are not unit-loaded for one organization may be forwarded to the army through one of these stations.

(3) *Distributing stations (Verteilerbahnhöfe).*
When a large number of units are dependent upon a single railroad for their supply, a distributing station may be set up to regulate the dispatch of supplies to the proper railhead or unloading point; apparently the combined functions of the collecting, forwarding, and distributing stations approach the functions of the U.S. regulating station.

(4) *Supply collecting areas (Nachschubsammelgebiete).*
Reserves of ammunition, fuel, and rations are kept loaded in trains in these areas subject to disposition by the Chief of Field Army Administration and Supply.

(5) *Field Army parks, bases, and depots (Heeres Parke, Stützpunkte, und Lager).*
Primarily concerned with the maintenance, repair, and forwarding of vehicles, including tanks and armored vehicles, these Field Army installations may be located well to the rear of the railheads.

(6) *Army parks (Armee Parke).*
Some of the army equipment parks may be located to the rear of the army railheads.

b. RAILHEADS (Kopfbahnhöfe).

Railheads are located as far forward as possible. While this generally results in army (*Armee*) railheads, each of which supplies a number of divisions or a corps (in the latter case the railhead may be called a corps railhead), a division railhead for each division is established whenever possible. On the Western Front, depending on the nature of the terrain and the effectiveness of Allied bombings, the railhead is found from 10 to 50 miles—usually about 25 miles—from the front. This is a great improvement over the conditions that existed in the early stages of the Russian campaign, when German railheads were on an average from 90 to 120 miles behind the front troops.

c. FORWARD OF RAILHEADS.

(1) *Army parks and dumps (Armee Parke und Lager).* Army fuel, rations, and ammunition dumps are almost invariably forward of army railheads, while army equipment parks generally are in the vicinity of the railheads.

(2) *Corps dumps (Korps Lager).* If army installations are far to the rear, corps dumps may be set up between army and division; in such cases the corps dumps function as advanced army dumps distributing to divisions. (3) *Division dumps (Divisions Lager).* The dump system may be pushed forward even into the division area, but this is the exception rather than the rule.

(4) *Distributing points (Ausgabestellen).* These are maintained by divisions and possibly other echelons in their areas for the distribution of rations, fuel, and ammunition. While stores are not generally retained at these points, small accumulations may occur.

(5) *Collecting points (Sammelstellen).* Although called collecting points, these centers, which are maintained by army and division; serve as supply points for new and repaired equipment as well as collecting points for damaged and captured equipment.

(6) *Reloading points (Umschlagstellen).* When long road movements are involved, reloading points may he set up by army or corps to facilitate supply movements.

(7) *Supply points.* Units lower than divisions have points analogous to collecting and distributing points.

5. Distribution of Supplies to Field Units

a. GENERAL SCHEME OF DISTRIBUTION.

(1) Supplies are transported by rail from home depots to army railheads where they are picked up by army supply columns and transported to army dumps and parks. Division supply columns receive rations, fuel, and ammunition at army dumps, and equipment at army parks. They carry the rations, fuel, and ammunition to division distributing points, and the equipment to

division collecting paints. At these points, supplies are transferred to battalion supply columns and carried to battalion or company supply points where the supplies are turned over to the troops.

(2) While this is the usual flow of supplies, it may be modified in a number of ways, most of which are shown in Figure 2. Operational conditions are the cause of most modifications of the usual system of distribution. Hence, if the army and divisions are short of trucks or gasoline, columns from units as low as companies may be forced to go as far as 20 miles to receive supplies from army railheads and dumps; if the lower echelons lack means of transportation, army supply columns may be used to bring supplies to the troops; if Allied strafing is expected, supply movements may be limited to the hours of darkness; if units are stationed in the near vicinity of army dumps, they may draw their supplies direct from the dumps.

b. DISTRIBUTION OF RATIONS.

Normally home rations depots ship supplies direct to Army Rations Dumps (*Armeeverpfdegungslager*). A number of such dumps may be set up, each with stores of less than 100 tons. In some cases, these dumps have been known to store small amounts of clothing, individual equipment, and office equipment. As they are not permanent installations, they may move from time to time. Forward army dumps sometimes are controlled by corps and called Corps Rations Dumps (*Korpsverpflegungslager*); in such cases, the corps dumps supply the division and corps troops, while army dumps supply units and individual detachments attached to army headquarters, and form a permanent organization for the support of future military operations. Rations supply within the division is handled through a rations distributing point (*Verpflegungsausgabestelle*). Supplies are received at this point and are distributed to division units. Usually livestock is sent to field butchery platoons for dressing, and flour to field bakeries for bread production.

(1) A butchery platoon can process the following number of animals per day:
- 40 beef cattle = 40,000 meat rations.
- 80 pigs = 24,000 meat rations.
- 240 sheep = 19,000 meat rations.

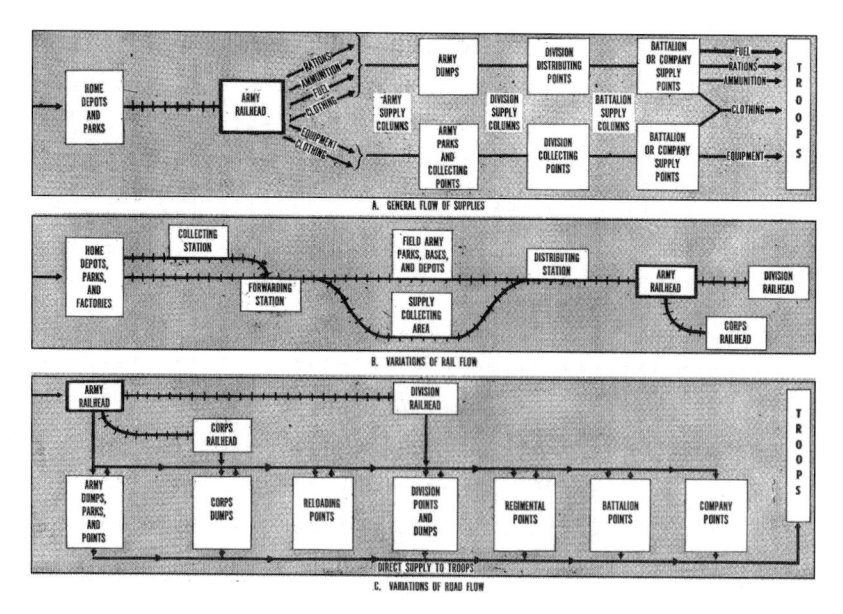

Figure 4 - Flow of supplies

(2) A field bakery company can produce between 15,000 and 19,200 bread rations, according to the weather and the time of the year. After passing through the rations supply points of the division units, the supplies finally reach field kitchens and troops. Field kitchens of two types are found: large, with a capacity for supplying 125 to 225 men; and small, with a capacity for supplying 60 to 125 men.

c. DISTRIBUTION OF AMMUNITION.

The home ammunition depots forward supplies to the Army Ammunition Dumps (*Armeemunitionslager*) which usually store from 3,000 to 6,000 tons. Any forward army dumps taken over by corps are called Corps Ammunition Dumps (*Korpsmunitionslager*). From these dumps, the ammunition is taken to Division Ammunition Distributing Points (*Divisionsausgabestellen*). One or more well camouflaged distributing points are established, located out of the effective range of Allied artillery and, if possible, on terrain protected from tank attacks. Ordinarily artillery ammunition and infantry ammunition are handled by different distributing points so as to facilitate the loading and unloading of supplies. In some cases Division Ammunition Dumps (*Divisionsmunitionslager*) are set up in the division area, especially if the front lines have been stabilized. From the divisions, ammunition is sent to infantry andi artillery ammunition supply points maintained by regiments, battalions, and companies. As German regulations permit the setting up of temporary ammunition dumps at these points, small reserves may be present only a few miles behind the front lines.

Unused ammunition, empty shell cases, packing cases, and faulty ammunition must be returned by the troops to army dumps from where they are sent to the home areas. The rapid return of this material is considered as important as ammunition supply.

d. DISTRIBUTION OF FUELS AND LUBRICANTS.

Fuel from home fuel depots or from Field Army mobile reserves is directed to the railheads. Sometimes the fuel is kept loaded in tanker trains (*Eisenbahntankstellen*) near the railhead and transferred from these directly to fuel columns, but preferably it is laid down in 20- and 200-liter containers in Army Fuel Dumps (*Armeebetriebsstofflager*) forward of the railhead. From these dumps the fuel is taken forward to Division Fuel Distributing Points (*Divisionsbetriebsstoffausgabestellen*) or, in the case of some motorized and armored divisions, to Division Fuel Dumps (*Divisionsbetriebsstofflager*). Fuel is forwarded from the division area to lower echelon supply points and to fuel points that are set aside for the use of single vehicles (*Tankstellen für Einzelkraftfahrzeuge*). The latter may also be supplied from the army fuel stores.

e. DISTRIBUTION OF CLOTHING AND INDIVIDUAL EQUIPMENT.

Stores are dispatched from the Zone of the Interior to the field rations dumps and to field equipment parks and collecting points, from which the stores are distributed to units.

f. DISTRIBUTION OF EQUIPMENT.

(1) Equipment is handled by parks of two different categories: the *Heeres*, or Field Army type, and the *Armee*, or army type. Although performing functions analogous to those of the Zone of the Interior Home (*Heimat*) and Corps Area (*Wehrkreis*) Equipment Parks, the field parks have a number of distinct characteristics. They are concerned only with military vehicles. Furthermore, they are

dependent upon Zone of the Interior depots, parks, and factories for fifth echelon maintenance. Lastly, the field parks are responsible for the storage of reserve equipment as well as the distribution of new and repaired equipment.

(2) The most numerous *Heeres* type park is the Field Army Motor Transport Park (*Heereskraftfahrpark* or *HeKP*). Unlike the Home Motor Transport Park, the *HeKP* normally does all repairs itself, without farming vehicles out to workshops, with the already existing repair facilities which it customarily takes over. Usually a number of *HeKP* are established in each army group area. Each *HeKP* may hold a reserve of about 200 new vehicles in addition to vehicles arriving from home equipment parks and depots, and damaged vehicles coming from Army Motor Transport Parks (*Armeekraftfahrparke* or *AKP*). In conjunction with army parks, the *HeKP* establish and maintain gasoline stations at certain selected points, usually along important roads. Not ascertained are the functions of reported Motor Transport Repair Parks (*Kraftfahrinstandsetzungsparke*) and Winterization Parks (*Winterlager*) which may be specialized *HeKP* or *HeKP* branches.

(3) Perhaps even more important than the Field Army Motor Transport Parks are the Field Army Tank Parks or Bases (*Stützpunkte*). These presumably are established on the basis of one per army group. Their importance is increased by the fact that armies do not ordinarily maintain fixed installations for the repair of tanks, although armies may have semi-permanent tank workshops. The tank bases are reception or control centers from which tanks are dispatched to workshops in the near vicinity for repairs, or returned to home depots and factories for fifth echelon maintenance.

(4) Also under Field Army control are Spare Parts Depots (*Ersatzteillager*), Tire Depots (*Reifenlager*), Track Depots (*Gleiskettenlager*), Tank Spare Parts Depots (*Panzerersatzteillager*), Armored Car Spare Parts Depots (*Panzerspähwagenersatzsteillager*), and Tractor Spare Parts Depots (*Zugkraftwagenersatzteillager*). The Depots furnish supplies to maintenance sections, workshop units, army parks, and Field Army parks.

(5) Army Parks (*Armee Parke*) are primarily for repairs but they also are supposed to maintain a reserve of between 5 and 10 per cent of the arms and equipment of the army, and to forward equipment either directly or through collecting points to units. An army has the following parks:

    (a) Infantry Park, for infantry weapons and trucks.

    (b) Artillery Park, for artillery weapons and trucks.

    (c) Anti-gas Equipment Park, for gas masks, decontamination suits, anti-gas clothing, and smoke equipment.

    (d) Engineer Stores Park, for engineer materials.

    (e) Signal Park, for radio and telephone materials.

    (f) Motor Transport Park, for vehicles and spare parts.

    (g) Army Equipment Park, for harness, horse carts, cooks equipment, and general items.

    (h) Medical Park, for medical equipment.

    (i) Veterinary Park, for veterinary equipment.

    (j) Horse Park, for riding and draft horses.

(6) When equipment is forwarded from army to division, it passes either directly from the army parks to Division Equipment Collecting Points (*Divisionsgerätesammelstellen*) or through an Army Equipment Collecting Point (*Armeegerätesamanelstelle*) to the division. In turn the division directs the equipment to the supply points maintained by its units. Equipment repaired by field maintenance sections and workshop units may be returned directly or through any of the collecting or supply points to the troops; because the procedure is greatly variant, Figure 6 pictures this latter flow as only direct to the troops.

6. Supply Movement

a. RAILROAD SUPPLY TRAINS.

(1) *Standard supply trains.*

German logistical manuals outline the use of standard rations, ammunition, and fuel supply trains with a maximum net load of 450 metric tons (or Approximately 500 short tons) on a standard gauge (4 feet 8 1/2 inches) railway. The text-book theory has generally been followed out in practice, although in some cases two or more locomotives have been sighted pulling unusually long fuel trains, and in some areas standard rations trains seldom are used. Standard equipment supply trains, with great variations in net loading weights, also are employed. In most cases, however, equipment of all kinds is loaded on the same train.

(2) *Rations supply trains (Verpflegungszüge)*

Tith an average of 40 cars per train may be composed as follows:

(a) Iron rations: 300,000 full and 300,000 half iron rations, totalling 442 metric tons.

(b) Full rations with fodder: 180,000 human and 40,000 animal rations, amounting to 454 metric tons. These may be loaded into three parts, each containing 3 days' supplies for 20,000 men and 4,000 animals.

(c) Full human rations with no bread but only baking materials: 300,000 rations, totaling 450 metric tons.

(d) Flour train (*Mehlzug*): 833,000 rations, amounting to 450 metric tons.

(e) Oat train (*Haferzug*): 90,000 rations, totaling 450 metric tons.

(f) Animal trains (*Viehzüge*): 360 cattle weighing 180 metric tons, 1200 pigs weighing 120 metric tons, or 1800 sheep weighing 72 metric tons.

(3) *Ammunition supply trains (Munitionszüge)*

With an average of 30 cars per train, are of three types:

(a) Unit-loaded trains, loaded according to the proportion of different types of ammunition needed by a particular division.

(b) Caliber unit trains, in which each car is loaded with Approximately 15 metric tons (16 1/2 short tons) of ammunition of a specific caliber.

(c) Single caliber unit trains, in which all cars are loaded with ammunition of the same caliber.

(4) *Fuel supply trains* (*Betriebstoffzüge*)

Two types are used:

(a) 20 gasoline tank cars, holding between 340 cubic meters (around 89,800 gallons) and 440 cubic meters (around 116,200 gallons) of fuel.

(b) 25 cars, holding gasoline in 200-liter (53-gallon) and 20-liter (5-gallon) cans and carrying 400 cubic meters (105,600 gallons) of gasoline, and five cars with oil, engine oil, gear oil, paraffin, and (in winter) anti-freeze barrels and cans.

(5) *Horse supply trains (Pferdersatzzüge)*

Consisting of 55 cars, each holding eight riding or light draft horses per car or 440 horses per train; six heavy draft horses per car or 330 horses per train; or four very heavy horses per car or 220 horses per train.

(6) *Signals and engineer construction materials trains (Baustoffzüge)*

Averaging 40 cars, of which 39 are open cars, with a net tonnage of about 820 metric tons (900 short tons).

(7) *Tank trains*

Carrying up to 25 medium tanks or up to 8 heavy tanks have also been reported. The average number of cars per tank train is about 33, with widely varying net loads.

(8) *Mixed equipment trains*

Very frequent and may contain from 25 to 60 cars with a total net tonnage of up to 850 metric tons.

b. ROAD SUPPLY COLUMNS AND TRAINS.

There are four types of road supply columns in the German Army:

(1) *Motorized columns (Kraftwagenkolonnen)* are, in general, employed on good roads. They can cover up to 125 miles per day. They are organized into very large, large, and small motor transport columns with a capacity of 120 metric tons, 60 tons, and 30 tons respectively for the transportation of supplies other than fuel. In addition, mountain divisions may have a special 10-ton capacity column. Fuel generally is trans-ported in motorized fuel columns of two types—heavy columns with a minimum load of 50 cubic meters of fuel, and light columns with a minimum of 25 cubic meters. Motor transport columns are designated with reference to their employment as Field Army, army, corps, or division motor truck columns.

(2) *Animal-drawn columns (Fahrkolonnen)* normally have capacities of 30 or 17 metric tons, and mountain animal-drawn columns 15 metric tons. In general, they are equipped with one-team wagons; in cavalry units two-team wagons are used. According to German training instructions, well cared for and trained horses can

SUPPLY COLUMNS AND TRAINS		
	Capacity (metric tons)	Capacity (short tons)
Very Large Motorized Column	120	132
Large Motorized Column	60	66
Small Motorized Column	30	33
Large Animal-Drawn Column	30	33
Small Animal-Drawn Column	17	18 1/2
Mountain Animal-Drawn Column	15	16 1/2
Mountain Motorized Column	10	11
Pack Train	5	5 1/2
	Minimum Amount (cubic meters)	Minimum Amount (gallons)
Large Motorized Fuel Column	50	13,200
Small Motorized Fuel Column	25	6,600

cover 12 to 15 miles per day and under favorable conditions up to 20 miles, with a clay of rest following. If oxen are employed, the rate of movement is slower. The Germans have been relying more and more upon animal-drawn columns for the movement of their supplies.

(3) *Pack trains (Tragtierkolonnen)*, generally consisting of 40 mules or horses each, usually are employed in mountainous terrain. A pack train can carry up to 5 tons, but its capacity and speed are dependent on the trails and grade. Even in level country, pack trains usually march more slowly than foot troops.

(4) *Mountain carrier units (Gebirgsträgereinheiten)* consist of mountain carrier battalions and companies whose men are employed in terrain where not even pack animals can be used effectively. Each man can carry between 45 and 75 pounds of materiel on his back.

c. SUPPLY ROADS.

Whenever possible a supply road is designated for each self-contained unit such as a division. In general, the main route of advance of the unit is designated as its supply road. This principal route may be called a *Rollbahn*, or rolling road, to distinguish it from any secondary supply roads. When the main supply route is used for troop movements as well as for supply purposes, it generally will be called a *Durchgangsstrasse*, or through road. Great importance is attached to the upkeep of these routes and the placing of gasoline stations (*Tankstellen*) at strategic points close by the routes.

IV. MAINTENANCE REQUIREMENTS

1. Total Requirements

a. VARIABLES INVOLVED.

The determination of the over-all requirements necessary to maintain German troops presents a number of difficulties. This is best shown by a review of the German supply expenditures in Russia in 1941. Armored divisions averaged some 30 tons daily when inactive and about 700 tons a day when engaged in heavy fighting; infantry divisions required 80 tons a day when inactive and some 1,100 tons during a day of heavy fighting. When engaged in defensive, mopping-up, or minor offensive activities, the divisions required supplies in amounts somewhere between the two extremes. By far the most important variable in this campaign was the amount of ammunition expended; requirements of fuel and equipment also varied considerably, while rations and clothing consumption remained relatively static. Expenditures depended upon the nature of the action involved, the types of units engaged, the zone of action, the season of the year, the amount of materiel available for consumption, and the facility with which supply movements could be made.

b. ESTIMATES OF TOTAL REQUIREMENTS.

When the variables evident in the 1941 Russian campaign have become relatively constant, as is the case at present, the German supply requirements can be estimated with some degree of accuracy. Under present conditions the average total supply requirements per German soldier are estimated to vary as follows:

- Inactivity: 5-10 pounds per man per day
- Mopping-up: 15-20 pounds per man per day
- Defensive fighting (but not against a major Allied push): 20-25 pounds per man per day
- Heavy defensive fighting: 25-50 pounds per man per day
- Offensive fighting: 25-50 pounds per man per day

2. Rations

a. HUMAN RATIONS SCALES.

The daily ration quantity (*Portionsatz*) is the amount of food

REPRESENTATIVE BREAKDOWN OF MAXIMUM RATION ALLOWANCES IN GRAMS PER DAY

Item	Component Class	Duty Class			
		Ration I	Ration II	Ration III	Ration IV
Rye bread	(a)	700	700	700	600
Fresh meat with bones	(b)	136	107	90	56
Soy bean flour	(b)	7	7	7	7
Headless fish	(b)	30	30	30	30
Fresh vegetables and fruits	(c)	250	250	250	250
Potatoes	(c)	320	320	320	320
Legumes	(c)	80	80	80	80
Pudding powder	(d)	20	20	20	20
Sweetened condensed skim milk	(d)	25	25	25	25
Salt	(e)	15	15	15	15
Other seasonings	(e)	3	3	3	3
Spices	(f)	1	1	1	1
Fats and bread spreads	(g)	60	50	40	35
Coffee	(h)	9	9	9	9
Sugar	(i)	40	35	30	30
Supplementary allowances	(l)	2	2	2	2
Total Maximum Ration in grams		1,698	1,654	1,622	1,483
Total Maximum Ration in lbs		3.74	3.64	3.57	3.26
Wine (in summer) (quarts)	(j)	.026	.026	.026	.026
Cigarettes (pieces)	(k)	7	6	3	2

consumed by one man for one day. It consists of three meals, the noon meal amounting to one-half of the total, the evening meal to one-third, and the next morning's breakfast to one-sixth. The Armed Forces High Command has laid down an over-all plan specifying the maximum amount of any ration item that may be served. The amount depends upon two factors: the duty class of the man receiving the ration, and the component class of the particular item being served.

There are four main types of rations served to troops. Ration I (*Verpflegungssatz I*) is for troops committed to combat, for those that are recuperating from combat, and for troops stationed in Norway north of 66° N. Lat. Ration II is for occupation and line-of-communication troops. Ration III is for garrison troops within Germany. Ration IV goes to office workers and nurses within Germany. Hospital cases may fall within any of these classes depending on the seriousness of the cases.

The most important items of the component classes are as follows: (a) bread; (b) meats, soy bean flour, cheese, fish, and eggs; (c) vegetables; (d) puddings and milk; (e) salt, mustard, vinegar, and other seasonings; (f) spices such as pepper, cinnamon, and cloves; (g) butter, lard, marmalades, fats, and bread spreads; (h) coffee and tea; (i) sugar; (j) spirits and wines; (k) tobacco.

Substitute issues may be made within a component class but not among different component classes. Thus the daily maximum allowance of vegetables for a soldier is 60 grams [In dealing with captured German documents, the American soldier will invariably find the rations allowances computed in grams or kilograms. A gram equals .0353 ounce or .0022 pound. A kilogram (1000 grams) equals 35.3 ounces or 2.2 pounds.] of dried vegetables, or 1200 grams of kidney beans, or 400 grams of salted vegetables, or equivalent quantities of any of about 30 other substitutes. It is not possible to predict which items will be served on any given day. The following chart, however, sets forth a likely breakdown of these maximum ration allowances.

b. SPECIAL TYPES OF HUMAN RATIONS.

(1) *March ration (Marschverpflegung)*.

The march ration is a cold food ration issued for not more than three or four consecutive days to units in transit either on carrier or by foot. It consists of Approximately 700 grams of bread, 200 grams of cold meat or cheese, 60 grams of bread spreads, 9 grams of coffee (or 4 grams of tea), 10 grams of sugar, and six cigarettes. Thus it has a total weight of about 980 grams.

(2) *Iron ration (Eiserne Portion)*.

An iron ration consists of 250 grams of biscuits, 200 grams of cold meat, 150 of preserved vegetables, 25 of coffee, and 25 of salt. Total weight is 650 grams without packing and 825 grams with packing. An iron half-ration is composed of 250 grams of biscuits and 200 grams of preserved meat; thus its total weight is 450 grams without packing and 535 grams with packing.

(3) *Combat Package (Grosskampfpäcken)* and *Close Combat Package (Nahkampfpäcken)*.

The Germans have begun to use these types of rations for troops engaged in combat. They include chocolate bars. fruit bars, candies, cigarettes, and possibly biscuits.

c. ANIMAL RATIONS.

An animal ration is the amount of food consumed by one horse, draft ox, dog, or carrier pigeon for one day. The quantity of an animal ration allowance (*Rationssatz*) depends on the type of animal, the area in which he is serving, and the content of the ration he is being fed. Horses, for instance, are divided into four groups: draft horses of the heaviest breed, draft horses of heavy breed, saddle-horses and light draft horses, and small horses. On the Eastern front, draft horses of the heaviest breed receive a maximum ration allowance of 5650 grams of oats, 5300 grams of hay, and 5750 grams of straw (including 1500 grams of bedding straw). The allotments to other horse groups are proportionately less. On fronts other than the Eastern Front, the allotments for all horses are generally smaller. In addition, substitutes such as preserved forage, barley, corn, etc., may change the ration weight. If the horse is being fed an iron ration, he is given a single item such as oats or hay or straw.

d. RATIONS IN THE FIELD.

Local stores obtained by purchase or confiscation play a greater part in the supply of rations in the field (*Feldportionen* for men and *Feldrationen* for animals) than is the case for any other class of supply. It is part of the German planning principle to live off the land as much as possible and to obtain only the remaining requirements from stocks procured through channels. The Germans fully appreciate the difficulty of employing such methods during periods of combat and do not count upon local stores during operative periods. Usually a normal reserve of about 10 days' rations for each man of an army is maintained within the army. The rations consist of full and iron rations, although the latter may be eaten only upon the receipt of special orders.

Rations carried in an army for each man:

	Full rations	Iron rations
With the man	-	1 (half)
On a combat vehicle	-	1
In the field kitchen	1	1
In the unit ration train	2	-
In the division train	1	-
In the army dumps and train	a total of about 3	

Ordinarily there are two full and two iron horse rations carried either on the horse or in unit supply columns. Other rations are carried by the army and the division.

For staff planning purposes, the weights of rations are computed by the Germans as follows:

Type of Rations	Weight in grams	Weight in pounds
Human rations:		
Standard ration with packing	1,500	3.3
Iron ration with packing	825	1.82
Iron half-ration with packing	535	1.18
Horse rations:		
Standard ration	10,000	22.
Iron oat ration	5,000	11.
Iron hay ration	5,000	11.
Iron straw ration	2,500	5.5

3. Fuels and Lubricants

Distribution of fuel is calculated in the consumption unit (*Verbrauchssatz*) which is the amount of fuel that will move each vehicle in a formation 100 kilometers or 62 miles. The allowance of consumption units per formation is systematically replaced as it is expended. Under normal conditions it was standard for German formations to maintain three consumption units at army dumps: in addition, armored formations carried four units, reconnaissance elements carried six and a half units, and all other formations carried five units. Because of present fuel shortages, the allowances of consumption units are now determined by the amount of fuel which the General Staff believes is the minimum necessary for the desired tactical uses.

4. Equipment and Clothing

The replacement of equipment and clothing is based upon the allowances authorized for units and individuals in the table of organization (*Kriegsstärenachweisung*), the table of basic allowances (*Kriegsausrüstungnachweisung*), and the various annexes (*Anlagen*) to these tables. When the materials allotted under the tables are destroyed, damaged, lost, or worn out, they are repaired or replaced as quickly as possible.

5. Ammunition

a. AMMUNITION ALLOWANCES.

The initial issue (*erste Ausstattung*) of ammunition is the total ammunition carried by a formation in columns, in dumps, and with the troops. The initial issue is systematically replaced as it is expended, on the basis of reports of ammunition remaining on hand sent from the divisions through corps to army, except as operational conditions modify the system. The allowance per formation is based on the number of weapons called for in the table of organization of the unit. Each weapon, in turn, has a number of rounds which is allotted to it as an ammunition quota or unit of issue (*Munitionsausstattung*). Two units of issue for all weapons of the division are carried within the division, while another unit of issue for all weapons in the army is held on army columns or trains as an army reserve. Thus each army has three ammunition quotas or units of issue for all weapons of the army.

b. AMMUNITION ISSUES.

Of the two ammunition units of issue that are found within the division, over one unit is found forward on the men, with the guns, and as company and battalion reserves, while less than one full unit of issue is retained as a division reserve in division columns and dumps. The exact quantity issued to each man is largely determined by the amount held by the battalion and company as their reserves. The following charts exemplify the units of issue found in infantry and artillery units of an army.

Units of Issue for Artillery Units:
- 37-mm AA: 1,500 Rounds
- 75-mm AA: 300 Rounds
- 88-mm AA: 300 Rounds
- 105-mm gun: 125 Rounds
- 150-mm how: 125 Rounds
- 150-mm gun: 75 Rounds
- 210-mm how: 50 Rounds

c. AMMUNITION EXPENDITURE.

The unit of issue of ammunition is not to be confused with the daily expenditure amount of ammunition. The latter does not arrive at any constant figure, but varies with the type of action, the area of fighting, and the other factors mentioned in paragraph 1. By analogy with the reserve amounts of other expendable supplies, however, it is possible that three units of fire are judged by the Germans to be sufficient to maintain an army for a period of roughly eight to ten days.

Weapon*	Forward Issue	Division Reserve	Probable Army Reserve (Unit of Issue)
9-mm automatic pistol	18	16	17
9-mm machine pistol	690	512	601
7.92-mm machine pistol	720	540	630
7.92-mm rifle	99	75	87
7.92-mm rifle (for troops other than infantry troops)	25	20	22
7.92-mm semi-auto rifle	159	135	147
Rifle grenade launcher	75	70	70
7.92-mm LMG	3450	2505	2977
7.92-mm LMG (for arty and AT troops)	1350	1020	1185
7.92-mm HvMG	6300	4750	5525
88-mm bazooka	5	5	5
81-mm mortar	150	126	138
120-mm mortar	150	90	120
37-mm AA	1200	none**	?**
75-mm inf how	192	151	171
75-mm AT (mtz)	150	100	125
75-mm AT (SP)	255	-	-
105-mm gun how	225	126	175
150-mm how	150	60	105

Ammunition Issues (Rounds) for a Volks Grenadier Division.
* Not included are 75-mm gun and flame thrower.
** AA ammunition reserves are usually kept by army and not by division.

V. EVACUATION

1. Maintenance and Repair of Equipment

a. GENERAL.

Perhaps the fundamental German principle of repair and maintenance is that equipment should be repaired as far forward as possible.

Practically all the installations that deal with repair and maintenance of equipment also participate in the flow of supplies, both in transferring repaired equipment back to units and in moving newly manufactured equipment to units (see Sections II and III). In the following paragraphs, therefore, they will be treated solely from the point of view of rearward flow.

b. MOTOR TRANSPORT.

Maintenance of an individual vehicle is the responsibility of the driver and the crew, but for repairs it is sent to one of a number of repair centers. While the procedure that determines which center shall undertake the repair has changed from time to time, it probably is determined by two factors: the number of working hours; and the facilities needed to effect the repair. Thus maintenance (*Instandsetzungs*) detachments and sections probably carry out repairs requiring less than four working hours with the tools at their disposal, while mobile field workshop (*Werkstatt*) units carry out repairs requiring less than 12 working hours. If the damage inflicted is too extensive for the facilities of the mobile workshops, the vehicle is sent to an Army Motor Transport Park (*AKP*) or to a Field Army Motor Transport Park (*HeKP*). The difference of functions between these two types of installations is not clear: it is likely, however, that the more difficult repair jobs are sent to the *HeKP*, while the *AKP* handle repairs that can be completed in less than 24 working hours. The disposition of the vehicle from these centers may be as follows: it may be repaired or scrapped; it may be forwarded to a Home Motor Transport Park (*HKP*), which is capable of carrying out all types of repairs; or, in the case of an *AKP*, the vehicle may be forwarded to a *HeKP*.

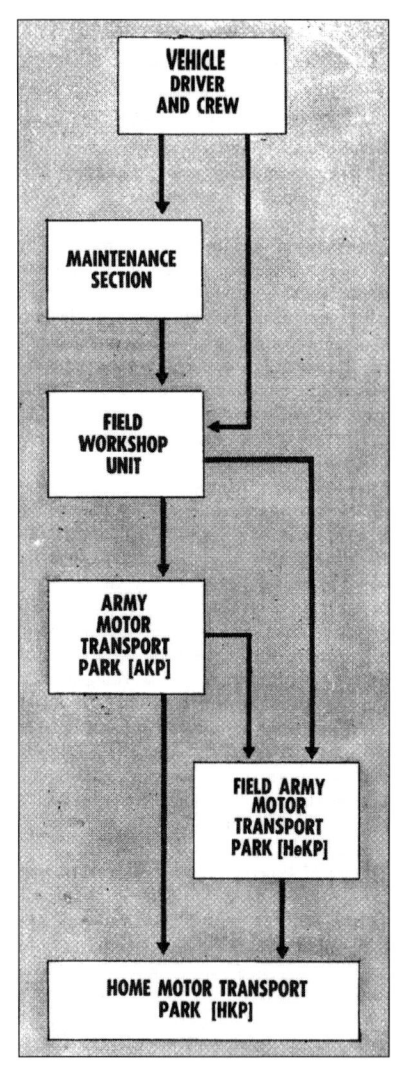

Figure 5. Motor vehicle repair and maintenance

While the exact position of collecting points in the rearward movement of damaged vehicles is not certain, it is very likely that whenever possible vehicles move directly to repair and maintenance centers under their own power without passing through collecting points.

c. TANKS, ARMORED VEHICLES, AND SELF-PROPELLED WEAPONS.

Minor repairs to armored vehicles (including tanks, self-propelled weapons, and other armored vehicles) are made by unit mechanics and by mobile tank-workshop units. If the repairs cannot be completed in the division area within three days, the vehicles may be sent to semi-permanent army tank workshops or to Field Army Tank Parks or Bases. When armored vehicles are so badly damaged that they cannot be repaired in the field, they are cannibalized or forwarded to tank equipment depots or factories in the home area. In the latter case the vehicles are no longer under Field Army control and are not returned to the units to which they were originally assigned.

Armored vehicles are repaired on the spot if possible. Otherwise they are moved rearward under their own power. Tank transporters are used only when long movements are contemplated or when vehicles cannot move under their own power.

d. OTHER EQUIPMENT AND CLOTHING.

All types of equipment including weapons, signal equipment, bicycles, and clothing are repaired within the division area if possible. If the equipment (other than clothing and individual equipment) requires more specialized attention, it is forwarded either directly or through equipment collecting points or workshop units to one of the army parks. Equipment which

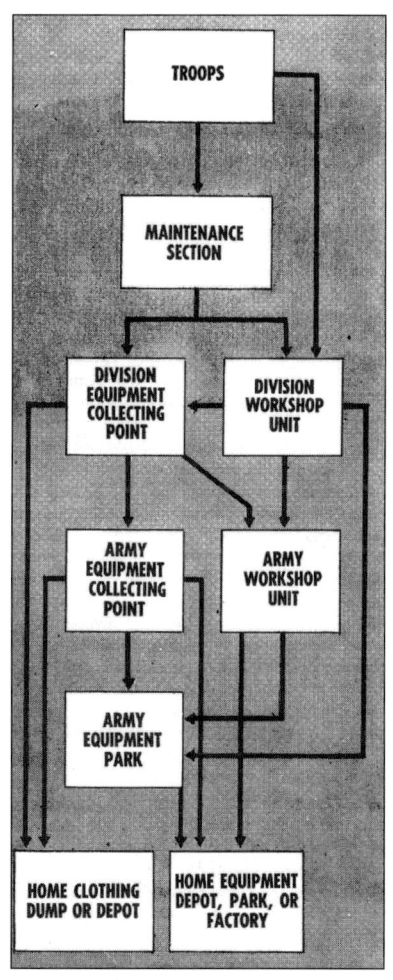

Figure 6. Repair of equipment and clothing

cannot be repaired in the field is directed to a home equipment park, depot, or factory. Damaged clothing and individual equipment generally pass from collecting points direct to home clothing depots and dumps. Figure 6, which is largely compiled from German schematics, should be examined for other details of the German repair methods.

2. Evacuation of Installations

With the narrowing of the Zone of the Interior, the Germans have been faced with the problem of what to do with depots that were formerly part of the Zone of the Interior system of supply. Variant courses adopted have been the conversion of the installation into a field installation, the evacuation of the depot to the new Zone of the Interior, and the operation of the depot as though it were still within the Zone of the Interior.

3. Evacuation of Wounded

a. GENERAL.

The German system for the evacuation of casualties is based upon an immediate sorting of the wounded so that soldiers who are not seriously injured can be returned to their units as quickly as possible, and those who are severely wounded can receive medical care with maximum speed. Under combat conditions the accomplishment of these ends in many cases will cause deviations from the normal system. A good example of this was shown in the early part of the Russian campaign when the great distances between the combat zone and the Zone of the Interior forced the Germans to use a chain of Casualty Collecting Points to control and expedite the rearward movement of sick and wounded.

Now that the combat zone has moved into Germany proper, deviations of an integrating nature should be anticipated.

b. CHANNELS OF EVACUATION.

(1) Casualties unable to walk are carried from the battlefield by battalion stretcher bearers, while those still capable of walking are directed to the Battalion Aid Station (*Verwundetennest*) which is located as close to the front line as is practicable. The Battalion Aid

Station gives first aid in emergency cases. As quickly as movements can be made, it passes the wounded to the Regimental Aid Station (*Truppenverbandplatz*), which is generally some 200 to 500 yards to the rear of the front line. At this station the wounded receive first aid and are sorted into ambulatory cases and stretcher cases. Stretcher cases are carried by litter to an Ambulance Loading Post (*Wagenhalteplatz*) for rearward movement, while ambulatory cases are instructed to make their way rearward on foot.

(2) Usually the stretcher cases are sent to a Main Dressing Station (*Hauptverbandplatz*), whereas the walking wounded move to a Collecting Point for the Slightly Wounded (*Leichtverwundetensammelplatz*). The latter two installations, both controlled by the regimental medical officer, sometimes operate as a combined unit, and in practically all cases are located reasonably close to each other. Their functions are as follows:

The Main Dressing Station attends the serious cases. It contains a surgical unit which performs amputations, applies dressings and splints, checks hemorrhages, gives blood transfusions, and administers sedatives and preventative injections. After treatment the casualties are evacuated further rearward.

The Collecting Point for the Slightly Wounded administers to casualties whose treatment requires only a few days. When the treatment is completed, the men are returned to combat. If, however, a case has taken a more serious turn, the wounded soldier is evacuated rearward.

(3) From the regimental area casualties may be taken to any of the various types of hospitals (*Lazarette*) found in the field or at home. Casualty Collecting Points (*Krankensammelstellen*) usually are set up along the line of evacuation to facilitate the grouping of casualties and their distribution to the rear. These points are generally established at railheads and other traffic centers by ambulance units. They do not handle casualties whose condition will not permit movement. Mobile Field Hospitals (*Feldlazarette*) serve as way stations for casualties who cannot be moved through the Casualty Collecting Points. They may be operated either by an army or by a division. Wherever possible, the Field Hospital is set up in available permanent buildings. It is equipped

to handle any casualty and has a capacity of 200 beds.

(4) Casualties who are physically able to be evacuated after treatment at the Main Dressing Station or the Field Hospital are moved either directly, or via the Casualty Collecting Points, to a Base Hospital (*Kriegslazarett*) or sometimes to a General Hospital (*Reservelazarett*).

Base Hospitals are large and relatively permanent installations which may be established by an army or the Field Army well to the rear of the combat zone. These hospitals are of two types: General Base Hospitals (*Kriegslazarette*), with normal accommodations for 500 cases, for casualties who require up to eight weeks' treatment before being discharged and for those who require a period of convalescence before moved to Reserve Hospitals; and Base Hospitals for Minor Cases (*Leichtkrankenkriegslazarette*), with accommodations for 1,000 patients, for casualties who need up to four weeks' of treatment or convalescence prior to discharge.

General Hospitals are permanent installations located inside Germany and are supervised by the Chief of Army Equipment.

(5) A man may be pronounced fit for duty by any hospital. If he is in a forward hospital, he will be returned to his unit. If he is in a General Hospital for more than eight weeks, he will he returned to the Replacement Army for reassignment.

c. TRANSPORTATION FACILITIES.

Hospital trains (*Lazarettzüge*) can carry between 358 and 386 lying cases or 920 sitting cases.

Standard German ambulances transport four lying cases, or two lying and four sitting cases, or eight sitting cases.

Horse-drawn vehicles, trucks, and hospital planes also may be used in evacuating the wounded.

4. Evacuation of Horses

a. CHANNELS OF EVACUATION.

Sick and wounded horses are marched by foot from the battlefield to a Horse Dressing Station (*Pferdeverbandplatz*), where emergency cases are treated. They then are marched or transported in horse transport columns to a station set up by the Division Veterinary Company (*Veterinärkompanie*). This station can be established within a minimum of six hours and can treat 150 cases. If the horses require further treatment, they are moved by horse transport columns to the Army Horse Hospital (*Armeepferdelazarett*) or to the Field Army Horse Hospital (*Heerespferdelazarett*). Such field hospitals can be established within a minimum of 12 hours and can handle 500 sick horses. Horse Collecting Points (*Pferdesammelplätz*) are formed generally to expedite the evacuation of horses to the rear. Normally there is an Army Horse Collecting Point (*Armeepferdesammelplatz*), intermediate between division and army, and a Division Horse Collecting Point (*Divisionspferdesammelplatz*) at division. Evacuated horses may be moved either directly or through these collecting points to the rear. Horses which require special surgical operations and those not likely to be fit again for army use are moved by rail from the field hospitals to the Zone of the Interior Home Horse Hospitals (*Heimatpferdelazarette*).

b. TRANSPORTATION FACILITIES.

Horse transport trains (*Pferdetransportzüge*) are composed of 55 cars, each carrying six sick or wounded horses, or a total of 350 horses per train. The standard horse transport road column can move 40 sick or wounded horses about 90 miles in one day.

5. Evacuation of Prisoners of War

Guard details drawn from the military police or from the combat unit itself take prisoners to the Division Prisoner of War Collecting Point (*Divisionsgefangenensammelstelle*). The Prisoners of War are next moved to the Army Prisoner of War Collecting Point (*Armeegefangenensammelstelle*), the guard details being drawn from military police, combat troops, or guard units. The Prisoners of War are lastly transferred from the jurisdiction of the Field Army to the Replacement Army Command. This is accomplished when the Prisoners of War are moved by rail to one of the Prisoner of War Camps within Germany. Officers are incarcerated in Officer Prisoner of War Camps (*Offizierlager* or *Oflag*); enlisted men are confined in Enlisted Men's Prisoner of War Camps (*Mannschafts-Stammlager* or *Stalag*).

VI. TROOP MOVEMENTS

1. Introduction

In movements of entire bodies of troops with their equipment, the space occupied, rather than the total weight, is the important factor. A very large proportion of the space is taken up by personnel, horses, and organic equipment; daily maintenance requirements that accompany the troops occupy much less space.

2. Rail Transportation

a. MAIN MILITARY ROUTES.

German railways generally are used jointly for military and civilian traffic, although military trains are given priority. Perhaps the only instances of railways designated solely for military uses are found in the combat zone, either on already existent railways or on railways constructed by the Army.

Normally double-track standard-gauge (4' 8 1/2") railways have a daily capacity of 30 military trains in each direction, while single-track standard-gauge railways can move 10 trains a day in each direction. Air damage can materially decrease these capacity figures.

b. STANDARD TROOP TRAINS.

The Germans have found it desirable to use troop trains of a reasonably constant composition. The standard trains found in the Balkans, Italy, and Norway are composed of fewer cars than the base types in Germany, Denmark, and the Netherlands which are described below. All types are designed as far as possible to carry a self-contained unit such as a company or a battalion. Nonstandard trains also may be used for troop movements.

K-trains (*Kraftfahrzüge* or motor vehicle trains) average 51 cars per train and carry Approximately 250 soldiers, 20 heavy vehicles (weighing up to 22 short tons per vehicle), and 20 light vehicles, plus other equipment. If lighter equipment is carried, the number of soldiers can be increased.

S-trains (*Sonderzüge*, or special trains) are made up for the movement of very heavy tanks and self-propelled guns. The number of men carried per train averages 125; the number of cars forming the

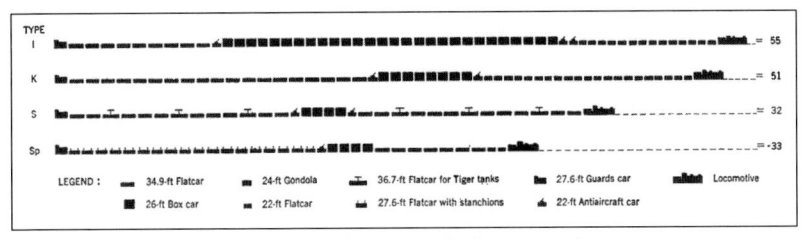

Figure 7. German basic standard troop-train types

train is between 30 and 35. An S-train usually carries from four to six Tiger tanks or from six to eight Panther tanks, interspersed with lighter equipment.

Sp-trains (*Sonderpanzerzüge*, or special tank trains) carry Approximately 20 medium tanks together with personnel and other equipment. The standard Sp-train is composed of about 33 cars.

I-trains (*Infanteriezüge* or infantry trains) of about 55 cars per train hold some 350 officers and men, 10 light vehicles, 10 heavy vehicles of a maximum weight of 22 short tons per vehicle, and 70 horses, together with other equipment. If a minimum of equipment is carried, up to 800 troops can be moved. It is possible that the I-trains seldom are used by the Germans at present.

Replacement troop trains with 50 to 60 cars per train can hold over 2,000 replacements. The use of this type of train probably has been discontinued.

c. ENTRAINMENT AND DETRAINMENT.
Troop trains generally are formed at railroad stations. The speed with which entraining can be accomplished varies according to the number of units being loaded, the number of stations used, the facilities available at the stations, and the importance attached to speedy loading. Depending on these conditions, loading of a single train can be accomplished within 2 to 12 hours. If all the unit trains can be loaded simultaneously at the entraining stations, an entire division can be loaded within that time. In practice, however, the time taken to assemble trains and troops and the limited number of entraining stations will materially increase the loading time of divisions.

It is estimated that a troop train can be unloaded in about half the time taken to load. Detrainment of infantry units may occur far forward, while armored units usually are detrained in rear areas.

d. SPEED OF MOVEMENTS.

The average German movement appears to average from 150 to 200 miles per day for long movements within Germany, and about 60 miles daily in areas near the combat zone.

e. TRAIN REQUIREMENTS.

At present the number of trains required to transport an infantry division is about 35 to 40. An armored division needs about twice that number. If a large number of divisions are being moved, additional trains will be necessary for corps and army units.

3. Road Transportation

a. MAIN MILITARY ROUTES.

Certain roads have been selected by the High Command to form a system of through routes (*Durchgangstrassen*) for military traffic in Germany and occupied areas. For the most part the through routes comprise the national highways and *Autobahnen*. In Denmark, however, the through routes more frequently consist of secondary roads than main arteries. Through routes generally run either east and west or north and south. When supply or troop movements are to be made over these roads, all civilian traffic is diverted to other roads.

b. MARCH SPEEDS.

(1) The average speeds of division marches in miles per hour are as follows:
- Infantry division: 3 by day, 3 by night
- Motorized division: 16 by day, 10 by night
- Armored division: 12 by day, 7 by night

(2) The average speeds of march columns in miles per hour are as follows:
- Infantry (long marches): 3
- Infantry (short marches): 4
- Mounted troops: 6
- Cyclists: 8
- Motorcycles and cars: 22
- Trucks: 22
- Trucks with trailers: 16
- Half-track vehicles: 16

- Tanks: 12

c. MARCH DISTANCES.

The infantry division normally can march about 20 miles in a day; under adverse weather or road conditions the rate of march may fall to 10 miles a day. The motorized division can maintain an average daily march of between 90 and 150 miles; the armored division from 60 to 90 miles a day. In the near vicinity of the combat zone, road movements without motor transport average 10 to 15 miles a day, while movements by motor transport approximate 30 miles a day.

INFANTRY DIVISION (at 5 kilometers or approximately 3 miles per hour.)		
	Yards	Meters
Inf Regt (each of three)	6,234	5,700
Rcn Bn	3,116	2,850
AT Bn	2,734	2,500
Arty Regt	7,382	6,750
Sig Bn	3,193	2,920
Engr Bn	2,570	2,350
Div Serv	4,155	3,800
Div Hq	1,553	1,420
Total Inf Div (approx.; without intervals between elements)	43,405	39,690
Total converted to miles	24.7	

ARMORED DIVISION (at 20 kilometers or approximately 12 miles per hour.)		
	Yards	Meters
Tank Regt	21,325	19,500
Pz Gren Regt (each of two)	13,145	12,020
Pz Rcn Bn	9,154	8,370
AT Bn	3,838	3,510
Pz Arty Regt	14,458	13,220
Pz Sig Bn	3,762	3,440
Pz Engr Bn	6,365	5,820
Div Serv	11,702	10,700
Div Hq	1,444	1,320
Others	5,468	5,000
Total Armd Div (approx.; without intervals between elements)	103,806	94,920
Total converted to miles	59	

Road spaces

d. ROAD SPACES.

While the road spaces occupied by divisions on the march are not constant, the road spaces of individual units may prove of some value. The examples on the previous page are from German sources and do not indicate the intervals maintained between elements.

If distances between the individual units are included, the average length of the infantry division would be about 30 miles (at 3 miles per hour), of the armored division 70 miles (at 12 miles per hour), and of the motorized division 80 miles (at 16 miles per hour).

4. Sea Transportation

a. GENERAL.

In the sea movements referred to in the following text, the basic shipping measurement is the gross registered ton (G/T), which is 100 cubic feet of the entire enclosed space of a ship.

The Germans use all types of cargo and passenger vessels for the transportation of troops. Generally the depth of water of the embarkation and debarkation ports determines the size of ship to be used. Thus many of the Baltic ports are limited to cargo ships up to 2,000 G/T. Cargo between Norway and Germany, on the other hand, ordinarily can be carried on much larger vessels.

The average speed of a ship is estimated at 200 nautical miles per day, although fast ships may average much more.

b. LOADING AND UNLOADING TIMES.

The time required for the loading of a vessel varies with a number of factors, such as the size of the vessel, the plan of the vessel, the port facilities, and the efficiency with which loading is conducted. The following average loading times are based upon German estimates. They apply for loading during day and night; considerable delays, however, may occur on account of adverse weather conditions.

- 100 men: 8 minutes loading time
- 100 horses (led over a ramp): 1 hour loading time
- 100 horses (lifted by cranes): 6 hours loading time
- 100 light motor vehicles (lifted by cranes): 6 hours loading time
- Supplies sufficient to load a 2,000 G/T vessel: 16 hours loading time

c. TONNAGE REQUIREMENTS.

Among other factors, the amount of tonnage required to transport troops depends upon the type of unit being transported, the efficiency of loading, the types of ships used, and the amount of nonmilitary stowage transported. Hence the following figures give only a general indication of the amount of space which is occupied by items when efficiently loaded.

- 1 man: 2 Estimated G/T requirement
- 1 horse: 8 Estimated G/T requirement
- 1 light motor vehicle: 10 Estimated G/T requirement
- 1 truck: 20 Estimated G/T requirement
- 1 heavy field gun: 20 Estimated G/T requirement
- 1 medium tank: 25 Estimated G/T requirement

It is likely that an infantry division requires between 50,000 and 70,000 gross registered tons for its movement, or a mean average of five or six gross registered tons per man. If loading is inefficient or if light loading is used, the G/T requirements per man will rise considerably. Thus in short movements such as ferry crossing, as much as 15 gross registered tons per man and equipment have been employed.

A BATTALION COMMANDER LOOKS US OVER

Intelligence Bulletin, January 1945

These enemy comments have a special value for U.S. junior officers and enlisted men, not only because U.S. combat methods are seen through German eyes, but because of the marked emphasis on German counter-measures.

Several weeks ago a Panzer Grenadier battalion commander prepared a report on his unit's recent experiences in combat against U.S. forces, and recommended possible improvements in German methods.

U.S. INFANTRY

During the past week of operations, the U.S. infantry has not gone in for aggressive action. When possible, they avoid close combat. When attacking, they mass behind tanks or sit on the tanks. They very seldom take advantage of darkness or fog to begin an attack. As a rule, an attack is preceded by a strong artillery preparation in which the Americans employ all calibers, including their heaviest. Planes are used for fire direction, and excellent results have been obtained. The infantry shoots wildly into areas where the presence of our troops is suspected, or into our principal sectors. Most of the fire is unaimed.

U.S. ARTILLERY

Artillery directed by observation planes places fire on each of our movements. The infantry main effort usually is supported by good fire concentration and by tanks. German counterattacks are harassed by U.S. fighter bombers, which strafe and bomb German infantry.

Fire concentrations on road crossings and identified positions are always placed at irregular intervals.

U.S. TANKS

If a U.S. tank is hit by our antitank weapons, the other tanks immediately turn away. In breaking through to our positions, they fire on our troops in foxholes with automatic rifles and machine-gun fire.

It is therefore recommended that: we dig our foxholes at a right angle underground. In attacking U.S. tanks at close range, the large rifle grenade and bazooka have proved to be valuable weapons. The small rifle grenade was found to be ineffective and unable to penetrate the tanks.

GERMAN ATTACK METHODS

As to our own attacks, we found them to be more successful when they were launched without artillery preparation, so as to gain surprise. Also, we have made the most of darkness and fog.

If artillery support is used, it is best to camouflage the concentration in the sector of our attack by simultaneously covering the other sectors with fire.

Whenever possible, attack preparations should be avoided during the day. U.S. air observation detects every movement, and directs sudden and heavy fire concentrations on the deployment area.

To avoid losses, the line of departure should be reached by infiltration. Attack in depth cuts down our own losses and allows us to employ our troops flexibly.

When our troops have been caught by U.S. artillery fire, we have found it very hard to escape trying to go around this fire. Therefore, it is recommended that our troops take cover immediately. If this is done, our troops should work their way close enough to be inside the minimum range of artillery and mortars. It has often proved advisable to attach 81-mm mortars to the assaulting units.

It is also useful to have an observation post well forward at the point of main effort, to direct fire from the captured positions.

With reference to the lack of cooperation by the artillery, it must be emphasized again and again that everyone must help the infantrymen.

At the point of main effort, double communication must be ensured by telephone and radio.

GERMAN DEFENSE METHODS

The following are recommended:

1. Deployment in depth in the sector. Always have a reserve available even though it is only a small force.
2. Establishment of three observation posts simultaneously—in the main line of resistance, in the advanced sector of resistance, and in the immediate vicinity of a gun position.

In previous engagements the installation of three observation posts proved very valuable, because the enemy—always was under our observation and fire, even though a penetration had been made.

Only one 81-mm mortar should be attached to the attacking company. Readiness and quick changing of positions make this a valuable weapon. The remainder of the weapons should be under the control of the mortar platoon leader for concentrated use in any one sector.

GERMAN INFANTRY DIVISION CUT TO MEET MANPOWER SHORTAGE

Tactical and Technical Trends,
No. 51, October 1944

A large percentage of German infantry divisions have been reorganized within the past year with their strength reduced but with virtually the same, or even increased, firepower. Two new types of six-battalion divisions have been encountered. One of them has two three-battalion regiments, and the other, a more common type, has three two-battalion regiments. Significant differences of both new types from the normal infantry division of 1943 are summarized below:

1. Total personnel is reduced from about 17,200, normal 1943 strength, to a maximum of about 12,400.
2. Infantry reduced to six battalions—either two regiments of three battalions each, or, more commonly, three regiments of two battalions each.
3. Infantry platoons usually reduced from four to three squads.
4. Reduction in personnel of supply columns and medical units.
5. General economy in use of personnel throughout the division, either by elimination or by doubling-up of duties.
6. Reconnaissance battalion replaced by a divisional Füsilier battalion, with an organization identical with that of the usual infantry battalion, but with more mobility given by extensive use of bicycles. With the change from offensive to defensive warfare, and the shortage of manpower, this mobile reserve takes the place of the reconnaissance unit.
7. Bridge column in the engineer battalion withdrawn to GHQ.
8. Firepower maintained, and even increased in some components.
9. Increase in caliber, though decrease in total number, of mortars and antitank guns, some of the latter being self-propelled.

Weapons	Old Type Inf Div, about 17,200 men	New Type Inf Div*, not over 12,400 men
LMGs	527	643
HvMGs	116	62
20-mm AA/AT Guns	11	40
50-mm, 75-mm, 76.2-mm, or 88-mm AT Guns	75	---
75-mm, 76.2-mm, or 88-mm AT Guns	---	48
75-mm, 76.2-mm, or 88-mm AT Guns (all SP)	---	14
Mortars:		
50-mm	84	---
81-mm	58	48
120-mm	---	28
Inf Hows:		
75-mm	20	18
150-mm	6	6
Arty:		
105-mm Hows	36	36
105-mm Guns	4	---
150-mm Hows	8	12
Flamethrowers	20	20

Three two-battalion regiment type only.

	Div Hq	Div Fusilier Bn	Sig Bn	Inf Regt	Inf Regt	Inf Regt	Arty Regt	AT Bn	Eng Bn	Div Serv	Total
MGs, Lt	2	51	12	111	111	111	69	32	31	61	591
MGs, Hv	-	8	-	16	16	16	-	-	6	-	62
AT guns, 75, 76.2, or 88-mm	-	-	-	12	12	12	-	12	-	-	48
AA/AT guns, 20-mm	-	4	-	8	8	8	-	12	-	-	40
AT, SP guns, 75, 76.2, or 88-mm	-	-	-	-	-	-	-	14	-	-	14
Mortars, 81-mm	-	6	-	12	12	12	-	-	6	-	48
Mortars, 120-mm	-	4	-	8	8	8	-	-	-	-	28
Inf. How, 75-mm	-	-	-	6	6	6	-	-	-	-	18
Inf. How, 150-mm	-	-	-	2	2	2	-	-	-	-	6
F. Hows, 105-mm	-	-	-	-	-	-	36	-	-	-	36
F. Hows, 150-mm	-	-	-	-	-	-	12	-	-	-	36
Flame-thrower	-	-	-	-	-	-	-	-	20	-	20

New-type German infantry division: strength and weapons (with three 2-battalion regiments)

10. Increase in number of 20-mm dual-purpose guns provides strengthened organic antiaircraft defense.

In all types of German units, the trend has been to supplement German manpower to an increasing extent by the use of a substantial minority of foreign auxiliaries (Hilfswilligen). These are usually Italian or Soviet prisoners of war.

There will be considerable differences, of course, in the strength and equipment of the various divisions. These differences will increase with shortages of matériel and personnel and with the consequent need for improvisation.

THE GERMAN KAMIKAZES

German Leaders Failed to Recognize a New Counteramphibious Tactic
Intelligence Bulletin, June 1946.

One of the most hushed up secrets of the war, back before the surrender of Japan, was the damage and inconvenience caused by the suicide-bent Kamikaze pilots of the Japanese Air Force. Troops who sailed to the invasion of Okinawa remember the Baka bomb, the winged aerial torpedo with its human pilot. But not until the end of the war, when intelligence officers began nosing around in the former Nazi domain, was it disclosed that a small group of fanatical Nazis had also organized a suicide corps for the purpose of breaking up the seaborne invasion of the continent with a German version of the Japanese Baka.

In fact, there is much evidence to indicate that the Nazi suicidists were laying their plans long before their Japanese allies conceived the idea for this unconventional tactic. Only bureaucratic inefficiency, and disinterest in official circles as high as Hitler himself, forstalled the appearance of Nazi Kamikazes in the air over Normandy on D-day.

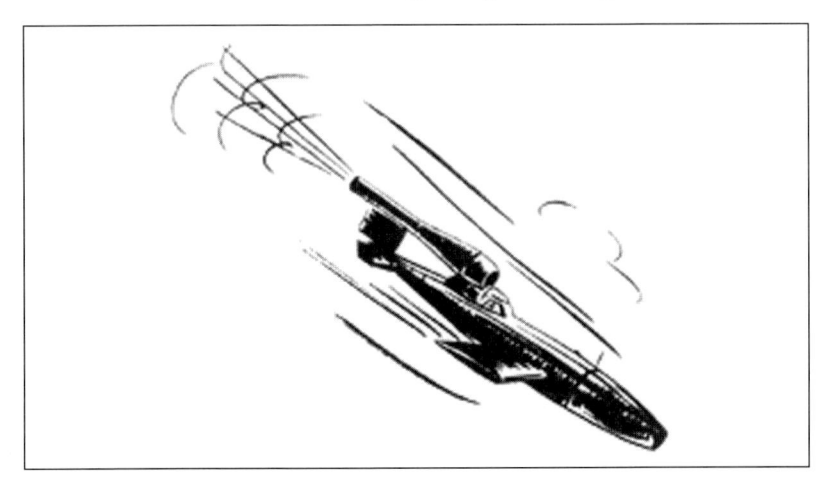

The inception of this strange project goes back to the year 1943, when the fortunes of war were beginning to turn against the hitherto victorious German Army. At that time, many people in Germany were beginning to see that the Fatherland would ultimately go down to defeat, unless some miraculous event produced a severe set-back to the Allied cause. Among these thinking Germans was a small group of idealists who were determined to do something about it. These people, who at first numbered no more than 30 or 40 persons, came together from all walks of life. Some of them were from the Army, others were civilians, and one of the leaders was a well-known German woman flyer.

It was the common belief of these people that the war was lost unless a most decisive blow could be struck against the Allies. They believed that this could only be accomplished by the complete disruption of the eventual Allied assault upon the continent, thus convincing the Allied leaders that Germany was secure and impregnable within her "fortress Europe."

AN IDEA IS BORN

From this line of reasoning, the idea of a suicide corps was born. It was thought that a weapon could be devised in the form of a flying bomb which, when piloted to its target, could sink a large warship or troop transport. Enough of these, the idealists believed, could completely wreck any seaborne invasion with an expenditure of less than 1,000 volunteer pilots. The members of this strange group were ready to volunteer. They asked only that they be given a weapon which would be certain to achieve its end, and they felt there were persons among their membership who had the skill to design such a weapon.

By October 1943, under the leadership of the woman flyer, a doctor of the Institute of Medical Aeronautics at Rechlin, and a first lieutenant of the Luftwaffe, organizational plans had advanced to a point where it was necessary to obtain official recognition and cooperation in conducting the project further. Because of her unique position in German aviation circles, this duty fell to the aviatrix.

The woman first presented the idea to the Luftwaffe High Command, and met with immediate rebuff. The German Air Force was not interested in an idea they considered to be the unstable reasoning of a group of psychopaths. After much delay, the Luftwaffe was by-passed, and the aviatrix went directly to Field Marshall Milch, at that time the head of the German Air Ministry. Again no progress was made.

After more weeks had passed, the woman determined to exploit her position and reputation in German aviation circles, and succeeded in gaining a hearing before the German Academy of Aeronautics. This Academy had the power to assemble the necessary scientists, technicians, and air tactical authorities, and eventually a meeting was called by the Director of the German Aeronautical Research Council. After a lengthy conference, the committee of authorities decided that the idea was indeed operationally sound.

With this authoritative evidence in hand, the next step before the group of idealists was to obtain official support and leadership for the suicide plan. Application was made for an interview with Hitler, and in February 1944, the woman leader of the project was summoned to Berchtesgaden for a 3-hour discussion with the Fuehrer.

INTERVIEW WITH HITLER

Hitler did not approve. He objected to the philosophy of suicide entailed in the plan, and pointed out that there was no precedent in German history like it. Therefore, he said, the whole idea was not in keeping with the character of the German people. The woman countered this with the argument that never before in German history had the fate of the country been in such a precarious position. This, apparently, was the wrong thing to say, for Hitler replied emphatically that the position was *not* precarious, and that if it ever became so, then he, Hitler, would personally give the orders for such desperate measures to be taken.

The interview was anything but successful, but before she left, the aviatrix did obtain Hitler's permission to continue with the development and planning so that the organization would be ready to operate if ever the Fuehrer felt the time had come to take such desperate steps. His parting remark was to the effect that he did not want to be bothered with the idea again until the time for action was ripe.

Meanwhile the group of suicide volunteers had grown to about 70 or 80 members. As yet no concerted recruiting effort had been made, and such volunteers as were accepted were a very select group. Once accepted, a candidate for membership in the suicide corps was required to take a pledge to the effect that "I hereby volunteer as a pilot of the manned glider-bomb. I am convinced that this action will end with my death."

On the basis of Hitler's permission to continue with the development of the program, the matter was laid before the Chief of the General Staff of the German Air Force. He half-heartedly assigned the official direction of the project to the commander of a Luftwaffe bomber wing that was engaged in all sorts of special operations and clandestine activities. At first it appeared that the plan was finally on the road to fruition, but it soon became evident that the new commander accepted the assignment mostly because he saw in it the means of receiving the glory and credit which would be brought by the self-sacrifice of the volunteers under him.

THE WEAPON

But at the same time, the German Air Ministry was ordered to perfect the technical preparations which would be necessary to put the plan into effect. The Messerschmitt 328, originally designed as a fighter or fighter bomber, was selected as the flying weapon to be used by the volunteers. Production of the plane was ordered, but proceeded so slowly that the volunteers began to suspect that some sort of official sabotage was afoot. As a result, the suicide group began to look around for another weapon—one which was easy to produce and would be available on short order. The V-1 "buzz bomb," rebuilt to carry a pilot, was decided upon. In less than 3 weeks, four types of this piloted missile were ready for testing.

Contrary to the wishes of the volunteer group, the Luftwaffe testing division insisted upon using their own pilots for the test flights. The two Luftwaffe men were soon seriously injured, and it was then that the woman pilot was called in and permitted to do the test flying. It was not an easy proposition. In order to train the suicide pilots, a two-seater "buzz bomb" had been built. Of course, it was necessary to land this model, if trainees were to be kept alive for the D-day mission. But since it was necessary to glide to a landing without power, and since the missile was not of conventional aircraft or glider design, the approach to the runway was necessarily steep, and landing had to be

This is the Nazi version of the Japanese "Baka" bomb. It is driven by a typical V-1 jet engine. Carrying a load of explosive in the nose of this craft, Nazi suicide pilots planned to wreak destruction among our D-day fleet with this weapon. Although the weapon was developed, the plan went astray through official indifference and bungling among the higher echelons of the Nazi command.

made at speeds approaching 155 miles per hour.

But as the technical development of the weapon went on with fair success, the rest of the program began to go astray through the bungling of the Luftwaffe officers put in charge of the volunteers. Although the suicide group at first believed the Luftwaffe wing commander—the one who had been appointed their official leader—was fully behind their plan, it soon became evident that he had little sincere interest in the project. What was worse, he appointed a staff of other Luftwaffe officers to responsible planning and operational positions. These officers apparently had no conception of the original mission of the volunteers—to destroy the eventual Allied invasion fleet. Instead, they were continually fostering half-baked ideas, such as suicide attacks upon Soviet ammunition trains on the Eastern Front. Although the volunteers were willing to give their lives to deliver a smashing blow to the Allies, they were reluctant to die on some comparatively non-essential mission. Meanwhile the training program had also bogged down. Much time was spent in physical education and pistol shooting, but little attention was paid to establishing a sound flight training program. The Luftwaffe Lieutenant, one of the original volunteers and who had been the spark plug behind the whole idea, found himself helpless because of his low rank. Although he tried repeatedly to make improvements, he could do nothing but take orders.

Again the woman flyer was called upon to use her influence to try and revive the rapidly failing program. This time she went to Himmler, in hopes that he might be able to do some good for the cause of the suicide volunteers. Himmler was not much help. He was not opposed to the suicide idea, but he was of the opinion that the membership of the corps should be made up of criminals and the incurably diseased. He offered to take over the program if one of his officers was permitted to assume the leadership of the entire plan. It was evident that under Himmler the plan would not receive any better treatment than it was getting under its present supervision, so his offer was turned down.

D-DAY ARRIVES

About this time, the Allies took a hand in things by staging their invasion in Normandy. Neither the suicide weapon, nor adequately trained suicide pilots were available, greatly because of the mishandling the whole program had received from its selfish or uninterested directors. The disappointment of the volunteer group was profound. Within 6 or 7 days after D-day, they realized that the invasion was a success, and that the moment for which they had been preparing had passed.

But, several days after the invasion had started, and all other efforts to halt it had failed, Herman Goering suddenly remembered that somewhere in his Luftwaffe there was a group of pilots who had volunteered for a suicide mission. In due course, Goering reached the commander of the bomber wing under whom the volunteers had originally been placed. The commander, a colonel, immediately declared that the group was ready for action. The volunteers were astounded. They knew that no planes or "buzz bombs" were available, and that only a few of the men had any more than the briefest of preflight training. Nonetheless, the commander and his technical assistants, without consulting the volunteers, set to work on plans to use a Focke Wulf 190, carrying a 4,000-pound bomb, to crash into selected targets. Now no one in the German Air Force had ever flown this plane with such a large bomb load, and it was highly doubtful that the plane would be able to get off the ground without crashing. Consequently, regular test pilots declined the honor of testing this experimental makeshift. Undaunted, the commander announced that his suicide pilots—none of whom had ever flown an FW 190, if any other plane—would within the next few days conduct the test flights themselves. If they were killed, he said, their names and loyal sacrifice would be recorded in German history with the same honor they would have received if they had crashed their plane onto the deck of an enemy ship. Any enthusiasm that had remained among the volunteers disappeared completely at this point.

Fortunately for these men, Hitler heard about the plans for using the FW 190, and ordered the project abandoned. The bomber commander was removed, eventually, and his successor set about trying to salvage some of the finer ideas of the original project. But by then it was too late. The Allies were established in force on the continent, the hour to strike had passed, and so the group of suicide volunteers was disbanded.

"And so," to quote the woman flyer, "did an idea that was born of fervent and holy idealism, only to be misused and mismanaged at every turn by people who never understood how men could offer their lives simply for an idea in which they believed."

CONCLUSION

Were it not for the grievous damage done to our fleet units a year later by the Japanese *Kamikaze* corps, this German project might be passed off as just another unconventional tactical venture which the German leaders were smart enough to recognize as nothing but foolishness. But in the light of our later experience with the Japanese, it is possible to draw the conclusion that the Nazi command failed to realize they were being offered an impressive counterweapon to seaborne invasion. It is useless, in retrospect, to attempt a reconstruction of what might have happened off Normandy on D-day, if the Nazi command had recognized the potentialities of these volunteers and their piloted bomb. Although it is unlikely that the suicidists could have thus defeated the invasion, the introduction of such an unconventional tactic, if exploited on the scale later used by the Japanese, would certainly have offered another serious threat to an already difficult amphibious operation.

EXTRACT FROM THE TELEPHONE DIARY OF THE 352ND INFANTRY DIVISION (COASTAL DEFENSE SECTION BAYEUX)

D-Day

1.00 hours: LXXXIV AK to 352nd Infantry Division: State of readiness II. Parachutists jumped on 716th Infantry Division sector.

1.15 hours: Putting all units on the alert by telephone ended.

1.45 hours: Report from 914th Grenadier Regiment: From fifty to sixty enemy parachutists jumped near Carentan Canal south of Brévands.

2.00 hours: Report from 914th Grenadier Regiment: A new landing of parachute troops from thirty to fifty aircraft south of Brévands. Individual parachutists landed near 2nd Battalion of 352nd Artillery Regiment in the vicinity of Cardonville.

2.07 hours: Report from 916th Grenadier Regiment: No enemy contact yet on our sector.

2.09 hours: Call of the Ia on the Commander of 726th Grenadier Regiment: How is the situation? No enemy on the sector of Bessin.

2.13 hours: Ia of the Division reports to Ia of Gen Kdo LXXXIV AK: On the left wing of 914th Grenadier Regiment sector an estimated strength of one battalion parachutists near Carentan Canal southwest of Brévands. Individual parachutists, who evidently have missed their goal, are near Cardonville. Up to the time, on all other sectors quiet prevails.

2.14 hours: Report from Naval Commandant Normandy: Enemy sea targets located 11 kilometers north of Grandcamp.

2.15 hours: Report by Naval Commandant Normandy transmitted to 352nd Artillery Regiment.

2.35 hours: Information from our right neighboring 716th Infantry Division: Parachutists near Amfreville, Berville, Conneville,

Herouvilette.

2.46 hours: Report from the 352nd Army Post Office: 2.35 hours two airplanes with troop-carrying gliders sighted, direction S-N.

2.48 hours: Report by the 352nd Army Post Office transmitted to 726th, 914th, 915th, 916th Grenadier Regiments.

2.55 hours: Report from 914th Grenadier Regiment: Approximately from eight to ten parachutists sighted near 4th Battalion of 352nd Artillery Regiment. Near Cardonville two parachutists with camouflage parachutes and in camouflage uniforms were taken prisoner. Apparently near Isigny landing of seventy paratroopers. Confirmation not yet on hand.

3.10 hours: Order from Gen Kdo LXXXIV AK (transmitted by Ia): Enemy parachute landing on either side of the Vire outlet. In the meadows south of Carentan, troop-carrying gliders landed Approximately one company. Presumably they are going to advance to Carentan.

3.10 hours: 352nd Infantry Division keeps open the routes with its left neighboring 709th Infantry Division via Carentan and for this purpose moves Task Force Meyer to Isigny-Carentan. The task force is assigned to the corps reserve. The start of the movement is to be reported.

3.15 hours: Ia order to Obstlt Meyer, 915th Grenadier Regiment: The whole of the task force to be made ready and moved forward over the bridge west of Neuilly into the area Montmartin-Deville. The march is to be made in several columns and small groups. Readiness to march and the roll-call is to be duly reported.

3.20 hours: 01 Gen Kdo LXXXIV AK to the Division (upon inquiry): Order No 1200/ 44 g. Kdos (Fuhrer order) is to be released.

3.22 hours: Report from 352nd Artillery Regiment: Since 03.20 hours 4th Battalion of 352nd Artillery Regiment is covered by pattern bombing. Strong air formations with troop-carrying gliders flying to the south.

3.25 hours: Ia of the Division to 914th Grenadier Regiment: Instruction concerning the bringing up of Task Force Meyer. Reconnoitering to be started against enemy troops landed in the depression south of Carentan.

3.30 hours: Report from 352nd Artillery Regiment: At present air attacks are being made on 4th Battalion of 352nd Artillery Regiment.

3.35 hours: Report from 916th Grenadier Regiment: Strongest bombing attacks on Le Guay, Point du Hoc and Grandcamp.

3.44 hours: Report from the Naval Commandant Normandy: One reinforced battalion of paratroops southwest of Brévands; here only a weak enemy detachment had landed. Bombing attacks are taking place continuously.

3.50 hours: Report from 915th Grenadier Regiment: Task Force Meyer ready to march. Roll-call at 04.15 hours.

3.53 hours: Ia reports to Chief-of-Staff Gen Kdo LXXXIV AK: Locating of sea targets has been disrupted at the time. March of Task Force Meyer to commence at 04.15 hours, one battalion to Carentan and two battalions into the area around Montmartin.

4.01 hours: Report from the Aviation Report Center Caen: On the sector of our right neighboring 716th Infantry Division, approach flight of strong four-motored formations with troop-carrying gliders heading south-west to Houlgate-Cabourg. Jumpings of parachutists near Morsalines, St Come and Ste Mere-Église with the left neighboring 709th Infantry Division. Three prisoners captured, carrying maps of the Vire river mouth.

4.07 hours: Information from our right neighbouring 716th Infantry Division: Current reinforcements in the form of airborne gliders and parachute formations east of Orne.

4.08 hours: Report from theAviation Report Center Caen transmitted to 726th Grenadier Regiment.

4.19 hours: Information from Ic Gen Kdo LXXXIV AK to the Division: The situation at the Seine outlet is probably worse than with us; strong enemy parachute and airborne troops have landed there. Details are not yet known. At the time, enemy observes complete radio silence.

4.20 hours: Report from 915th Grenadier Regiment: Task Force Meyer—915th Grenadier Regiment and Fusilier Battalion (Artillery Battalion of 352nd Artillery Regiment)—is marching off and its arrival can be expected to take place in three or four hours.

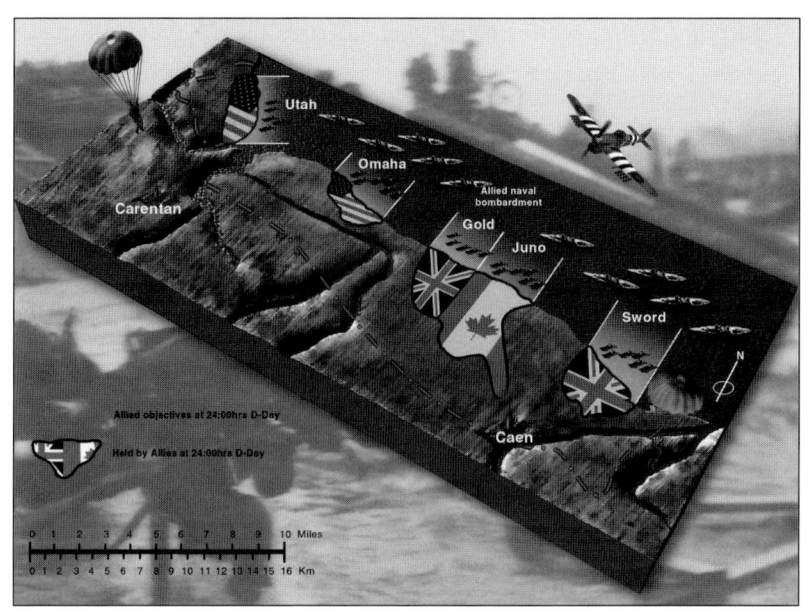

Operation Overlord

On the sector of 726th Grenadier Regiment, artillery fire can be heard.

4.30 hours: Report from 914th Grenadier Regiment: Report on the start and progress of the attack launched by the two battalions of 914th Grenadier Regiment against parachute troops southwest of Brévands. Details are not yet known. Near Carentan Canal the enemy is forcing his way from Le Moulin to the south.

4.34 hours: Report from 352nd Artillery Regiment: Landing craft have not yet been sighted ahead of Grandcamp.

4.35 hours: Report from 916th Grenadier Regiment: An American 1/Lt taken prisoner near St Pole Guay testified that along with the parachute troops also dummy dolls are being dropped, which explode when contacting the ground.

4.45 hours: Report from 726th Grenadier Regiment: Between 04.00 and 04.10 hours, Defense Works Nos 44, 47 and 48 were bombed heavily.

5.02 hours: Report from 352nd Artillery Regiment: Off Port-en-Bessin one big and four smaller naval units were sighted. Ahead of Grandcamp light naval units are reported.

5.03 hours: Report from 352nd Panzerjager Battalion: Single troop-carrying gliders were sighted at an altitude of 2,000 meters heading to the west.

5.06 hours: Report from 726th Grenadier Regiment: Defense Works, particularly near Arromanches, St Honorine and Colleville, in continuous air attacks, are covered with bombs of the heaviest caliber. Over Sully parachutists were observed, which probably were a crew which jumped from an airplane shot down.

5.10 hours: Report from 914th Grenadier Regiment: 2nd Battalion of 914th Grenadier Regiment brought in three American prisoners with aerial photos and maps of the Cotentin peninsula, particularly of the area around the mouth of the River Vireo For the time being, the prisioners cannot be forwarded, as enemy parachute forces have blocked the way.

5.15 hours: Ia exchanging information with Ia of the left neighboring 709th Infantry Division: In Carentan itself there are no enemy troops, but north of Carentan stronger parachute forces have been dropped. Ste Mere-Église is held by enemy parch ute troops.

5.20 hours: Report from 352nd Artillery Regiment: Advanced observers of 2nd and 4th Battalions of 352nd Artillery Regiment report to have ascertained noises which probably originate from naval units, at approximate distance of two kilometers, heading toward the Vire outlet. Furthermore, 29 ships, including four bigger type naval units (at least destroyer or cruiser class) are reported to be observed at a distance of from six to ten kilometers heading toward Le Guay-Point du Hoc. Three or four aircraft have been shot down near Formigny; one pilot (a Pole) was taken prisoner. The number of landing craft off Port-en-Bessin has increased to fifty.

5.22 hours: Report from the Naval Commandant Normandy: Our naval units were firing at sea targets. One enemy ship blew up. Ia informed the Naval Commandant that about fifty landing craft, together with four bigger naval units, probably destroyers, were lying off Port-en-Bessin.

5.25 hours: Report from 726th Grenadier Regiment: 10 kilometers north of Port-en-Bessin, thirty ships have been observed proceeding slowly, keeping course to the west. Marine Battery

Longue presumes them to be gunboats or destroyers.

5.27 hours: Report from 352nd Artillery Regiment: Off Port-en-Bessin, four bigger naval units. Close by the coastline, our own small naval units were observed.

5.32 hours: Report from 916th Grenadier Regiment: In the Bay of Colleville-Vierville, landing boats are nearing the beach. Farther on, bigger naval units have been sighted, keeping course to the west. A naval formation consisting of five men-of-war is heading toward the east; small landing boats have taken course landward. Apparently, the enemy enshrouds himself in a mantle of artificial fog.

5.35 hours: Ia reports to the Chief-of-Staff of Gen Kdo LXXXIV AK: Transmission of the report delivered by 916th Grenadier Regiment; in addition, five naval units have been observed further off from St Laurent, three of them units approaching the coast, together with a larger number of landing craft. Up to this time, twelve prisoners have been made.

5.36 hours: Ia reports to the Commanding General, Gen Marcks: Report identical to that made to the Chief of Staff.

5.37 hours: Report from 726th Grenadier Regiment: Between Defense Works Nos 56, 59 and 60 and ahead of Asnelles, numerous landing boats with their bows toward the coast are debarking. Naval units began to deliver fire on the beaches from their broadsides.

5.45 hours: Report from 914th Grenadier Regiment: North of Defense Work No 88, twenty-six landing boats, including bigger units, have been observed.

5.50 hours: Ia of the Division reports to the Chief of Staff Gen Kdo LXXXIV AK: Report by 726th Grenadier Regiment on landing boats ahead of Defense Works Nos 56, 59 and 60 and at Asnelles, also about firing of the beaches by naval units. The Commander of the Division suggests halting Task Force Meyer in view of the altered situation. The Commanding General agrees and orders the task force to be halted.

5.52 hours: Report from 352nd Artillery Regiment: Approximately from 60 to 80 fast landing boats are approaching the coast near Colleville. Our own artillery cannot reach these boats. The region of Maisy is kept under fire from heavy naval artillery; likewise Marcouf. The naval units on the high sea are too far away for our own artillery.

5.55 hours: Report from 916th Grenadier Regiment: Ahead of Vierville, forty-five smaller and middle-sized landing boats were observed, which opened fire on the coast.

5.56 hours: Report from 914th Grenadier Regiment: From ten to fifteen kilometers north of Defense Work No 88, three big naval units were observed, which delivered fire to the region of Maisy.

6.03 hours: Order transmitted by the Divisional Ia to 352nd Fusilier Battalion (it had switched in to the telephone network): Halt the Battalion; await further orders from the Commander of 915th Grenadier Regiment. Fusilier battalion located in the woods of Cerisy on the march road.

6.04 hours: Report from 916th Grenadier Regiment: By 05.45 hours, altogether 140 ships were assembled in the Bay of Vierville. The coastal defenses are subjected to a heavy naval fire.

6.15 hours: Report from 726th Grenadier Regiment: Defense Work No 60 is subjected to particularly heavy artillery fire. In the neighborhood of Defense Work No 37, twenty smaller landing boats are approaching the beaches.

6.17 hours: Report from 726th Grenadier Regiment: Some of the naval units off the coast near Defense Work No 37 turn away to the west.

6.20 hours: Report from 916th Grenadier Division: In the Bay of Vierville, tank landing craft have been clearly observed.

6.25 hours: Ia of the Division informs 352nd Panzerjager Battalion of the appearance of the first tank landing craft in the Bay of Vierville.

6.26 hours: Report from 352nd Artillery Regiment: The coast between Defense Works Nos 59 and 60 is held under the heaviest artillery fire. Large naval formations lie far away on the high sea. By heavy bombing attacks on 1716th Battery Emplacement, some of the guns were buried by rubble; three of them have been set free again and emplaced anew. At the time the artillery regiment maintains good connections with the observation posts.

6.32 hours: Report from 126th Grenadier Regiment: Landing boats off the coast between Defense Works Nos 59,61 and 62 and ahead of Asnelles. The enemy is enshrouding sea targets in a mantle of artificial fog and placing a wall of fog before the coast. Up to this time, the companies of the reserve battalion have suffered only a few casualties.

6.37 hours: Report from 126th Grenadier Regiment: The first landing boats are debarking on the beaches ahead of Defense Works Nos 65 and 69. Some of them are tank landing craft.

6.45 hours: Report from 914th Grenadier Regiment: The attack of 2nd Battalion/914th Grenadier Regiment against parachute troops southwest of Brévands is making but slow progress in the terrain not easy to survey. Grandcamp is lying under enemy naval artillery fire.

6.50 hours: Ia of Gen Kdo LXXXIV AK to the Division: According to the testimony of prisoners, one airborne division landed in the Carentan area has the mission to take the town of Carentan. Information by Ia of the Division to Ia of Gen Kdo LXXXIV AK about the newest reports received by the Division on the enemy (see above).

6.57 hours: Report from 914th Grenadier Regiment: Ahead of Defense Work No 92, twenty landing boats are keeping course toward the coast.

7.05 hours: Report from 916th Grenadier Regiment: Near Defense Work No 68, east of Vierville, enemy in the strength of fifty men landed; weaker enemy forces also near Defense Work No 62.

7.06 hours: Report from 126th Grenadier Regiment: Enemy near Defense Work No 60, northeast of Colleville, landed forty men and one tank. Defense Work No 60 engaged in a fire duel.

7.08 hours: Report from 914th Grenadier Regiment: 2nd Battalion/914th Grenadier Regiment, with altogether four companies, is attacking the parachute forces. Against a tenacious resistance of the enemy our attack can gain ground but slowly.

7.20 hours: Report from 126th Grenadier Regiment: Landing of enemy forces on beaches in front of Defense Works Nos 60, 61, and 62, and further to the west. Between Defense Works Nos 61 and 62, enemy in the strength of one company is on the beach, which is under fire from our own artillery. At Defense Work No 61, the 8.8em antitank gun was put out of action by a direct hit. In front of Defense Works Nos 37 and 37a on the right divisional boundary line, landing boats are approaching the coast; landing will begin presently. Defense Work No 37 lies under a heavy artillery and rocket fire.

7.25 hours: Report from 726th Grenadier Regiment: One company is attacking in front of Defense Works Nos 60 and 62. Near Defense Work 61, a further four enemy boats have landed; one boat was put to fire by a 5-cm tank gun. The enemy has penetrated into Defense Work No 62, while No 61 is being attacked both from the beach and from the rear. Telephone connections to Port-en-Bessin and to 1 Battalion/726th Grenadier Regiment are disrupted. Inquiry ofIa to 726th Grenadier Regiment: When and by whom is a counterattack to be carried out between Defense Works Nos 61 and 62 to throw back the enemy?

7.30 hours: Report from 352nd Artillery Regiment: At the time there is no connection to the observation post near Colleville. Landing boats between Defense Works Nos 61 and 62 were contended by cones of concentrated fire. From ten to fifteen smaller landing boats are entering the mouth of the River Vireo

7.35 hours: Ia to the Chief of Staff of Gen Kdo LXXXIV AK: Near Arromanches, on the right divisional boundary line, the enemy landing boats are approaching the coast; the landing is bound to begin immediately. Near Defense Works Nos 6~2, northeast of Colleville, enemy forces of from 100 to 200 men have penetrated our lines. In the Bay of Vierville, there are no enemy troops nearby, but a large number of landing boats are quickly approaching. Request one battalion (1/915th) to be assigned from Task Force Meyer for a counterattack in the neighborhood of Defense Works Nos 60-62. The request was granted by Corps HQ.

7.45 hours: Report from 914th Grenadier Regiment: On the sector of our left neighboring 709th Infantry Division, fifteen landing boats lay at the water's edge in the neighborhood of Le Grand Vey.

7.45 hours: Report from 916th Grenadier Regiment: Near Defense

Work No 70, northeast of Vierville, three tanks are rolling up the hill; three tanks penetrated into Defense Work No 66; the upper casemate of Defense Work No 62 was put out of action by a direct hit.

7.50 hours: Commander of Division to the Commander of 726th Grenadier Regiment: One battalion from Task Force Meyer is moving to Colleville to launch a counterattack near the coastal Defense Works Nos 6~2.Will arrive there within one and a half hours.

7.55 hours: Report from 352nd Artillery Regiment: Radio report from 1st Battalion/ 352nd Artillery Regiment, saying that our situation at Defense Work No 60 is uncertain.

7.57 hours: Report from 726th Grenadier Regiment: On the sector of our right neighboring 716th Infantry Division, between Defense Works Nos 35 and 36, thirty tanks have already been landed.

8.01 hours: Report from 916th Grenadier Regiment: Near Defense Work No 68, north of St Laurent, four tanks; near DW No 66, three tanks are already on the beach; at DW No 65 the situation is still unsettled. The antitank platoon is committed.

8.04 hours: Information from the right neighboring 716th Infantry Division: The Orne bridge near Benouville is in enemy hands. East of the Orne, our counterattack is being launched. 1716th Light Battery is out of action.

8.05 hours: Report from 916th Grenadier Regiment: Weak enemy forces have penetrated into Point du Hoc. One platoon of 9/126th Grenadier Regiment will be committed to launch a counterattack.

8.10 hours: Report from 126th Grenadier Regiment: Situation at Defense Works Nos 61 and 62 unaltered; fighting is going on also at Defense Work No 52.

8.12 hours: Report by Ia to the Chief of Staff of Gen Kdo LXXXIV AK: Transmittance [sic] of the newest reports (see above). On the sector of our right neighboring 716th Infantry Division, about 35 tanks are heading via Defense Works Nos 35 and 36 toward Arromanches.

8.19 hours: Report from 916th Grenadier Regiment: Enemy troops have landed near DW No 62. Details are still lacking. A battalion ofTask Force Meyer has been committed against the enemy landed north of Colleville. Some tanks have been landed north of Vierville. The enemy ahead of DW Nos 66 and 68 is being attacked by our forces. Near Point du Hoc, the enemy has climbed up the steep coastline (by means of rope ladders falling from the shells); the strongpoint has started fighting.

8.20 hours: Report from 914th Grenadier Regiment: The battle against the parachute troops in the Brévands area waged by 2nd Battalion/914th Grenadier Regiment has not yet come to an end.

8.21 hours: Information from the right neighboring 716th Infantry Division: The thirty tanks on our left wing have turned to the south and are heading to Meuvaines.

8.22 hours: Radio report from 914th Grenadier Regiment: Fifteen landing boats entering the mouth of the River Vireo

8.25 hours: Report from 352nd Artillery Regiment: 3rd Battalion/352nd Artillery Regiment reports: Of The tanks landed near Defense Work No 35, several (about six) have been put to fire or made immobile by antitank and land defense guns.

8.30 hours: Report from 352nd Artillery Regiment: On the sector of 716th Infantry Division, Defense Works Nos 35 and 36 have been overrun. The enemy infantry and thirty-five tanks are lying before Meuvaines. The right-hand division is throwing the 642nd Eastern Battalion to the hill east of Meuvaines. Defense Work No 37 continues fighting. The antiaircraft gun of Defense Work No 40 has shot three or four tanks; besides which, two or three landing boats are burning.

8.31 hours: Ia to 126th Grenadier Regiment: 2nd and 1st Battalions/916th Grenadier Regiment have to prepare for an attack to the right in the direction to Meuvaines. Readiness to be reported.

8.35 hours: Commanding General -Divisional Commander: Gen Kraiss reports: Situation on the right wing near Meuvaines and Asnelles is difficult; Meuvaines is in enemy hands. Ahead of Asnelles, our antiaircraft guns have shot six tanks. Gen Kraiss proposes to launch an attack by Task Force Meyer (minus one battalion), reinforced by the bulk of 352nd Panzerjager Battalion, in order to throw back to the coast and into the sea the enemy

Allied troops come ashore on Fortress Europe.

infantry and tanks penetrating our right wing. Portions of 352nd Panzerjager Battalion are to be kept in readiness. General Marcks authorizes the commitment proposed.

8.40 hours: Ia to 352nd Artillery Regiment: The connection with the observation points is to be established again latest before the tide is coming in again, as it may be presumed that the second wave of enemy forces will try to land then. An artillery liaison detachment of 3rd Battalion has to be held in readiness immediately with the object of supporting the attack of Task Force Meyer.

8.46 hours: Report from 352nd Artillery Regiment: North of St Laurent, Defense Works Nos 65, 66, 67, and 70 have probably been taken by the enemy. Ahead of Defense Work No 68, strong enemy forces are landing, from larger-size boats, an approximate strength of 150 men.

8.55 hours: Report from Telephone Switching Central: Telephone connections to 916th Grenadier Regiment are all disrupted for the time being.

9.05 hours: Report from 126th Grenadier Regiment: Defense Work No 61, northeast of Colleville, is in the hands of the enemy; DW

No 62 is firing with but one machine gun; DW No 60 is still intact. Enemy forces are pushing forward between Defense Works 61 and 62 to 63. Further stronger forces are being landed from fifty boats near Defense Work No 62. Reserves of 1st and 4th Companies are being brought up there. Near DW No 52, quiet prevails again. DW No 37 asks for reinforcements. Enemy infantry and tanks are heading to Meuvaines.

9.12 hours: Report from 914th Grenadier Regiment: Ahead of Defense Works Nos 92 and 99, numerous landing boats are entering the Carentan Canal. Debarking has not yet begun. 5th and 6th Battalions/914th Grenadier Regiment are engaged at the Carentan Canal defending against enemy parachute troops.

9.15 hours: Report from 916th Grenadier Regiment: Ahead of Defense Work No 65, northeast of St Laurent, sixty to seventy landing boats are debarking at present. No reports have been received from St P. Point du Hoc. Situation ahead of Grand camp is unaltered. Defense Works 65-68 and 70 are occupied by the enemy. Further considerable debarkments near Defense Works Nos 65 and 66 have been ascertained.

9.25 hours: 126th Grenadier Regiment reports: Three enemy tanks on the eastern wing of Defense Work No 38; reconnoitring has been started.

9.30 hours: Ia to 916th Grenadier Regiment: The self-propelled company of 352nd Panzerjager Battalion is subordinated to 916th Grenadier Regiment; the company itself is still at Engreville. 2nd Battalion/916th Grenadier Regiment is to be committed to a counterattack against Defense Works Nos 65-69.

9.35 hours: Report from Ic to Ia: Enemy radio message intercepted reading: To all commanders of the units: Everything is going OK, only a bit too late. Alaska. (presumably a request for reinforcements or artillery fire.)

9.45 hours: Report from 914th Grenadier Regiment: On the sector of the right neighboring 709th Infantry Division, tanks are being landed between Defense Works Nos 3 and 5; the Division, having no connection with its superior command, asks for support in the form of armor-piercing antitank weapons.

9.47 hours: Division to Corps HQ: Transmission of the request of the left neighboring regiment for support by antitank weapons against landed enemy tanks, as the Regiment is no longer able to get connection to 709th Infantry Division.

9.55 hours: Ia - Chief of Staff of Gen Kdo LXXXIV AK: Discussion and estimation of the general combat situation.

10.00 hours: Ia to 352nd Artillery Regiment: Information pertaining to the enemy landed near Defense Works Nos 3 and 5 on the left neighboring sector. Commission: With all available guns of 2nd Battalion to contend the enemy between Defense Works Nos 3 and 5 and to intercept his supply lines. Report from 352nd Artillery Regiment: The situation re ammunition with the heavy 4th Battery is very strained.

10.12 hours: Report from 726th: Three auxiliary craft in the harbor of Port-en-Bessin were sunk by direct hits of bombs.

11.00 hours: Radio message of the Division to Task Force Meyer: When are you going to start? In what direction?

11.01 hours: Information from the right neighboring 716th Infantry Division: Out in the bay of the mouth of the River Orne there are thirteen cruisers and a large number of landing boats. On either side of Vaux Chateau the enemy has succeeded in making a penetration.

11.10 hours: Report from 3rd Battalion/726th Grenadier Regiment: Defense Works Nos 66 and 68 north of St Laurent, contrary to previous reports, are still firmly in our hands. On the other hand, the enemy, with the strength of two companies, has penetrated into St P. Point du Hoc. Reserves, which were available, have been committed against Point du Hoc with the object of restoring the previous situation. From the men-of-war on the high sea the enemy is firing at the steep coastline with special shells from which a rope ladder is falling out, with the help of which the steep slopes can be climbed. The occupational troops of Defense Works Nos 71 and 73 are very weak; the construction pi-units (Bau-Pi-Ernherten) have been brought up for reinforcements.

11.12 hours: Report from 914th Grenadier Regiment: Somewhat to the north of Point du Hoc, twenty bigger naval units on the high seas, including troop transporters, and Approximately from two to three hundred landing boats, have been observed.

11.14 hours: Report from 726th Grenadier Regiment: At 11.10 hours, 1st Battalion/ 916th Grenadier Regiment started an attack against the enemy occupying Hill 22 east of Asnelles. Allegedly, the enemy has taken Asnelles. The situation on the left wing is critical, as the enemy has already advanced up to the church in Colleville. Defense Works Nos 60 and 62 proceed defending themselves gallantly.

11.32 hours: Information from the left neighboring 709th Infantry Division: Further landings are effected along the whole front. The enemy has succeeded in making some breaks.

11.38 hours: Report from the Aviation Report Center Caen: At 11.21 hours, fourteen larger-sized naval units were sighted on the the high seas ahead of Grandcamp.

11.40 hours: Report from 126th Grenadier Regiment: The southwestern exit of Colleville has been taken by the enemy. Further tanks are being debarked ahead of Defense Work No 62. A great number of tanks are congested before the antitank ditch.

11.42 hours: Report from 914th Grenadier Regiment: The enemy is extending his landing place on the sector of our left neighboring 709th Infantry Division spectacularly. On the sea there are at present twenty-two ships with barrage balloons.

11.47 hours: Report from 914th Grenadier Regiment: 1st Battalion/914th Grenadier Regiment has not yet contacted the enemy. In the bay of the River Vire there is a strong enemy concentration with barrage balloons. The attack of 2nd Battalion/ 914th Grenadier Regiment against the parachute troops in the Brévands area is progressing slowly.

11.48 hours: Information from the left neighboring 709th Infantry Division (inquiry of Ia): There is no connection to Carentan. The situation in the sector of our left neighbor next but one is perfectly quiet.

11.55 hours: Report from 916th Grenadier Regiment: The enemy has occupied the southwestern exit with one platoon. Further landings of tanks are taking place ahead of Defense Work No 62.

12.05 hours: Ia to 914th Grenadier Regiment: Concentrated cones of artillery fire are delivered by 2nd Battalion/352nd Artillery Regiment on Defense Works Nos 3 and 5 on the left neighboring sector, where the enemy is landing in companies. Defense Work No 1 is encircled.

12.20 hours: Information from the left neighboring 709th Infantry Division (inquiry of Ia): The penetration by enemy tanks extends already to a depth of four kilometers. Ahead of Defense Works Nos 3 and 5, there are twenty-two landing boats with barrage balloons. Countermeasures with antitank weapons from the north and from the southwest are under way.

12.25 hours: Ia reports to the Chief of Staff of LXXXIV AK: New report on enemy activities is submitted; see report at 12.20 hours. The occupation troops at St P. Point du Hoc are encircled by two enemy companies. A counterattack with portions of 3rd Battalion/126th Grenadier Regiment has been launched. The Corps HQ will have 30th Mobile Brigade brought up and subordinated to the Division, assuming, probably, the defense of the right wing.

12.35 hours: Report from 126th Grenadier Regiment: Colleville has been reconquered from the enemy. Defense Works Nos 62 and 62b are in our own hands; 61 is still occupied by the enemy, including one tank.

12.48 hours: Ia reports to Grenadier Kdo LXXXIV AK on the successes attained by 2nd Battalion/915th Grenadier Regiment near Colleville.

12.49 hours: Report from 916th Grenadier Regiment: Defense Works Nos 60, 62, and 62b are in our own hands; at 61 there is still one enemy tank.

13.17 hours: Report from the right neighboring 716th Infantry Division: Artillery reports forty tanks of the heaviest type heading to Ryes.

13.40 hours: Report from 2nd Battalion/915th Grenadier Regiment: On the left wing of the Battalion, the enemy is infiltrating to the south between Defense Works Nos 62a and 62b; the wing is being extended to the south.

13.45 hours: Report from 914th Grenadier Regiment: Two companies from 2nd Battalion/914th Grenadier Regiment have been committed for the defense at the Carentan Canal, one company attacking the parachute troops from Defense Work No 100c to the south and the other one from Villadon.

13.46 hours: Ia of the Division reports to Ia of the Army the estimate of the general combat situation.

13.58 hours: Report from 352nd Artillery Regiment: 1st Battalion reports that Colleville has again been taken by the enemy. The tanks ahead of Asnelles have turned to the east; the beachhead there has grown to be very big already.

14.00 hours: Report from 916th Grenadier Regiment: 5th Company/916th Grenadier Regiment started a counterattack against the enemy, infiltrating between Defense Works Nos 62a, 62b, and 64, and is going to join the attack carried on by 2nd Battalion/916th Grenadier Regiment.

14.05 hours: Report from 126th Grenadier Regiment: The attack of 1st Battalion/916th Grenadier Regiment on Meuvaines had to be turned to the direction of St Come, as eight tanks with mounted infantry were attacking Defense Works 40a, 40b, and 40c. DW Nos 60 and 620 are in our hands as heretofore.

14.26 hours: Report from 2nd Battalion/915th Grenadier Regiment: Our attack came up against tenacious resistance offered by the enemy, resulting in heavy casualties. Defense Work No 62 is still holding; DW 62c has no mortar ammunition any longer. The enemy, in the vicinity of the church and the Chateau Colleville, is infiltrating to the south. A counterattack has been started. Order of the Ia to 2nd Battalion/915th Grenadier Regiment: "The enemy at the chateau must in any case be thrown back again. Defense Works 60 and 62 must remain firmly in our hands."

14.34 hours: Information from the right neighboring 716th Infantry Division (inquiry by Ia): A considerable break has been made by the enemy troops near the mouth of the River Orne. Several defense works west of the Orne are encircled. The troops landed have established contact with the parachute troops in the rear. Near Ryes, forty tanks of the heaviest type are said to be moving to the southwest.

14.55 hours: Report from 914th Grenadier Regiment: 2nd Battalion/

914th Grenadier Regiment has been involved in heavy engagements in a hedgerow terrain in the Catz area. At 14.45 hours a further one hundred paratroopers jumped north of Defense Work No 100. Up to this time, twenty-three prisoners have been brought in.

15.50 hours: Report from 915th Grenadier Regiment (Task Force Meyer): We have established contact with 1st Battalion/916th Grenadier Regiment, which is committed left of us. The general direction of the attack is Meuvaines-Asnelles. The assault guns have arrived at the Regiment.

16.00 hours: Report from 915th Grenadier Regiment: The task force is going to attack from a line of departure with its right wing at Villiers-le-Sec, and left wing at Bayernville. Enemy tanks near Creully have pushed through to the south.

16.02 hours: Report from Ie of the Division to Ia: According to a radio message intercepted, the enemy forces in the Meuvaines area have to be estimated as one full division.

16.10 hours: The break at St Laurent has been extended by the enemy; Defense Work 71 c and the village of St Laurent are in enemy hands.

16.12 hours: Report from 726th Grenadier Regiment: Defense Work No 39 has been taken by the enemy. DF38 is encircled, and even DF40 is being attacked by six tanks and one infantry company. Furthermore, seven tanks are located ahead of Defense Work No 42, and several tanks in front of DW 44. Strong enemy landings are going on ahead of Defense Work No 62.

16.17 hours: Ia of Gen Kdo LXXXN AK to Ia of the Division: Our left neighboring 709th Infantry Division has great anxiety about the increasing debarkments on the right wing.

16.34 hours: Report from 916th Grenadier Regiment: Between Defense Works Nos 62 and 64, the enemy is removing staggered obstacles with tanks in order to prepare a broader passage for his tank forces.

16.38 hours: Report from 726th Grenadier Regiment: Ryes is in enemy hands.

16.50 hours: Report from 352nd Artillery Regiment: 4th Battalion reports heavy debarkments of tanks and trucks heading landward between Defense Works Nos 62 and 64.

16.58 hours: Report from 352nd Artillery Regiment: Further strong landings of tanks and trucks between Defense Works Nos 67 and 73.

17.10 hours: Report from 2nd Battalion/915th Grenadier Regiment: Battalion has been bypassed by the enemy in the rear near Chateau Colleville; he has broken through to the south. Wounded cannot be brought back any longer.

17.21 hours: Report from the 4th Battalion/352nd Artillery Regiment: Further strong landings on the coast near Vierville.

17.25 hours: Report from 352nd Artillery Regiment: 2nd Battalion/915th Grenadier Regiment is contained by the enemy.

17.30 hours: Report from 915th Grenadier Regiment (Task Force Meyer): At the time of our movement into the assembly position, the enemy infantry and tanks have taken Villiers-Ie-Sec and the hill south of it. In face of a superior enemy, the fusilier battalion (on the right wing) had to withdraw to St Gabriel, as the assault guns could not come up against a superior number of enemy tanks. There is no longer any connection to the left 1st Battalion/915th Grenadier Regiment near Bazenville. The Commander, Obstlt Meyer, presumably seriously wounded and made prisoner.

17.43 hours: Report from 126th Grenadier Regiment: The enemy has pushed forward from St Honaire to the south, toward Russy.

17.50 hours: Ia reports to the Chief of Staff of Gen Kdo LXXXIV AK on the whole of the combat situation.

17.50 hours: Report from 916th Grenadier Regiment: The enemy, who is continuously receiving reinforcements, has penetrated into Vierville, Asnieres and Louvieres. The Commander of the Division, from the command post of126th Grenadier Regiment to IA: General information about the situation on the right wing. Southwestern edge ofRyes has been occupied by a fortress pi-company. 1st Battalion/916th Grenadier Regimentis to establish contact to the left; connection to the Battalion, however, has been disrupted for hours.

18.00 hours: Chief of Staff of Gen Kdo LXXXIV AK to Ia of the

Division: On the sector of the right neighboring 716th Infantry Division, the enemy has made a particularly deep penetration. 30th Mobile Brigade, subordinate to 352nd Infantry Division, because of lack of heavy infantry weapons, can only be used for sealing purposes.

18.25 hours: Ia of the Division to 352nd Pi-Battalion: Together with the 17th Landes Bau Battalion, 17th Pi-Battalion is to reach the St Laurent area via the command post of 916th Grenadier Regiment.

18.25 hours: The Commander of the Division, from the command post of 916th Grenadier Regiment to **IA:** 1st Battalion/914th Grenadier Regiment has the order to clear up the situation at the Point du Hoc strongpoint by a counterattack. A counterattack from the east with detachments from the Le Guy strongpoint has also been started.

18.26 hours: Division to 352nd Field Replacement Battalion: The Field Replacement Battalion and portions of the March Battalion, which have already arrived, have to reach the region south of Mosles.

18.28 hours: Report from 126th Grenadier Regiment: Enemy tanks are forcing their way from Sommervieux to Magny. In order to stave off this thrust, six or seven assault guns are being brought up to the Regiment.

18.40 hours: Division to 32nd Antiaircraft Regiment: One heavy battery on either side east and west of Bayeux is to be committed for the defense of the town against enemy tanks.

19.35 hours: Report from 916th Grenadier Regiment: Fifteen larger transporters and thirty smaller craft at a distance often kilometers from the coast, headed to southeast, have been observed. Enemy in Vierville has been reinforced by one company.

19.40 hours: Ia of the Division to Commander of the Division at the command post of 916th Grenadier Regiment: Information concerning Task Force Meyer. Assault guns have been moved from St Gabriel to the west in order to ward off enemy tanks ahead of Bayeux. Divisional Commander to the Ia: The defensive line on the sector of 916th Grenadier Regiment extends from the eastern suburbs of Colleville over 69c, 69 to 71cc. Beginning with Defense

This picture taken on June 7th provides a vivid impression of the huge scale of the undertaking which was operation Neptune.

Work No 74 to the west, everything is in order. The enemy at St P. Point du Hoc is contained from east and south by 9th Company/726th Grenadier Regiment.

1945 hours: Report from 916th Grenadier Regiment: Parachute troops landing near St P.le Guay.

20.40 hours: Ia of the Division reports to the Chief of Staff of Corps HQ on the combat situation.

20.59 hours: Report from 914th Grenadier Regiment: Fifty troop-carrying gliders have landed west of the Carentan Canal.

21.00 hours: Report from 726th Grenadier Regiment: 1st Battalion/915th Grenadier Regiment reported by radio that it has been pocketed in the neighborhood of Bacenville, and that it has taken prisoner a British general.

21.07 hours: Ia of the Division reports again to Chief of Staff of Corps HQ on the combat situation.

21.12 hours: Report from 726th Grenadier Regiment: Ahead of Port-en-Bess in, fifteen large and thirty small landing boats have been ascertained.

21.35 hours: Report to the Division from Fusilier Battalion 352: Enemy infantry and tanks have taken St Gabriel; remnants of the Battalion are retreating to Brecy.

21.42 hours: Ia of the Division to Chief ofStaff ofCorps HQ: By prisoners' statements, the 50th British Infantry Division has been ascertained near Sommervieux. The fifteen large and thirty small transporters reported as being at sea are heading [on] course [toward] Port-en-Bessin. The battleships have already proceeded [to fire] broadside[s]. The landing of further strong enemy forces is imminent.

22.10 hours: Ia of the Division to Chief of Staff of Corps HQ: One battalion of 30th Mobile Brigade in the middle sector is to be subordinated to 916th Grenadier Regiment as the situation near Grandcamp is uncertain. The parachutists there have joined with the terrorists [French Underground movement].

22.33 hours: Ia of the Division to 726th Grenadier Regiment: 513th and 518th Battalions of30th Mobile Brigade will be brought up and subordinated to the Regiment. New defense line has to be built up in the line Brecy-Esquay-Sommervieux-PouhgnyTracy.

22.55 hours: Report from 352nd Fusilier Battalion: The strength of the Battalion is but forty men, plus additional fifty men from 1st Battalion/915th Grenadier Regiment; furthermore, there are six assault guns intact. In face of strong enemy pressure, the task force has withdrawn toward Ducy.

23.07 hours: Ia of the Division to 726th Grenadier Regiment: Portions of 94th Bau Pi Battalion (360 officers and men) will be subordinated to the Regiment.

23.20 hours: Divisional Commander, Gen Kraiss, to Commanding General, General Marcks: Tomorrow the Division will be able with all available forces to offer the same kind of hard resistance to the supreme enemy, as was the case today. Because of the heavy casualties, however, new forces have to be brought up the day after tomorrow. The losses of men and materiel in the islands of resistance are total. By the heaviest kind of bombing and cones of concentrated fire from naval artillery, greater numbers of the guns built in at field strength were buried under rubble and had later to be set free again.

Divisional Commander, Gen Kraiss, to the Commanding General, General Marcks (continued): The occupational troops in the defense works have fought gallantly. Defense Works 74—91, despite the losses they have suffered, are still in full readiness to defend themselves. At the time, 352nd Pi-Battalion, together with 7th Company/916th Grenadier Regiment, is attacking from Formigny Defense Works Nos 68-70. 6th Company/916th Grenadier Regiment regained Defense Work No 65a, but was then entirely covered by heavy enemy naval artillery fire. 2nd Battalion/915th Grenadier Regiment, in an energetic attack, captured the defense work north of Colleville, but is now encircled near Colleville and is clamoring for ammunition. Defense Works Nos 37 and 38 have been fighting gallandy and have shot altogether six tanks. On the left wing, the counterattack by 1st Battalion/914th Grenadier Regiment against St P. Point du Hoc is still progressing. The Field Replacement Battalion and the March Battalion have been moved forward in order to defend Formigny and St Laurent against an enemy heading to the south. No news has been received from 3rd Battalion/352nd Artillery Regiment southwest of Ryes. Almost all of the radio stations of advanced observation posts have been put out of action.

Commanding General Marcks to the Division Commander, Gen Kraiss: All reserves available to me have already been moved up. Every inch of the ground has to be defended to the utmost capacity, until new reinforcements can be brought up.

24.00 hours: By prisoners' statements, the following enemy divisions have been ascertained up to the present: 1st American Infantry Division; 29th American Infantry Division; 50th British Infantry Division; 79th British Armoured Division; 101st American Airborne Division.

THE 21ST PANZER DIVISION ON 6 JUNE 1944

*By Generalleutnant Edgar Feuchtinger,
General der Panzertruppen Leo and
Freiherr Geyr von Schweppenburg*

0030-0130 hours: The 125th Panzer Grenadier Regiment makes the first report of airborne landings near Rauville, Bréville, Escoville, Troarn, Truffreville, Bannerville, and Demcuville.

0035 hours: Third and highest stage of alert ordered for divisions.

Starting at 0100 hours: The 2nd Battalion/125th Panzer Grenadier Regiment leaves shelter, one company at a time, to engage the airborne enemy troops which have landed in the reported localities.

0200-0400 hours: Continually arriving reinforcements for the airborne enemy troops as far as the Dives area reported by 125th Panzer Grenadier Regiment, 716th Division (static division at Caen), 711th Static Division (east of the Orne), Commander of the Caen area, 305th Army AAA Bn (the AAA Battalion of the 21st Panzer Division) in the antiaircraft position north of Caen, on the Caen-Lion-sur-Mer road.

Approximately 0230 hours: 3rd, 9th, 10th Companies, 125th Panzer Grenadier Regiment, and 4th Company of the 200th Assault Gun Battalion (Cagny) put at the disposal of the 125th Panzer Grenadier Regiment. Two companies of the 22nd Panzer Regiment put in readiness north of Maezieres. Ever since the first reports concerning enemy landings were received, the Divisional Commander has been in constant telephone communication with the CG of the Seventh Army. Army Group B would not release the Division for commitment.

Approximately 0245 hours: Division takes first prisoners. Confirmation that 6th British Airborne Division is landing east of the Orne (between Orne and Dives). From 0230 hours on: Continued news of further airborne landings, also west and south of Caen. Later found to be erroneous. Mock landings on Carpiquet airfteld and surroundings with explosive dummies.

Approximately 0400 hours: 1st Reconnaissance Battalion/21st Division ordered to investigate reported landings south and west of Caen. From 0500 hours on, reports to the effect that entire area is clear of enemy.

Approximately 0550 hours: Heavy naval artillery fire in the area around Caen. Artillery positions and 305th AAA Battalion positions hit. Six guns disabled. Pattern bombing on MLR along the coast and on rear positions.

Approximately 0640 hours: Reports of landings along the coast north of Caen. Still no orders for the Division to join battle. Situation on the coast increasingly more threatening. The weaker elements of the 125th Panzer Grenadier Regiment in heavy fighting against 6th British Airborne Division.

0730-0800 hours: Independent decision taken by Division to attack 6th British Airborne Division east of the Orne, in order to keep this area open for a further attack across the Orne against the enemy landing from the sea west of the Orne. The Division was assembling in the woods at Bellegreville and Chicheboville, and was subordinated to the Seventh Army and LXXXIV Corps at St Lo. After the 2nd Battalion/125th Panzer Grenadier Regiment had been involved in hard fighting east of the Orne from 0100 on, 2nd Battalion/192nd Panzer Grenadier Regiment (Hill 61, east of Periers), 1st Battalion/155th Panzer Artillery Regiment (in position in the area Periers-St Aubin-Beuville), and 200th Panzerjager Battalion (in the area Periers-Plumetot-Gazelle-Beuville) were subordinated to the 716th Division as soon as the landings from the sea began. This was only rescinded during the night of 6 June 1944. The absence of two Panzergrenadier regiments, one artillery battalion, the antitank battalion and the Army AAA battalion, the spreading of the Division over a wide area, and the combat tasks which cropped up on both sides of the Orne, all had a fateful influence on the course of the combat on 6 June 44.

Situation, 6 June 1944

The first Panzer division to be engaged was the 21st Panzer Division, located in the vicinity of Caen. The disposition of this division on D-Day was a striking example of wretched Panzer tactics and the result of Rommel's orders. Before the invasion started, the division was scattered in four groups and quartered on both sides of the Orne river. The 125th Panzer Grenadier Regiment, northeast of Caen, formed the first group; the 6th Airborne Division (British) jumped into the midst of their billet area. The second group-the division staff and the Panzer regiment, with one artillery battalion and weak elements of the Panzerjager (antitank) battalion-was in reserve southeast of Caen. The third group, consisting of a battalion of the 192nd Panzer Grenadier Regiment, was on the west bank of the Orne. This battalion was attached to the 716th Infantry Division and was committed in the front-line positions along the coast. Behind it was the bulk of the Panzerjager battalion. The 193rd Panzer Grenadier Regiment, less a battalion, was located north of Caen.

The main body of the 21st Panzer Division had received strict orders not to move; it was not to be committed without the consent of Genfldrn Rommel. Thus it happened that these troops had to stand by as spectators while the enemy paratroops jumped on their comrades. Only after an investigation of the situation by the Ia-who believed in the doctrine of Panzer Group West to attack an airborne enemy without delay-was the main body of the division committed against the British. Thus, this group acted on its own responsibility, against orders. After issuing the attack order, the division commander had left his command post to meet Gen Infantry Marcks, who was at that time Corps Commander. The latter officer was at the command post of the 716th Infantry Division in Caen. The meeting took place at about 1000 hours. The Ia, the only man who knew tank warfare, remained behind.

At 1300, just at the time the tank regiment made contact with the enemy, an order was received from Corps to break off this engagement and to attack those forces of the enemy which had reached the heights north of Caen. This entailed crossing the Orne and running the gauntlet of narrow defiles in the town of Caen. By noon, the enemy had established a beachhead between the Orne and the Vire, 25 kilometers wide and five kilometers deep. About this time, Seventh Army subordinated the 21st Panzer Division to the 716th Infantry Division;

the latter had ceased to exist as a fighting unit.

Before the invasion, when the controversy over the use of Panzer divisions as local tactical reserves was at its height, Panzer Group West had pointed out that the unavoidable consequence would be the subordination ofPanzer divisions to commanders who had received no training in the employment of tanks. No decision had been made with regard to this controversy.

Seventh Army, meanwhile, had requested the Luftwaffe to direct its main effort against the beachhead, west of the Orne. In the afternoon of D-Day, the 21st Panzer Division was ordered to continue the attack on the west bank of the river in the direction of Riva-Bella.

Counterattack of the 21st Panzer Division

1200 hours: After the assembly of the division, Corps HQ ordered an attack on the enemy who had landed from the sea west of the Orne, north of Caen. All marches in that terrain, which did not boast trees and which was under constant surveillance by enemy planes, had to be made with the units well dispersed. Due to the heavy air activity (constant bombing of the marching columns and attempts to destroy the Orne bridge) and the heavy fire from naval artillery, the march through the narrow places in Caen was still more difficult.

There was only one usable bridge in Caen. A further light bridge was available in Colomoelles. The approaches of the various combat teams had to be fixed correspondingly.

1600 hours: At 1600 hours the division was ready to attack north of Caen with two combat teams:

Armored Combat Team:

22nd Panzer Regiment, I Bn (light armored half tracks), 125 Panzer Grena Regiment (less 1st Co), 1st Co (light armored half tracks), 220 Panzer Engr Bn, III Bn, 155th Panzer Art Regiment in the area west of Heronville-west of 23 [sic].

Combat Team:

192nd Panzer Gren Regiment, consisting of: 192nd Panzer Gren Regiment, less its II Bn, 2nd Co, 220th Panzer Engr Bn, II Bn, 155th Panzer Art Regiment in the St Contest-Cussy area.

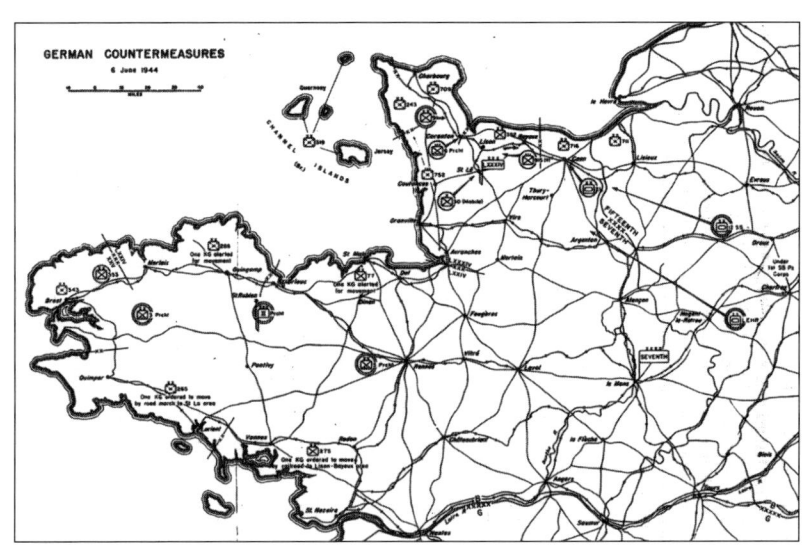

German countermeasures, 6th June 1944

The 125th Panzer Grenadier Regiment less its 1st Battalion, the 21st Reconnaissance Battalion, and the 200th Assault Gun Battalion were involved in fighting against the 6th British Airborne Division east of the Orne.

Objectives of the attack:
- Armored Group: the coast between the mouth of the Orne and the eastern outskirts of Lion-sur-Mer.
- Group 192 Panzer Grenadier Regiment: area around Lion-sur-Mer.

The attack by the armored group threw the enemy out of Lebussy and reached the heights north of Lebussy. When it was north of Mathieu-Combes, the group, continuing the attack through Epron, came under heavy fire from tanks and artillery, corning from the direction of Periers and Hill 61.

A number of Mark IV tanks were lost. The British tanks were firing from a distance of approximately 2,000 meters, whereas the fire from the Mark IV tanks on the British tanks, although scoring definite hits, was not effective, as the projectiles had no more power of penetration at that distance. (600 meters was about the greatest distance at which fire on such targets was effective.)

Although it would rob us of a lot of time, it had now become necessary to move the Combat Team to the west in order to evade the fire. This move was made still more complicated by the fact that all radio communications were interrupted by the enemy, and that no orders could be radioed through to the tank crews. Finally, it was possible to carry out the attack on Hill 61 in the direction of Periers under cover from southwest of Gazelle.

At about 1900, there was another heavy enemy airborne landing. On both sides of the Orne, it cut off the fighting groups from each other and isolated them. It was particularly difficult to combat these airborne landings, for the most part consisting of troop-carrying gliders, as the tanks could not fire at targets in the air and the Division AAA Battalion, in position north of Caen, had been destroyed by the British naval artillery. Machine-gun fire from the Panzer Grenadiers accounted for about 26 gliders in the air.

By a local advance through Plurnetot, the Combat Team, 192nd Panzer Grenadier Regiment, had reached the coast at Lion-sur-Mer. A heavy tank attack, together with the airborne landing, had meanwhile engaged the left wing of the Combat Team and threatened to destroy it. Despite the airborne landing and the tank attacks, we succeeded in keeping the Combat Team together, but lost a large amount of men and materiel, in particular a number of self-propelled guns and the largest part of the 1st Company/192nd Regiment, which was cut off in a signal communications strongpoint near Douvren. This company, although isolated, resisted for eight days, until lack of ammunition and food forced it to surrender. Radio contact with it was maintained until the end.

Under cover of darkness, the division had to be put in some sort of order in the line Havent Wood-south of Escoville-north of Honorine-Blainville (2nd Battalion/192nd Regiment here)-northern outskirts of Herouville-heights north of Leboussy-north of Epron-north of St Contest-Buron. This was carried out successfully. Contact could also be made with the 2nd Battalion/192nd Regiment in Blainville. This battalion gradually fought its way back to the northern outskirts of Herouville and there took over connection with both sides of the Orne.

At approximately 2200 hours, the division was subordinated to I SS Panzer Corps. At approximately 2300 hours, the divisional commander at his advanced command post was in telephone contact with the Commanding General and the Chief of Staff of I SS Panzer Corps, who were at the command post of the 21st Panzer Division.

This evaluation of the situation was given to them:

In the course of 6 June 44 the enemy had succeeded in making his landings on both sides of the Orne from the sea and from the air with strong forces. Opposed to the 21 st Panzer Division east of the Orne was the 6th British Airborne Division; west of the Orne were the 3rd British Infantry Division, at least one armored brigade, and parts of the 3rd Canadian Division. The enemy was supported most effectively by his air force and naval artillery.

An attack along the whole front of the division was impossible with the available forces, particularly as the static 716th Division had to be written off. Even now, an attack east of the Orne would hold the greatest promise of success. For this it would be necessary to direct those elements of the 12th SS Division which were only just coming into this sector and to subordinate them to the 21st Panzer Division. From the beginning of the invasion, the division had considered it of paramount importance to recapture this sector, as otherwise

a. It would be a standing menace to the division's east wing;
b. The enemy would be in a position to reinforce this bridgehead with troops at his convenience;
c. It would constantly tie down strong German forces;
d. It would, due to the favorable terrain, be the area from which the enemy would carry out his large-scale attacks in the direction of Falaise, after gathering his forces.

On the other hand, to the German Command the recapture of this sector, and the immediate forming of a bridgehead at Ranville, would mean the possession of the eventual starting point for an attack on the east flank of the landed enemy and his supply bases. In the division's opinion, based on the enemy's strength and on personal impressions, an attack with any hopes of success [si~ and with the aim of throwing the. enemy back into the sea could only hold out any hopes of success ifit was carried out on 7 June 1944 with not less than three concentrated Panzer divisions and a guarantee of the corresponding Luftwaffe support needed for dealing with the enemy air force and forces out at sea. These conditions would promise success on either the west or the east of the Orne.

Corps could not agree to these suggestions. Corps stated that the 12th SS Division would take up contact with the 21st Panzer Division during the night, and that both divisions together would attack west of the Orne in the morning of 7 June 1944.

Thus, it never came to a counterattack any more, as only one Panzer Grenadier Regiment and one Panzer Battalion from the 12th SS Division had arrived as neighbor to the 21st Panzer Division by 1600, and these forces were not enough for a combined attack.

THE 711TH INFANTRY DIVISION ENCOUNTERS THE INVASION

By Generalmajor Joseph Reichert

Once during the night a volley could be heard from the sea, which, however, soon died out. Later on, it was reported that a German convoy had encountered an enemy invasion fleet. Otherwise the night was quiet, until about dawn, when the main operation, the landing from the sea, commenced. It began with a sort of heavy barrage lasting for a long time against the coast from the sea and the air, which extended in some places-in the east-as far as Cabourg and to the heights south of Houlgate. The whole horizon appeared to be a sole mass of flames, until the fIre, perhaps after the landing of the first elements, was gradually reduced to single-shot fire.

It lasted a little more than an hour until reports came in, according to which the enemy landing had only taken place west of the Orne. Our own positions had suffered very little from the enemy fIre; losses in men were very slight, because the main body of the occupying forces had taken shelter during the bombardment.

Thus, we could start with the further mopping up of the hinterland. The two reserve battalions were charged with this task, that is, the reserve battalion of the left regiment had to mop up the sector between the coast and the road St Arnould-Varaville (inclusive) and the other one, of the right regiment, the area between the mentioned road Pont l'Eveque-Troarn (inclusive). At first our main efforts were directed along the roads, so as to render free the lines of communications. Parts of the antitank battalion were subordinated for this purpose. This mopping-up action had more or less been completed by the evening of 6 June.

The parachutists who had landed did not succeed, probably owing to the countermeasures which were immediately taken locally, in forming groups of any considerable fighting strength, so that in most

An aerial view of the thousands of ships gathered together to support the Normandy landings gives an impression of the overwhelming logistical advantages which lay with the Allies.

cases only slight resistance was offered, which could be broken very quickly. Most of them kept in hiding and surrendered, offering no resistance. The prisoners taken, who belonged to the 1st (English) and 1st (Canadian) Battalions of the 6th British Airborne Division, made only very meagre statements, from which it could be assumed that they belonged to elements which became lost and scattered. They were to bail out between the Dives and the Orne and had taken the Dives river, claiming it to be the Orne because the former looked much bigger than the latter. One man in particular reported that originally a landing had been envisaged from the sea as far as Cabourg, but that modern obstacles ahead of the beach, the presence of which had been ascertained there, had caused them to abandon this plan. This was to some extent confirmed by British maps, which were found later with the most accurate markings of individual strongpoints and the obstacles ahead of the beaches. A number of the latter ones in the Cabourg sector had been marked with question marks.

The connection—with the neighboring 716th Division directly affected by the landing operation—which, owing to the overloading of the wire net, was achieved there only after considerable time, indicated that along the entire divisional sector and farther to the west the enemy had forced a landing and had penetrated the coastal area to a depth of two to three kilometers. It was blocked up in a preliminary makeshift way. From the noise of battle, which could be heard from the coast, it could be concluded that single strongpoints on the coast were still holding out. Further countermeasures had been taken. With regard to elements of 716th Division to the east of the Orne, I could find out that the coastal strongpoints were being held and that there was contact between the 716th and 711th Divisions on the coast as well as near Varaville.

By noon, the roads in our own divisional sector had already been cleared by fighting to such an extent that I could drive by car to the command post of my left regiment (744th). In the thick brushwood, we were well able to evade the fighter-bombers which occasionally appeared over the sector. On my way to the regimental command IR 744, I saw a number of parachutes hanging from trees and telephone wires. The terrain in the vicinity of the regimental command post was rather shell torn; the command post itself, however, had not been hit. From the roof of the castle one could see the enemy fleet outside and observe a lively coming and going of boats to and from the coast. The coastal battery near Houlgate fired against the landing enemy near Quistreham west of the Orne. From the regimental command post I drove to the heights east of Brucourt, four kilometers to the south of Cabourg, from where one could take a good view of the terrain between the Orne and the Dives. Here we had more and more proof of the airlanding of the enemy. A hundred meters away from the road there was a shattered four-motor bomber lying on the ground, and damaged and undamaged troop-carrying gliders were scattered about on the fields or caught in clusters of trees. The terrain to the west of the Dives was dotted with yellow points (parachutes). The noise of battle close by could not be heard. Only from the direction of Ouistreham could the weak sound of MG fire be heard, and one could see single artillery impacts.

THE ALLIED ATTACK: THE 6TH FALLSCHIRM REGIMENT REACTS

By Oberstleutnant Friedrich, Freiherr von der Heydte

Although the authorities were frequently at odds in their estimates as to where and how the Allied invasion would take place, it was nevertheless apparent that since the middle of May commanders as well as troops were agreed in assuming that an invasion was to be expected during the first ten days of June. Consequently, the lower headquarters were astonished when all division commanders and one regimental commander from each division, the corps artillery commanders, and the commanders of corps headquarters reserves were ordered to report to Rennes on 6 June 1944 at 0830 in order to spend the entire day in an army group map exercise. It was rumored that this map exercise had been ordered by the Wehrmacht High Command, although the possibility existed that it was an idea of Rommel, who, in North Africa, liked to issue his orders in the form of map exercises.

The majority of the officers who had been ordered to report left for Rennes on the evening of 5 June and spent the night there. Consequently, about 50 percent of the division commanders and possibly 25 percent of the regimental commanders were not with their troops during the night of 5 June 1944.

On 4 June there had been increasing signs that the invasion was imminent. The French civilian population openly discussed the fact that an Allied landing was close at hand. On 4 June a cousin of General Leclerc laughingly told me a rumor that the invasion had been planned for the night of 4 June. During that night, all the French-speaking soldiers from Alsace-Lorraine, who had been serving in the regiment as drivers, deserted, with the exception of one who was found shot the next morning. These drivers had presumably been in contact with French Resistance groups and had deserted immediately upon hearing

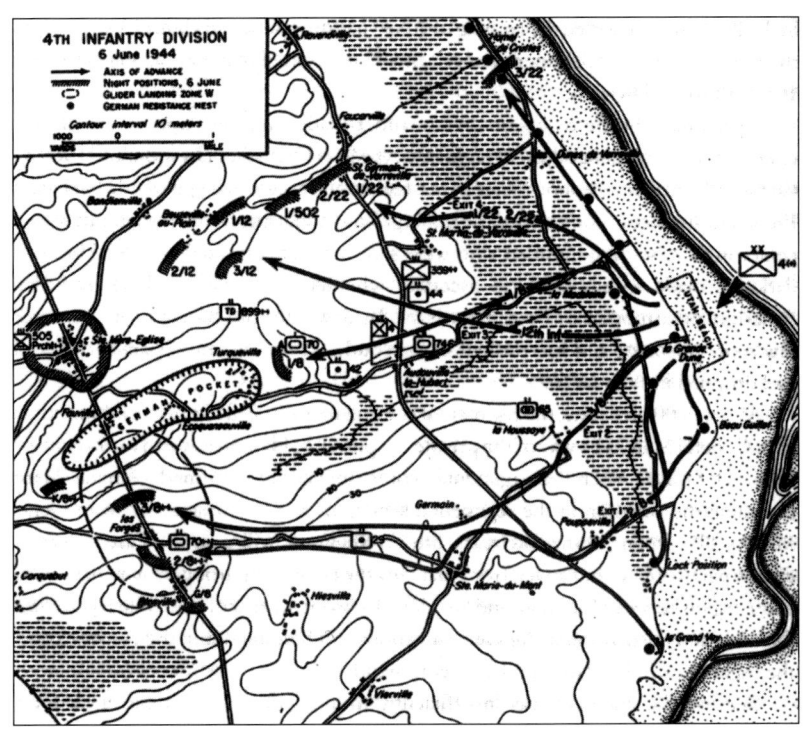

4th Infantry Division, 6th June 1944

that the invasion was imminent.

Since the middle of May 1944, the 6th FS Regiment had, in accordance with instructions, been distributed over a long line in field type positions in the Lessay-PeriersRaids-Mont Castre area. The regiment was subordinated for tactical purposes to LXXXIV Corps, for supply matters to the 91st Grenadier Division, and for administration to II FS Corps. As an "LW unit," the parachute troops being considered "LW personnel," the regiment had been linked with the Cherbourg aircraft warning network.

The 91st Grenadier Division, the so-called airlanding division of the Army general reserve, was, at the beginning of 1944, activated as an Army unit at the troop training grounds at Baumholder. Generalleutnant Falley was the division commander and Lieutenant-Colonel Pickel was the operations officer. The division command post was located near Etienville. Originally, the 91st Division had probably been designated for combined parachute and airlanding operations-Operation Tanne (fir tree) or Operation Fichte (pine tree), planned for the beginning of March 1944-in conjunction with the 6th FS Regiment in one of the northern countries, possibly Finland. After this plan was abandoned, the 91st Grenadier Division, like the 6th FS Regiment, was sent to LXXXIV Corps about 1 May 1944. The combat efficiency of this division was poor. On the morning of 6 June 1944, the division commander, who was on his way back from Rennes, was killed in front of his command post either by American paratroopers or by members of the French Resistance. Command of the division was temporarily taken over by one of the regimental commanders, Colonel Klostermeyer, and later by Generalmajor Kohler, the commander of an adjacent division. The division was decimated during the first three days of the invasion; its remnants were for the time being attached to other divisions or withdrawn. The division staff was employed as a special assignments staff for the purpose of reconnoitering and preparing defensive positions behind the invasion front.

However, apart from the disruption of telephone connections, the death of the commander of the 91st Grenadier Division, and the demolition of the railroad tracks south of Periers, there was, during the first days of the invasion, not the slightest sign of any activity by the French Resistance movement in the district of the 6th FS Regiment and its immediate neighbors.

Late in the evening of 5 June, about 2230, the commander of the aircraft warning service in Cherbourg, a lieutenant serving with the signal troops, informed his regimental commander by telephone that Allied ship movements and the concentration of transport aircraft at British airfields seemed to indicate the possibility of an invasion that very night. Soon after, the signal officer of the 6th FS Regiment made the same report, and, from 2300 on, the regimental commander was able to follow the approach of the Allied transports and fleets on the aircraft warning chart. At 2300 the regiment was alerted.

A few minutes after the alert order had been transmitted to all elements of the 6th FS Regiment, a severe air bombardment began to the north and northwest of the regimental sector, about twenty kilometers from the regimental command post, which was located north of Periers. Shortly after midnight, the 1st Battalion, which was located in the Raids area, reported the landing of Allied paratroopers, and about 1300 it reported the capture of the first prisoners, Americans, who reported that they belonged to the US 101st Airborne Division.

After midnight the regimental commander made futile attempts to establish telephone contact with the adjacent regiments, the 91st Grenadier Division, and LXXXIV Corps. All German telephone lines in the regimental sector had apparently been cut by French Resistance groups, as had the underground connection with the aircraft warning center in Cherbourg. Linesmen who were sent out were attacked at several locations; darkness made it impossible to ascertain whether they were fired on by isolated American paratroopers or French partisans. By dawn, the 3rd Battalion had captured a few score prisoners and had pushed to the southeast the American paratroopers who had dropped in their sector.

About 0600 on 6 June, the regimental commander succeeded in establishing contact with General Marcks by way of the private telephone of his landlady and the French post office at St Lo. After the regimental commander had informed General Marcks regarding the situation in the regimental sector, he received this order from General Marcks: "Beginning immediately, the 6th FS Regiment will clear the Carentan area of enemy paratroopers and attack from that area the enemy paratroopers who have landed in the region between Carentan and Ste Mere-Église in the rear of the 709th [?] Grenadier Division and destroy them. All German troops still holding out in the combat zone of the regiment will be placed under its command."

Because the regiment was insufficiently motorized, it was no easy task for the battalion commanders to withdraw their units from the widely separated strongpoints and to assemble them in the Meautis area, west of Carentan. South of the Carentan-Periers road, the 3rd Battalion was still engaged in combat with scattered groups of enemy paratroopers who fought stubbornly; to the southeast and east, the battalion covered in that area the assembly of the rest of the regiment. The 1st and 2nd Battalions reached the assembly area in the early afternoon without making contact with the enemy.

The regimental commander had driven to Carentan in the morning in advance of the regiment. He found Carentan free of Allied troops and almost free of German troops; and between 1000 and 1100, without encountering enemy troops, he reached St Come du Mont, where a German battalion had dug in. There he awaited instructions.

An overwhelming picture presented itself to the regimental commander from the church tower of St Come du Mont. Before him lay the coast and the sea. The horizon was strewn with hundreds of ships, and countless landing boats and barges were moving back and forth between the ships and the shore, landing troops and tanks. It was an almost peaceful picture; in the combat report which I submitted at the time to the Parachute Army, I wrote that it reminded me of a beautiful summer day on the Wannsee. The noise of battle could not be heard, and from the church tower of St Come du Mont there was no sign of German defense activities. Only a shot rang out here and there whenever the sentries of the German battalions came in contact with Allied paratroopers.

The regimental commander established his command post in a defile just south of St Come du Mont and ordered the 1st and 2nd Battalions to be brought forward to the area of St Come du Mont via the Douve Canal. He issued the following order to the battalion commanders: ''The 2nd Battalion will advance on Ste Mere-Église on both sides of the St Come du Mont-Ste Mere-Église road; it will attack the enemy troops immediately upon contact and annihilate them. The 1st Battalion will cover the regiment on the line of Ste Marie-du-Mont against enemy troops who have landed from the sea. The 13th Company will cover the advance of both battalions.''

The 3rd Battalion of the regiment remained in the Carentan area in order to protect the rear and the deep flanks of the regiment; the battalion of the Seventh Army reserve was placed under the control of the 6th FS Regiment and remained in its positions around St Come du Mont.

At 1900, the 1st and 2nd Battalions advanced from the area ofSt Come du Mont. At first, both battalions proceeded rapidly. By nightfall they had not yet come into serious contact with the enemy. Around midnight, the advance elements of the 1st Battalion had arrived at Ste Marie-du-Mont, while the 2nd Battalion had reached a point about 500 meters from the southern edge of Ste Mere-Église. Both battalions sent a number of prisoners back to the regiment.

Some time after midnight (the author can no longer recall exactly when), matters took an unexpected turn. Throughout the entire combat zone of the regiment, American parachute and airlanding units were again descending in large numbers. American paratroopers (members of the 82nd Airborne Division, according to statements by prisoners), who had landed northwest of St Come du Mont (I have forgotten the name of the exact place), threatened the rear and the deep left flank of the 2nd Battalion; the units which had landed to the north and northeast of St Come du Mont cut off the 2nd Battalion from the regiment and from the 1st Battalion, while the American paratroopers who had descended east of St Come du Mont in the very center of the area of the 1st Battalion, which was still advancing, threw this battalion into hopeless confusion.

INVASION

By General der Panzertruppen Leo,
Freiherr Geyr von Schweppenburg

In the early morning of 6 June 44, my Chief of Staff informed me of a large-scale enemy landing at the Plateau de Calvados and, to the west, on the Cotentin peninsula. In a few hours, I learned that Army Group D had ordered the movement to the front of the 12th SS (Hitlerjugend) Panzer Division and, later, Panzer Lehr Division. I personally requested of Genfldm von Rundstedt that Panzer Lehr Division be moved only after darkness because of enemy air action. This request was refused. The Division lost 123 personnel carriers and five trucks in the Panzer Grenadier battalion alone, as soon as it started to march. When the commander of the Panzer Lehr Division received the order to move out at once, he made the same request to Seventh Army to move at night, with the same negative result. Genlt Beverlein, Commander of the Panzer Lehr Division, and Gen Panzer Geyr von Schweppenburg, Commander of Panzer Group West, had experienced for years a considerable amount of stubborn Panzer fighting. Rundstedt, Jodl, and Blumentritt had not. The resulting two schools of thought represented the difference between the tactics of horsedrawn divisions of the Napoleonic Age and the 19th Century and that of mechanized divisions of the 20th Century. The tactical methods of one were hardly understandable to the other.

The decision to move these two Panzer divisions to the front was a very significant one. Hitler had reversed his recent decision (formed after bitter controversy between Rommel and von Geyr, von Rundstedt remaining aloof) and abandoned the idea of a strategic reserve. The Panzer divisions were committed in the same manner as a reserve battalion in 1918 might have been thrown in to take back a segment of a trench captured by the enemy. Since Hitler had the last say, one would have hoped that experts were consulted. This was not the case. Neither Panzer Group West nor Genobst Guderian was asked to express an opinion.

LXXXIV CORPS COUNTERATTACKS WITH LOCAL RESERVES ON THE AFTERNOON OF D-DAY

By Oberstleutnant Friedrich von Criegern

By 1100 the enemy had been able to establish an almost continuous beachhead as far as Asnelles, with about two kilometers' depth of penetration. There was severe fighting near Asnelles, where the reserve battalion of the 716th Infantry Division launched a counterattack that at first was successful but later was repelled. Thus, Bayeux was endangered by an enemy thrust. Therefore, Corps ordered the reinforced 915th Grenadier Regiment of the 352nd Infantry Division (the Corps reserve)—which had already been put on the march so as to keep open the Vire river crossings east of Carentan—to pivot and attack via Bayeux-Ryes the enemy that had landed near Asnelles and throw him back into the sea.

While the first landing attempt had been repelled east of Grandcamp, the enemy succeeded in establishing a beachhead east of Ste Mere-Église on the eastern coast of Cotentin. Elements of the 709th Infantry and 91st LL Divisions and the 6th FS Regiment had been attacking the airlandings concentrically, in order to annihilate the enemy that had landed from the sea east of Ste Mere-Église. The following units attacked: one Kampfgruppe of the 91st LL Division and elements of the 709th Infantry Division from the north from the Emondeville area, one Kampfgruppe of the 91st LL Division from the west from the area of Pont l'Abbe, and the 6th FS Regiment from the south from the Carentan area.

In spite of the fact that confirmation of their assignment had not arrived as yet, the 243rd Infantry Division, near Cherbourg, received orders to immediately start on the march to Montebourg one reinforced regiment, to be assigned to the 709th Infantry Division.

Strong concentrations of ships were observed offshore along the

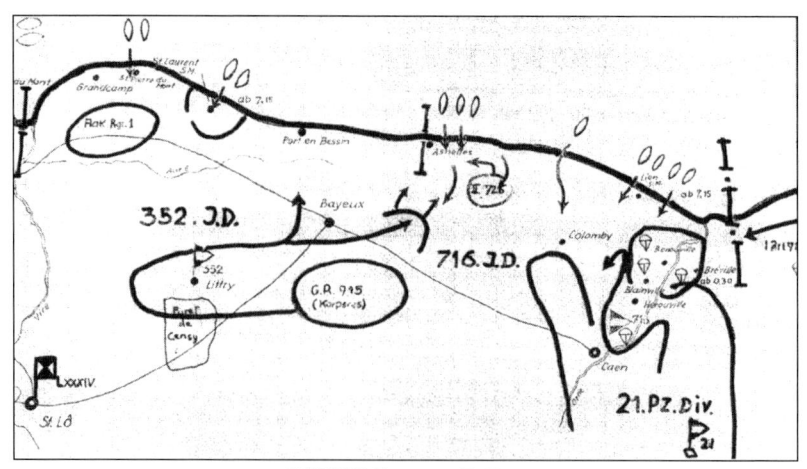

LXXXIV Corps on D-Day

east coast of the peninsula. The enemy landings, with fighter escort, continued during the course of the whole day.

At 1500, the 12th SS Panzer Division was subordinated to the Corps. But, as it was still in the process of approach, the counterattack by the 21st Panzer Division could not await the arrival. The Commanding General (Marcks), who during the morning had visited the Valognes area to determine countermeasures, returned to 21st Panzer Division at Caen.

At 1620 the counterattack began. When the general returned in the evening, he reported to Army that the counterattack by the 21st Panzer Division had failed. On one hand, this was due to an enemy airlanding in the rear of the attacking troops; but it was especially true that the attack was not conducted in a concentrated manner by the troops, which had been jumbled together in during previous battles in the commitment east of the Orne river.

The counterattack near Ryes by the 915th Grenadier Regiment of the 352nd Infantry Division also failed. In the evening, the enemy reached the Bayeux-Caen road east of Bayeux.

Counterattacks against the beachhead east of Ste Mere-Église from the north and west were ineffective. The attacking troops were delayed, weakened and partly jumbled on the approach by battles with airlanded enemy forces.

About 1900, the 6th FS Regiment attacked from the southern areas

328

of St Come du Mont and with one battalion advanced as far as Ste Marie-du-Mont. Another battalion advanced to a point south of Ste Mere-Église. We at least succeeded in annihilating strong elements of the airlanded enemy or pressed them together in the area of Ste MereÉglise.

The result of the first day of the invasion was not very hopeful. It was not possible at any single spot to prevent a landing. The coastal defense was broken through at three points, even though individual islands of resistance still held out inside the points of penetration. The bulk of the coastal artillery was put out of action. Heavy losses were caused by ship artillery. We did not succeed in taking full advantage of the favorable situation, caused by the temporary weakness of the enemy, immediately after the landing. Corps had hoped that it would be possible at that time to mop up the situation with its own forces. The weak reserves were already delayed, and weakened to such an extent by the enemy airborne troops (one division at the Orne river, two divisions west of the Vire river) that, during the day, they were no longer able to carry out a decisive attack.

The success of the invasion is mostly due to the heroic fighting by troops in the first landings of enemy airborne divisions. Decisive, however, was the lack of German Luftwaffe and Navy. Only this made it possible for the enemy to approach unobserved and unharassed and to bring to its full effectiveness during the landing his supremacy in the air and on the sea.

There was little hope of successfully continuing the counterattack with our own forces before the arrival of large reserve. Since Gen Marcks had his doubts that the High Command would take countermeasures in good time, he considered the invasion as already successful on the evening of 6 June.

During the night of 6/7 June, I SS Panzer Corps assumed command in the Caen sector in order to conduct, after the arrival of the 12th SS Panzer Division and together with the 21st Panzer Division, a counterattack west of the Orne river. Thus, the 716th Infantry Division was assigned to I SS Panzer Corps. The former right boundary of the 352nd Infantry Division became the Corps' right boundary.

I SS PANZER CORPS MOVES UP TO COUNTERATTACK, 6 JUNE 1944

By Generalmajor Fritz Krämer

In May of 1944 there were increased signs that an invasion was imminent. The Commander-in-Chief West kept the Corps currently informed of developments. The Channel coast, the Dieppe sector, Caen and the Cotentin peninsula were named as probable landing points. Since mid-May, large-scale troop movements were also carried out. By 1 June, Commander-in-Chief West was keeping the Commanding General or Chief of Staff informed on Hitler's opinions on the invasion, the latest of which presumed that the date would be about mid-June. As OKW reserve, the Corps was directly subordinate to OKW, but the divisions envisaged for commitment were not yet known.

On 6 June 1944, at about 1000 hours, the Chief of Staff was informed by Chief of StaffPanzer Gruppe West of the landing of strong enemy forces near Caen. Still nothing was known concerning the probable commitment ofCorps. Nevertheless, orders were given to the staff and troops to be prepared for immediate commitment.

At about 1400, Ia of Seventh Army, Oberst iG Helmdach, telephoned that Corps was assigned to Seventh Army. The Commanding General and Chief of Staff were to come immediately to Seventh Army headquarters at Le Mans for briefing, and Corps troops were to start immediately in the direction of Caen. However, the Chief of Staff I SS Panzer Corps pointed out to Chief of Staff Seventh Army the lively enemy air activity already observed by Corps, and the long distance involved, stated that it was not possible to cover the distance by a Fieseler Storch airplane, and asked fora telephone or written order.

At about 1500 hours, Corps received the following order by phone:
- I SS Panzer Corps, subordinated to Seventh Army, will throw the

A wrecked German half-track from an SS division lies on its side next to one of its fallen occupants. The American soldier is standing aboard a Wespe, one of the new breed of German self-propelled artillery which provided effective fire support for the Panzer divisions. They were, however, never available in adequate numbers; only 635 of these very useful vehicles were produced to satisfy the unceasing demands of both the Western and Eastern fronts.

enemy landed near Caen back into the sea. Following units will be subordinated: 21st Panzer Division near Caen, 12th SS Panzer Division, and probably Panzer Lehr Division.
- 21st Panzer Division is already committed near Caen.
- Division CP Caen.
- Since 5 June 1944, 12th SS Panzer Division is on march from Dreux area into the Elbeuf area.

To thwart espionage activity, we had been ordered to check the authenticity of every important telephone order a short time after its receipt, by telephoning the headquarters which had issued it. Enquiries by telephone at General of Panzer Troops West and Seventh Army confirmed the correctness of the aforementioned order.

Counterattacks In the Caen-Bayeux Area

Since Corps staff and troops had been alerted on the forenoon of 6 June 1944, the march in the direction of Caen could be started at about 1600 hours along the Nantes-Foreux-Trun-Falaise road. The main road was avoided because of the great danger from the air, and the units

German prisoners under the guard of a British Tommy who looks particularly pleased with his haul. The Germans themselves had endured the massive aerial and naval bombardments and were probably very pleased to be out of the fighting.

moved in extended columns. Already there were burning vehicles of all kinds everywhere on the road. No considerable Flak formations or air forces were available for defense against enemy fighter planes, so these were able to attack as though carrying out exercises. Air attacks had a paralyzing effect on some of our drivers. German soldiers were not accustomed to this type of attack, and it was several days before they became accustomed to it, placed observers in vehicles, and took necessary countermeasures. Whenever enemy fighters approached, the vehicles were raced, if possible, to a house, tree, slope of the road, or other cover, and the crew alighted. High Command soon ordered that march columns and supply vehicles move only at night.

While on the way, the Corps Chief of Staff met the Commander of the 12th SS Panzer Division, who gave some valuable hints about camouflage during marches, and also said that the command post of the 21st Panzer Division was no longer at Caen but at St Pierre-sur-Dives. Sections of wood south of Falaise were the intermediate goal of Corps troops and the main body of the staff. The combat train echelon had been ordered to assemble in a forest about four kilometers north of Falaise. To prevent loss of valuable headquarters radio cars, the echelon had been ordered to keep radio units very small and widely separated during the move.

In a verbal order to its commander, the 12th SS Panzer Division was diverted by way of Elbeuf-Lisieux-Caen. Marching was to start in the early hours of the evening, making full use of the darkness. Guides and persons who were to receive orders had been ordered to proceed to the road junction five kilometers north of St Pierre. At 1800 hours no contact had been established with the Panzer Lehr Division, which had not yet been subordinated.

Apparently, the news about the enemy landing had quickly passed to the civilian population. Groups of civilians were standing before the doors of their houses in towns and villages. Their attitude was not hostile; rather, they showed a strong resentment towards the Allied air attacks, which oftentimes did not discriminate between German motor- and horse-drawn vehicles and French civilian vehicles. Likewise, the civilians were aware that enemy air attacks had almost demolished Falaise.

When Corps arrived at Falaise, it was impossible to pass through the burning town, and we had to detour along a road that the local military police had cleared. This roundabout way was passable for tanks and heavy motor vehicles, so that delay was the only obstacle the air attack created.

At 2000 hours on 6 June 1944, the Commanding General and Chief of Staff met at the command post of the 21st Panzer Division at St Pierre-sur-Dives. Repeated enemy air attacks, detours, and the conversation with the division commander of the 12th SS Panzer Division had delayed arrival. Already it was apparent that men and vehicles could be saved from destruction only by restricting daytime traffic, and moving at night with dimmed lights. Avoidance of the main roads and use of subsidiary roads were not sufficient, as the enemy fliers also kept the subsidiary roads under observation.

The old maxim of Panzer troops, "It is better for both driver and vehicle to use good roads even if the distance is greater," proved to be true also at night. Troops moving at night arrived at assembly areas in full strength and earlier than if they had moved by day with very great distances between units. Unfortunately, it was a long time before higher headquarters was convinced of this and correctly calculated time and distances.

Upon his arrival at the command post of the 21st Panzer Division on 6 June 1944 at 2000 hours, the Commanding General ofI SS Panzer Corps was confronted with the following situation:

1. Only the first general staff officer was present at the command post of the division. As early as the forenoon of 6 June, the 21st Panzer Division had been committed to support of the 716th Infantry Division employed on the coast. The division had not yet attacked compactly, as, for reasons not yet ascertained, it had been committed first on the right and later on the left bank of the Orne. Elements of the division were still on the right bank of the Orne, as the commander of the 719th Infantry Division, employed there, wanted the tanks. The command post had no contact by telephone with the individual combat groups of the division. The division commander was at the command post of the 716th Infantry Division. Telephonic communication with him was frequently interrupted, and audibility was poor at times. He had no contact with his combat groups, except through messengers and special-mission staff officers. He had failed to take a radio set with him. (For a commander of a Panzer or motorized division to leave his headquarters without a radio set was considered tantamount to traveling without his head.)

   The Panzer regiment of the division was committed on the left bank of the Orne and had contacted the enemy. The situation was vague. Approximately 60 tanks (panzer IV and V) were ready for action. They were adequately equipped with ammunition and fuel.

2. The 12th SS Panzer Division was on the march. We could not expect its arrival before noon on 7 June 1944. (Actually its assembly was not completed until the morning of 8 June.)

3. The 716th Infantry Division, committed at the coast, was split up into several parts, but details of its situation were not available at division headquarters. Some of its elements were employed in individual shelters. In the vicinity of the coast, contact was maintained by radio or telephone.

4. There was delay in establishing telephone contact with Seventh Army at Le Mans, and, when contact was established, audibility frequently was practically nil. The relay station at Falaise was operating under severe difficulties due to the damage to the town by bombing. In a teletype conversation with Seventh Army at about 2400, Corps requested subordination of the Panzer Lehr Division and reported assumption of control of the 716th Infantry Division, and also that a coordinated attack of Corps units was not expected to take place before 8 June 1944. Further increased support was requested from the Luftwaffe, and the impossibility of daytime marches was pointed out. Seventh Army made it clear that it was essential to carry out a compact attack by Corps as soon as possible.

Reports received by the 21st Panzer Division during the night showed that elements committed on the left bank of the Orne, together with such elements of the 716th Infantry Division as were still capable of action, were on the point of establishing a line of resistance roughly from Blainville (north) to the Caen-Douvres railroad. The divisional sector was opposed by British troops. The enemy had pushed his beachhead inland for about seven or eight kilometers.

Computation of time during the night of 6/7 June made it clear that the most advanced elements of the 12th SS Panzer Division would not arrive south of Caen before early on 7 June. Their assembly could not be completed before the night of 7/8 June. We had to consider delays due to enemy air activity.

The most advanced elements of the Panzer Lehr Division could be expected to arrive at the bridge near Thury-Harcourt on the morning of 7 June.

A Panzer division without supply troops required nine or ten hours to pass a given point, so the assembly of divisions could not be completed before the evening of 7 June. This was only possible if there were no mishaps, an assumption that could not be depended upon. Corps considered that the morning of 8 June was the earliest it could attack.

The only possibility of an earlier attack would have been by the commitment of individual elements of the division within sectors fixed on the map, without awaiting the arrival of artillery, and consequently without artillery support. This would have resulted in splitting up the division, and it could never have been brought together again. The committed elements of the division might have been exterminated by the advancing enemy, had it been called upon to fight against artillery with mere rifles and machine guns. Even if the most favorable results were achieved, the division would be tied up in such a manner as to deprive it of its chief advantage-mobility. Our higher headquarters could have computed this time as well as we, but during the teletype conversation it became evident that they indulged in the desirable but ill-founded hope that the Panzer corps could move mountains.

In this vague situation it was imperative not to lose our nerve. The Commanding General, therefore, decided to prevent an extension of the beachhead by the combined efforts of the 21st Panzer Division and the still-active combat elements of the 716th Infantry Division, in order to launch a compact attack after the approach march and assembly of the other division was completed. During the night of 6/7 June 1944, I SS Panzer Corps issued the following order:

1. We have to reckon with the extension of enemy beachhead during 7 June 1944.
2. In order to prevent extension of enemy beachhead, I SS Panzer Corps, which on 6 June 1944 assumed control of the Orne sector, inclusive of 716th Infantry Division, will assemble for attack on 7 June 1944, and throw the landed enemy back into the sea. Probable time of attack on 8 June 1944.

Therefore:
   a. 21st Panzer Division will hold the line hitherto reached on either side of Blainville. Elements of 716th Infantry Division employed there will be subordinated.

   The reinforced Panzer regiment will conduct offensive action with limited objectives, in order to simulate the presence of strong Panzer forces. Ground gained has to be occupied immediately. It is not essential to establish a continuous MLR. During the night of 6/7 June, the elements of the division which are not employed on the right bank of the Orne have to be moved to the left bank.

   b. 716th Infantry Division will hold its present strongpoints and assemble its scattered elements north of Caen. Caen has to be prepared for tenacious defense. All formations of Army, Navy, and Luftwaffe located there will be subordinated.

All elements capable of combat located in sector of 21st Panzer Division will be subordinated to this division.

   c. Corps Artillery Commander (Arko I) will move Corps Artillery Battalion to its firing position south of Caen and will support 21st Panzer Division in resistance and attack. Artillery of 716th Infantry Division, 21st Panzer Division, and other artillery formations employed at the coast will be incorporated into the plan of fire.

3. 12th SS Panzer Division will go into its jump-off position in the region of Caen (excl.)-Verson-Fleury.

The assembly of Division has to be accomplished speedily. Further orders will follow.

4. Panzer Lehr Division, placed under control of I SS Panzer Corps immediately, will secure crossing of Division near Thury-Harcourt and assemble in the area around Evrecy. Further orders will follow.

5. Heavy Panzer Battalion/I SS Panzer Corps will reach forest west of Bretteville.

6. CP of 21st Panzer Division to be transferred immediately to the region of Caen.

7. Corps CP will transfer into the May-sur-Orne area. Corps Signal Battalion will establish radio contact with Seventh Army, 84th Artillery Commander (AK), and with subordinate divisions. Telephone connections will be established according to verbal directions.

For Corps Headquarters, Chief of Staff

GROUND TACTICS OF GERMAN PARATROOPS

Intelligence Bulletin, June 1944.

The commander of a German parachute demonstration battalion recently issued to his companies a directive which affords useful insight into some of the ground tactics that enemy paratroopers may be expected to employ. The following extracts from the battalion commander's order are considered especially significant:

1. For parachute and air-landing operations, I have given orders for section leaders and their seconds-in-command to carry rifles, and for the No. 3 men on the light machine guns to carry machine carbines. There are tactical reasons for this decision. The section commander must be able to point out targets to his section by means of single tracer rounds. The No. 3 man on the light machine gun must be able to give this gun covering fire from his machine carbine in the event that close combat takes place immediately after landing. This last should be regarded as a distinct possibility. He must provide this covering fire until the light machine gun is in position and ready to fire. Before the assault, the No. 3 man on the light machine gun must also be able to beat off local counterattacks with his machine carbine until the machine gun is ready to go into action.

2. Since so many targets are likely to be seen only for a fleeting moment, and since the rifleman himself must disappear from hostile observation as soon as he has revealed his position by firing, the German paratrooper must be extremely skillful at "snap shooting" (rapid aiming and firing). The following three points are to be noted and put into practice:

    a. Snap shooting is most useful at short ranges. It will not be employed at ranges of more than 330 yards, except in close combat and defense, when it will generally be employed at ranges under 1,100 yards.

    b. Even more important than rapid aiming and firing is rapid

disappearance after firing, no matter what the range may be.
   c. Movement is revealing, also. Men must move as little as possible and must quickly find cover from fire at each bound.
3. I leave to company commanders the distribution of automatic and sniper rifles within companies. I wish only to stress the following principles:
   a. Wherever possible, sniper and automatic rifles will be given to those paratroopers who can use them most effectively. In general practice, this rules out commanders and headquarters personnel (who have duties other than firing).
   b. There seems to be a general but incorrect impression that our sniper rifles improve the marksmanship of men who are only moderately good shots. These rifles are provided with telescopes only to make more distinct those targets which are not clearly visible to the naked eye. This means that an advantage accrues solely to very good marksmen firing at medium ranges—and, what is more, only where impact can be observed and the necessary adjustments made. Since the sniper is seldom in a position where he can observe for himself, a second man, with binoculars, generally will be detailed to work with the sniper.
4. I wish company commanders to make the report on the battle of Crete the subject of continual reference in their own lectures, and in the lectures of platoon commanders who are training noncoms. I particularly desire that those passages in the report which deal with the importance of the undertaking as a whole be drilled into every man. The last three exercises I have attended have shown me that this principle is by no means evident to all platoon commanders. Platoon commanders in this battalion are still too much inclined to fight their own private brands of war instead of paying attention to the larger picture.
5. It is extremely likely that, during a parachute or air-landing operation, this battalion will land in hostile positions not previously reconnoitered, and will have to fight for the landing area. Such fighting will be carried out according to the same regulations which would obtain if we had fought our way into the heart of a hostile

position.
6. Inasmuch as we shall soon be receiving our new machine guns, [Here the German battalion commander is probably referring to a consignment of regular or modified M.G. 42's.] training with those new machine guns we already have must be pushed forward in our light companies—at least to the extent of giving the No. 1 men about 1 1/2 hours a day on it. The most important point to be driven home is that this weapon is to be fired in very short bursts to avoid waste of ammunition.[No doubt the enemy also hopes that this precaution will help to keep the fire on the target.]
7. During the exercises and field firing demonstrations I have witnessed—I admit they have been few—I did not once see yellow identification panels used to mark our forward line, nor did I see the swastika flags used to identify our own troops to friendly aircraft. Henceforth, these panels and flags will be carried on all occasions and will be spread out at the proper times.
8. I wish platoon exercises to include more emphasis on the attacks on well prepared defensive positions. This Will Include cooperation between two assault detachments and a reserve assault ("mopping-up") detachment.

Each German paratroop company commander, it is reported, must designate five to seven of his best men as a tank-hunting detachment. These men perform their regular duties, but are prepared to act as a team in their tank-hunting capacity whenever they may be called upon. The infantry training of German paratroopers is usually very thorough, covering all normal training and, in some instances, use of the light machine gun, heavy machine gun, mortar, and antitank rifle, as well. Cunning and initiative are stressed. Many men are taught to drive tanks and other vehicles. Use of simple demolitions and the handling of antitank and antipersonnel mines are often included in the training.

88-MM GERMAN ANTITANK GUN USED IN FRANCE: GENERAL DATA

Tactical and Technical Trends, No. 51, October 1944.

Detailed information is now available concerning the German 88-mm (3.46-in.) antitank gun *Pak 43/41* which was first encountered by United States forces in France, although it had been employed previously against the Soviets.

General data:
- Length of tube, including muzzle brake: 258.66 in.
- Length of muzzle brake: 17.35 in.
- Maximum traverse (30° R, 30° L): 60°.
- Rate of traverse: 1 turn per 34".
- Maximum elevation: 36°.
- Maximum depression: 7°.
- Height of wheels: 48 1/2 in.
- Maximum recoil: 28 in.
- Minimum recoil: 24 in.
- Length of carriage without gun: 216 in.
- Length of carriage with gun: 360 in.
- Height of carriage in traveling position: 78 in.
- Total weight of equipment: 9,660 lb.

The carriage of this equipment follows orthodox lines with trail legs hinged to a bottom carriage upon which is mounted a cradle providing lateral deflection and carrying the usual layout of traversing and elevating gears. The wheels, on cranked stub-axles, are independently sprung but there is no compensation between the wheels, and the carriage is on four-point support when firing. In general, the carriage appears as if it might be one of the earlier designs of field carriage adapted to take the *Pak 43/41* gun.

The barrel is made in two sections. The front end of the rear section has an enlarged diameter which is prepared for the reception, jointing, and securing of the rear end of the front section. The correct positioning of the rifling is ensured by a key which is inserted from the outside. A locking collar, similar to that used on all German guns to lock barrel to breechring, locks the front section to the rear section, thus preventing longitudinal movement. Use of this locking collar obviates the necessity for start of thread. A gas seal is provided by inserting a steel expansion ring between the two sections of the barrel. This ring fits into recesses cut in each section.

The front section is supported by the rear section for a length of 32 inches and has two bearing surfaces, one at the front end and one at the rear end: these have a clearance of 0.004 and 0.003 inch respectively.

The lug which takes the recoil cylinder is not connected to the breech ring but is a part of a bracket welded to a band which splits into halves and is forward of the breechring. Breechring and mechanism are similar to the 75-mm *Pak 40*, slightly simplified. The gun is fired electrically, with two 2-volt batteries in series provided on the left side of the carriage. The muzzle brake is similar to that found on the *Pak 40*, *Pak 36*, and other guns. but in this case the rear baffle only is bushed.

The cradle is a welded design. It is attached to the carriage by a pintle at the rear and two adjustable rollers in the front. These rollers bear on a plain machined arc. Underneath the cradle a flat machined plate is attached by two bolts, and this plate in turn fits underneath the plain arc and serves as a stop to any upward movement of the cradle in firing.

The hydropneumatic recoil mechanism is on top of the gun. The pressure is 800 pounds per square inch. The buffer is housed in the cradle underneath the gun and is of orthodox design.

The elevating gear is arc-and-pinion type and is normal with the exception of two hand wheels, one on each side. The left handwheel can be used for final aiming, as it has a ratio of one and one-half turns to one of the right handwheel. The gun is fired from the left wheel. The traversing gear is normal, controlled by a handwheel to a worm on the center of the cradle, then to a worm-and-pinion onto the traversing rack on the carriage.

The trail is split and of riveted construction. It is rather short, only 10 feet 6 inches in length.

Attachment of the spades is interesting. They are forward, on top of the legs, in the traveling position and fold back over the legs for firing. The legs are locked in the traveling position by two locking devices, one of which also locks the cradle, and the other also locks the lunette in position. The lunette folds back and locks on the inside of the right leg when in the firing position.

The 88-mm *Pak 43/41* may be confused with the 88-mm *Pak 43* because of similar designation. While both have tubes based on the tube of the 88-mm *Flak 41*, the *Pak 43* has a cruciform carriage not unlike that of the 88-mm *Flak 18* and *36*. However, the *Pak 43* carriage does not permit sufficient elevation for AA fire.

Ammunition listed below is fired by the 88-mm *Pak 43/41*:

Type	Approximate weight of projectile (pounds)	MV (f/s)
HE (with point-detonating quick and delay fuze)—88-mm Sprgr Patr 43, Kw. K. 43 m. A. Z. 23/28	20.68	2,296
HE (with combination point-detonating quick and time fuzes)—88-mm Sprgr Patr 43, Kw. K. 43 m. Dopp. Z. S/60 Fl. or Dopp. Z. S/60 V	20.68	2,296
APCBC—88-mm Pzgr Patr 39/43, Kw. K. 43 m. Bd. Z. 5127	22.44	3,280
AP40—88-mm Pzgr Patr 40/43, Kw. K. 43	16	3,775

GERMAN ANTITANK TACTICS: TEXT OF A CAPTURED DOCUMENT

Tactical and Technical Trends, No. 51, October 1944.

Don't split up antitank units, give them definite tasks in combat, maintain close liaison with the infantry, set up antitank nests under unified command, employ self-propelled companies in mobile operations—these are some of the antitank tactics outlined in a recently obtained German document. The translation from the German follows:

The tendency to split up antitank units completely, to have a proportion of antitank firepower everywhere, is wrong. The smallest unit permissible is the half-platoon (two guns), except for defense of streets for which less may be employed.

Companies in their entirety, or at least whole platoons, should cover likely tank approaches. To use a single antitank gun is to invite destruction. Other terrain over which tanks might approach will be covered by mines, obstacles, or tank-destruction detachments.

Antitank units will normally be in support; they must be given definite tasks and allowed to make their own tactical dispositions.

Engagement of even worthwhile infantry targets must be the exception rather than the rule. Such employment is limited by lack of mobility, by the bulkiness of the gun as a target, by the sensitivity of the barrel which is subjected to great strain, and finally by the small issue of high-explosive shells. In addition, accuracy diminishes with bore wear.

On the move, regimental antitank companies are normally distributed throughout march groups by platoons—one platoon always with the advance party. No heavy antitank guns [should be] with the point, as too much time is needed to bring them into action. Divisional antitank battalions are normally brought forward as a body.

In assembling, locate in areas from which the final movement can also be protected; local protection [should be] by machine guns. Positions for antitank guns not immediately employed will be reconnoitered and prepared. Antitank warning arrangements must be made by the officer commanding the antitank unit detailed for local protection. Advantage will be taken of unexpected gains of ground to push forward the antitank defenses.

CLOSE INFANTRY LIAISON

In attack, antitank units follow the advancing infantry in areas likely to favor tank counterattacks, moving from cover to cover in such a manner that the antitank guns always have advantageous positions. The leading infantry must not be beyond the range of the antitank guns. As many guns as possible must be ready to fire simultaneously. There must be close liaison between the antitank units and the infantry before and during the attack. When the objective has been reached, or if the attack is held up, a solid belt of antitank defenses must be organized immediately. This is the responsibility of the antitank unit commander.

In defensive operations, an antitank defense plan will be drawn up by the responsible antitank commander. Location of the main defensive belt must give the antitank guns suitable fields of fire; this is a prerequisite for effective antitank support for the infantry.

Antitank positions must be established at some distance to the rear. These positions must be camouflaged so they will not be seen and concentrated on before the attack. However, in the selection of positions it must be remembered that these should be sufficiently far forward to cover the ground in front of the main defensive belt. Normally, regimental antitank companies are forward, and divisional antitank units are to the rear.

Alternative and dummy positions are essential for continued surprise. Mines and obstacles should be used in suitable areas. Tank-hunting detachments should be held ready in villages, wooded areas, and close country.

Nests of antitank guns under one unified command should be set up. Units arriving subsequently will be incorporated in the general antitank defense plan.

Open fire as late as possible. Do not be deceived by feint attacks.

Use one uniform system of tank warning. It is important to keep in contact with artillery OP's. Take advantage of all radio and telephone facilities. Tank warnings have priority over everything.

If there is any possibility of creating an antitank reserve, the reserve units must reconnoiter a number of possible positions and prepare them for occupation.

In the employment of self-propelled antitank guns the following will apply:

Companies are controlled by radio, in emergency by flag signals. Normal formations for movement on the battlefield are file, arrowhead, broad arrowhead, or extended line. Self-propelled antitank guns use fire and movement, their constant readiness for action making them the ideal mobile reserve. They are, therefore, the very weapon to use at points of main effort. The tactical unit is the company; exceptionally, the platoon. Disadvantages at present are low speed (up to 10 miles per hour), tall silhouette, weak armor, and restricted traverse. Immediate counterattack, such as can be carried out by assault guns, is impossible. Self-propelled antitank guns can be employed only on open flanks if adequately covered by infantry. Whenever possible, ground reconnaissance, preferably on foot, must precede the occupation of positions.

CHECK BRIDGE CAPACITIES

On the move, one self-propelled antitank half-platoon should be as far forward as possible; the remainder of the platoon should be with the advance party. The rest of the company will remain together. Road reconnaissance must include investigation of the carrying capacity of bridges.

In an attack, the infantry will be accompanied by self-propelled antitank platoons, each giving the other mutual support. The enemy should be engaged by surprise, when possible from defiladed positions or from positions on reverse slopes, with all guns firing simultaneously. Fire should be opened, when possible, by whole companies, since it will frequently be necessary to fire in several directions at the same time. Platoons can fire effectively only in one direction at a time.

The only completely successful method of employing self-propelled companies is in mobile operations. Flank attacks are very effective, especially if they are combined with a small frontal attack.

In defense, the main task of self-propelled antitank guns is the destruction of tanks which have broken through. Self-propelled units will therefore be held as mobile reserves and employed all together, especially for the point of main effort. An efficient warning system, using radio whenever possible, is especially important. Gun commanders must thoroughly reconnoiter probable operational areas, the ground in the main defensive belt, tank approaches, and the rear areas of the position. Close liaison with the infantry is essential. It is wrong to dig in self-propelled guns because of their lack of traverse, but firing and alternative positions must be prepared for them.

FIGHTING IN NORMANDY

Combat Lessons - Rank and file in combat: What they're doing; How they do it, No. 4

Bucking the Hedgerows

The terrain in the area selected for the initial penetration of French soil was generally level or gently sloping. However, it was broken up into a "crazy quilt" pattern of small fields separated by "hedgerows." These consisted of an earthen mound or wall 8 to 10 feet in width and 4 to 6 feet in height, covered with a scrub undergrowth.

Along the top of this wall grew rows of trees. Forming an important part of the obstacle thus created was the ditch which ran along one or both sides of the mound. The roads, narrow and winding, ran between these hedgerows, and offered the defenders many advantageous positions for ambuscades or surprise attacks on advancing foot-troops and armor. Observation was normally limited from one hedgerow to the next, although an occasional structure, such as the church tower in a village would widen the horizon.

These peculiarities of terrain led to the development of special operational techniques in the application of tactical principles. Quoted below are some experience reports, from the battlefield, of hedgerow fighting.

The German Defense

Ever since August 1940 the Germans have been studying and organizing the beach defenses of the French coast. They are past masters of the art of utilizing the terrain to advantage.

As set forth in a letter from the *Commanding General, U. S. XIX Corps*: "The Germans have been thorough in their defense. Their weapons are normally sited to provide long fields of fire. The 88-mm dual purpose gun, the Tiger tank with its 88-mm gun, or the Panther tank which has a 75-mm high-velocity gun, normally takes you under fire at ranges up to 2,000 yards. All weapons are well dug in. The mobility of their tanks is often sacrificed in order to secure the protection of a ditch or the walls of a building.

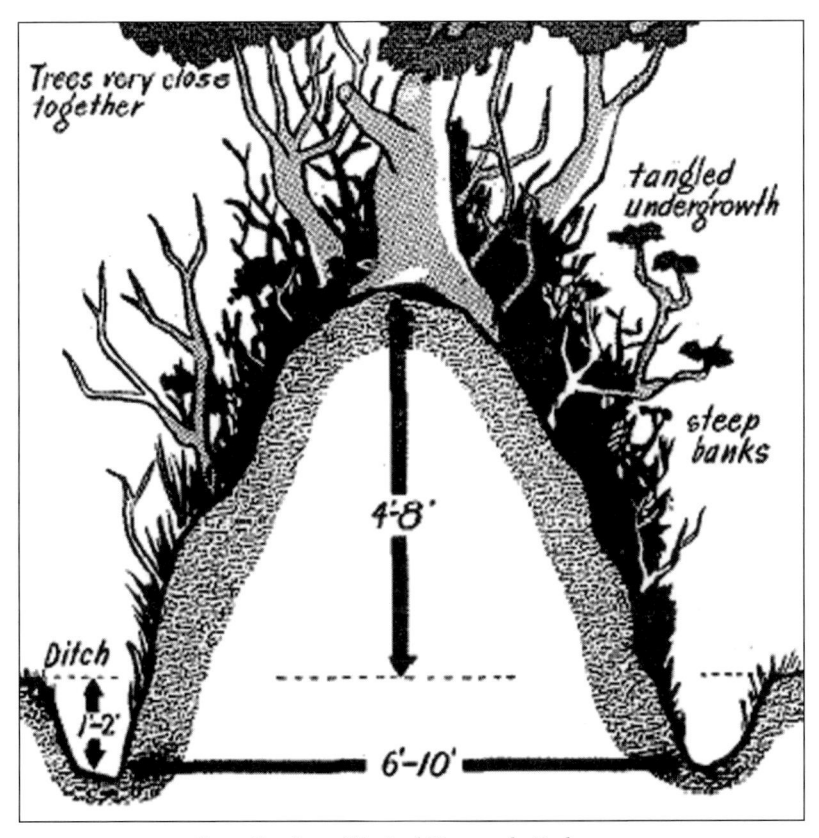

Cross Section of Typical Normandy Hedgerow.

Sniper Trouble

"The German soldiers had been given orders to stay in their positions and, unless you rooted them out, they would stay, even though your attack had passed by or over them. Some of their snipers stayed hidden for 2 to 5 days after a position had been taken and then popped up suddenly with a rifle or AT grenade launcher to take the shot for which they had been waiting.

"We found fire crackers with slow burning fuse left by snipers and AT gun crews in their old positions when they moved. These exploded at irregular intervals, giving the impression that the position was still occupied by enemy forces.

"High losses among tank commanders have been caused by German snipers. Keep buttoned up, as the German rifleman concentrates on such profitable targets. This is especially true in villages. After an action the turret of the commanders tank is usually well marked with rifle bullets.

Enemy in Ambush

"On several occasions the Germans have allowed small patrols of ours to enter villages and wander around unmolested, but when stronger forces were sent forward to occupy the village they would encounter strong resistance. The Germans will permit a patrol to gather erroneous information in order to ambush the follow-up troops acting on the patrols' false report."

German Weapons

One infantry regimental commander has given a good detailed description of the defensive organization: "We found that the enemy employed very few troops with an extremely large number of automatic weapons. All personnel and automatic weapons were well dug in along the hedgerows in excellent firing positions. In most cases the approaches to these positions were covered by mortar fire. Also additional fire support was provided by artillery field pieces of 75-mm, 88-mm, and 240-mm caliber firing both time and percussion fire. Numerous snipers located in trees, houses, and towers were used.

Our Attack

"The most successful method of dealing with these defensive positions was the closely coordinated attack of infantry and tanks, with artillery and 4.2-inch chemical mortars ready to assist where needed. The use of these supporting weapons was severely handicapped by the limited observation."

TANK-INFANTRY COMBINE

Teamwork the Key

The great emphasis placed on the importance of tank-infantry teamwork is reflected in the many reports and training instructions that have been issued by combat commanders. For example the *Commanding General, VII Corps* published the following narrative of such an action in a training memorandum: "The capture of the high ground north of the MONTEBOURG-QUINEVILLE ROAD was accomplished by the 3d Battalion, 22d Infantry, closely supported by the 70th Tank Battalion, which was operating at a reduced strength of

18 tanks.

"Upon receiving the order for the attack at 1830, 13 June, the tank battalion commander immediately initiated a route reconnaissance to a suitable assembly area and arranged for a conference between his key officers and those of the infantry battalion.

Elements of the Plan

"At this conference the following essential elements to effect coordination were agreed upon:

"1. H-hour would be at 0930.

"2. An artillery preparation would be fired from H-15 minutes to H-hour.

"3. When the artillery fire lifted, the tank mortar platoon, from positions immediately in rear of the Line of Departure, would fire on all known and suspected AT gun locations.

"4. Each of the two infantry assault companies would be directly supported by six tanks. The remaining six tanks would be in general support.

"5. All tanks would be held 800 yards in rear of the LD, moving forward in time to cross the line with the infantry at H-hour.

The Advance

"The attack jumped off on time, the tanks advancing very slowly, spraying the hedgerows with machine-gun fire. The infantry advanced abreast of the tanks, mopping up as they proceeded. The supporting tank company remained about 500 to 600 yards in rear of the assault companies and covered their forward movement by overhead fire.

"The objective was seized at 1500 after an advance of over 2,000 yards against a well-organized resistance which utilized both open and concrete emplacements."

Corp Commanders Comment:

In discussing this attack the Corps Commander made the following comments on infantry-tank cooperation:

"Tank companies require at least 3 hours and tank battalions a minimum of 5 hours of daylight in which to prepare for an attack.

"Tank assembly positions should be selected well in rear of the Line of Departure.

"Tank officers and infantry commanders should discuss and arrange all details of their cooperative effort by personal conference at some prearranged location. If possible this location should allow visual reconnaissance of the zone of activity.

"The tanks should not be advanced to the LD until the time of the attack.

"Artillery observers should be with the leading wave of tanks.

"Radio communication between the infantry CP and the tanks should be maintained.

"The speed of the tanks should conform to the infantry rate of advance. Gaps should not be allowed to develop between the two elements.

"The infantry can assist the tanks in passing through hedgerows by protecting them from hostile AT personnel using AT grenades or rockets.

"In the absence of definite targets forward infantry elements should fire at the nearest cover to the front and flanks. Rifle fire directed along the lower structures of friendly tanks will discourage enemy use of magnetic mines.

"Enemy AT guns firing at our tanks should be immediately smothered by our mortar and automatic-weapons fire, thus forcing the gun crews to take cover and permitting the tanks to outflank and destroy the enemy guns.

"Tanks should be employed on both sides of hedges when advancing along a hedgerow.

"If at all possible tanks should avoid roads during the attack.

"The tanks in general support should mop up any positions which are bypassed by the first wave of tanks.

"Once the final objective is reached the tanks should immediately withdraw to a predetermined rally point. If they remain with the infantry they will attract heavy enemy artillery fire which will seriously interfere with the infantry reorganization."

Limited Objective

A letter from *Headquarters, XIX Corps*, stresses the importance of the limited objective in controlling the combined infantry-tank action: "The major objective given in corps, division, and even regimental plans and orders is reached by a series of limited-objective attacks by infantry and tank platoons and companies. Thus the designation of the major objective should be considered as indicating an axis of advance and an ultimate goal for the smaller assault units. Here in Normandy the normal objective of each attack is the next hedgerow where there will be a pause for reorganization and for planning the next advance. Keep the distance to be traversed short so that the tanks will not outstrip the infantry, thus losing the close support that is mutually necessary to make the fight effective. It is very desirable whenever conditions permit that each limited objective be visible from the line of departure.

Personal Reconnaissance

"The closely coordinated team play that is called for in hedgerow fighting requires a maximum of personal reconnaissance. The key to success in each fight from hedgerow to hedgerow is personal reconnaissance by the commanders concerned."

Bulldozer Tanks

An infantry battalion commander wrote from Normandy: "The light and medium tank equipped with a bulldozer blade was successfully used to plow through the hedgerows, cutting openings through which the other tanks would file to fan out and cover the next field. The steep banks which line the roads would be cut down at predetermined crossing points."

Fighting Infantry

Infantry Regimental Commander, Normandy: "Fire and movement is still the only sound way to advance your infantry in daylight fighting. Build up a good strong base of fire with automatic rifles and light machine guns. The heavy machine guns are much more effective, but it is difficult to keep them up with the advance. Use your 60-mm mortars to deepen and thicken your covering fire. When you are all set, cut loose with all youve got to keep Jerrys head down while the riflemen close in from the flanks and clean him out.

Hedgerow Hints

"Because of the limited range of observation, scouts tended to operate too close to their units. They should try to keep at least one hedgerow ahead of the remainder of the squad.

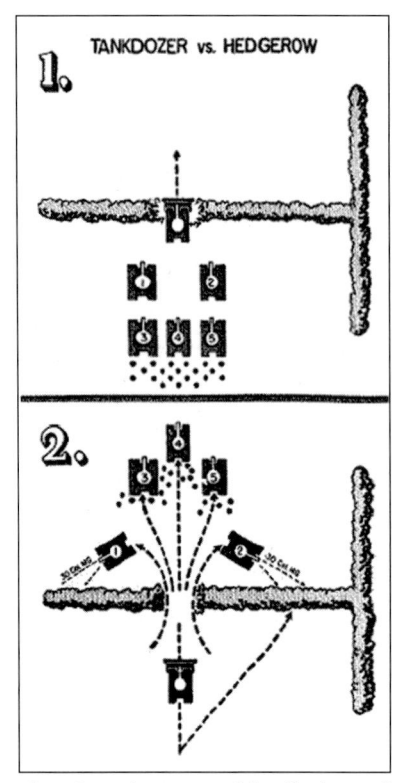

"Riflemen still have a tendency to wait for a definite, visible target before shooting. Each man should cover with fire any assigned sector which he believes occupied. Only then will he provide the needed protection to his comrades on the move.

"Avoid the areas in the vicinity of large trees when digging in. Enemy artillery fire in these trees will cause tree bursts with the same effect as time fire."

Hedgerow Explosives

Observers Report, Normandy: "The engineers played their part in the tank-infantry team. The sketches show graphically how the closely coordinated tank-infantry-engineer team worked in one of our divisions.

"The tank would place covering fire on the far hedge from a position behind the hedge to be breached. Under this fire the infantry would move into the field ahead to cover the engineer operations. The engineers would place explosive charges to breach the hedge during the infantry advance.

"When the tank fire had to stop to avoid endangering our own infantry, the tank would momentarily withdraw, and the charges would be detonated. The team would then move forward to the next hedgerow to repeat the performance. It was found that two charges of 50 pounds each placed as shown were adequate to breach any type of hedgerow."

Lean on the Artillery Preparation

Commanding General, 79th Division, Normandy: "Heavy artillery preparation fires, terrifically expensive in ammunition, have been wasted because they were not closely followed up by the attacking infantry. Remember these supporting fires do not destroy the enemy but merely force him underground for a brief period. You must be on top of him when he pops up again."

The Useful 4.2
Infantry Battalion Commander, Normandy: "The 4.2-inch chemical mortar has proved to be a wonderful close-support weapon. Captured prisoners stated that they feared it more than artillery shell because they could not hear the projectile. The Germans have shown a marked dislike for WP, and on many occasions a few rounds, thrown in their hedgerow positions have caused their precipitate withdrawal.

"We fired the mortars like artillery pieces, using forward observers with the assault rifle companies. The mortars did their best work at ranges of 1,500 to 2,000 yards, but on occasion they have done deadly execution at 3,500 yards."

Battlefield Recovery Under Fire
Letter, first *U. S. Army Group*, Normandy: "A tank battalion used the following procedure to recover one of their tanks which had been immobilized only 200 yards from the German lines:

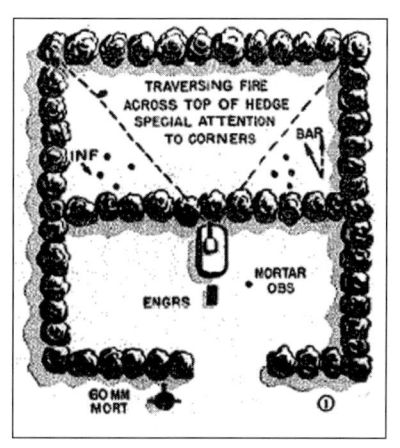

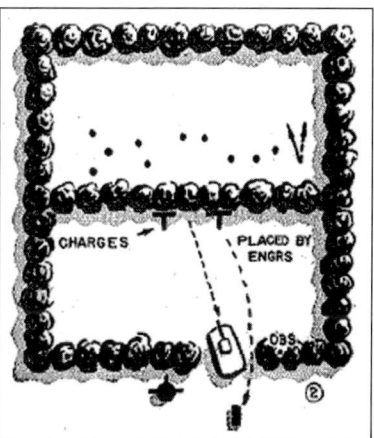

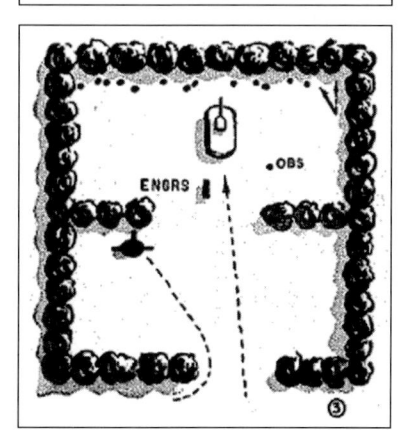

"An infantry platoon was placed in concealment in the hedgerow facing the German position and disposed so that its fire would cover the disabled tank. An 81-mm mortar was emplaced on the right flank of the infantry platoon. Then the tank recovery vehicle (T-2) started forward. Almost immediately a German machine gun opened fire but was silenced in short order by the mortar.

"When the recovery vehicle reached the disabled tank, the German infantry opened fire and moved forward, but the heavy fire from our infantry platoon, coupled with a concentration from the mortar, caused their precipitate retirement. The recovery vehicle hooked on to the tank and towed it to safety with no further difficulty and no casualties."

ALLIED FIRE POWER FORCES ENEMY TO STRESS NIGHT INFILTRATION

Tactical and Technical Trends, No. 51, October 1944

Increasing emphasis on the importance of infiltration of Allied positions at night, and an admission of Allied superiority in fire power and air power, are significant points in a recently published German army document. Translation of an extract follows:

The incredibly heavy artillery and mortar fire of the enemy on the Western front is something new, both for seasoned veterans of the Eastern front and new arrivals from reinforcement units. Veterans get used to it comparatively quickly, but inexperienced reinforcements require several days to do so.

The Allies have complete mastery of the air. They bomb and strafe every movement, even single vehicles and individuals. They reconnoiter our area constantly and direct their artillery fire. Against all this the German Air Force is conspicuous by its complete absence.

From the operations point of view, our own offensive operations by day, after completed assembly, etc.—i.e., attacks prepared "according to the book" have little chance of succeeding. Assembling of troops is spotted immediately by enemy reconnaissance aircraft, and smashed by bombers. fighter bombers, and artillery directed by aircraft; and if the attacking troops go forward they become involved in such dense artillery and mortar fire that heavy casualties ensue and the attack peters out within the first few hundred yards. Losses suffered by the infantry are then so heavy that the impetus necessary to renew the attack is spent.

Better results have been obtained through attacks by assault detachments operating at night on a broad front. These detachments penetrate enemy positions noiselessly and, in each instance, surprise and overcome the enemy without enemy artillery or air units having a chance to intervene.

The primary condition for this is that each individual assault detachment be fully acquainted with its task and know what to do in various circumstances, that it be in close liaison with its neighbors, and that the heavy weapons and artillery know exactly when to come into operation. But this is usual only in the event of local failure, when surprise has not been achieved.

Direction of infiltration operations is less a question of large-scale, elaborate planning than of practical instruction and reminder. The fact that "assembly has been completed" before the attack begins is of less importance than the fact that every company and platoon commander has thought of everything necessary to ensure the success of his assault detachment.

It is an essential duty of the staff planning the operation to put everyone down to the lowest ranking commanders completely in the picture. An attack of this nature attains no far-distant objective, but proceeds only by small stages, night after night. Yet in the end it reaches its objective without paying a heavy toll in manpower. The more cunning and variable the fighting, the more successful the operation.

TERRAIN MURALS IN A NORMAN FORT

Tactical and Technical Trends, No. 51, October 1944.

German troops who manned one strongpoint on the Norman coast had a constant reminder of the directions from which the Allied invasion would come. Murals of the surrounding terrain had been painted in colors on the concrete walls of the several open-top emplacements of the position. Each sector of the ground dominated by the position was depicted on the wall from which it was visible. Thus, even if visibility was limited by fog, the occupants of any particular section of the position had a bird's-eye view of the specific area for which they were responsible. Evidently the maps were used to indicate fields of fire and approaches that would most likely be used by amphibious forces. The strongpoint consisted of 12 emplacements, connected radially to an underground command post. All weapons had been removed from the position, but some 60-mm mortar ammunition was found.

GERMAN EMPLOYMENT OF HEAVY ARMORED PLATOON

Tactical and Technical Trends, No. 47, June 1, 1944.

A German source states that in the attack heavy, armored reconnaissance vehicles mounting the 75-mm Kw K are extremely effective as support weapons because of their high speed, their armor protection against small-arms fire and shell splinters, their ability to open fire instantly and their high rate of accurate fire. It is stated that the heavy armored platoon can be used to build up or quickly switch a concentration of fire that will decisively influence the fighting at a crucial point, but that the platoon or a single heavy armored car cannot undertake independent reconnaissance or combat tasks without infantry support because they can only fire in the direction of movement and because they are not equipped for close combat. The following details have been extracted from a German source.

a. General

In order to increase the probability of scoring hits, the effectiveness of the firing, and to save ammunition, it is essential that the vehicle be driven as near to the target as the enemy's fire permits. The gun will be fired only when the vehicle is at the halt. Use will be made of all available cover.

The heavy armored platoon will be given objectives which either cannot be engaged (or engaged quickly enough) by the artillery or other support weapons, or it will be held ready to engage such objectives as are encountered during the course of the battle. The small amount of ammunition carried necessitates moderation in its use.

If the platoon or single vehicles cannot be given specific targets during a battle, especially during and immediately after penetration, the platoon will keep in close proximity to the infantry and engage enemy objectives hindering the advance. Every armored commander must be able to recognize where his assistance is required. As a rule platoon commanders will indicate targets to vehicle commanders but the latter will issue their own fire-orders. The platoon will not normally be employed as a covering force. For greatest effect, the platoon should always be used as a whole, but single vehicles may be placed under command of rifle platoons or armored units on the march or on reconnaissance if superior enemy armor is anticipated, during fighting on a broad front in close country, or when the rifle platoons or armored units are given independent objectives.

b. On the March

On the march the heavy armored car may move well up with the point company to enable it to neutralize with concentrated fire any resistance suddenly encountered.

Single vehicles may be employed to reinforce the forward covering troops or armored car patrols if enemy armor is anticipated.

c. In the Attack

The platoon will accompany the attacking infantry and support the attack in co-operation with the other support weapons, especially during penetration and in the fighting in the depth of the main defense zone. As a rule the platoon will be employed as a weapon to be used at the main point of effort under the direction of the infantry commander.

The tasks of the platoon will be to neutralize particularly stubborn centers of resistance, field works and pillboxes, enemy tanks or antitank weapons.

After the objective has been gained, the platoon will take over protection against an enemy counterattack especially if tanks are anticipated.

d. During the Pursuit

During the pursuit the platoon will be kept well up with the leading elements to enable them to break quickly, in co-operation with the other arms, any enemy resistance which may be encountered, and to disperse the enemy.

In the pursuit it may be necessary to place single vehicles in support of pursuing troops or of reinforced armored patrols.

e. In Defense

The platoon will also be used offensively, especially in support of local or deliberate counterattacks. For this purpose, especially thorough reconnaissance and preparation is necessary before employment. During enemy tank attacks the platoon is specially suitable for rapid engagement at the decisive or most threatened point. The platoon can also be used to isolate enemy penetrations.

Only under exceptional circumstances may the platoon be included in the unit fire-plan, and will then be employed as flexibly as possible. The vehicles must be given cover against enemy artillery and air attacks by digging in.

Together with the infantry the heavy armored car platoon can be used to cover disengagement. The platoon can support local attacks, can hold up the enemy for a considerable time from covered positions, and is able to disengage quickly. It may be necessary to put single vehicles under command of rearguards.

f. In Static Warfare

The platoon can be used to give effective support in attacks upon static and field works.

It is necessary for complete success that there be thorough reconnaissance, discussion with the attacking infantry, and cooperation of all arms.

The tasks of the platoon in static warfare will be:
- Engagement of embrasures
- Engagement of field pillboxes and houses
- Blinding of weapon pits and centers of resistance
- Blasting a way through obstacles
- Support of the attack over the front area, especially by firing air bursts
- Protective fire for assault troop raids
- Together with infantry, the platoon can be held as a mobile reserve to be pushed through any lanes or gaps made and attack enemy positions from the rear.

g. Ammunition
- Up to 800 yards, fire for effect is recommended without ranging; HE 34 over 800 yards should normally be used only after preliminary ranging.

  HE 34: range up to 6,000 yards.

Instantaneous fuze is used against centers of resistance, antitank guns and large targets (bunched troops).

Delay fuze is employed against defiladed targets or targets under cover (field pillboxes, houses, etc), air-burst against live targets.

AP: range up to 1,400 yards, and is used against light armored vehicles, and embrasures of static positions. It also may be used at all ranges for possible nuisance effect against roads as well as against tanks which cannot be otherwise engaged.

Hollow charge 38: range up to 2,200 yards and used against the heavier tanks. At ranges over 800 yards the probability of registering hits is small.

TRANSCRIPT OF QUESTIONS PUT TO GENERALFELDMARSCHALL WILHELM KEITEL AND GENERALOBERST ALFRED JODL

Note by Kenneth W. Hechler, Major, Infantry (Res)

This was not an oral interview, but rather constitutes the translated answers of Keitel and Jodl to a questionnaire on the invasion, the questions for which were forwarded by the ETO Historical Section. The questions were at a high enough level, and the answers allowed sufficient play for judgment, so that considerable weight can be given to the answers, despite the fact that neither Keitel or Jodl had access to German documents or maps at the time they prepared their answers.

I recall that Keitel and Jodl both signed the German text of their answers, and this text was then translated by Sergeant Kiralfy. I forwarded the English text to the Historical Section, but I do not know what happened to the German text.

It is unfortunate that I did not have sufficient time to go back and orally interview Jodl and Keitel at greater length regarding their observations on these important issues. At the time, I told General Jodl that we had so many issues to take up with him that I felt that it would be better for him to summarize his answers in brief form, and perhaps we could then expand on them after the members of the ETO Historical Section had had a

Chief of Operations Staff: Generaloberst Alfred Jodl

chance to digest his preliminary reply. In this way, I hoped to skim off the cream of his observations during the entire European campaign, before he was yanked off to the War Crimes Trials in Nuremburg. It was obvious that Jodl was doing most of the work in preparing the answers. Keitel's major role seemed to be to question Jodl quite excitedly as to whether he had included any material which might be useful for War Crimes prosecution.

Q: Did the German General Staff feel that its forces would be able to stop the assault on the beaches, or did it figure that, once landings were made, mobile reserves could be moved to the assault areas soon enough to prevent a build-up of Allied forces and also drive the American and British forces into the sea? Did the Germans, assuming the Allies would have to have ports immediately, expect frontal assaults to be made on ports or on the beaches as they actually were? What were the estimates of the German General Staff as to the capabilities of the Allies as regards building up their forces and supplies over beaches once a beachhead was established? When were the Germans convinced that the Normandy assault was the main attack and not a diversion or just one of several attacks?

A: In OKW, before the invasion, we anticipated several landing points on the open coast, but they were in the vicinity of large harbors, that is to say, primarily on both sides of Dunkerque, Boulogne, Le Havre, or Cherbourg. We believed that, in a concentric land attack with support from the sea, one of these harbors would be captured for a port of debarkation. In view of the reported massing of invasion forces in southern England, we further were of the opinion that one group would jump off from the Dover-Folkestone area and the other from the Portsmouth-Weymouth area.

We did not anticipate direct frontal assaults on the ports from the sea; accordingly, we thought that debarkation on the open coast could only take place very slowly-much more slowly than actually happened-and that the rough water in particular would cause you serious delays.

We judged the timing and extent of the first major landing would be as follows: some three divisions would be disembarked at each of the two main landing points and their debarkation would require five or six days; besides these, two divisions of airborne troops would be set down at each of the two points. This calculation as to time justified our hope that we would be able to bring up superior forces on our side for a counterattack, even should the actual landing not be repulsed.

When the landing occurred in Normandy, we considered it as only one major assault, and expected a second in the German Fifteenth Army sector.

Q: Prior to the assault, what knowledge did the Germans have of the Allies' equipment or preparations for the establishment of artificial beach ports? Did the Germans have knowledge, perhaps through the Japanese and our amphibious operations in the Pacific, of our experience and experimentation with artificial ports? Did they underestimate our ability to build up the capacity of these beach ports?

A: We had observed, through aerial reconnaissance, the device which was used to form an artificial beach harbor. We believed its purpose was to form new quays in place of those destroyed in the port. We had no information from the Japanese as to the possibility of your producing artificial harbors. It came as a surprise to us.

Q: In view of later experience with the defenders of ports such as Brest, Cherbourg was surrendered after a relatively short fight. Why wasn't the siege prolonged? Was there a shortage of ammunition at Cherbourg?

A: The inadequate defense of Cherbourg was also a disappointment for the Supreme Command. We found a reason for it in the fact that a large part of the troops we contemplated to defend the fortress were employed in the fighting on the eastern coast of the peninsula, and that, contrary to the express orders of OKW, a great part of the troops brought into the peninsula after the invasion allowed themselves to be forced out toward the south or even suffered a breakthrough. So far as one can properly judge from so far away, the conduct of the Commandant of Cherbourg [Genlt von Schlieben-Ed.] did not come up to expectations and fell short of the example of Brest or St Malo.

Q: The Germans must have realized, before the fall of Antwerp, that this port would be of tremendous importance to the Allies. Why wasn't Antwerp defended more tenaciously and why, when the Allies approached the port, didn't the Germans destroy the port facilities as they did at Cherbourg, Brest, and other places?

A: The sudden loss of Antwerp caught OKW completely by surprise. We are unable to explain the reasons as we have not been acquainted with them. We refer you to Gen von Zangen, Commander of Fifteenth Army.

Q: Had the Germans made prior preparations for a siege-type defense of ports in France before the invasion, or was the tenacious hanging on of the German defenders the result of a post-D-Day realization of Allied supply difficulties or needs?

Chief of Staff: Generalfelfmarschall Wilhelm Keitel

A: All the important ports were more or less strong as fortresses, and had complete all around defenses. They were to be defended to the last in order to deny the enemy the opportunity to disembark quickly and on a large scale. This plan had still been maintained; therefore, when it became necessary in August 1944 to evacuate almost the entire coastline, we determined to leave certain coastal fortresses garrisoned in order to impede the supplying of the invading army for a long time. In addition, it was only in this way that we could benefit from the years of fortifying, the stationary artillery, the stocks of food, and the munitions of every kind.

Q: Why did the Germans allow the build-up over the beaches to proceed so relatively uninterrupted? Why didn't they bomb the artificial ports more than they did? What determined the German policy to lay mines via air at night in the Utah and Omaha areas rather than bomb beach and supply installations and ships?

A: The invasion came at a moment most disadvantageous for the Luftwaffe. The bomber units were being converted to the new airplane models Me 262 and Ar 234. Putting it generally, the relatively weak employment of bomber units, against the southern English port towns before the invasion as well as against the landing points after it began, is explained by the necessity of weakening severely the bomber arm even before the production of the new plane models for the strongest possible fighter arm.

The assault on the landing points, which was ordered as the main air effort, could be carried out by day only with fighter planes kept on call. The slight effect of these attacks is explained by the fact that it became more and more difficult for the fighter bombers to penetrate the fighter screen extending from the beach, which was warned by the radar stations you installed in the very first stages of the landing. At night, all available bomber units in the West were employed. Although torpedoes and guided bombs were used, preference was given to the air-dropped mine. Through this and cooperation with E-boats, we promised ourselves the most comprehensive mine infestation possible of the sea in front of the landing points and artificial ports.

Q: What type of craft attacked the LSTs in the exercises off Portland on the night of 27/ 28 April 1944? Were the Germans aware that exercises were taking place, or did they suspect that the mounting of the operation had begun, or was it a case of a chance patrol discovering the unprotected Allied craft several miles off the coast?

A: I do not remember the circumstances now, but I am pretty certain that the clash of the practice units with German E-boats or torpedo boats was accidental.

Q: Was the light bombing of Plymouth, Torquay, Dartmouth, and other places just prior to D-Day aimed at concentrations or marshaling areas known to be there, or was it just chance that some of these were either hit or nearly hit?

A: In the southern English ports referred to, the assembly of shipping for a landing was observed by our aerial reconnaissance. On the other hand, bombers were employed to a slight degree when the weather permitted. See also the answer to Question 6 [i.e. that concerning the build-up over the beaches].

Q: To what extent did weather affect reconnaissance activities in the Channel by both planes and E-boats just before D-Day?

A: Channel reconnaissance, especially by air, of the southern English ports, was often obstructed by the weather.

Q: Were the Germans aware that the mounting was taking place in southern England in the two weeks prior to the invasion?

A: We were aware at the end of May 1944 of the movement of troops into southern England. From that time on, the troops of Army Group B (Rommel) were in a constant state of alert for any emergency.

Q: How near completion were the beach defenses along the Omaha and Utah areas? Was there a target date for the completion of these defenses, or were construction activities to continue indefinitely?

A: The complete construction of the coastal defenses was not yet finished and never would have been; therefore, no date for their completion had been set. It was ordered that, by the beginning of April 1944, the military installations must be put into a defensible state and the Organization Todt's construction offices, etc., be evacuated.

Since the Spring of 1944, no more permanent installations had been built, as the necessary sand and cement no longer could be brought up. Further improvement was limited to camouflaging the batteries and building small field fortifications, dugouts, and minefields and obstacles. Although construction of the Atlantic Wall was started as early as 1941, it had been constructed without any fixed uniform building plan by various branches of the service. Later, the construction work was carried on uniformly through the Inspector of the Engineers and Fortresses and with the aid of Organization Todt. The work was strongly influenced and personally supervised by the Führer himself.

THE INVASION BY GENERAL WALTER WARLIMONT

Q: Did you anticipate that the invasion would take place where it actually did?

A: Hitler was the first one who decided for himself that this was the most probable spot for landing. On 2 May 1944, he ordered that antiaircraft and antitank weapons were to be reinforced all through Normandy and Brittany, counting mainly on an invasion in Normandy. Hitler's view was based on intelligence received as to troop movements in the British Isles. Two main troop concentrations had been noticed there: one in the southeast with mainly British troops, and one in the southwest, in Wales and on both sides of Wales, consisting mainly of US troops.

Q: Where did most of the other high-ranking officials believe that the invasion would take place?

A: Up to May 1944, when Hitler first spoke of it, we were all prepared for a landing in the Channel zone between the Seine and the Somme, by Abbeville and Le Havre. Therefore, throughout 1942-43, the coastal defenses were built up mainly in the Fifteenth Army zone.

Q: At what particular point?

A: I cannot say that we expected the landing at any particular point in Normandy. We expected it all along the coast with special reference to the small ports (which are mainly in the Bayeux area). We were not quite convinced that Hitler was right in expecting that attack, but he kept harping on it and demanded more and more reinforcements for that sector.

Q: Why did the generals predict that the invasion would strike at a different point than Hitler predicted? You both had access to the same sources of information, did you not?

A: We generals figured along the lines of our regular military education, but Hitler figured out of intuition as he always did. We figured on the Channel zone because

(1) it is the shortest crossing from the British Isles, (2) once across

the Channel, it is the shortest way to Germany and its industrial Ruhr, (3) it has at least one big harbor, Le Havre, better situated than Cherbourg and with better routes and lines of communication into the interior, and (4) your air force had better possibilities to support the attack closer to its bases.

Q: Upon what else besides intuition did Hitler base his conviction that we would invade Normandy?

A: Besides his observations from troop movements, Hitler based his theory on the idea that you would aim to build up a stable front, including one big harbor, and there was no better place on the whole coast than the Cotentin peninsula for this purpose.

Q: Did the regular army officers and High Command lean any more toward Hitler's view as the invasion date approached?

A: We recognized too that a landing in other parts of Europe further north was becoming more and more improbable as the British troops were grouped more and more to the south. The position of the US troops especially led Hitler to anticipate an attack launched against the west coast of Normandy.

Q: We, of course, did our best to deceive you into thinking that we would land in the Pas de Calais area, and, after the landing in Normandy, we still carried out elaborate deception plans in order to tie down your Fifteenth Army in this sector. What led you to feel that we would land in the Pas de Calais area?

A: The first air attacks were against fortifications of the Seine, and, since we had many standing fortifications in this sector, we took it as further evidence of your plans. We attached great importance to the Resistance movements in the interior and tried to determine the place of landing by noting where most parachute baskets, etc., were dropped. As time went on, however, this became so widespread that it no longer gave us any help.

We also managed to get into some of your radio nets. Radio transmitters were dropped from planes to be used by your agents in France to inform you about our movements. We intercepted some of these and got into your radio nets and used them ourselves, and also used them to communicate with your stations. We had the impression that this action of ours had passed unnoticed by you. We found out that there were special catchwords with which you prepared your operations and by means of which you were going to inform the French Underground as to the day and hour of your attack.

Q: To what extent was it possible to complete the fortifications along the Normandy coast where the invasion was later made?

A: The fortification of Normandy was not at all complete. Such fortifications require a long time. In Picardy we had more workers from occupied countries and better communications, and no one had thought of Normandy much before. The Normandy fortifications were just the same as those of other parts of the French coast, with one big position every 20 to 30 kilometers.

Q: Was it a case of shortage of troops or shortage of materials for the fortifications?

A: Not many more troops could have been put in there, but we could have done much more in the way of fortifying. Materials, such as cement, were also rare, having to be divided among all the armed forces. Furthermore, railway transportation was getting worse all the time as a result of air attacks on the big junctions. So, we were well aware that the fortifications were by no means complete, but it was too late to complete them as we should have liked.

Q: What would you have liked to have done in the way of better fortifications on the Normandy coast?

A: We should have had more standing fortifications built by the troops and not by Organization Todt. As it was too late by this time, all we could do was to put more troops in Normandy and improve their equipment.

Q: What troops did you have available to repulse the invasion?

A: By about 2 May 1944, we had, so far as I can remember without diaries, maps, or operations books, one static division of old men [716th] (comprising two regiments around the mouth of the Orne), the 711th [Infantry-Ed.] Division, which was a static division, and the 352nd [Infantry-Ed.] Division in front of Bayeux, to cover a coastline of at least 60 or even 80 kilometers. There was a special force in Cherbourg. We had three divisions (352nd, 716th and 711th) on the north coast of Normandy, another one (709th [Infantry-Ed.] Division) around Cherbourg, and the 243rd [Infantry Division-Ed.] on the west coast of Normandy. On 2 May 1944, Hitler put in the reinforcements of the antiaircraft and antitank weapons which were given to the units with a view in particular to their being better able to combat paratroops and airborne units. On 4 May 1944, he ordered the 2nd FS Division, then on the Eastern Front, to be transferred to the West. One regiment of this division, 6th FS Regiment, which was already in Germany when the order was given, came at once to Normandy, somewhere near St Lo. Hitler then ordered the 91st (LL-Ed.] Division, one of the very few divisions we had in Germany as an operative reserve, to be transferred to Normandy, also as a reserve. Most of this strength was on the base line of the Cotentin. So, actually only one parachute regiment and one division were sent in as we had no operative reserve to dispose of. Rundstedt, as C-in-C West, tried to send reinforcements, but had no reserves either and could do nothing worth mentioning. All our troops were required to defend the various coastlines, and your attack in Italy was making great progress. One division of Fifteenth Army, the Luftwaffe Feld Division (number not known) even had to be sent to Italy.

Rommel, at the next echelon, had always fought for a more tactical defense of the coast. He wanted to put in reserves as close to the coastline as possible. This was possible, of course, once you knew where the enemy was going to strike. But when you did not know, and had a coastline of thousands of kilometers, it was too hazardous to risk. As soon as Hitler decided that Normandy was the likely spot, Rommel had his way and sent in his Panzer divisions, which were attached to him as Wehrmachtbefehlshaber [Military District Commander in Occupied Territory Ed.] ofWestern Europe (Netherlands Headquarters). Army Group B extended right down to La Rochelle. Rommel had a reserve ofPanzer divisions and, in accordance with his line of thinking, he now put in the 21st Panzer Division somewhere near Caen, the 12th SS Panzer Division around Falaise, and the 2nd Panzer Division around St La (or a little east of it).

Rommel had one Panzer division left. He had two in Normandy, one quite close to the coast, and two just 40 to 50 kilometers behind it. He had one division behind Fifteenth Army. This took place about the middle of May 1944. Rommel took no infantry divisions from Fifteenth Army. Maybe this was due to uncertainty as to the division of spheres of Rommel and Rundstedt. I am not sure whether Rommel and Rundstedt were convinced Hitler was right. Rommel claimed it made no difference where the attack came as his defenses were now so good all along the coast.

There were four more armored divisions farther east which were reserved for the disposition of OKW. Two were in the neighborhood of Paris, the Panzer Lehr Division and the 2nd SS Panzer Division.

Q: Did you expect us to land only where there were ports and harbors, or did you know about our artificial ports? Why did you not bomb our artificial ports after you discovered how much we were using them to land supplies?

A: We always expected your attack with the aid of harbors, and if we had known more about your artificial ports, we should have done more to stop it. If you ask why the air force did not bomb more effectively the places where you landed, the answer is that our air force was unable to break through your defenses in order to find and hit the targets at all.

Q: Were you able to estimate the rate at which we could build up supplies and troops on the beaches after the initial landing?

A: We knew the capacity of the small (natural) harbors, but, not knowing about the artificial ports, we could not estimate your rate of supply. We were able later to gauge the rate at which you were landing troops, but confined ourselves to strength figures and the number of divisions as our reconnaissance did not give us much information on your troops and still less on your supply circumstances.

Q: Did you suspect that the invasion would take place on the date which it did?

A: The weather was right for an invasion and we had been alerted to the possibility for some weeks prior to 6 June 1944. Our chief intelligence source was the radio, and our intercepts revealed that the invasion would take place on the morning of 6 June 1944. This information was relayed to headquarters on the afternoon of 5 June 1944. Hitler knew it and Gen Jodl knew it, but the information was not made available to the troops in Normandy.

Q: Was this considered a great mistake by Hitler?

A: In Hitler's eyes, Gen Jodl, unlike other men, did not make military mistakes. Gen Jodl knew the state of alarm or alert under which the troops in northern France were operating and did not consider it necessary to give out another order. Furthermore, there had been a number of other false alarms prior to this one.

Q: Was your reconnaissance hampered any in the days immediately prior to the invasion?

A: Unfortunately, we had no regular air reconnaissance because of the superiority of your air power over the area. Air reconnaissance was made perhaps every fortnight, and even then was confined to photographs of possible points of embarkation. Sea reconnaissance also was rather difficult; it was difficult to keep boats in the open sea when the British Navy dominated the area.

Q: Do you recall any of Hitler's specific comments immediately prior to the invasion?

A: More and more in recent months, since Hitler had assumed his role of military expert, he would talk at great length and in broad terms at the semi-daily operational meetings. These meetings, attended by up to twenty high officers, would be held at 1300 and close to midnight. Hitler would speak honestly, but seldom directly to any individuals or individual. He would speak "out of the window." To answer your question, just before the invasion his line was that the impending invasion of France would be the decisive event of the coming year. Hitler said, "It will decide the issue, not only of the year, but of the whole war. If we succeed in throwing back the invasion, then such an attempt cannot and will not be repeated within a short time. It will then mean that our reserves will be set free for use in Italy and the East. Then we can stabilize the front in the East and perhaps return to the offensive in that sector. If we don't throw the invaders back, we can't win a static war in the long run because the materiel our enemies can bring in will exceed what we can send to that front. With no strategic reserves of any importance, it will be impossible to build up sufficient strength along such a line. Therefore, the invader must be thrown back on his first attempt."

VON RUNDSTEDT EXPLAINS
Intelligence Bulletin, March 1946.

"Had I been able to move the armored divisions which I had behind the coast, I am convinced that the invasion would not have succeeded."

Lack of air power, and interference from higher levels, played major roles in the defeat of the German Army after the Normandy invasion, according to Field Marshal von Rundstedt. But the former German commander-in-chief in the West has admitted that the Allied commanders outsmarted him several times to make the situation even worse.

Caught in the position of a boxer up against an opponent with both a good left hook and a good right cross, Von Rundstedt guessed incorrectly that the right cross—the invasion of the Cotentin Peninsula—was merely a feint to the landing of the left hook—an invasion of the Belgian or French coast farther north. By the time he and his successors discovered that the right cross was really the knockout blow, it was too late to save anything but remnants of the German Army in France.

A great deal of the interference from higher levels developed later during the Battle of Germany, Von Rundstedt declared, the worst instance being the Ardennes counteroffensive of December 1944 and

"Rommel's asparagus" was "well meant" said Von Rundstedt, but it was not much of a success because in some places the sea simply turned the obstacles around and sanded them up or rolled them away.

January 1945.

"The Ardennes offensive bore my name quite wrongly," the former West Front commander protested. "I had nothing to do with it. It was ordered from above down to the smallest detail."

He thought, too, that interference from above had wrecked his earlier plans for the defense of France against the invasion. In the first place, he did not have enough troops to cover the areas in which the invasion might come, and higher officers interfered with the distribution of what he had. When it finally became necessary to shift troops around, it was too late—by that time Allied planes had such overwhelming air superiority that they blasted his reinforcements to bits, or stopped their movement by cutting communications facilities.

BASIC GERMAN WEAKNESSES

The situation immediately prior to the invasion of June 1944 was not good, Von Rundstedt said. He and his former Chief of Staff, General Blumentritt, recognized at least three basic weaknesses: their inadequate number of troops had to cover enormous stretches of coast line, some divisions as much as 35 to 40 miles; the Atlantic Wall was "anything but a wall, just a bit of cheap bluff"; and there was no counterattack reserve or so-called "Armee centrale," a strategic army under central command to counterattack where the invasion came.

Von Rundstedt, like many other German generals, said he did not control Germany's best troops. He complained that many of his best units were sent to Italy, and he asserted vigorously that it was "madness to continue the war in Italy that way."

After the collapse of Italy, "that frightful 'boot' of a country should have been evacuated. Mussolini should have been left where he was, and we should have held a decent front with a few divisions on the Alpine frontier. They should not have taken away the best divisions front me in the West in order to send them to Italy. That's my private view."

Whether he could have gotten more troops for the West, Von Rundstedt did not know. He did know that the High Command was hard pressed for troops on all sides, but nothing was ever done about it.

"It was only decent to do something" after Mussolini was reinstated,

Von Rundstedt admitted, but he added, "of course it was absolutely a matter of politics and nothing else. I assume, though I have no positive knowledge, that the High Command was in favor of it."

"I thought that was nonsense, too," Von Rundstedt said of the occupation of Norway. "What was the point of occupying it?"

He termed the Norwegian operation "purely a naval affair" in which he had no interest. In fact, his major interest all along was to accumulate the proper armored divisions, mobile forces which could be quickly sent where they were needed.

HIGH COMMAND INTERFERED

"Had I been able to move the armored divisions which I had behind the coast, I am convinced that the invasion would not have succeeded." Von Rundstedt made this emphatic statement as he told of continued interference from higher levels with the disposition of his inadequate forces. "If I had been able to move the troops, then my air force would also have been in a position to attack hostile ships."

If he had had his way, Von Rundstedt indicated that the Allies would first of all have sustained prohibitive losses during landing operations. In addition, they would not have been able, "with relative impunity," to bring up battleships close to the coast to act as floating gun batteries.

"That is all a question of air force, air force, and again air force," he commented.

The Normandy invasion would have been "like Dieppe on a big scale"—Von Rundstedt believes—if he had been able to move his armored divisions as he desired. He summarized the situation with the statement:

"We would certainly have been better off if a good many things had been different as regards the distribution of forces."

ATLANTIC WALL MYTH EXPLODED

"The enemy probably knew more about it than we did ourselves," Von Rundstedt said in referring to the so-called Atlantic Wall as a "mere bluff." He confessed that such a wall did exist from the Scheldt to the Seine, "but further than that—one has only to look at it for one's self in Normandy to see what rubbish it was."

According to Von Rundstedt, the wall consisted of a few pillboxes in holes in the sand so far apart that "you needed field glasses to see the next one." The only good thing was the fortresses, such as Cherbourg and Brest, but they were all fortified only toward the sea. He described the wall as "a dreary situation" south of the Gironde toward the Spanish border because "there was really nothing at all there."

All the ballyhoo about the Atlantic Wall was simply propaganda, Von Rundstedt said, but he admitted that people believed it—"at least we believed it." He thinks, however, that it was no mystery to the Allies because their air photography probably revealed the bluff.

Although a lot of material went into the defenses, Von Rundstedt complained that the Navy got most of the concrete. He pictured the German Navy as building higher and thicker roofs on their U-boat shelters every time the Allies dropped a heavier bomb.

"It doesn't suffice to build a few pillboxes," Von Rundstedt pointed out. "One needs defense in depth. Moreover, the requisite forces were lacking—we couldn't have manned them, even if fortifications had been there."

ARTILLERY WEAKNESSES

The former German commander in the West really warmed up on the subject of coastal batteries and artillery. Admitting that he was not an artilleryman, Von Rundstedt nevertheless severely criticized the mounting of the coastal guns. They were mounted as on ships, and could fire only out to sea. They were of no use to land forces because they could not fire in all directions. To make things worse, the coastal batteries included many captured guns, thus hampering the supply situation.

As if things were not bad enough, Von Rundstedt complained, the last divisions he got were very weak in artillery, some of them having only three light batteries. A good division on land should have nine light batteries and at least three heavy batteries, in his view.

CAUGHT WITH PANZERS DOWN

Von Rundstedt confessed that the Allies caught him flatfooted with their thrust out of the Cotentin Peninsula. If he had been in the position of his enemy, intent on taking Paris and the interior of France, Von Rundstedt explained, he would have landed to the left and right of the Seine and taken the shortest route.

He admitted that he was puzzled because he believed a landing on the Cotentin was aimed at securing a harbor. At the same time, he could see no point in getting a harbor there because the route to the interior of France was three times as long.

Believing the most powerful thrust would come through Belgium toward the Ruhr, Von Rundstedt considered the area northeast from the Seine to be the most dangerous. For that reason, the division sectors on that coast were shorter, and the fortifications there were constructed as strongly as possible.

Adding to Von Rundstedt's belief that the landing would come further north was the fact that the Navy believed a landing could be made on the Cotentin only at high tide. Even then the rocks and reefs below the water would wreck the ships, thus making a landing extremely hazardous. Here, too, the Allies fooled him by landing at low tide and using the rocks as cover against the fire from land.

"We probably didn't know about the floating harbors." he commented in explaining that he had not considered the Cotentin a likely landing area. "I, at least, didn't. Whether the Navy knew of them I don't know."

SECOND INVASION EXPECTED

Von Rundstedt said there were definite grounds for anticipating another invasion further north, primarily front tactical and strategic considerations. Projecting himself into the mind of the Allied high command, he reasoned: "I will land here, wait until the Germans have gathered all their forces to meet me, and then land at the other place."

An additional motive for a second landing was the fact that the launching ramps for the V-bombs were in the Belgian area—if the effect of these bombs was as unpleasant as German propagandists declared.

"I can't believe it was." Von Rundstedt commented, "because so far I've seen no results of V-weapons here (in England). But it would have counted for something, perhaps, if they were as unpleasant for the English as they afterward were for us in the Eifel, when they all went back into our own lines.

"The V-weapons as such had nothing to do with us in the Army," he said. "The actual protection of them was undertaken by the Flak."

He argued that he was afraid of an Allied thrust north from the Seine more because of the strategic importance of an attack toward the Ruhr and Lower Rhine than because of the V-bombs.

"A landing which for a long time we considered very likely before the invasion actually began was one to get rid of the U-boat bases—namely, Brest, St. Nazaire, and Lorient—from the rear," Von Rundstedt declared. "Then when the U-boat business collapsed so completely, we said that was no longer of interest and wouldn't come off. Attention was then concentrated more and more on the northern part."

GERMAN ARMORED SITUATION

Although Von Rundstedt could not remember his exact tank strength in France at the beginning of June 1944, he thinks he had Approximately six or seven Panzer divisions, but they were spread out. Two were immediately available when the invasion came, and two others were able to come up on the first day. Another one came from Belgium, and then one came from southern France. He complained that one division never did make it from southern France because it had "some difficulties" with the Maquis.

"The defensive role played by the armored divisions near Caen during July and August was a great mistake." Von Rundstedt confessed, "but it was done on the orders of higher authority. We wanted to relieve the armored divisions by infantry, but it was impossible in the bulge in front of Caen where they were also under fire from ships' guns. You can't relieve any troops then."

Von Rundstedt's plan, which was turned down, was to withdraw the armored forces behind the Orne, form up the relieving infantry there, and then take away the tanks from in front and use them as mobile units to attack U.S. forces on the flanks. He was backed up by the senior tank commander, General Beyr von Schweppenburg, but to no avail. The armored divisions were left where they were "on the Führer's own orders."

"Whether similar orders were likewise responsible for the Avranches counterattack, I don't know," Von Rundstedt commented, "since I left on 1 July."

He said he had wanted to make a counterattack while German forces were still north of St. Lo. His plan was to thrust between the British and American landing troops, attacking the Americans and merely screening off the British, because the terrain was more favorable and the battle prospects were better.

AIR POWER AT WORK

Systematic preparations by the Allied air forces caused the general collapse of the German defense, Von Rundstedt said. He cited three important factors.

First, there was the smashing of the main lines of communication, particularly the railway junctions. Although Von Rundstedt had planned the defense so that reserves could be moved to the threatened areas, Allied planes knocked out railway lines and made the shifting of troops impossible.

The second factor was the attack on roads and on marching columns, individual vehicles, etc., so that it was impossible to move by day. This made it extremely difficult to bring up reserves, and it also created a supply problem because fuel and ammunition could not be brought up.

Carpet bombing constituted the third factor. In certain respects, Von Rundstedt said, it constituted an intensified artillery barrage and knocked out troops in pillboxes or dug in ahead of the front line. It also smashed reserves in the rear.

Although the GAF "did what it could," Von Rundstedt pointed out that he had practically no air reconnaissance. German planes which did take to the air were outnumbered 10 to 1, and any long-range reconnaissance was "absolutely nonexistent."

"Rommel's asparagus" (beach obstacles) was "well meant," according to Von Rundstedt, but it was not much of a success because in some places the sea simply turned the obstacles around and sanded them up or rolled them away.

In reinforcing German troops fighting in the Cotentin, men were immediately withdrawn from the southern front. Troops were held on the northern front, however, because the Germans were afraid of a landing on the Belgian or French coast. As explained by Von Rundstedt, the Germans believed that "Phase I is here, but Phase II will come there."

When it became apparent later on that the Normandy invasion was the real thing, the destruction of the Seine bridges "made itself felt very unpleasantly." The reserve troops had to be detoured around or brought over in ferry boats.

THE ARDENNES OFFENSIVE

Turning to the Ardennes offensive, Von Rundstedt said that every protest on our part, including those from the late Field Marshal Model, was turned down."

If he had directed the attack, Von Rundstedt said, he would have confined himself to a smaller objective. His plan would have embraced an attack on the Aachen pocket from two sides in an attempt to destroy it.

"For a far-reaching operation such as the Ardennes offensive, aimed first at the Maas and possibly still further, the forces were much, much, much too weak. The possibility of driving inland with armored divisions, with no GAF, was purely visionary. Reinforcements and supplies, with their railheads back on the Rhine, took longer and longer to move, and it was impossible to get them up. That offensive was bound to fail. There was no other possibility."

Pointing to the German offensive in 1940 from Trier toward Luxembourg and Calais, Von Rundstedt explained that a vast number of troops were available simply to cover the flanks and protect the spearhead. The forces in the Ardennes offensive were far too weak for the exercise of a comparable function, he explained, using as examples the actions at Bastogne and near Stavelot-Malmedy.

"If I do anything like that, I must have large, very large forces." Von Rundstedt concluded, "but those suggestions were not heeded and things turned out as I'd expected. The root of the whole trouble was air power, air power!"

Allied troops sift through the wreckage of a German supply column destroyed from the air as it retreated through the Falaise gap. In the foreground are the remains of a German half track and a motor cycle.

The German armies which took to the field in Normandy included over one million men, supported by over 1500 tanks and some 3500 guns. This vast assemblage needed over 20,000 vehicles and 20,000 horses. By the end of the campaign, the Germans had lost some 240,000 men killed and wounded, a further 200,000 as prisoners of war and practically all of the tanks, guns and vehicles. In that respect, the battle for Normandy must rank as a strategic victory on a par with the destruction of the Army Group Centre, the outcome of Operation Bagration which was taking place in Russia, at the same time. Taken Together these two campaigns represent the decisive blows from which there was no possible prospect of recovery.